"In this honest and sensitive memoir, Tankersley vividly illustrates how God comes to us disguised as our life. Recounting the ups and downs of his personal life and ministry . . . , he shares his lifelong struggle to balance with integrity a compassion for the suffering of people with a prophetic proclamation of the gospel. Truly a worthwhile read."

—WILKIE AU
Professor emeritus of Theological Studies,
Loyola Marymount University

"Tankersley's new book . . . is a beautiful and clearly written account of how a Presbyterian pastor lived the faith and encouraged so many others to do so as well. . . . I commend these memoirs to all who seek to live and give leadership the power of the gospel for our time."

—CLIFTON KIRKPATRICK
Professor of World Christianity and Ecumenical Studies,
Louisville Presbyterian Theological Seminary

"Tankersley is a beloved pastor whose wise and gentle spirit guided Laguna Presbyterian Church through the wild and tumultuous last decades of the twentieth century and into the early years of the twenty-first. . . . All of this is unveiled in *A Pastor's Highways*. . . . At times humorous and other times deeply and transparently vulnerable, Tankersley takes us on a ride through those various issues and challenges."

—MICHAEL REGELE
author and retired PCUSA Pastor

"In this book, Jerry tells his story to help us see better than ever what makes him the special pastor and servant of Christ that he is. I am humbled and inspired by the example of his candor, and I am inspired to remember our calling as he ascribes all the glory to the God of the 'New Creation' in Jesus Christ. Beautiful insights into an enigmatically excellent pastor."

—STEVE YAMAGUCHI
Pastor, Tokyo Union Church

A Pastor's Highways
on the Way to
the New Jerusalem

A Pastor's Highways
on the Way to
the New Jerusalem

Arthur Jarrell Tankersley

Foreword by John Huffman

RESOURCE *Publications* · Eugene, Oregon

A PASTOR'S HIGHWAYS ON THE WAY TO THE NEW JERUSALEM

Copyright © 2021 Arthur Jarrell Tankersley. All rights reserved. Except for brief quotations in critical publications or reviews, no part of this book may be reproduced in any manner without prior written permission from the publisher. Write: Permissions, Wipf and Stock Publishers, 199 W. 8th Ave., Suite 3, Eugene, OR 97401.

Resource Publications
An Imprint of Wipf and Stock Publishers
199 W. 8th Ave., Suite 3
Eugene, OR 97401

www.wipfandstock.com

PAPERBACK ISBN: 978-1-6667-1333-6
HARDCOVER ISBN: 978-1-6667-1334-3
EBOOK ISBN: 978-1-6667-1335-0

OCTOBER 27, 2021 11:19 AM

Contents

Permissions | *vii*

Foreword by John Huffman | *ix*

Preface | *xiii*

INTRODUCTION
Interpreting the Highways:
From West Texas to the New Jerusalem | *1*

CHAPTER 1
The Highways of God's People | *7*

CHAPTER 2
The Highways of My Story | *29*

CHAPTER 3
The Highways from Westmont College
to Fuller Theological Seminary, 1959 – 1962 | *49*

CHAPTER 4
The Highways to Princeton Theological Seminary, 1964 Th.M. | *52*

CHAPTER 5
The Highways Back to California, 1963–1964 | *57*

CHAPTER 6
The Highways from Wilshire Presbyterian Church
to the La Canada Presbyterian Church, 1964 – 1972 | *59*

Chapter 7
The Highways from La Canada to Laguna Beach, 1963 – 1972 | *66*

Chapter 8
The Highways to Laguna Beach
and the Laguna Presbyterian Church, 1972–2018 | *86*

Chapter 9
The Highways to Louisville and beyond, 2000 to 2018 | *204*

Chapter 10
The Highways into the Storms, 2016 to 2020 | *318*

Chapter 11
The Highways to the New Jerusalem | *329*

Bibliography | *346*

Permissions

The Scripture quotations contained herein are from the New Revised Standard Version Bible, copyright 1989 by the Division of Christian Education of the National Council of the Churches of Christ in the U.S.A. and are used by permission. All rights reserved.

Song Title: God Moves in a Mysterious Way, Isaac Watts/William Cowper/ From Greatorex Collection/Richard E.Gerig, 1968, renewed 1996 Lillenas Publishing Company (admin. By Music Services) All Rights Reserved, SESAC, Used with Permission.

Excerpt from The Second Mountain: The Quest For A Moral Life by David Brooks, copyright 2019 by David Brooks. Used by permission of Random House, an imprint and division of Penguin Random House LLC. All rights reserved.

Excerpts from The Sacred Journey and Telling Secrets, Frederick Buechner Literary Assests, LLC. Used with Permission.

Excerpts from The Case for Orthodox Theology, Estate of Edward John Carnell, Used with Permission.

Excerpt from Surprised by Joy by C.S. Lewis, copyright CS Lewis Pte Ltd 1955, Used with Permission.

Excerpts from The Jesus Way, Eugene Peterson, The Jesus Way, Wm. B. Eerdman's Publishing Co. 2007, Used with Permission.

Excerpts from The Holy Longing: The Search for A Christian Spirituality by Ronald Rolheiser, copyright 1999 by Ronald Rolheiser. Used by permission of Doubleday, an imprint of the Knopf Doubleday Publishing Group, a division of Penguin Random House LCC.

Excerpt from Educated, A Memoir, Penguin Random House LCC, Used with Permission

Foreword

I'VE KNOWN OF THE AUTHOR the Rev. Dr. Arthur Jarrell Tankersley since our lives overlapped briefly in the early 1960s as fellow students at Princeton Theological Seminary. But his formal given name quickly became "Jerry" as he became one of my lifetime best friends in 1978. It was then that as pastor of the Community Presbyterian Church of Laguna Beach, California, he gave invaluable counsel to me as Anne and I struggled to find God's guidance as whether or not to leave the historic pulpit of the First Presbyterian Church of Pittsburg, Pennsylvania, to accept the call to become the pastor of the St. Andrew's Presbyterian Church of Newport Beach, that next city up the coast from his. He helped me work through the complexities of that tough decision in a way that enabled me to see my way through to accept the call. He also instantly became my soul brother, the marvelous personal confidant with whom for well over four decades I have been able to share the tears of tragedy mingled with the joys of pastoral ministry. And through all these years as we have addressed impossibly painful, complex professional and personal challenges he has inevitably helped us identify a humorously absurd angle of each issue confronting us, enabling our initially somber conversation to conclude in the mirthful reality that this too shall pass.

For almost half a century we have been in a pastor's covenant group that has met monthly sharing honestly and confidentially the deepest realities of both family and pastoral life. I know this man, Jerry. I respect him as a human being of utmost Christ-centered integrity. In-spite of his distinguished forty-six-year Laguna Beach pastorate he remains a humble servant of our Lord. For all these reasons and much more he is most qualified to share with the world in written form this realistic record of and reflection on his multifaceted life.

This could be four books, each looking through a somewhat different lens at life and ministry. Instead, Jerry has enriched us by integrating these four, somewhat distinct, literary genres into one carefully constructed, thoughtful expression.

One, this is a highly personal expose—what one would call a memoir. He reveals his life as a youngster in Texas. He grew up facing challenging family of origin issues. One would not have expected the product of such a family environment to be as spiritually and academically motivated as he has ended up being. Elvis Presley was his musical hero. To this day he can still surprise the unexpecting with his pretty good Elvis impersonation. As a teenager he was, along with other influences, led to personal faith in Jesus Christ through the evangelistic ministry of Billy Graham. He was nurtured by the "Old Fashion Revival Hour" radio ministry of Dr. Charles Fuller. Through these and other influences he describes making his way to California's Westmont College and Fuller Theological Seminary.

He tells his story of falling in love, getting married, becoming a Presbyterian, doing a graduate degree at Princeton Theological Seminary, and accepting an assistant pastorate position back in California only to stumble into the heartbreaking reality that his wife had become romantically involved with other men. Devastated by an unwanted divorce, he was convinced his days as a pastor were over. He describes with great gratitude how through the wise counsel of trusted friends he discovered gracious personal and professional restoration. This led ultimately to God's gift of Kay in a fulfilling marriage continuing now for half a century along with their adopted son Jeff, his wife Rachel, and their two sons. Jerry shares the joys and sorrows of local parish ministry in a way that lends an "Amen" of recognition to the pastor reader with whom he is so sensitively relatable.

Two, this is a spiritual autobiography, yet Jerry moves beyond the factual and feeling data of memoirs into deep personal, theological, ethical, and spiritual interwoven reflections. He describes honestly his own dark nights of the soul. He shares how he has benefitted from early years of psychotherapy and in more recent years the accountable relationship with a personal spiritual director. I found his honest sharing of his internal personal life to be both encouraging and inspirational. Jerry's reflections are both honest and insightful.

Three, this is a superb record of a history of American religious and social life from World War Two to the present. As careful and thoughtful as he has been as a pastor, Jerry's interests go beyond this to integrate both professional ministry with first rate theological and political reflection. With superb theological training at both Fuller and Princeton seminaries he has additionally earned doctoral degrees from Claremont Graduate School and the Claremont School of Theology in both political science and ministry. He continues to read widely in both areas. Jerry's life experience for these two disciplines has been the laboratory of Laguna Beach, Orange County, California, the United States, and the world. He is highly knowledgeable in book learning and in practical life experience. He is a world traveler who brings his intellectual curiosity to all he does and everywhere he goes. He knows history and has in this book distinguished popular ministry and societal trends from spiritual and social movements of lasting significance. He is quite uniquely a global Christian who has invested his life in missiological reflection that has led to servant ministry action of both a domestic and international nature.

Jerry has complemented his biblical preaching with mid-week teaching that has endeavored to develop a congregation of thinking followers of Jesus. In both venues he has gracefully and biblically addressed the controversial issues of our day including race, gender, human sexuality, and consumerism. He has done this in a relationally sensitive and ethically nuanced manner. He has masterfully maintained his ethical and theological integrity while lovingly and pastorally ministering to the binary realities of a congregation that combines both blue state and red state identifying constituencies.

Four, there is a governance integration into all the above of Jerry's love and institutional involvement at all levels of the Presbyterian Church U.S.A. As a gracious evangelical he has been a faithful presbyter serving the larger denomination in an irenic fashion. In 2002 he accepted the invitation to allow his name to be put forward as a candidate for Moderator of the General Assembly. Although not elected, the kindly expertise with which he carried out his candidacy opened nearly a quarter century of leadership of numerous opportunities to serve the larger church. Jerry has seen that involvement as crucial to who he is. He explains his steadfast refusal to join with those who have for various political and theological reasons chosen to leave our denomination. He has stayed engaged in all these denominational controversies with dignity and grace. And he has contributed extensively to the various theological and ecclesiastical debates that have marked the life of the larger Church. Instead of footnoting various theological and governance documents to be included in an appendix, he has with care selectively integrated these materials into the main body of this manuscript highlighting their importance to his entire enterprise.

In short, Jerry Tankersley has succeeded in providing an informing and inspiring weaving of these four strands of his life experience. I commend this book to you as a worthwhile read not only for what you will discover about his highways traveled, but for the enhanced understanding you personally will receive, thus enlightening the view of the highways you have traveled, are traveling, and will yet travel.

Dr. John Huffman

2021

Preface

THE PRESBYTERY OF LOS ANGELES ordained me to the gospel ministry on August 18, 1963. I was honorably retired by the Presbytery of Los Ranchos on June 30, 2018. The Presbyterian Church (U.S.A.) has blessed, inspired, troubled, and faithfully sustained my personal, family, and pastoral life. For this I am deeply grateful. I dedicate this writing project of biblical and theological reflection to the members of the PC (U.S.A.) with deep thanksgiving.

I also dedicate this work to my wife, Kay Hoppe Tankersley. We are approaching our 53rd wedding anniversary. She has been a champion for me and our son, Jeffrey Jarrell Tankersley. My family has been God's gift to me. I have learned much from them and have tried to bless them. Not always have I succeeded, but always we have been together in mutual forgiveness and graceful living. Thankfully, Rachel Rao Tankersley and my two grandsons, Quinn, and Luke, have come into our family. There has been much joy through them.

A special thanksgiving for the three Presbyterian congregations I served: the Wilshire Presbyterian Church in Los Angeles; the La Canada Presbyterian Church in La Canada, California; and for 46 years the Laguna Presbyterian Church of Laguna Beach, California. Words cannot express what I have learned through these three churches and the devoted disciples who have faithfully stood beside me, laughed and wept with me, challenged me, forgiven me, and advanced the kingdom of God with me and within me.

What I have written is more than a spiritual memoir. My story and my family's story are interwoven with the American story of the 20th and early 21st century's story. Years ago, I read The Autobiography of Harry Emerson Fosdick, *The Living of These Days*. His final chapter was entitled, "Ideas That Have Used Me". In that chapter he reflected on the great ideas and issues that had shaped the life of America in the 20th century and how he thought about them from the perspective of the pulpit in dialogue with the people in the pews who listened and struggled with theological conflicts, dangerous spiritual challenges, economic depressions, racial protests, the afflictions of various diseases, political divisions, wars, and peace. He saw it all and became a blessing to a nation living through tumultuous times. He was identified as a modernist, but he now reads like a Christ-centered, Scripture centered, man of God whose voice at Riverside Church in New York City, the nation needed to hear through trying decades.

In my journey story I have reflected on the great issues of the decades of my service and shared how they have "used Me", "driven me to my knees in prayer", and "transformed Me" in the light of the authority, the presence, and the power of the kingdom of God. There was no escape from the struggles of the church and the world. The controversies of my days and years, in which I was alive to God in ever deepening ways, used me, and made me who I am today as a man in his early eighties still seeking to understand the mystery of life, death, and the inbreaking of the living God in human history and experience. As a pastor within the PCUSA, I have been pressed to address the issues of our lives and the challenges to the church. I cannot say that I have solved all the issues that have questioned my mind and heart, but I have given myself to the task in the context of my family, my churches, my friends, my nation, and the larger world.

This has been a journey into which I was called by the Word and the Spirit of the Living God. I have sought to live beneath the cross of Jesus, my Savior and LORD. At times I failed, but the LORD never failed me. God's grace sustained me, forgave me, and empowered me to live with abandon and adventure. Always, the mission of moving "further up and further in", in the words of C.S. Lewis, to the reality of the kingdom of God has drawn me toward the fullness of Eternal Life in the presence and the hope of the promised New Creation. My journey began in the flatlands of Northwest Texas. At long last I trust that I will walk into the New Jerusalem in the presence of the Holy One who created me, called me, blessed me, and has given meaning to each moment of the journey.

Included in the body of these reflections are papers I wrote seeking to interpret for the people I served what was happening in the light of the mission of God in our troubled world. Over the years I have been reminded in reading the New Testament that the church came to know Jesus and the apostles through their written testimonies and letters inspired by the Spirit of God.

Preface

Especially I think of the Apostle Paul. Luke's presentation of the mission of God through Paul the Apostle in the Acts of the Apostles was foundational for the spiritual life of the new disciples and for the movement of the church's mission from Jerusalem to Rome. He introduced the Apostle to churches that would spread to the ends of the earth. But also, the Letters Paul wrote to the churches that he planted, expressed his personal story and his insights into the power of the Gospel of God in calling forth historical expressions of God's kingdom in the life of the church and its surrounding contexts. Within those letters Paul allowed his readers to know him in all his strengths and weaknesses, with his faith in the sovereign purpose and plan of God in his missionary journeys, along with his take on the great issues and ideas of the Greco-Roman and Jewish cultural worlds into which he was born and to which he was called. Faith, Hope, and Love inspired and guided him in helping his church's grow up into the grace and knowledge of the LORD. His personal experience of grace became a model for all who would believe and follow in the way of the Cross into the kingdom of God. (2 Corinthians 11- 13; Galatians 1 and 2; 1 Timothy 1:12-20)

Therefore, rather than place my written pastoral letters to the churches I have served in this document's Appendix, I have included them in the body of the larger narrative. These letters and papers were written to build up the church in the knowledge of God's grace, love, and truth. I have not pretended to write Scripture, simply to expound and to allow the Spirit of God to speak through my human words and reflections. The book speaks of my passion for the pastoral ministry, but also of the challenges of the various decades to my understanding of God's grace at work in and through human conflict, aspiration, and longing for the truth of the Gospel. I invite the reader to seriously read them in the light of one pastor's effort to document his journey over several decades of walking, running, praying, suffering, and loving the people of God.

Welcome to my journey from West Texas toward the City of God, the New Jerusalem. Thankfully, I have not been alone, but have shared the journey with a large host of the people of God who travelled with me. Most of all, the living LORD has journeyed with me. In trust I live into the future which only the LORD may give.

Dr. Jerry Tankersley
Laguna Beach, California
August 2021

INTRODUCTION

Interpreting the Highways

From West Texas to the New Jerusalem

TOM HANKS IS ONE OF my favorite actors. Two of his movies have caused me much reflection, "*Forest Gump*" and *"Cast Away." "Forest Gump"* tells of the journey of a boy in Alabama through great difficulty and developmental challenges. His dying mother told him, "Forest, life is like a box of chocolates. You never know what you are going to get." In the movie the symbol of the surprising highway of his life journey was a white bird's feather being lifted from the ground by the air and blown in every which direction. Forest's life travelled on highways of chance and amazing accomplishment.

In "*Cast Away*," the story of a Fed-Ex time and motion man was told. Chuck Noland, played by Hanks, spent his life problem-solving for Fed-Ex. At a moment's notice he could be called to the ends of the earth to fix a problem. He was engaged to a wonderful lady with whom he was spending the Christmas Holidays. At the last moment he was called to take a Fed-Ex flight to the South Pacific to address a problem. During the flight, his Fed-Ex airliner went down over the South Pacific. He was the only survivor. He floated on a raft from the wreckage. He arrived at a small uninhabited island. For the next four years he endured great hardships in seeking to survive. Everyone at home was sure he was dead. At last, he was declared dead. His fiancé married and life went on.

Amazingly, a piece of his crashed plane was washed ashore, and he was able to use it as a sail for his newly constructed raft. He put together the raft and sail to escape the island with the winds lifting him over the incoming tides and waves. At last, a cargo ship saw him, picked him up, and he made it home. He had chosen a floating Wilson volleyball, with his bloody handprint upon it, as an image with whom he conversed. Also, with Wilson there was a Fed-Ex package addressed to a place near Canadian, Texas. The package had angel's wings imprinted upon it. He did not know what the angel wings meant. Perhaps there was some angel watching over him? Chuck was determined to deliver the package if he survived.

Upon return he visited his now married fiancé. They were both traumatized and affirmed each other as the love of their lives. But she had a husband and a child. She had saved Chuck's car in her garage. After tears and kisses he drove away into an unknown future.

In Northwest Texas near Amarillo, he delivered the package with the imprinted angel wings to a farm with the same insignia over the gateway. No one was at home. He left it at the front door with a message that the package had saved his life. Then he drove away to a nearby crossroads. They ran from north to south and from east to west in the middle of the flatlands of northwest Texas. The scene from high above haunted me as he stopped his SUV, took out his maps, placed them on the hood of his car, and was busy making a choice of the highway he would choose. Where was he headed?

As he did this a pickup truck came down the highway and turned in front of him and stopped. A beautiful red headed lady stepped out and asked him where he was headed. He answered that he was trying to decide. She told him that one road led south to the Gulf of Mexico; the other to Amarillo and on to California; the other made its way to Canada and beyond. Then she jumped into her truck and pulled away. As she did, she called out to him with a very seductive smile. "Good Luck Cowboy". As she drove away, Chuck saw on the back of the truck the insignia, the "angel wings", that were on the package he had just delivered. The look on her face said it all. Perhaps this was the guidance he needed. "Good Luck Cowboy". This was an invitation to act, to choose one's destiny, to choose life. Everything within me wanted to cry to him, "Go after her Cowboy!" This was guidance for a new life of love and meaning. All he needed to do was to choose and to act!

"Good Luck Cowboy!" What is it that makes sense of our life's journey? Is there any power of providence that is at work in the events of our lives? Or is our life story and journey a series of accidental events and required choices that we weave together at the multiple crossroads of life through time and space? Is life a feather being blown through the air by the winds with no rhyme or rhythm? Is life really like a box of chocolates? You never know what you are going to get? Is there a connection between divine guidance and human choice? What role does fate have in our ultimate choices? Could Oedipus have avoided marrying his own mother? Dare we trust the work of a higher power in guiding our choices, even though we may not be aware of this guidance? Does life have any meaning? Or is our life journey the result of a combination of powers beyond us, working upon us, possibly pulling strings to determine our destiny? Could William Shakespeare's *"Macbeth"* be correct as he heard the report of Lady Macbeth's death? He said:

"To-morrow, and to-morrow, and to-morrow Creeps in this petty pace from day to day, To the last syllable of recorded time, and all our yesterdays have lighted fools the way to dusty death. Out, out brief candle! Life's but a walking shadow. A poor player that struts and frets his hour upon the stage, and then is heard no more; It is a tale told by an idiot, full of sound and fury, Signifying nothing."[1]

During my first semester at Texas Tech, I majored in speech and had an opening role in Shakespeare's Twelfth Night. I was given an entrance role, spoke a line, and then made my exit, never to appear again in the play. A lot of my study time was wasted to make my dramatic entrance and exit. My parents came from Amarillo and brought a young lady who was my childhood friend. I was hoping to impress her with my potential and importance. The role did not achieve much, but it was an expression of my highway choice with little awareness of where that choice might finally lead me.

It was the beautiful red head at the crossroads of Chuck's life, with the panoramic view of Texas highways that crisscrossed the awesome flatness of the geography of the Panhandle of northwest Texas that raised in my mind the philosophical questions of human freedom and some guidance greater than the character's decisions.

"Good Luck Cowboy", and the attractive lady was on her way with the "angel wings" posted on the tailgate of her pickup truck. In that moment of choice, the mysterious connection of freedom and destiny were playing out. The movie ended and each viewer was allowed to write his or her own ending. Stories with no endings have frustrated me. Or

---

1. Harbage, *Shakespeare, Macbeth*, 15–30.

sometimes a given ending by the author does not satisfy and we rewrite the ending anyway. Perhaps good story telling leaves us at the crossroads still ruminating on which way to choose or why we chose the highways we have travelled.

When I met my wife Kay on a blind date, the first image of her as she opened her apartment door was her beautiful dark red hair and creamy complexion. My attention was captured. Through my time at the La Canada Church, I kept a Peanuts cartoon tacked to my office bulletin board. In the cartoon the central character had become fascinated by the "Little Red Headed Girl". I chose to marry that "Little Red Headed Girl" and I have never regretted it. From time to time, she has reminded me that she preserved the beautiful green silk dress she wore on our first date. Also, the wine bottle from that evening's dinner has been a candle holder for us and sits on one of the shelves of our kitchen. Perhaps this was why I wanted to cry out to Chuck, "Go after that red-headed girl." Providence was at work.

For years I have loved the ancient Greek story of voyage, travel, and journey. On one of our family vacations in the early 1980's on the island of Maui, Hawaii, my goal was to seriously read and to reflect on The Iliad and the Odyssey. I think I was searching for a metaphor through which to interpret my family story and my own story. In more recent years I visited the ruins of Troy discovered by the German archeologist, Heinrich Schliermann, who in 1870 excavated the site. I bought my son and I a wood model of the Trojan horse made famous at Troy. What drew me to this story was the long journey back home of the central character. There were many obstacles and temptations. The struggles to make it home in hopes of being reunited with loved ones whom he had left behind for so many years during the battle for Troy spoke to my inner longing to find my way back to the ground of my own being. I did not see my personal story as one of going to war and returning home, but I did see my journey as embracing suffering and longing to enter the reality of the biblical vision of peace in the fullness of the New Creation.

Something of this longing for home I strongly identified with in the memoirs of Tara Westover. She wrote,

> "Tyler said he would miss me, then he let me go, stepping into his car and speeding down the hill and onto the highway. I watched the dust settle.
>
> Tyler rarely came home after that. He was building a new life for himself across enemy lines.

It would be many years before I would understand what leaving that day had cost him, and how little he had understood about where he was going.

Tyler stepped into a void. I don't know why he did it and neither does he. He can't explain where the conviction came from, or how it burned brightly enough to shine through the black uncertainty.

But I've always supposed it was the music in his head, some hopeful tune the rest of us couldn't hear, the same secret melody he'd been humming when he bought that trigonometry book or saved all those pencil shavings."[2]

(A younger sister's reflections about her older brother's leaving home)

Tara's brother left home to discover a life. Tara ultimately needed to leave home to discover reality and life. Her family, in the name of some form of survivalist fundamentalism, was oppressive and nearly destroyed the entire family. There was much abuse from the parents and from other siblings. Somehow Tara courageously left home to become educated at BYU. That separation ultimately gave her the courage to move toward a larger reality and to rewrite her personal narrative for the sake of life. Her journey toward life and love severed her relationship with home and her parents. Her parents sought to bring her home from Harvard Graduate School, but she refused. Home was too toxic for her to return. Although, in listening to her CSPAN interviews, she still longs for home. In that sense, she is doing what we all do and that is to sort out our identity and to connect with a new story that gives meaning, hope, and love.

My desire in this memoir is to pursue this tension in my life's journey on the highways that I have chosen in faith that a divine benevolent sovereign was calling, guiding, and leading me toward a destination that I could not see except by inner intuition. Comfort has come to me through the Apostle Paul's affirmation in Romans 8:28 and 37, "We know that all things work together for good for those who love God, who are called according to his purpose. For I am convinced that neither death, nor life, nor angels, nor rulers, nor things present, nor things to come, nor powers, nor height, nor depth, nor anything else in all creation, will be able to separate us from the love of God in Christ Jesus our Lord." NRSV. This passage, along with Psalm 139, have nurtured my faith.

---

2. Westover, *Educated*, 51.

The paradoxes of divine providence and human freedom have haunted the highways of my life that I have chosen. I am a mixture of Greek and Hebrew world views that will not always live together in philosophical/theological harmony. Often, I have stood at the crossroads with my maps figuratively spread while seeking to discern my way in the overall scheme of things. Thankfully, persons and events have opened doors to my future, and I have stepped out into the unknown.

One summer vacation time I was especially asking for guidance. One day while in prayer the answer came in my inner reflections: "Wait and see what I will do." That was not exactly the answer I was seeking. It has never been easy for me to wait, to pray, and to surrender to the will of God. So, I have waited and moved forward one day at a time, one breathe at a time as the character in *"Cast Away"* chose to do. My journey has been filled with surprises. God has come to me over and over as Paula D'Arcy wrote, "God comes to you disguised as your life."[3] My story will trace how this has been true over and over.

---

3. Au, *Aging with Wisdom and Grace*, 16.

Chapter 1

The Highways of God's People

"Happy are those whose strength is in you, in whose heart are the highways to Zion. As they go through the valley of Baca they make it a place of springs; the early rain also covers it with pools. They go from strength to strength; the God of gods will be seen in Zion."

(PSALM 84:5–7 NRSV)

EUGENE PETERSON CLARIFIED WHEN HE spoke of the way we come to God and the way God comes to us in Jesus. He wrote,

> "What is God doing? Jesus tells us what to do; at the same time, he tells us what God is doing. Jesus is God in action. Jesus is God speaking. Jesus is God touching lepers. Jesus is God forgiving. Jesus is God blessing children. Jesus is God weeping over Jerusalem.
>
> Jesus is the way we come to God. Jesus is the way God comes to us. And not first one and then the other but both at the same time. Psalm 84 speaks of men and women 'in whose hearts are the highways to Zion.' Jesus. Our way to God. God's way to us."[1]

In 1990 I was drawn to the Summer Institute of Theology at Princeton Theological Seminary. I had not seen the Seminary campus since I left in June 1963, after completing my class work for the Th.M. degree in History of Doctrine. The theme of the 1990 Institute was "Pilgrimage". I

---

1. Peterson, *Jesus*, 38.

had a growing conviction that I had been on a lifelong pilgrimage that had led me through an open door toward the fulness of life. What I trusted was that God my Creator had a purpose and plan for my life which required me to journey by faith as the Spirit of God led me. The sovereign presence and power of the Lord who created me and who had been with me and for me through all the valleys and mountain top experiences of the journey was the God of love. (Psalm 23; Romans 8, C.S. Lewis, *The Horse and His Boy, The Chronicles of Narnia*)

The Institute was an opportunity to do theological reflection on my journey. One of the reading assignments was John Bunyan's Pilgrim's Progress. From that summer of reading and reflection the metaphor of "journey" or "pilgrimage" became helpful for interpreting my personal salvation story. Years later it was a joy for me to visit Bunyan's hometown in England and to experience the context of his vision of God's salvation and the City of God. While he was in prison Bunyan wrote this allegory of Christian's journey from the Worldly City toward the New Jerusalem, the City of God.

I believe "pilgrimage" is a central metaphor for the Christian story. It is the Bible's story. The Bible tells God's story, Israel's story, Jesus' story, the Church's story, and invites us to interpret our personal stories, our family stories, our tribal stories, our political stories through the lens of God's interactions with the elect people. From the Bible's perspective human history had a beginning and will have an ending, an alpha, and an omega. Time began in a garden and will end in the City of God, the New Jerusalem, the new heaven, and new earth where the River of Life flows and where the Tree of Life produces leaves for the healing of the nations. (Ezekiel 47; Revelation 21–22)

The Greek story was often shaped by endless repetitive cycles of events that were controlled by the gods, by fate, and were, therefore, ultimately meaningless. The Bible's story struggles with life through the lens of God's creation love and providence. Paradise was created; Paradise was fallen; and Paradise will be restored. I suspect those of us in the western tradition carry both Greek and Hebrew highways or narratives in our minds and hearts. Big parts of our personal narratives reflect the inner arguments between Greek and Hebrew worldviews. Perhaps these narratives shape and form the "flesh and the Spirit" within us and likely give rise to "faith and doubt" during the long journey to reality.

My faith, hope, and love inform me that the story that needs to be reclaimed is the Christian's responsibility for this world in which he or she journeys on the way to the City of God. This is the narrow highway that leads to life and blessed are those who walk in this way. It is an inner and outer journey as Elizabeth O'Conner framed it years ago. The pilgrims plant the seeds of God's blessings, and through the power of God, transform the deserts into fruitful places. To be sure, a pilgrim's journey is one of pain, of suffering, of unknowing, yet profound meaning. Central to the journey is God's project of healing the world, of making peace, of reconciling the world, and working toward justice through his people, of setting the world right. This, as New Testament scholar N.T. Wright has said, is God's project. Jesus said in Matthew's Sermon on the Mount,

> "Enter through the narrow gate; for the gate is wide and the road is easy that leads to destruction, and there are many who take it. For the gate is narrow and the road is hard that leads to life, and there are few who find it." (Matthew 7:13–14)

In John's Gospel Jesus taught,

> "I am the gate. Whoever enters by me will be saved and will come in and go out and find pasture. I came that they may have life and have it abundantly." (John 10:9–10)

The church has been invested with a stewardship responsibility for planet earth. The New Creation will mean the transformation of human history and the cosmos. This is God's mission through God's people, the church. (Isaiah 40–55; John 20; 2 Corinthians 5) "As the Father has sent me, so send I you."

I remember my teacher at Westmont College, Dr. David Hubbard, suggesting an explanation for the difference between the students at UCSB and those of Westmont College. He said that Westmont students lived within the tensions of "the flesh and the Spirit" and struggled with internal "faith and doubt". They were Christians and were not entirely at home in this world and were not sure of their responsibility for the world. The UCSB students likely had greater internal peace because they were more conformed to the ways of the world. Therefore, they could do, say, and embrace the fallenness of human history without many pangs of conscience. Of course, this was a generalization.

There were Christians at UCSB as well, along with many good persons on their way travelling their own highways. Nevertheless, what all of us pilgrims learn along the way is that our journey is not escapist, of seeking to move from this troubling world to the joys of eternal life or heaven.

God's mission through his people is one of restoration to Life, to what God intended Life to be from the beginning. When the New Creation arrives the brokenness of our sin sick, death enslaved world, will be made whole in a transformed heaven and earth that overlap and interconnect with the Sovereign reign of Israel's God over God's people. In that moment, justice, peace, and love shall have arrived and the kingdom of God will have become fully realized. (For this insight I am indebted to N.T. Wright's biblical theology interpreted in his many books.)

Eugene Peterson wrote, and I agree,

> "The people who told the Jesus story, primarily Matthew, Mark, Luke, and John, were also conversant with earlier narratives that anticipate this story. They tell the story of the way of Jesus in the narrative context of centuries of storytelling in such a way that the stories of the preceding two thousand years are filled out and completed in the story of Jesus.
>
> If we want to get the full impact of the story of Jesus and the way of Jesus, there is no substitute for taking a long, slow, leisurely pilgrimage through the pages of Genesis to Malachi, getting that river of narrative flowing through our bloodstream, observing the enormous attention given to place and person, so that this story is rooted in the immediate and the local, in named people in the neighborhood, among the animals and angels alive in those forests and deserts." [2]

I share Peterson's perspective. In reading my personal narrative you will discover that the central pursuit of my life has been to know the Jesus story whose personal narrative was deeply grounded in Israel's story. Over the years I have heard the voice of the living God speaking to me and through me the grace, the truth, and the love of God. I believe that the spiritual renewal of the church is and will be contingent upon the people of God living their life together in the worship of the triune God, Father, Son, and Holy Spirit. Through God's story, Israel's story, the door to the kingdom of God has been opened, but also the door into the meaning of human existence and the purpose and plan of God for human history and the ever – expanding cosmos.

Through faith the Christian confesses that God the Creator spoke his powerful word and everything that there is came into being. Genesis 1 and 2 were poetry, two Confessions of Faith, two true myths, narratives that invited humans to sing and to dance together in joy at the goodness

---

2. Peterson, *Jesus*, 39.

and beauty of life. The Lord is good, and the steadfast love of the Creator is to be celebrated. (Psalm 33:6-9; 136:1-9; Revelation 4:11) The reader of the creation stories should not think of these theological confessions as scientific accounts, but rather as profound calls for each of us to reflect on the mystery of the Creator's sovereign authority, power, and grace to call forth out of nothing the created order. At the end of each day of creation the Word of God declared that the divine work was good.

The crown of the creation story in Genesis 1 was of the human created in the image of God and declared to be very good. As male and female the Lord created the human in God's image. The Creator gave to the humans the stewardship responsibility to work the garden of the earth, to be fruitful and to multiply, to live in harmony, in right relationship with the Creator and with each other. God's shalom, peace, and justice would characterize the blessings of the LORD. On the seventh day of Creation God rested in the well-being and majesty of what God had done.

Genesis 2 told the story of Creation in a different way than the first account in Genesis 1. According to this narrator the Lord reached down into the soil of earth, formed Adam from the dust of the ground, breathed into his nostrils the breath of life and Adam became a living person full of the life of God's Spirit, fully animated to do God's creation work. After naming all the animals of the garden, Adam was aware that he was alone and that he needed a helper fit for him, to work with him, to fellowship with him, to listen and to speak in communion with the Creator and with each other. Adam needed a walking companion, if you will, to journey with him in the adventure of living life to his fullest and as God intended. Unmarried and married persons were made for life in community, the "beloved community" of the people of God. The need for fellowship witnessed to the humans as being created in the image of God.

The grace of the Creator looked with compassion upon Adam in his loneliness and provided the gift he needed. The Lord caused a deep sleep to fall upon Adam and while he was asleep took one of his ribs and fashioned the gift into a woman whom Adam named Eve. Awakened, he exclaimed, "This at last is bone of my bone and flesh of my flesh; this one shall be called Woman, for out of Man this one was taken." "Therefore, a man leaves his father and his mother and clings to his wife, and they become one flesh. And the man and his wife were both naked and were not ashamed." Genesis 2:18-25

Central to the mystery and wonder of the story was that the Lord gave to Adam and to Eve the freedom to love and to be loved. Some have said this was God's greatest risk. How would the first couple use their freedom? They were not robots programed to always live within the boundaries established by the Lord. They were abundantly blessed and given all they would need to walk in faithful covenant fellowship with the Lord and with the human community. But they were required to choose life by obedience to the Lord.

The LORD provided one who would look Adam in the face, stare into his eyes, and experience joyful union with him in sexual intercourse to which they were both powerfully drawn as an expression of the mystery of life, love, and human intimacy. From this union would come children who would continue the Lord's creation work!

The two were permitted to eat from all the trees in the Garden of Eden, except for one, the tree of the knowledge of good an evil. On the day they ate of that tree they would surely die. The two could only maintain their full humanity by living in obedience to this command.

The narrator did not say why a voice of rebellion was also heard in the Garden. It was a voice that suggested that Adam and Eve could become more than they were created to be, servants of the living LORD living in right relationship with their Creator and with one another. The tempter's voice suggested to Eve that the Creator could not be trusted. He was seeking to keep something from them. He knew that on the day the couple ate from the one prohibited tree their eyes would be opened to see that they could be like God, knowing good and evil. Since the fruit of the tree was delicious looking and was to be desired to make one wise, Eve ate the fruit and gave some to her husband and he ate. Their eyes were opened, and they knew they were naked. The result was that they hid from the Creator.

When the LORD came walking in the Garden at the set time for fellowship, he called out to them, "Where are you? What have you done?" He knew what they had done. They had eaten from the forbidden tree and incurred guilt and shame.

The confrontation with Adam was painful and accusatory. Adam said, "It was the woman you gave to be with me who caused this. She gave me the fruit and I ate it. It is her fault. Don't blame me!"

Eve excused her act by blaming it upon the snake, a voice in God's Garden. "The serpent tricked me, and I ate." The consequence was that the humans fell away from God. If not completely lost, the image of God was clouded, and they incurred the wrath and curse of God upon themselves and the created order.

Theologians have sought to interpret this simple, yet profound story of human lack of trust in the goodness of God, or rebellion in pride against the Creator. Surely, their act was one of disobedience to the will of God in seeking to become like God to replace God. They assumed they could be their own gods. The consequence was that they lost their original relationship with God; they came under the dominion of sin, experienced the futility of life, and were driven from the Garden to live East of Eden without access to the Tree of Life. They were caught up in endless cycles of power seeking and conflict. The result of this chaotic state of nature would be human violence and death.

Through their transgression, their misuse of human freedom, they introduced into human life lack of trust, prideful rebellion, competitive self-seeking, the processes of aging, vaulting ambition, endless conflict, and all the seven deadly sins that have led to wars and rumors of wars and even to the potential destruction of the created order. The human family characterized by all these destroying attitudes and behaviors became broken and enslaved to the powers of sin and death.

Thus, Cain murdered his brother Abel. The Lord asked Cain about the well-being of his brother Abel. Cain responded, "Am I my brother's keeper?" God became sorry that he had ever created the humans. (Genesis 6) The whole earth was full of violence and the way of peace had been lost. The judgment of God was poured out in the Great Flood. Noah, the one man rescued from the waters, turned out to be a disaster. The LORD made a covenant with Noah and the sign of the covenant was a rainbow. With a new beginning after the flood, the humans built the Tower of Babel to climb up into heaven and to be like God. The LORD confused the languages at Babel and chaos reigned. "All have sinned and fallen short of the glory of God. No one is righteous; no not one." The wages of sin are bondage, futility, and death. (Romans 3 and 6) The Creator could have given up on the humans, but God developed another strategy to rescue humanity from its fallen-ness to restore what was lost and to renew the hope of salvation.

In an act of divine grace God chose one man, Abraham, and his wife Sarah, to carry the promise of blessing, to become the father and the mother of a multitude of nations. The Lord cut a covenant with them, and circumcision was the sign of the covenant. (Genesis 15–17) Through the offspring of this family peace and hope began to spring up. Thus, began the journey of Abraham and Sarah into a future of blessing and judgment for the sake of a new humanity.

The story of the creation and the fall of the first humans is just that. I do not look at the story as a literal story of history. Nevertheless, I read it as a poignant story that interprets what is true about each of us, including me. I am a child of Adam and Eve. I have struggled to awaken to life as a gift of God to be celebrated with the spirit of gratitude. Unbelief, lack of trust, pride, and sensuality have taken deep roots in my soul. I have discovered that the line of sin runs through my heart. I am a person that has experienced inner emptiness and relational brokenness. I understand the reality of being asleep and insensitive to the love and justice of God. Like the Narnian Prince held in bondage in a dark, underworld cave ruled by the usurping wicked witch, placed under a spell, and anesthetized by the witch's magic, I have slept through *kairos* moments of opportunity. If help had not come from the overworld of freedom, I would have remained in the darkness of spiritual sleep. Puddleglum, the Marshwiggle, the Christ disciple from the overworld, had entered the dark underworld, moved his foot into the witch's fireplace, experienced the pain that awakened him, and me to the reality of a Way or Highway out of slavery toward the restoration of true freedom.[3]

Jesus, the Word of God incarnate, was wounded for my sins and the sins of humanity to release us all from the dark bondage of this world of spiritual darkness. If the LORD had not intervened in my life journey to begin the long process of transformation, I would not have lived the life I have lived.

Not only is this true of me and my family, but it is true for the entire human family. We are lost and trapped in a foreign land. If God does not do for us that we cannot do for ourselves there is no hope. The amazing grace of the story is that our clouded images of God may yet be allowed to respond to the love of God revealed in Israel's story and in the life, death, and resurrection of Jesus, Israel's anointed One.

Yes, the Voice of the Creator may speak into our spiritual darkness and call us forth to Abraham's journey on a desert highway into the destiny God has planned for us. This is the highway to Zion and blessed are those whose hearts are paved with desire for the City of God. (Psalm 84:5–7) To choose this road is to walk on the way to restored freedom.

Dr. Armand Nicholi, Jr. wrote a book entitled, *The Question of God; C.S. Lewis and Sigmund Freud Debate God, Love, Sex, and the Meaning of Life*. In this imagined debate Freud argued that the humans needed to

---

3. Lewis, *Silver Chair*, 181.

grow up, to face the facts of life and death, and make the best of it. C.S. Lewis responded with the argument that growing up was not what the humans were called to do. Rather, the human task was "to wake up" to the reality of God, respond to the revelation of the Creator, and begin the lifetime journey of transformation by the illumination of the light of God's Word and Spirit. (2 Corinthians 4:3-6; Ephesians 5:8-14)

The biblical story is filled with the theme of waking up to the reality of the meaning of life in the light of God's grace. This was the human journey to which humanity was invited. Abraham was elected and called by the LORD to leave his native country with the promise of God's blessings upon him. (Genesis 12-22) He and Sarah would become the father and the mother of a multitude of nations. They would become nomads in search of a land and in hopes of a family that would bless all people. Having heard the Voice of the Lord and believing the Lord's promises, they travelled the Fertile Crescent from Ur of the Chaldeans up the Tigress/Euphrates Valley to Haran. By welcoming this journey, they began what Eugene Peterson named *"A Long Obedience in the Same Direction"*.

The irony of the story was that Sarah was barren and could not give her husband an heir. Together they suggested various ways to provide an heir. After they were well beyond the years of bearing children and all hope was nearly lost, the promise was fulfilled by the grace of God. Isaac was born. Abraham and Sarah laughed. Isaac represented their future and the future of the Covenant people of God. The old couple had to face the fact that they could not guarantee their own future. Only God could do that. Abraham circumcised Isaac. Abraham's family would bear the sign of God's covenant promises. Amid faith and doubt they journeyed with an awareness that they were citizens of the Heavenly City to which Hebrews 11:8-22 witnessed. They carried the promise of blessing for all nations. They were welcomed and resisted because of the promise they carried and the hope they inspired for the nations, and for the Creation.

Finally, Abraham witnessed to his trust that the future blessing could not be guaranteed by Isaac, but only by the God who made the promise and who gave the child. The future of Israel was not in the gift but in the giver of the gift. The sacrifice of Isaac (Genesis 22) foreshadowed the sacrifice of the Son of God by the God of grace on the altar of Golgotha. The sparing of Isaac's life was a witness to the resurrection power of God and to the strong purpose of God to "unite all things in Christ". (Romans 4;

Ephesians 1; Hebrews 11; James 2:18–24) Abraham's faith was reckoned to him as righteousness. His works of obedience witnessed to his faith.[4]

The Bible's story struggles with the question of why it was that God chose this nomadic couple through whom to build a covenant family and through whom the nations would be blessed? At midway of the first decade of the 21st century, I was part of a group of Presbyterian pastor/theologians dialoging with leadership from the American Jewish community. We were writing a new paper for the PCUSA on *"The Relationship Between Christians and Jews."* We studied the Abraham story together. The Rabbi's suggested that Abraham was called and chosen because he was the best of men, the first team. Abraham was a righteous man obedient to the will of God. He was a perfectly observant man. God chose the very best through whom to accomplish his rescue of humanity. (We did not discuss the birth of Ishmael to Abraham and Hagar. That is another story line, and it is central to Muslim faith.)

Of course, I believe that if one honestly reads the Genesis story of the patriarchs and matriarchs, our fathers, and mothers in faith, what is seen is an imperfect family who had doubts, and who demonstrated lack of trust as they laughed at the promises of God. Sarah may have come to think that her old husband was unstable and full of fantasy. He had difficulty in being honest. She knew that. She must have been perplexed by her husband's ambivalence. To save his own skin, Abraham lied to the Egyptians and said that Sarah was his sister. (Perhaps she was his half-sister.) She was taken into Pharaoh's harem because she was beautiful. If Pharaoh had not been warned in a dream, the mother of the Promise could have been lost and perhaps the project of salvation through Israel terminated. Sarah tried to help God by offering her handmaid, Hagar, to Abraham, through whom to bring a promised child into the world. But no, the promised child was to come through the power of God to old Abraham and Sarah. (Galatians 4:21–31) When they were beyond the age of childbearing, the gift of Isaac, their future, was given.

At the end of their earthly journey, the only part of the Promised Land that they owned was a burial cave for the family. A Palestinian tour guide in Israel commented to me in private one day that at least Abraham bought the cave rather than stealing it.

The theologians of Israel had a larger story to tell about the faithfulness of God to God's promises and to the grace of God that was always

---

4. Sanders, *God Has a Story*, 30–40.

at work even in the midst of human sinfulness. Deuteronomy 7 asked why God chose this family through which to bless the world. The answer given was that God chose Israel as an act of Divine Love. In 1 Corinthians chapter 1 the Apostle Paul reminded the believers in Corinth of their humble origins and limited accomplishments. God chose what was imperfect, weak, broken, and lowly to confound the wisdom of the world. Thankfully, the aging couple, Abraham, and Sarah, received an unconditional covenant promise from the LORD; Grace empowered their gratitude. Nevertheless, they laughed at the promises of God. Their life story was a mixture of laughing, weeping, and struggling.

After the near sacrifice of Isaac in the land of Moriah, the LORD intervened and saved the boy. What this must have done to Isaac we do not know. What it did to the old couple we dare not guess. Soren Kierkegaard explored this test of faith in *Fear and Trembling*. He suggested there were multiple ways of looking at the story. To be sure, the test revealed the obedient heart of the father and the mysterious ways of the Lord. Abraham and his son Isaac moved forward having come to trust that the Lord was good and had a mission for this family.

Eugene Peterson, in *The Jesus Way*, in his chapter on Abraham entitled *"Abraham: Climbing Mt. Moriah"*, wrote,

> "The way of faith does not serve our fantasies, our illusions, or our ambitions. Faith is not the way to God on our terms, it is the way of God to us on his terms."[5]
>
> "The sacrifice of Isaac had to be read in the total context of Abraham's life. There had been many times of leaving securities and of moving into the unknown of the journey into which the Voice of God had called him. He had built many altars along the way to remember and to celebrate the faithfulness of God. It had meant surrendering to the Voice's guidance without knowing where he was going. Repeatedly, Abram left behind what he might have permanently worshiped. But from beginning to end he had learned to leave and to trust in the sovereign God who had often tested him." [6]

Peterson witnessed,

> "At Mount Moriah we accept and worship a God beyond our understanding. At Mount Moriah we embrace a mystery that is light-filled, but no less a mystery for all that."

5. Peterson, *Jesus*, 55.
6. Peterson, *Jesus*, 55.

"Faith means that we put our trust in God—and we don't know how he will work out our salvation, only that it is our salvation that he is working out. Which frees us for anything. We must be the ones tied down, so that we can be the ones set free." [7]

"Still, even after many years of reading this story I am surprised to find myself surprised. I am surprised that Abraham, Isaac bound, and knife raised, is not surprised to hear the Voice tell him that there is a ram in the thicket. And Isaac is not surprised to end up not sacrificed."[8]

"The text is a summing up and clarification of a long life of reorientation from the ziggurat in Ur to the altar on Moriah, from self-aggrandizement to God-gifting. To live by faith—to live a faith life—means to be tested". [9]

So, it was for Jesus. The synoptics place the story of Jesus' testing by the devil at the beginning of his mission. Having been baptized by the Holy Spirit, the same Spirit led him into the desert to be tempted. The devil offered him everything our broken, pride filled, self-centered world had to offer. All he had to do was worship the devil, make a deal with the devil, and allow the evil one to show him how to be a successful Messiah. He could have chosen the way of "upward mobility". Thank God, Jesus rejected the devil's deal and chose the way of suffering, obedient trust in the purpose and plan of God. He recapitulated Israel's 40 years of wilderness testing, but was faithful to the God of resurrection life, trusting God's loving plan, even though he moved through the valley of the shadow of death. This is the pilgrimage into which the Voice calls us each and through which the Lord proves himself faithful to his people, the new humanity, the New Israel, the church. (1 Corinthians 10:13; Romans 8:28–39)

Abraham sent his servants on a journey to find a wife for Isaac among his relatives in Haran. (Genesis 24) Rebekah was identified and accepted the invitation to return to Canaan to marry Isaac. Soon the twins, Jacob, and Esau, were born to Rebekah and Isaac. They came from the womb in conflict. Jacob, the younger son, stole his older brother's birthright. By deception he and his mother schemed to gain Isaac's final blessing. Jacob had to flee Esau's wrath. Facing a long journey, Jacob now

---

7. Peterson, *Jesus*, 55.
8. Peterson, *Jesus*, 56–57.
9. Peterson, *Jesus*, 57.

carried the blessings of the family. God had promised to bless him, to keep him, and to bring him back to the Promised Land. (Genesis 28)

Wilkie and Noreen Au referred to the Jacob story in their book on aging. What they wrote has become an interpretive story of my life. The first words out of Jacob's mouth when he awakened after the dream were these:

> "Wow, God was in this place, and I did not know it." "This biblical story conveys a consoling message: no matter how life challenges us, God will be there to support us."
>
> "By the time we reach the afternoon of life, we have lived long enough to know that aging is not a smooth road but has its ups and downs. Like Jacob, we need to know that God is with us when rocky times leave us feeling vulnerable and afraid. While faith assures us of God's abiding presence, disruptive life events can disorient us and blur our perception. To find God in turbulent times may require some rummaging. Just like rummaging through a drawer looking for something we know is there but can't quite put our hands on, rummaging for God involves sorting through our experiences until we discover how God is present."[10]

There were many children fathered by Jacob through the sisters Leah, Rachel, and their two handmaids. Jacob learned how painful the consequences of deceit could be. Uncle Laban betrayed his promises to Jacob. Therefore, Jacob had to work extra years to marry Rachel, the younger sister that he loved. When he decided to take his wives and children back to his parent's home in Canaan, he returned with fear and trembling for how he might be encountered by Esau, the brother whom he had cheated out of his birthright and final blessing. His approach to Esau was measured. He placed his family and animals ahead of him while he waited at the Jabbok River. It was there, alone in the darkness, that he was encountered by a man with whom he wrestled all night. Neither prevailed in the struggle. At sunrise the mysterious man asked him to release him. Jacob demanded the man bless him first. As the sun was rising, he discovered that he had been wrestling with the angel of the Lord. The angel left him with a new name, "You shall no longer be called Jacob, but Israel, for you have striven with God and with humans, and have prevailed." Jacob called the place Peniel, saying, "For I have seen God face to face, and yet my life is preserved." Not only had he received a new

---

10. Au, *Aging*, 16–17.

name. The mysterious man had touched him in his hip and Jacob walked with a limp the rest of his life. (Genesis 32)

In one of my Israel trips I bought a small silver statue mounted on a lava rock depicting Jacob's wrestling with the Lord. It showed the angel and Jacob wrestling hand in hand, face to face. The small statue has sat on my church desk as a reminder that I too have wrestled with God and been wounded. In the waters of baptism, I have received a new name. In my old age I have walked with a limp as a reminder of my journey with Christ. Nevertheless, I say with the Apostle Paul, "I want to know Christ and the power of his resurrection and the sharing of his sufferings by becoming like him in his death, if somehow I may attain the resurrection from the dead.

Not that I have already obtained this or have already reached the goal; but I press on to make it my own, because Christ Jesus has made me his own. Forgetting what lies behind and straining forward to what lies ahead, I press on toward the goal for the prize of the heavenly call of God in Christ Jesus." (Philippians 3:10–16)

The 12 tribes of Israel came from the family of Abraham, Isaac, and Jacob. The family was troubled by Jacob's favoritism to Rachel's children. The final chapters of Genesis tell the story of Jacob's beloved Joseph and his brother's hostile fears.

With resentment and anger Joseph's brothers sold him into Egyptian slavery. As a young man Joseph taunted his brothers about his own favored position in the family. Years later the guilty brothers travelled to Egypt to buy food in a time of famine only to discover that Joseph had become second only to Pharaoh and was the administrator of Egypt's social welfare program. By God's providence Jacob's family moved to Egypt and there was a surprising reunion. The final theological commentary upon the flawed family and the faithfulness of God were Joseph's words to his guilty, anxious, angry, and fearful brothers, "You meant it for evil, but God meant it for good for the sake of saving the elect family as well as the nations of the earth." (Genesis 50:15–21) God's grace was at work in the midst of human sinfulness. Some have said that this is the central message of the entire Bible.

A Pharaoh arose who did not know Joseph. Jacob's family, which had settled in Egypt, was enslaved. They were seen as a national security risk for the Egyptians. They became the victims of state genocide. Not the last time this family would suffer from genocidal hatred. They cried to the heavens and the LORD delivered them through the leadership of

Moses, who was a murderer hiding in the Sinai. Yet, the LORD called him for the mission of leading his people to the Promised Land. Kicking and screaming, Moses resisted and yet, obeyed. (Exodus 3–4) In the journey his sense of inadequacy was transformed into a meek, courageous faith. In a mighty exodus story of rescue the LORD set his people free to journey toward the land promised to Abraham and Sarah. What commenced was a 40-year journey through the wilderness of Sinai. After much purification and the strengthening of faith through times of testing and the death of Moses, Joshua, by the presence and power of the LORD, led the people across the Jordan River into the Promised Land.

The Old Testament story made the point that the LORD travelled with his people. The LORD'S presence was with them. The LORD led the former slaves by a cloud of glory during the daytime and by a pillar of fire at night. The mobile tabernacle in the wilderness was the center of the worship of the LORD. At Mt. Sinai the LORD'S glory shined upon Moses and a conditional covenant based upon legal obedience was cut and sealed in the blood of the animal sacrifice. The Law, the Torah, the ten words, were written upon the stone tablets given to Moses for him to carry down the mountain to the people.

The first four commandments called for love for the LORD. (Exodus 20; Deuteronomy 5) The second six commandments called for the Israelites to love their neighbors as they loved themselves. (Leviticus 19:18) When Moses arrived with the commandments, the people had convinced Aaron, Moses' brother, to make a "golden calf" to lead them back to Egyptian security. Being free to move into the future led by the glory of the LORD created an excess of anxiety and fear. Idolatry, the worship of gods that were no gods, gods that they thought they could see and touch, stirred the wrath of the LORD and of Moses. There was a crisis of leadership. Moses cast the tablets to the ground, and they shattered. Then he confronted his brother Aaron; commanded Aaron to grind up the golden idol to fine dust, and then made the people drink the crushed gold in their water. They had broken all the commandments before Moses came down from the mountain.

The LORD was ready to abandon this people and start anew with Moses, but Moses prayed and asked forgiveness for them. Forgiveness was given, but there were consequences. The wrath of God allowed the people to suffer the results of their disobedience. The story of Israel continued, but the tensions between cheap grace and the costly grace of God were alive each day of the journey.

Joshua, after 40 years in the wilderness and the death of Moses, was given the spirit of Moses to lead the conquest of Canaan. Gradually, the tribes settled, but they were unable to drive out their enemies from all the land.

The LORD, *YAHWEH*, was a God on the move in history for the sake of redeeming his people. (2 Samuel 7) The Judges held the Tribal Confederacy together as the tribes did battle with their enemies. The people longed for a king so that they might be like the surrounding nations. Samuel warned them. The LORD relented and Saul, David, and Solomon came to the throne. The people came to understand the dangers of having a king over them. (1 Samuel 8) The Davidic Covenant was established. However, rather than King David building God a house, the Lord would build David a dynasty through the hands of Solomon, the Son of David. Neither David nor Solomon was perfect, but at their worst they still had in their hearts the highways to Zion.

After Solomon the tribes of Israel separated into the northern and southern kingdoms. The word of the LORD was spoken through the prophets to both kingdoms. Major and minor prophets called the people to covenant faithfulness: "to do justice, to love kindness, and to walk humbly in the way of the Lord." (Micah 6:8) But Israel had played the harlot with other gods and the people of the promise were corrupted and defiled by their idolatry.

God's judgments led to the Assyrian and Babylonian Exilic stories. First, Israel, the northern ten tribes, were carried away in 722 B.C. into Assyrian captivity to ultimately assimilate and to disappear on the stage of world history. In 587 B.C., Judah was carried away into Babylonian captivity. After a remnant returned to the Holy Land in a New Exodus, Israel's journey continued toward Bethlehem and the birth of the Son of David, the Son of God, Jesus, the Son of Mary. (Matthew 1) His bodily presence was the living Temple through which God's True Light shined into the human neighborhood for the sake of revealing grace, truth, and the love of God to a world enslaved in the darkness of unbelief, pride, sin, and death. (John 1, *THE MESSAGE*)

Centuries after the Golden Age of King David and Solomon, God's judgments fell upon Israel, the Davidic monarchy and Jerusalem. The unconditional blessings of the Abrahamic Covenant would not be received by Israel without obedience to the Mosaic Law. God's grace was not cheap. The blessed assurance of the *"Royal Theology"* of the Davidic Covenant proved unreliable as security for the future. (Jeremiah 7; Ezekiel 34) Only obedience to the Mosaic Covenant would guarantee the blessings of the promises. The glory of the LORD, in judgment upon Israel's idolatry and covenant breaking, led the people into Babylonian captivity where they lived in exile for nearly 100 years.

In the 6th century B.C., the Babylonian armies razed the Jerusalem Temple and the City. Thousands died. The remnants of the people were removed to a foreign land where they were mocked and required to sing the LORD'S song. (Psalm 137) It was a time of great physical and spiritual suffering. The king, the land, the city, the temple, symbols of God's promises and blessings, were taken away. It seemed as if Israel's journey had ended, and God had rejected his people. The result was that an exilic identity was forged. A longing for return to the Promised Land never left them. Somehow, the highways to Zion were still in the hearts of God's covenant people. Through their long exilic years, the theologians of Israel studied, contemplated, prayed, and interpreted their history. Obedience to the Law of Moses, as interpreted by the exilic theologians and lawyers, became everything. The Exile was seen as God's judgment upon the law breaking of the leadership and the disobedience of priests and prophets. (Ezekiel 34) Nevertheless, the LORD promised a New Covenant, which he would write upon Israel's heart by the presence of the Spirit of God. (Jeremiah 31; Ezekiel 36; Hosea 11; Hebrews 8)

In God's providential purpose at work through Cyrus the Great the people were restored to the Holy Land and the Holy City. An effort was made to rebuild the Temple to its former glory. Israel had been disciplined and transformed by the love and justice of God. A New Exodus happened. The glory of the LORD went before his people into the Promised Land where they were resettled under God's blessings and judgments. (Isaiah 40–55)

At long last, James A. Sanders said in one of his sermons, "the glory of the LORD which had accompanied his people from Ur, to Egypt, to Syria, to Canaan, to Babylon, and back to Jerusalem crawled into a cradle in Bethlehem (Matthew 1 and Luke 2) and the Word became flesh, incarnate in Jesus the Servant-Son of God and Israel's Christ."[11] (John 1) Jesus journeyed up and down the land promised to his ancestors. Through the mighty acts of God in healing, restoring faith, renewing hope, mediating forgiveness to broken sinners, and ultimate obedience to the will of God, God's salvation took root in human history anew. In Jesus the kingdom

---

11. Sanders, *God Has Story*, 140.

of God was at hand. Jesus set his face to go up to Jerusalem. (Luke 9:51) "Salvation came not through a force in history, but through a human face."[12]

Along the way Jesus taught the twelve disciples about the call of God upon them to journey with him in doing God's mission. After his death, resurrection, and ascension, the Holy Spirit was poured out upon the believers in Jerusalem in fulfillment of the prophet's promises and they were empowered to witness to the gospel to the ends of the earth. (Luke 24; Acts 2) As Jesus had set his face to go up to Jerusalem, (Luke 9:51) so now the church was empowered to make its witness in Jerusalem, in Judea and Samaria, and to the ends of the earth. (Acts 1) The presence and power of the Spirit of Jesus filled his disciples, and the mission of God was launched that would carry the gospel to the nations. (See N.T. Wright: *How God Became King*; and *The Day the Revolution Began*)

The story of salvation moved on and came to fulfillment in the death of Christ upon the cross and his Easter Sunday resurrection. The story continued in the lives of those who followed Jesus. The LORD of the Abrahamic Covenant, an unconditional Covenant anchored in the faithfulness of the God of grace, fulfilled the promises made. People were coming from east and west, north, and south, to sit at table in the kingdom of God. The Word and the Spirit of God were advancing the reign and rule of God, the Kingdom of God. The journey with God and the search for the fullness of life continued in God's mission through the church, the family of Christ, the New Israel, the New Humanity. This was a people made up of believing Jews and Gentiles, slave and free, male and female, rich and poor, black, and white, from every tribe, nation, language, and race but now reconciled and adopted into relationship with the God of love, the God of justice and peace. In mercy God gathered his church, his New Covenant people. (2 Corinthians 5; Ephesians 2; Revelation 5)

Over time I have come to believe that the true Israel are children of the New Covenant reconciled in the blood of Christ poured out upon the cross and sealed with the promised Holy Spirit on the Day of Pentecost. This family shared a "salvation story". We are the New Israel. At the cross, on Good Friday, humanity was rescued from the powers of sin and death in order that we may move toward Life in the Kingdom of God, the Promised Land, the New Creation. This is our sacred journey. It is our pilgrimage toward the City of God, into our true homeland.

---

12. Gerson, Michael, Sermon at Washington National Cathedral.

The Highways Of God's People

The New Creation is already and is to come. The kingdom of God overlaps and interconnects with human history, as N.T. Wright affirmed. We live in the in-between times of the "already and the not yet". We walk with Christ as those who are receiving the mind of Christ, but also struggling with the internal conflicts between the "flesh and the Spirit". The Caesars of the political orders of the earth may have proclaimed themselves as lords of the world, but the church's confession was and is "Jesus is LORD". (Philippians 2:5–11) Through faith we have become citizens of the City of God. Along the way we pray for God's will to be done on earth as it is in heaven. The LORD'S Prayer is our prayer. Because we are forgiven sinners called out of our slavery to the "principalities and powers of this present darkness", adopted as the children of God, we walk with joy out of the shadow lands into the fullness of the bright colors of the real Narnia.

C.S. Lewis, in *The Chronicles of Narnia, the Last Battle*, wrote of the invitation for us to travel "further up and further in" to the joy of life healed by Aslan's death and resurrection, and set free by the breath of his mouth to journey with courage into the fullness of grace and truth. C.S. Lewis concluded his Narnian tales with these comforting words to the English children who had been guided by the presence and power of Aslan toward the fullness of reality:

> "For us this is the end of all the stories, and we can most truly say that they (the children) lived happily ever after. But for them it was only the beginning of the real story. All their life in this world and all their adventures in Narnia had only been the cover and the title page: now at last they were beginning Chapter One of the Great Story, which no one on earth has read: which goes on forever: in which every chapter is better than the one before." [13]

This is a summary of the Biblical story of God's grace at work in my days and years. My personal narrative interprets my "pilgrimage" through time and place with all its joys and sorrows, with all my strengths and weaknesses, with the conflicts between the old and the new, with successes and failures, with being conformed to the world and being transformed by the Word and the Spirit of God. Grace has filled my heart with gratitude to God. The desire to be like Jesus, to love God with all my being and my neighbor as myself has grown. The fruits of the Spirit are

---

13. Lewis, *Last Battle*, 173–174.

growing in my life, but the old person that still has a voice at the table can sidetrack my journey.

In *Mere Christianity*, C.S. Lewis said that each day we awaken "to dress up like Christ", to put on the "face of Christ" and "to pretend to be like Christ" knowing that we are not Christ. Nevertheless, over time we become like Christ; we begin to look like Christ, to have his mind and personality. We are becoming "Little Christ's". (Colossians 3) The truth is that God is pretending that we are "Little Christ's". The day will come when we will be fully like him who we love and who first loved us. Already we are the children of God by grace. It is not yet clear what we shall become, but when he appears, we will be like him for we shall see him as he is. (1 John 3) [14]

There is no perfect saint taking this pilgrimage. There are no plastic saints in the biblical story. All we know is that we have heard the same Voice that Abraham and Sarah heard calling them into their future for the sake of a fallen world yet radically loved and embraced by the God of grace. The City of God beckons, but so also the tantalizing attractions of a world filled with money, sex, conflict, aspiration, pride, ambition, violence, suffering, death, and the pursuit of power.

What about the Jewish people who were unable to believe in Jesus and to be united in the New Covenant? Has God abandoned his people, the people of the First Covenant? Has the church replaced Israel? In the history of the church, "replacement theology" has led to persecution of the Jewish people by the "New Israel", the church of Jesus Christ. In conversations with American Jewish leaders and representative pastor/theologians of the PCUSA, this was a point of discussion. They were clear that they continued to live under their Covenant that the Lord made with Abraham, Moses, and David. They argued that the Presbyterian Church dared not surrender to "successionist theology". If we did, this would lead us down the road of rejection of the Jewish people and to justification of identifying the Jews as wicked, unbelieving, Christ killers.

I will come back to this discussion later in the narrative. For now, let me say that our group of pastor/theologians desired to affirm with the Apostle Paul that God has not forsaken his people. (Romans 9–11) Rather, the New Humanity is bonded with ancient Israel and believes in Jesus as the expected Jewish Messiah. The church has been spiritually engrafted into the olive tree of Israel and we have been nourished through

---

14. Lewis, *Mere Christianity*, 193.

this tree's root system. The mercy of God is great enough to embrace all of humanity. This is not a theology of universalism, but the mystery of the sovereign grace of God our Creator, Redeemer, and Sustainer who has a purpose and plan of salvation for all who believe. Like Paul in Romans 9 the new humanity in Christ grieves for our brothers and sisters who do not believe in Jesus Messiah. We long for the salvation of all people and nations. We have been called to be a light to the nations telling and demonstrating the electing grace, love, and justice of our God.

I have been inspired by David Brooks in his latest book. In humility he wrote,

> "I suppose this happens to most of us as we age: We get smaller, and our dependencies get bigger. We become less fascinating to ourselves, less inclined to think of ourselves as the author of all that we are, and at the same time we realize how we have been the ones shaped—by history, by family, by forces beyond awareness. And I think what changed, in the most incremental, boring way possible, is that at some point I had the sensation that these stories are not fabricated tales happening to other, possibly fictional, people: They are the underlying shape of reality. They are renditions of the recurring patterns of life. They are the scripts we repeat.
>
> Adam and Eve experienced temptation and a fall from grace, and we experience temptation and a fall from grace. Moses led his people from bondage meanderingly toward a promised land, and we take a similar spiritual journey. The psalmist investigated himself and asked, 'Soul, why are you so downcast?' and we still do that. The prodigal son returned, and his father, infused by grace and love, ran out to meet him. Sometimes we, too, are outrageously forgiven. These stories are not just about common things that happen to people. They are representations of ongoing moral life. We are alive in the natural world, and we use science to understand that layer of aliveness. We are also alive in another dimension, the dimension of spirit and meaning. We use the biblical stories to understand that dimension of aliveness.
>
> "I can only answer the question 'What am I to do?'" Alasdair MacIntyre wrote, "if I can answer the prior question 'Of what story or stories do I find myself a part?'" If there are no overarching stories, then life is meaningless. Life does not feel meaningless. These stories provide, in their simple yet endlessly complex ways, a living script. They provide the horizon of meaning in which we live our lives—not just our individual

lives, but our lives together. These stories describe a great moral drama, which is not an individual drama but a shared drama. We are still a part of this drama, as Jayber Crow put it, created and being created still."

"A pilgrimage is a journey undertaken in response to a story." [15]

---

15. Brooks, *Second Mountain*, 212–213.

Chapter 2

The Highways of My Story

Poem by Robert Frost: The Road Not Taken

"Two roads diverged in a yellow wood,
And sorry I could not travel both
And be one traveler, long I stood
And looked down one as far as I could
To where it bent in the undergrowth,
Then took the other, as just as fair,
And having perhaps the better claim,
Because it was grassy and wanted wear;
Though as for that the passing there
Had worn them really about the same,
And both that morning equally lay
In leaves no step had trodden black
O, I kept the first for another day!
Yet knowing how way leads on to way,
I doubted if I should ever come back.
I shall be telling this with a sigh
Somewhere ages and ages hence:
Two roads diverged in a wood, and I—
I took the one less traveled by,
And that has made all the difference."[1]

---

1. *Norton Anthology*, Vol. 2, 1020.

U.S. 87, My Childhood Cross-roads.

> "Most, I fancy, have discovered that to be born is to be exposed to delights and miseries greater than imagination could have anticipated; that the choice of ways at any cross-road may be more important than we think; and that short cuts may lead to very nasty places."[2]

> "God has made it a rule for Himself that He won't alter people's character by force. He can and will alter them—but only if the people will let Him....He would rather have a world of free beings, with all its risks, than a world of people who did right like machines because they couldn't do anything else. The more we succeed in imagining what a world of perfect automatic beings would be like, the more, I think, we shall see His wisdom."
>
> C.S. LEWIS ESSAY, "THE TROUBLE WITH 'X',"[3]

Two highways intersected in my hometown of Amarillo, Texas. One of those roads was

U.S. 87. It ran from north to south in the Texas Panhandle. By the time I was in college I knew every little town between Amarillo and Lubbock. I had driven through each one of them on Highway 87. There was Canyon, Happy, Tulia, Kress, Plainview, Abernathy, Hale Center, and Lubbock. My mother's family lived primarily in Lubbock. There were four brothers and two sisters in her family. There were Roy, Mike, Leoda, Ruby (my Mom), Audrey Allen, "Sparky", and Paul. My grandmother, Layla Jane Perry Sparkman, was the center of the family.

Grandma's husband, Walter Sparkman, had abandoned her and the six children during the Great Depression years of the 1930's. Trying to carve out an existence in the Dust Bowl years as a farmer outside of Lubbock and to survive no doubt tried the soul of my grandfather and grandmother. But in such a time, to abandon his wife and children, was cowardly and not easily forgiven. That loss made its mark on grandma and her family. Grandfather Sparkman married again and lived in Ft. Worth with his wife. Grandma went to work and raised the children through difficult years. Grandpa visited us a few times as my sister and I grew up. I recall that he was a great storyteller and seemed to me a likeable man. I never asked Grandma about him because I understood she still carried

---

2. Lewis, *Selected Essays*, 153.
3. Snyder, Ponderingprinciples.com. January 26, 2019.

the grief, the pain, the loneliness, and the hardships of all those years in her heart. I loved her and she loved me and all her grandchildren. For years she labored in a hospital kitchen to support herself and her children. I often wondered why she and my Mom wept each time they parted and we would return to Amarillo. I can guess some of the reasons.

Technically, I was a middle child who functioned as the first child. When I was about three years of age my parents, with my younger sister Vivian Kay, moved 120 miles north to Amarillo. I was born on May 31, 1937, and she on July 27, 1939. Our older sister Billie Marie was born in 1934 and died at a year and a half. She was born with some defect that took her life after surgery in Oklahoma City. I'm not sure my mom ever got over that loss. She kept a picture of Billie in her bedroom but never spoke much of her.

Mom and Dad met in Lubbock. At age 16 they eloped to Clovis, New Mexico, to be married on September 6, 1930. My Dad's mom and dad were divorced, and my grandmother married a man named Blondie Stephens. Only on a few occasions did I meet my dad's birthfather, Percy. He was from Joplin, Missouri. I think he ultimately followed the crops to California and finally settled in Visalia, California, where he is buried. He had some sort of eye problem. Perhaps he was cross – eyed. The last time I saw him was in 1954 in Visalia. He lived in a small, run down trailer and was very poor. He frightened me and I did not want to spend much time near him. He died in the mid-50's and my dad and his sister Vivian drove to California to attend his funeral. Mom and Dad's families were part of the wreckage of the Great Depression and the Dust Bowl years. Their formative years were spent in trying to survive and to carve out a life during hardships of all kinds. Dad was a baker and had a job even through the Great Depression.

He was a hard worker. During WW11 Dad built a bakery that distributed cookies, breads, and pastries throughout the southwest and mid-west. It was named *"Art's Fine Cookies"*. The family bought a new Dodge in 1946. Dad purchased the longest conveyor belt oven west of the Mississippi River to rapidly bake his vanilla wafers with consistent quality. He was the cookie king of Amarillo. The challenge he faced during the war years was in getting sugar since sugar was rationed. Somehow, he got involved with black market sugar. As a child I watched him, and Mom, paste book after book with the rationing stamps. After the war the government moved in upon him and together with the impact of the post war recession the business failed. He moved his 60' long conveyor oven to Southern California to begin anew, but by 1948 the business was terminated, and he returned to Lubbock.

Alice Hamlin (Dad's mom), and Percy Tankersley (Dad's birth father) had four children, Arthur James (my Dad), Clarence (Bud), Vivian, and Fred Tankersley. My Dad was born in Eastern Oklahoma, near Fort Smith. The family story was that my dad's grandmother's husband, Frank Hamlin, rode with the outlaw Jesse James. My great grandmother was known as "Granny". She was born around 1851. She lived to 101 with her daughter Alice in California and was buried in Lubbock. Her funeral traumatized me and gave me death anxieties for several years. The Pentecostal preacher who had known her from years before in Lubbock cried through the whole service, as did everyone who packed the chapel. At the viewing I ran from the mortuary in tears. I was amazed at how much emotion a family could invest in a funeral. After all the loud cries and tears, the larger family gathered at my mom's brother's house, Mike and Nora Sparkman, and celebrated with a great dinner with much laughter. Somehow the conflicting emotional expressions did not all fit.

Blondie and Alice, my dad's mom, moved to Salinas, California, and later to Colton. Family of origin issues were a source of conflict in my parent's marriage. Mom went to school through the 8th grade. Dad finished in the 4th grade. The lack of education limited them. They were hard workers. An education would have made a big difference in their life stories.

Mom and Dad had a tumultuous marriage. Dad had a major problem with anger. When his anger flared, he could become violent. There were times when he physically abused Mom. Some of my memories are like still photographs of violent, frightening scenes. I must have been around 4 or 5 years old when we lived on Monroe St. in Amarillo. Mom stood at one end of the living room and my dad at the other. My sister and I were on the couch watching as he held a pistol on her. It was a 38-caliber gun. I did not understand but I was terrified. Somehow the family made it through that night, but the experience still fills me with anguish as I remember it.

One of my early memories from 4 years old was December 7, 1941. I was on the front porch of our Monroe St. house in Amarillo. I was playing with a toy airplane when Dad arrived. My parents were talking about the Japanese bombing of Pearl Harbor, Hi. The nation was at war. Two male relatives of my dad lived with us on and off during those years. They would come and go in their military service. Mom would always cook breakfast and place the food on large plates. When they left the table, she washed the dishes and put them away. She told them she would not use them again until they returned. I think she understood that many were not returning from the war because of their deaths. Thankfully, they both came home, and we celebrated. They were brothers, Titus and Pee Wee. They would get on the floor with me and my electric train, put on the engineer's hat and run the train with me. I was delighted. Dad was called up to be drafted. He went to the bus station to be taken away. For some reason, they did not call his name. When he asked about it, the man told him to go home and to not ask any more questions. So it was. It may have been that his business was deemed essential for feeding the troops.

There were other occasions of conflict and violence between my parents. From time-to-time Mom would provoke him to anger. They would have cussing verbal fights of loud screaming. Dad would go into a rage and hit her. A few times I remember seeing my mom's face black and blue and swollen. She was a battered woman who kept coming back for more. I do not know what they were fighting about. I think it was about mutual accusations concerning infidelities, business worries, or larger family conflicts. Their anxiety turned into anger and rage. My sister and I were traumatized. Dad would tear up the house and separate from the family. Mom would be sorry and use me as a pawn to negotiate my dad back into the house. I think I developed peacemaking skills through these experiences. For some reason members of the family thought I could fix it and keep the peace. What blossomed in me was a fearful, controlling co-dependent personality. As I grew older, and they fought through the night, I would lie in bed and pray for the fighting to cease. I would go into crying fits pleading for them to stop. I was looking out for my own welfare, serving my own interests. The family frequently tottered on the brink of chaos and catastrophe. Mom hated him and loved him, needed him, provoked him, but always wanted him to come home. Through the years I preached many sermons to my dad and Mom. Often, he came home. When I stopped enabling and preaching to them the final separation occurred.

My Dad carried heavy burdens with his business. There were years when there was tranquility, but my sister and I never knew when another season of rage might break out and we would move away from Amarillo to Lubbock, to live with Grandma, or to a small city like Borger, Texas, or to San Antonio, Texas, in the summer of 1950. We lived in my dad's bakery in Borger. All four of us were in one bedroom. It was not healthy.

I remember my dreams of going home to Amarillo and to grade school friends. We always found our way back to Amarillo and to 911 Austin St. When the Borger bakery was closed, we returned to our home base. I was much relieved and looked forward to joining my friends at Nixon Jr. High School. Much had changed between the 6th and the 7th grade, and I was behind in my academic development. Thankfully, during our high school years the family was somewhat stable. Dad started another bakery and did well throughout our high school years.

We moved to 1504 Bonham St. I had a basement room, participated in ROTC, and was chosen as an officer my senior year. I made it through those years, but always with academic troubles. I did not study. My sister and I had some good years, but the threats of unexpected outbreaks of violence were always lurking in our hearts. My sister Kay was bright, beautiful, and popular. In her senior year she was part of the Queen's court. Of the two of us, surely, she would succeed. I felt alone on the sidelines; she defended me; and I was known as Kay's older brother.

By my senior year of high school, I weighed nearly 200 pounds. I was fat and sleepy looking. Food was my comfort and drug of choice. I was often lost in fantasy. I never cracked a book. One night my friend Mike Ross asked me why I did not lose some weight? His question gave me courage to begin facing what my excessive eating was about. Recovery would mean learning to say "no" to bakery donuts and pies. Mom's cobblers were famous, and my friends loved to come over to our house after school and eat pie. Between Thanksgiving 1954 and May 1955 when I graduated from Amarillo High School, I lost 30 pounds. I was pumping iron at the YMCA and beginning to jog. It was an awakening. But the damage had been done. I had little self-confidence. I carried an image of myself as an ugly, dumb, fat kid who was afraid to compete. Self - confidence had been drowned in the pool of dysfunction that characterized our family.

I was almost without hope. At some level I knew I was facing a moment of truth. Would I choose to be a responsible adult willing to work, to risk, to compete, and to grow, or would I allow personal laziness to bury me and to strip me of promise? Who was I and where was I going? Did I have any future beyond the battlegrounds of our family and the limitations of the Texas Panhandle? I suspect I was depressed, anxious, and fearful. It was a dangerous time for me. I never contemplated suicide, but I was the kind of kid who could have been easily lost.

My childhood pictures showed me as a sad looking little boy. I finally recovered from childhood tonsil infections that stripped me of the desire to eat. My Mother would beg me to eat one bite. She did all she knew to do to nurse me to health. I looked like a refugee child in my first-grade picture. At 5 or so I had my tonsils removed, my appetite returned, and I began to eat. Mom told me that she promised herself that if I ever began to eat that she would stuff me. And she did. Being loved meant eating and welcoming the signs of Mom's affection.

During one of my parent's times of war when I was a student at Texas Tech, my sister and I found the 38-caliber pistol, (still a threat at that time) and took it out to a farm near Amarillo to bury it. That gun came to symbolize some of the misery of our childhood years. My life was headed in a positive direction and the burial of the gun was the closing of a door of a violent, threatening past. Nevertheless, my sister and I carried the wreckage deep in our souls of our parent's 34 – year marriage. Somehow, we would need to deal with that wreckage, face ourselves, and discover what it would mean to become adults who did not perpetuate the family system of fear, anger, and violence.

Near the end of 2018 my sister was diagnosed with Pancreatic Cancer. In early January 2019 she was in Hospice Care. She died on January 21, 2019, three years to the date on which we buried our 102-year-old Mother. Vivian Kay, my sister, was ready to go to be with the LORD. We spoke several times about her hope anchored in the promises of God's Word. She knew I loved her. While she was still aware, we spoke about the violence and troubled marriage of our parents. Her memories differed somewhat from mine. She thought I had seen more violence than she. For her, my parent's marital issues were their issues. As far as she was concerned Mom and Dad loved us both and she seemed to be at peace with that. I agreed about their love for us. Their last words to us were the assurances of their love. I was the peacemaker in the family, and I think I carried that burden. A child ought not to carry that responsibility. It will weigh the child down. Being a child and a counselor at the same time was damaging.

My sister must have felt secure in their love because she found difficulty in separating from them and always went home to Mom in her times of crises. Or, she simply did not have the self-confidence to separate, to educate herself, or to build an emotionally secure adult life for herself. Anxiety and fear dominated both my mom and my sister. Over the years Kay sought her way to freedom and happiness in marriage. Her last three husbands were financially successful. She married four times. Two boys were born to her and Charles Keeling, Jr., of Albuquerque, N.M. All four marriages ended in divorce. There was Steve, Charles, Lynn, and George. Each marriage was filled with anxiety, fear, and anger. She worked as a legal secretary and supported her boys. As a pastor I married her twice and was encouraged by her to marry her to number 4, but my conscience would not allow. In fact, the first wedding I did after ordination was my sister's and Charles' at the First Presbyterian Church of Albuquerque, N.M.

When she and George divorced, she returned to Lubbock to live the rest of her life in an emotionally symbiotic relationship with our mother. Mother suffered with this and yet bound Kay to her for emotional support. Mom bailed her out of financial messes repeatedly. In her final years the only income Kay had was Social Security of less than $1,200.00 a month. Her house was severely damaged by water leaking through the roof. My co-dependency was tempted to rescue her repeatedly. My wife helped me with this, as have several friends and counselors.

Route 66 to the West was seductive for my dad. There were trips to California over many years to visit my grandparents and other relatives on my dad's side. Our family was not unlike many American families drawn into the new frontier of the West seeking to escape from life in the East that held little promise for them. It may have been that this move was an expression of doing a geographic for the sake of leaving old problems behind. The truth was that these sojourners carried their problems in themselves to California. After they arrived at the Pacific Ocean there was no place to go. They had to deal with their personal and family issues and decide if they could survive and flourish on this new frontier. How many times I heard my dad say, "that blood is thicker than water."

During these childhood years there were regular weekend trips to visit with Mom's relatives in Lubbock. It took around two hours to travel the two-lane highway. High School football competition between Amarillo High and Lubbock High always drew the larger family together for Thanksgiving Dinner, either before or after the game. Often, we had healthy teasing between the Amarillo and the Lubbock families as to which team should have won or which team the referees cheated? My great fantasy was to grow up to be on the football team of the Amarillo High School Sandies. After we argued over the game, we settled in for delicious food prepared by my grandmother and my aunts.

My cousins and I played touch football in the backyard until we were called to the table with all the traditional foods of the season with the cakes and pies that we all loved. My cousins and I needed sideboards to stack the traditional foods of Thanksgiving. This was in the days when we thought little about overeating or becoming obese.

On the way back to Amarillo, late at night, my sister and I often fell asleep, me on the floorboard of the car, and she on the back seat. We were full and happy. Lying on the floorboard of the car was a pleasant experience for me, although awkward. I hated being awakened when we arrived late in Amarillo. My uncles and aunts, my cousins, and my grandmother made us feel at home. It was family. We travelled the same highway, U.S. 87, that ran North to Amarillo or South to Lubbock.

When Kay and I had conflict, our mom would put us in the same room, set us down in opposite chairs and make us look at each other until the crying stopped. By then we had forgotten what we were fighting about, and all was well. We often teased Mom about locking us both in the closet until our fight was over. We were childhood friends. She was always my protector and advocate. Kay was a Tomboy, played sports with the boys and participated in the neighborhood games. By high school she blossomed into a beauty. We both received piano lessons for three years and sang in the junior high choir. For me, neighborhood football won out over piano practices. We did, however, have parts in recitals at the music conservatory in Amarillo. I regret that I did not attend to my music training. I had a good singing voice, as Kay did. We would form a duo and sing "Baby Its Cold Outside". On one occasion we sang on the radio in Lubbock. Our Junior High, Nixon Junior High, each year had a talent contest. I sang the popular ballad, "If". I received high praise. With training on how to sing with a piano I might have won the contest.

When Rock n' Roll came to Amarillo we both joined the dance. All of us were buying 45 – inch records. I loved Elvis Presley. I dated my sister's girlfriends and thought I loved Judy Warren. I used to pick Judy up in my dad's yellow Studebaker after school and drive her home. One afternoon, we pulled up to her house only to see her dog lying dead in the middle of the street. I did not know what to do with her tears of pain. Thankfully, her dad was there to pick the dog up. She was a Southern Baptist and was often swayed by the Baptist evangelists who had suggested it was dangerous to kiss your boyfriend. She told me we could no longer kiss. After a while, in obedience to her convictions, we were driving home from a movie in the dark and she said to me, "Jerry, I want you to kiss me!" I was one happy fellow. Before long, we broke up, but that was for the best. By chance, I read her obituary in the Amarillo Newspaper. She died at age 81 having returned from Dallas to Amarillo.

When I graduated from Amarillo High School in 1955 my academic standing in the class of around 700 was 17th from the bottom. My friend Mike Ross was in the top ten of the 700. He was on his way to MIT, and I was on my way to Texas Tech. The tuition at Tech was $25 dollars per semester. I drove U.S. 87 to Lubbock and to Texas Tech. My first year at Tech, I lived with my grandmother. Her house on 8th Street was a few blocks from the university campus. Many cold mornings when the temperatures were dropping, and the winds were blowing across the flat farmlands, I walked to the campus to attend classes with the freezing winds blowing against me. I was grateful when my parents bought me an adequate coat to wear on those days.

My friend Sammy had connections with the nurses in training. I began to date one of them. Thankfully, I saw that she was not mentally balanced and broke off the relationship.

I lived in Doak Hall on the campus during my sophomore year. It was a wonderful experience with two different roommates. There was a growing sense of independence and great fun. 1955 to 1957 were beginning years of an intellectual and spiritual awakening for me. Every year the Student Union sponsored a track contest that invited the various organizations and fraternities to compete. The spring of 1957 I ran the one – mile relay with the Baptist Student Union. I had been running a lot. By then I was very thin. But in trying to keep up with some of the high school track stars during the second of four laps I burned out on the last 100 yards of the second lap. I finished, but I was embarrassed that I had not done better.

On the weekends I attended my uncle and aunt's church, Grace Chapel. I think it had been a Plymouth Brethren church. It was small, ultra-conservative, dispensational in theology, mistrustful of mainline churches, but the pastors were men of God whose faith touched me. On one childhood visit to Lubbock, Brother Lacy, the pastor, sang "The Holy City" as a solo. He sang with such passion that tears formed in his eyes, ran down his face, and spiritually transported me into the City of God. He planted the seeds of the vision of eternity into my soul. The spiritual highway to this City became the way of my life journey.

In my childhood years, weekend Saturday nights in Lubbock with my uncle and aunt, Estel and Leoda Rampy, were always a treat. They would gather my sister and I, with my three cousins, for prayer. We would get on our knees in their bedroom and pray with them. I felt uncomfortable. God's holy presence was there. The cloud of God's love settled in over us. Whenever my Uncle Estel had a chance, he talked with me about life and the Christian faith. He loved me and I enjoyed our serious conversations. They encouraged me to listen to the Old – Fashioned Revival Hour with Charles Fuller. We listened to Billy Graham on the radio. The Back – To the Bible Hour with Dr. De Haan's teaching was standard fare on Sunday mornings before church. Their family was a spiritual lifeline for me. I think Mom was jealous of my aunt and Uncle. Mom resented what she considered their religious and hypocritical personalities as seen through her eyes. But for me this family cared for my soul. They gave me a Scofield Bible with an inscription from Paul's Letter to Timothy. It was a Christmas gift that I have kept all these years.

My parents never prayed in this way. In Amarillo, our Austin street next door neighbor's, invited my sister and I to Sunday school at First Presbyterian Church. We ended up joining the church. Dr. Frances Pritchard baptized us. I believe it was in the summer of 1948. We were a part of a group sprinkled on a Sunday evening. He and his elders came to our home at 911 Austin St. and that visit led to our family's joining the church. My Dad insisted on being immersed in the baptismal tank of the First Christian Church. The family watched as he came up out of the water in the white robe with Dr. Pritchard. As my mom drove my sister and I away from church the night of our baptism she asked if I felt any different? Her question irritated me, and I answered, "No"! "Am I supposed to feel differently?"

First Presbyterian Church left me spiritually cold and bored. The formality of the sanctuary and the liturgy did not speak to me. However, the beauty of the sanctuary left a lasting impression in my memory. Sunday School was boring as the students negotiated the class content. The first half of the class the teacher would allow us to talk about the Friday night football game if we would allow him to present the Sunday School lesson in the second half. In 1970 when Dick Armstrong from Princeton Seminary visited the La Canada Presbyterian Church where I was an associate pastor, I shared my First Presbyterian memories with him. His answer was that I was not yet ready to see or to believe, but it was the planting of the seed of the gospel in my heart. That seed later bore fruit. I was grateful for his insight into my spiritual journey.

Surprisingly, in 1977 I was a commissioner to my first General Assembly of the United Presbyterian Church in the USA in Philadelphia, Pa. During a ceremony recognizing retiring missionaries of the denomination that later became the PCUSA, a name was called out: Dr. Frances Pritchard. This was the name of the pastor who had baptized me, my sister, and my dad in 1948. When the recognition was completed, Dr. Pritchard came walking down the isle of the Convention Center. As he neared, I recognized him. I stepped into the isle and introduced myself to him and asked if he was the pastor from Amarillo. He answered in the affirmative. I was thrilled. I told him my story and it made him glad. I shared that I was pastor of Laguna Presbyterian Church in Laguna Beach, California. He said he was retiring to a Presbyterian Retirement Home in California. Since Laguna Beach was only 90 miles from San Diego, I asked if he would come preach in our church. He said he would. By mail we arranged the date, and he came. He and his second wife visited for the day. After church they came to our home and shared lunch with us. I still believe it was a providential encounter and connection with the spiritual roots of my life and the journey that his pastoral ministry launched with our family.

Various images of U.S. 87 planted themselves in my memory. North Texas could have damaging winter ice storms. The trees would bend from the ice – covered branches and break, along with the power lines. The morning after, the sun made the world appear as beautiful Chrystal. It was a Narnian frozen world shrouded in mystery. During college years there was a huge snowfall about 3 feet deep spreading across the farm and ranching lands between the two cities. That weekend I drove home to Amarillo for a visit with my parents. It was a bright blue sky, and the snow almost blinded my eyes. It was a wilderness landscape transformed by the gift of white powder covering the farmlands. I loved it.

After my first two years at Tech, I packed all my belongings in the '56 Chevy Bel Air that my dad had given to me. I drove U.S. 87 back home to Amarillo. I remember thinking that I did not know what the future held for me, but I was convinced I was not returning to Tech to complete my final two years. Something had happened in my life and a new destiny was taking shape.

At the beginning of my freshman year at Texas Tech, the entering class was gathered in the quad of the Administration Bldg. There were 2500 of us. The Dean asked us to stand as our majors were called out. From major-to-major students stood. Finally, he asked all pre-ministerial students to stand. There was one poor guy who stood up. It was not I! Yet I was convicted that I should be standing, but I did not have the courage to take a public stand for the faith or a lifetime of following Jesus. I have often wondered whatever happened to that fellow. I owe him a lot.

My first year at Tech, my English professor assigned a term paper for us to write. We could choose the subject. For some reason I selected the subject of creation and evolution. My paper attacked Darwin's theory of evolution that suggested that humans evolved over time from lower to higher organisms and animals. I thought I was defending the Bible from atheistic science. The female teacher called me to her office after reading the paper. She gave me a lecture I will never forget about my closed mind and narrow worldview. It was embarrassing and humiliating. I passed the course, but barely. Looking back, I needed the lecture. I complained to my Aunt Leoda about the teacher's lack of faith, and she supported me. After all, we read the footnotes of the Scofield Bible that said the world was created in 4004 B. C. Nevertheless, the confrontation was jarring and an important part of my intellectual growth. I had not recognized how uneducated I was or what a long journey was before me.

Getting an education may cost one a great deal. Tara Westover's memoir, *Educated*, shared what becoming educated had cost her and two of her siblings. From the western mountains of Mormon Idaho and from a crazy family, she and two of her siblings ultimately earned Ph.D.'s. The result was that their parents rejected the three of them after many years of abusive treatment. I have been grateful that my parents supported my intellectual growth and took pride in my later accomplishments.

The summer between my freshman and sophomore years of college my Amarillo High friends gathered back home. Mike Ross, my best friend, returned from MIT in Boston. He had become identified with Tremont Temple Baptist Church in Boston and had become a Christian. I had always wondered what it would be like for my best friend to become a Christian. I was overjoyed. We decided to drive my new Chevy to Oklahoma City for the Billy Graham Crusade during that summer of 1956.

Mike, Gerry Shaffer, and I spent the night in Oklahoma City and attended the Crusade. I will never forget Billy's text. It was Youth Night and he spoke out of the Prophet Ezekiel,

> "And I sought for anyone among them who would repair the wall and stand in the breach before me on behalf of the land, so that I would not destroy it; but I found no one." (Ezekiel 22:30)

When Billy gave the invitation to go forward to accept Christ and to commit to serving him with our lives, Mike nudged me in the side and said, "Jerry, we have to go forward." The three of us went forward and stood at the very front looking up at Billy. It was a watershed moment in my journey. We had driven East on U.S. 66 from Amarillo to Okla. City. I began to weep. I blubbered. I knew it was a turning point for me. I had not had the courage to publicly risk confessing Christ in fear that I would not follow through.

Something profoundly shifted in me that night. Christ, who created me, loved me, graced me, and forgiven me, had touched the depths of my heart as I passed from being a lukewarm Christian to a young man called to stand in the gap, to be Christ's representative, to commit to becoming a servant of Christ in the building of the kingdom of God.

Life would be different from then on. The same summer of 1956, Mike, my sister, my mom, and I travelled to Houston, Texas, to see my girlfriend, Ruth. She was a bright, attractive, committed Christian whom I had met at Grace Chapel. I wanted to marry her. I asked her to wait for me, whatever that might mean for us. She said she was not ready for such a commitment. She pointed to a church hymn entitled, His Way:

> "God moves in a mysterious way His glorious wonders to perform; He plants His footsteps in the sea, and Rides upon the raging storm.
>
> You fearful saints, fresh courage take; the threat'ning clouds you so much dread Are big with mercy, and shall break In countless blessings on your head."[4]

God moves in mysterious ways in our lives. In the first semester of our sophomore year Ruth broke up with me and set me free to become the man God was calling me to become. It was a great gift from God through her. I began to understand that Jesus would not allow any earthly need or plan of mine to knock me off the road I was traveling into His future with hope.

In the words of Jeremiah,

> "For surely I know the plans I have for you, says the Lord, plans for your welfare and not for harm, to give you a future with hope." (Jeremiah 29:10–14)

---

4. Cowper, *The Hymnal*, 54.

By the second semester of my sophomore year, I decided that if I was going to follow Jesus that I needed to read the New Testament from Matthew to Revelation. A travelling preacher had provided me with an American Standard Version of the Bible. I still have it. Each afternoon in the privacy and quiet of my dorm room I systematically read the New Testament from cover to cover. I did not want any of my dorm friends to see me reading the Bible. Most of their rooms were papered with Playboy of the Month pictures. But alone with God I read, and I wrote notes in the margins of the Bible. By the time I was finished I knew I was a Christian, and that God had a future for me that I needed to choose.

My roommate Terry Savage, from Amarillo, who was an electrical engineering student, suggested to me one evening, as we discussed a section in my economics textbook, that I ought to consider studying for the ministry. His affirmation of my interests and gifts moved me to a deeper consideration of God's calling. During my freshman and sophomore years I became friends with Blake Martin who had acted with me in William Shakespeare's, Twelfth Night. He was a little older but a nice friend. Before long he shared with me that he had been a Church of Christ preacher, but had left his church when he and his wife divorced. Soon they reconciled and he became a pastor at a local Lubbock Church of Christ. This was a learning experience for me.

Across the years spiritual guidance has come to me from many unexpected sources. A friend has showed up with a word of encouragement and affirmation just when I needed it. What was fascinating to me was that as I fell in love with the biblical story, other stories and academic disciplines began to intrigue me. Education was beginning to have its way with me, and it was good. With fear and trembling I took the course on Zoology. I was determined to excel in the course. I studied hard. I arose in the middle of the night to go to the dorm lounge to go over my notes for an exam. I memorized everything I could. I received a B+ in the course. I loved dissecting the frogs and bugs. I began to think about medical school. The course in Botany followed. A whole new world opened for me, but I was too far behind.

My freshman year I had declared a major in speech. I did that because in my final semester of high school I took speech and was one of the speakers in a Speaking Chorus. I loved it. In the AHS ROTC assembly in which we competed in the rifle drills before the student body and they voted, I was runner up. My friends affirmed me.

At Tech I was a disk jockey on the campus radio station. "Tank's Record Hop," I called the program. It was a good experience. I auditioned for a role in Shakespeare's *Twelfth Night*. I opened the play. I neglected my studies in preparation for a possible acting career. I joined the debate team of the college. These things were signs of an awakening to life. I dated nurses in training. It was the fun I should have been having in high school. Yet, I wasted a lot of study time.

The summer between my sophomore and junior years of college I returned to Amarillo and became very involved with the Amarillo Bible Church, another dispensational church friendly to Moody Bible Institute and to Dallas Theological Seminary. There was a large group of student's home from universities across America. The summer group decided to conduct street meetings in downtown Amarillo on Saturday evenings. We had a portable loudspeaker and organ. The store across from the Post Office allowed us to plug the sound and organ into their electrical system. A fearful group would gather on the street as the men from the Amarillo Air Base arrived on buses looking for something to do other than drink in the bars. My uncle and aunt, John and Vivian Heket, owned the bus shuttle along with the Trailways Bus Co. out of Amarillo.

Since by that summer I had memorized more scripture than anyone else in the group, I was asked if I would do the preaching. After the Billy Graham meeting, I became involved in the Navigator's Bible Memory program. Psalm 119:9, 11, saved me and began to anchor my identity in God's Word. 1 Corinthians 10:13 assured me that God would see me through times of temptation. At great risk I decided to preach on the street. My voice carried up and down the street. Amazingly a group of curious people gathered. The sidewalk was crowded with puzzled observers and military men. I noticed my mom and Dad would come and stand a block away to watch and to listen. Perhaps they thought I had flipped my cookies. About all I did was quote scripture and give an invitation.

The conversations we had that summer were meaningful. The number of Air Force service men who came into our summer fellowship surprised us all. The group mushroomed in size. I made many friends. An adult leader at the Bible Church suggested to me that I had a call from God to be a preacher. The inner conviction of the Spirit encouraged me. My parents affirmed me. Before the summer was over a Southern Baptist evangelist came to town named Angel Martinez. Why I remember his name, I do not know. He wore a pink sport coat and white buck shoes. Many filled the convention hall, and many made decisions for Christ. I remember summer friends from the military and Amarillo Bible Church hugging each other and saying that we would meet in heaven. We had a premonition that our ways were getting ready to part but that something very powerful had occurred in and through our summer fellowship and mission.

There was a fellow named Tom Boyd, who had just graduated from Westmont College in Santa Barbara, California, and he had returned home. Westmont was a small Christian liberal arts college that was not yet accredited, but which would soon be. Tom was a 6 '8" basketball player who was a charismatic person. He had left a big impression on the Westmont College student body. He suggested I ought to investigate the school for the purpose of training for ministry. Sure enough, I applied the summer of 1957 and was admitted two weeks before school began in the fall. I graduated with a B.A. in June 1959 with a major in Bible.

U.S 66

Route 66 ran between Chicago and Santa Monica, California. As it passed through the Texas Panhandle it ran through the center of Amarillo. My Dad's bakery was on this famous route. I often watched cars travelling from West to East on their way to Oklahoma and beyond. The passing cars stirred an interest in the stories of people who had left Oklahoma, Arkansas, Missouri, and Texas to escape the Dust Bowl poverty of the 1930's. They sought new beginnings in California where there were jobs. I was on the verge of doing the same.

To my surprise, Route 66 became the way to my future. My parents and I packed up the '56 Chevy and drove to Southern California. On the way we went to Disneyland in Anaheim. We visited a bakery in Burbank that had a long oven that my dad had read about. When we arrived in Santa Barbara and the Westmont College campus in Montecito, it was like arriving in paradise. My folks left the Chevy with me and took the Greyhound bus back to Amarillo. It was a life changing separation, an important individuation for me. A few months later my dad closed his bakery in Amarillo and moved to Bakersfield, California, for a new beginning. It was the beginning of the end of their 34 years of marriage. Years later he shared with me how painful it had been to return to Amarillo without me. I did not appreciate that pain until the fall of 1988 when my wife and I drove our son Jeff to Spokane, Washington, to begin his freshman year at Whitworth College. Driving into our long driveway in Laguna Beach upon our return, I felt a surge of emotional and physical pain, the pain of having an empty nest and of life changing for us.

For me Westmont College was exactly what I needed. It was a small Christian college of 300 students with outstanding faculty. Dr. David Hubbard was my major professor. He had just completed his Ph.D. at St. Andrews University in Scotland. He challenged me to study and inspired me. Later, he would become the President of Fuller Theological Seminary in Pasadena. I had much catching up to do. God sent me into a place that prized academic excellence and spiritual commitment. My academic coasting would be challenged, and I would be inspired. Dr. Hubbard told me that if I were to become a minister, I would be required to work at it. Profound counsel from a man who had a plaque on his home wall that read, "My Grace Is Sufficient for You, For Power Is Made Perfect in Weakness." (2 Corinthians 12:9)

Westmont had a summer gospel team and a famous quartet. In the fall of 1957, I was appointed as the preacher of the college gospel team. We visited churches on Sunday evenings, sang, and I preached. The following summer the gospel team travelled around California singing and preaching in churches and summer camps related to Westmont. It seemed a confirmation to me that my call was valid. I was having the time of my life.

At Westmont I met my future wife. She was a freshman, and I was a junior. I was in search for a self to be, for work to do, and for others to love. For the Christmas holiday break my Santa Barbara and Westmont friend, Bob Richard, and I, traveled by TWA to Amarillo. It was my first commercial airline flight. My Dad invited the local television station to be at the airport for our arrival. Bob and I were budding evangelists. We swooped in on the wings of the TWA Super Constellation. We appeared on an afternoon TV program during the holiday. Underneath it all, I was longing for her, listening to romantic music, and yearning to hear from her.

The Westmont College basketball team toured through Amarillo during that vacation. Amarillo Bible Church invited me to preach on a Sunday evening and for the team to give their testimonies. These guys were the most popular people on campus. That evening I preached and "Doc Mead", the wealthy owner of Mead's Fine Bread, a huge bakery that distributed bread throughout the region, attended the service. He was a Southern Baptist layman whom my dad admired. This dear man came to hear me preach and following the service gave to me a small leather – bound New Testament inscribed by him with Paul's prayer for the Ephesian church. (Ephesians 3:14–21) I still have the Testament. I am grateful for it. It meant so much for "Doc" to be there, to take an interest in me. It was an affirmation of my dad's business position in the Amarillo community.

Bob Richard and I flew back to L.A. in early January. It had been snowing heavily in Amarillo the day before we left. The evening of our flight the storm clouds parted, and the moon was full. The light of the moon reflected off the newly fallen snow. From the air it looked like a fairy land of white landscape illumined by the light of the moon. I could not wait to see my girlfriend. After arrival the romance resumed. I was in love. The winter/spring semester our relationship grew deeper, and we discussed marriage. I was entering my senior year. The summer of 1958 I travelled with the Westmont Gospel Team around California. Being separated from her was difficult, but she and her parents were planning a wedding.

She was working in West Covina at a Clifton's Cafeteria. I went to pick her up and on the way was involved in a serious accident in my 1956 Belair Chevy. I turned on to a busy street and was rear-ended by a speeding car that I had not seen. The impact drove me into an orange orchard and the front end of my car was folded up against the driver's compartment. I had a smashed lip and loosened front teeth. I was emotionally shaken. I could have been killed. My Dad was in Colton at the time. I called him and he came the next morning. He was kind and helpful. The car was repaired, but it was never the same after the accident.

The fall of 1958 I lived in the Westmont dormitory. Bob Larson was my roommate. That summer I had preached one Sunday evening in his Dad's Baptist Church in South San Francisco. I will never forget a young man who was seated on the front row. He was dressed in a sport coat, wore white gloves, played a banjo, and sang while I tried to preach. In the fall my fiancé and I searched for a place to live in Santa Barbara. We found one and she moved in. It was a time of transition in which we were facing into adult realities.

On December 12, 1958, we were married at the Methodist Church in Upland, California. Marriage settled me and inspired me to study. I knew it was either make or break for me. My grades soared and I fell in love with history, Greek, philosophy, theology, and biblical studies. The Bible major was like a Classics major. When I arrived at Westmont, I thought I was called to be a Billy Graham type evangelist. I was lonely and needed someone to love me and for me to love. She seemed to be an intelligent, committed Christian, as were her parents. I was on the way.

Dr. Hubbard encouraged me after my graduation from Westmont in 1959 to attend Fuller Theological Seminary in Pasadena. Indeed, this was my goal. My uncle and aunt, Estel and Leoda Rampy, had encouraged me to listen to the Old-Fashioned Revival Hour on radio with Dr. Charles Fuller preaching. His voice moved my emotions to tears as I listened to him. It was as if the Voice of God's truth and love reached out to me and spoke to me of the reality of God's presence and power. He planted within me the desire to attend the seminary that he had founded.

Soon after my arrival at Westmont my friend, Bob Richard, and I, drove to Long Beach to attend in person the OFRH in the Civic Auditorium. It was the fulfillment of a dream.

Edward John Carnell was the President of Fuller. When he visited Westmont my senior year, he appeared to me an elegant, sophisticated philosopher striding into the campus dressed in a double-breasted grey suit and wearing a black top hat. I was in awe. He was a Harvard trained evangelical philosopher and theologian. I wanted to be like him. Little did I realize that he was afflicted with severe depression and at age 47 would die in a hotel room of an accident or an outright suicide. I attended his memorial service in Pasadena. Nevertheless, he was the model of a man I could aspire to become.

The newlyweds moved to Chino, California, to live with her parents for a couple of months before Fuller began. In September of 1959 we rented an apartment in Pasadena a few blocks from campus. I needed a job and through the job placement office found a part time position with a small technology firm in Monrovia. Since I had completed one year of college accounting at Texas Tech, they employed me to become their part-time bookkeeper. I was in over my head, but I learned a great deal. When the company was sold, I was released from the job and managed to scrape together a few jobs to see me through my senior year. One of the jobs was to work with a small team of students cleaning the telephone building in Alhambra in the evening hours. I felt like the prodigal in a foreign land with a longing to complete that season and to move on to the future. I hated it, but I learned some things about life, and I endured for several months until I graduated. At the same time, she graduated from college in 1962.

CHAPTER 3

The Highways from Westmont College to Fuller Theological Seminary

1959 – 1962

THE THREE YEARS AT FULLER were a strain upon us each. I worked and studied and so did she. I learned that several of the Fuller faculty were recovering fundamentalists and were in therapy after nervous breakdowns. She was unhappy and went into counseling. Her counselor recommended I see Dr. Harry Rosenthal. We worked at the marriage, but my anxieties grew. Underneath it all I think I knew our marriage was in trouble, but I was determined to stick with it. She found a part time job at a small business and dressed seductively to go to work. When she wanted to go to a business party in Hollywood without me, I suspected there was an office affair beginning. I pleaded with her not to go and she finally chose not to attend, but I was upset. Thankfully, she found a teaching job in my senior year at Fuller and my anxieties diminished.

While at Fuller the question of my future service captured my attention. I took a full load of classes and worked 20 hours a week while studying in the evenings and weekends. I was burning the candle on both ends. In Systematic Theology with Dr. Paul King Jewett, as we were studying the theologies of baptism, I remembered I had first been baptized by sprinkling at First Presbyterian Church in Amarillo. Later I had been dunked in the baptismal tank of Grace Chapel in Lubbock, as a believer. I had covered the bases. But in class, a light flashed in my head, and I knew I was first a Presbyterian and that this would be the direction of my call to ministry.

Studies at Fuller Seminary were rigorous. The faculties were seen as giants in the evangelical/conservative church. Academic excellence was foremost. The courses that were the hardest and required the most work I passed with A's. In what I considered the lower-level courses I received B's and C's. I graduated with a strong B average. There was Biblical Theology, Greek and Hebrew, Church History, Systematic Theology, Ethics, Pastoral Counseling, Theology, Homiletics, and Preaching. I was one of the preachers of the two Fuller Gospel teams.

The course in preaching during my second year I considered a slam dunk. After all, I had done a lot of preaching. Clarence Roddy was the respected teacher who had experienced many years of successful preaching in the Baptist Church. He was a great soul. He also taught pastoral theology. The stories he told us out of his experience were breathtaking and inspiring. Sometimes he would cry as he told them. Later, I learned that he had experienced a nervous breakdown and at one time had been led from the classroom weeping. He had the reputation of giving Dr. David Hubbard his only "C" grade in seminary. We all knew that Dr. Hubbard was brilliant. Perhaps his "C" validated my "C" in the preaching class.

I remember Dr. Roddy saying that he feared for those men who seemed to have all the gifts for preaching, who were handsome and intelligent, but who trusted in their own natural gifts without realizing that without the power of God they would soon burn out and give up. He said he preferred a man who had humility, normal intellectual capabilities, and understood he had to work hard just to keep his head above the water. By that time, I had come to think of myself as smart and handsome. Although, the self-image of being a lazy, fat, dumb kid still haunted me. But I tried to compensate for that insecurity. Nevertheless, Dr. Roddy took us all by surprise.

Each of the class students were required to select a text from First Peter and to deliver a sermon on that text. The sermon was to be a 10 - minute message for the class. The first two preachers were me and the other gospel team preacher. I preached on the subject of "the love of God". After the two of us had preached, Dr. Roddy asked the class what my subject was. They agreed, it was the "love of God". That reassured me and I was encouraged. Then he asked the class, "what did Mr. Tankersley communicate?" The class agreed that my non-verbal communication in the sermon was "anger". I was stunned. My ego was shattered. Not only that but he asked the class if they thought either of the preachers would ever get a call to a church? The class was unanimous, "NO!" To me this was the shaking of the foundations. It meant that I needed self-awareness and self-knowledge. It meant that I would need to work on more than a preaching manuscript but also upon my own soul and what was going on in my life.

I learned a lot at Fuller. More and more I wanted to go into teaching at the college or seminary level. A church pastoral ministry appealed less and less. Rather than fall in love with a pastoral calling, I felt I was being prepared for an academic teaching career, yet my previous grades simply did not rise to the level of what a first – rate graduate school would require. Practical courses in worship, spiritual formation, or prayer were barely provided. We were training to be scholars as if this were the most important role of a servant of the church. Fuller was establishing a School of Psychology and many of my fellow students were in counseling and troubled by their pasts and anxious about their futures. Some were having emotional breakdowns and for the first time were being intellectually and emotionally stretched. Some were smoking cigarettes and drinking alcohol. Most of us were married and some of the marriages were disturbed.

Life was difficult. When I came to faith, I assumed all these kinds of problems would disappear from my life. But now I was on a fast track with life and all the aspects of being human were catching up to me. I could not outrun them. There was no escape from the human condition and the limitations of my life.

This was a dilemma for me. Yet I had come alive to the discipline of study. I did not realize that pastoral ministry would require intense weekly preparation, that I would need to study, to pray, to live with integrity, to lead a business organization, to be an effective public speaker, to raise a lot of money, to be a pastoral counselor, to be in therapy, and to be a generalist in interests and gifts. Up to that time I had not seen a pastor who could handle all these things.

Chapter 4

The Highways to Princeton Theological Seminary

1964 Th.M.

It was not until I arrived at Princeton Seminary that pastoral ministry began to emerge as a possibility for me and that I might have gifts to that end. I remember visiting Union Theological Seminary in NYC seeking to gather information about their doctoral programs. I fantasized about the Ph.D. program in Classics at Princeton University.

We were on the quarter calendar at Fuller. Each ten-week quarter was a race to absorb all the facts one could, write a paper, and pass the final exam. Trying to be married, to go to school fulltime, and to work 20 hours a week were taxing. Looking back, I do not know how I did it.

While at Fuller, we joined the Glendale Presbyterian Church and worked with high school students. Soon I came under care of the Presbytery of Los Angeles. In those years the Presbytery required Fuller grads to attend an extra year at a Presbyterian Seminary. L.A. Presbytery did not trust Fuller grads to be faithful Presbyterians since Charles Fuller had divided a church in Orange County and Fuller was founded to replace the old orthodox Princeton, but on the west coast. This became an incentive for me to prove my loyalty to the denomination. This was the way of upward mobility.

I enrolled at Princeton and was accepted in the summer of 1962. We loaded our car, the '56 Chevy, and began the long journey on Route 66 by way of Lubbock to visit my parents. Before leaving Southern California to drive across the U.S. I had new treads put on the tires. As we were gassing up in Kingman, Arizona, it was so hot that the new treads were melting off and the two rear tires deflated in the Chevron station. Thankfully, her dad had given me his credit card and we put two new tires on the car. While in Lubbock, my dad insisted on buying us a newer used car, a '58 Oldsmobile with air conditioning. So off we went into an unknown future hoping that we would prosper on the east coast in New Jersey. We drove on U.S. 66 to Chicago and then across the northern part of the U.S. to Ohio, where we visited her grandmother. At one time the city was a vital steel town, but that was gone, and the town had grown stagnant. The Rust Belt was showing itself. We left our small dog "Charlie Brown" with grandmother and continued our journey to Princeton, N.J. We found a small house to rent in Princeton Junction near the train station.

New York City immediately beckoned. Neither of us had been to the East Coast and we were excited to see Manhattan. The Oldsmobile was still packed with our belongings. We found a parking lot. The attendant, an African American man, noticed our license plate from Texas. He warned us that we might trust our belongings in a Texas parking lot, but in NYC we would quickly be ripped off. Clearly, we were naïve and needed the warning. Somehow, we survived, enjoyed the city, and returned to Princeton Seminary to stay a few days in an apartment in the seminary center. We found a housesitting job for a month in the countryside of N.J. and moved in to discover that the house was flea infested. It was horrible.

When we left Lubbock for the journey east, we were both excited. She had taken a pregnancy test while in Lubbock and the result was positive. Thankfully, she managed to get an elementary school teaching position in Heights Town, N.J. Before school began, we received a call from my Uncle A.A. Sparkman informing us that Mom had been operated on for a hysterectomy and that she was in a life – threatening situation. My Dad was flipping out. Uncle Sparky, one of my favorites, suggested we needed to return to Lubbock before she died. We had little money. He loaned us $400 dollars for airline tickets on Braniff Airlines through Dallas. (Several years later I paid him back the $400.) I will never forget that flight. As the plane moved through storms out of Nashville, I contemplated 1 Corinthians 15. My death anxieties increased, and fear almost paralyzed me. My uncle picked us up at the airport in Lubbock. For a week or so we prayed and rooted for Mom. Mom recovered and we returned to Newark and Princeton to begin the school year.

While in the hospital my grandmother and I were seated in the lobby as Walter, my grandfather, her ex-husband entered. She bristled and was clearly offended that he had come to see my mom after abandoning the family so many years before.

The Presbytery had not informed me of the courses they thought I ought to take at Princeton. I called Dr. Thomas Gillespie, pastor at Garden Grove Presbyterian Church and chair of the Candidates Committee of L.A. Presbytery. He asked me to audit a course in polity and to take some historical theology courses. So, I enrolled in the Th.M. program in History of Doctrine. Why not get a degree? I loved the Seminary. The courses were a semester long and called for reading, reflection, and hard work. I took what I wanted to fulfill the requirements. I found the course in Early Church Doctrine taught by Dr. George Hendry to be difficult but stimulating. I received an A in the course. Dr. Edward Dowey taught the Theology of Luther and Calvin. I loved it. He became my Th.M. advisor. He joked about "Christianity Yesterday" rather than "Christianity Today". I wrote my Th.M. thesis on "The Debate Between the Puritans John Owen and Brian Walton on the Inspiration of Scripture."

Another course I took was "19th Century Opponents of Christianity". I chose to write my paper on Darwin and the impact of his evolutionary teaching on the Christian Faith. I barely scratched the surface even though I read good portions of his famous book on *The Origin of the Species*. I still was not intellectually mature enough to deal with Darwin. I passed the course but was puzzled by evolutionary theory. I had not considered that his understanding of "Natural Selection" and the "Survival of the Fittest" had been embraced by the Social Darwinians and applied to political and economic theory. The Hegelians as well as the Communist political philosophers Marx and Engels, took the idea of development and evolution in nature and applied it to political ideology, history, and economics.

Of course, evolution was the center of the debate between the fundamentalists of the early part of the 20th Century and the Progressive Protestant Churches seeking to be in sync with modern science. My engagement with Social Darwinism came later in my doctoral work in Government at Claremont Graduate School. The debate about Creationism continues to this day between ultra-conservative theologians and liberal devotees of Darwin's scientific discoveries. Faith and Science were pitted against each other. Could one be a Darwinian and a believer in the Bible's Creation stories? I confess that the Scopes trial and the argument of

William Jennings Bryan are now an embarrassment for me. This famous lawyer, presidential candidate, candidate for Moderator of the General Assembly of the Presbyterian Church, and Presbyterian layman, won the trial, but lost the battle. He died shortly after the trial was completed.

During that year at Princeton, I had a student intern job at Immanuel Union Church on Staten Island, NYC. The congregation had ties to the Presbyterian Church, but also to the United Church of Christ. I drove up from Princeton to Staten Island 2 to 3 times a week. Dr. William MacCalmont was their new pastor. He had been the President of Westminster Choir College in Princeton, N.J. It was a joy to work with him. My position description was to work with junior high and high school students. Bill allowed me to teach adult classes and to preach occasionally. I felt loved by the people and encouraged. The culture of Staten Island was interesting. The Prohibition Party had been organized on the Island in the early part of the 20th century, but the people of the church in the 1960's drank alcohol heavily. It was my first experience of drinking in the context of a church fellowship. I remember inviting a recovering alcoholic to speak to the high school group. He made a powerful presentation that functioned as a warning about alcohol and drugs. Our high school students needed the warning.

One night in Princeton we went to a movie at the local theater. It was the story of the suffering of alcoholism. The *"Days of Wine and Roses"* won many awards. After seeing the movie and falling in love with the musical score, the next morning I awakened with bright red eyes. I think I was carrying a lot of unrecognized anxiety and fear about death. A friend of mine at Fuller Seminary had died over a weekend from acute Leukemia near the end of our senior year. This occurred shortly before our graduation. My red eyes convinced me I was dying. I went to the eye doctor in Princeton and thus began a life – long battle with eye allergies that have made me appear debauched periodically. I think the redness came with response to allergens in the air in various places. But stress has always seemed to be a factor for my hay fever and other allergies. I learned to live with it until now, but it has deeply troubled me because of the way it made me appear. Endless explanations have resulted. Who knows the numbers of eye drops I have placed into my eyes over the years? Thankfully, my eyes are healthy, and my vision has been good. My Dad went blind at age 74 from diabetes. That has not happened to me for which I am deeply grateful.

In the late fall of 1962, my wife discovered she was not pregnant and had a DNC in a Trenton Hospital. Her mother came for a week to be with us. I was concerned. She was depressed. We sought a counselor. Pastor Bill recommended we see a psychiatrist in Brooklyn who was a friend of his. It was like entering the office of Sigmund Freud of the old European world. After one visit my wife's depression lifted, but the therapist reported to Bill that my wife was not a Christian. Bill told me this. At the time I did not understand such a report. However, later I concluded that she told the doctor something about herself that I did not know. At the time I was in the dark hoping that our marriage would work out.

One of the awakening experiences I had at Princeton Seminary was in October 1962 as I sat in my car in the parking lot of the seminary library listening to President Kennedy on the radio giving his speech about Cuba and the Soviet Union's placement of missiles and atomic warheads in Cuba aimed at the U.S. Princeton was within the range of those missiles. The reality of our troubled Cold War world came home to me.

That fall of 1962 I followed the elections in California when Richard Nixon was defeated as he ran for governor of the State. In my first voting in the 1960 national election, I had voted for Nixon as President of the U.S. Fuller students were convinced that John F. Kennedy would bring the Catholic Pope into the White House. I was heartbroken. I listened to Nixon's concession speech in California after his defeat in the governor's race. His political career seemed over.

On the 200th anniversary of Princeton Theological Seminary in October 2012, I visited Washington D.C. and the National Archives. On display were the recordings and other documents related to the Cuban Missile Crisis. It was sobering to listen to conversations of the President and his Cabinet and military counselors. Thankfully, the Soviets withdrew their missiles from Cuba and the world, threatened by another war, breathed a sigh of relief.

All in all, the Immanuel Union Church was a positive experience. However, in the springtime a group of church leaders came to me and said they would like me to be their next pastor because Bill would likely soon move on. I knew then that I needed to leave as soon as the school year was over. I left making public affirmations of the church and of the pastor and Bill returned the favor.

CHAPTER 5

The Highways Back to California

1963–1964

I HAD RECEIVED AN INVITATION from Wilshire Presbyterian Church in Los Angeles to become their assistant pastor to youth. We left Princeton on June 9, 1963, visited Washington D.C. a few days before M.L. King Jr. gave his famous "I Have A Dream" speech at the Lincoln Memorial. We travelled the southern route back to L.A.

On the journey through northern Alabama, Mississippi, and into Tennessee I saw African American poverty like I had never seen it. Being in the old South with all the remnants of poverty, slavery, racism, and lack of justice deeply moved and troubled me. I began to realize that this was the world into which I was born and that I carried the seeds of prejudice, privilege, and white supremacy in my own heart.

I passed my ordination exams I had written in the Princeton Seminary Library. The oral exam was at Immanuel Presbyterian Church in the Wilshire District of L.A. The Candidates Committee passed my written exams but some on the committee commented that I was still the conservative I had been at Fuller. They hoped I had grown beyond that. Yet, they confessed that I was among many other conservatives in the Presbyterian denomination. On August 18, 1963, the Presbytery of Los Angeles ordained me to the gospel ministry.

There was a nice reception after the service. I do not have a picture from that event in my life. It was an anxious time. Somehow, I had made the transition to ordination in the PCUSA. There was a sense of relief, but I could not have imagined what was coming into our lives.

CHAPTER 6

The Highways from Wilshire Presbyterian Church to the La Canada Presbyterian Church

1964 – 1972

OUR FAMILIES GATHERED FOR MY ordination to the gospel ministry by the Presbytery of L.A. at the Wilshire Presbyterian Church. I invited Dr. Chet Buley, a Presbytery Executive, to preach. He forgot and arrived late. He came running down the center isle in the middle of the service. I was glad he made it, but I was embarrassed. That summer I fell in love with the students from L.A. and Hollywood Highs. We went to Forest Home Summer Camp. One of our high school boys drowned in the Lake during the summer. At his memorial service my wife and I were seated in the front pew looking into his open coffin. It was a painful pastoral experience for me, yet an important learning time. The adults in the church had received me with open arms. I led a summer high school beach retreat in Goleta, Ca. on the message of the Book of Nehemiah. That fall I attended many six – man Culter Academy football games. The pastor, Dr. W. Clarence Wright had been at the church for 30 years. He taught my Presbyterian polity class at Fuller Seminary and did a good job. David Crawford at Princeton had told me that Wright was an honest conservative.

I had dreams of Ph.D. studies and applied at USC. I was admitted into the M.A. program in religion. I enrolled in a class on the Theology of Paul Tillich. It was in that seminar on Friday, November 22, 1963, that the door flung open, and a student or professor announced to the class that President John Kennedy had been assassinated in Dallas. My wife picked me up at USC and we sadly drove to our apartment in the Wilshire District of L.A. The following Sunday Pastor Wright made no mention of Kennedy's death. The church and the nation were in grief, but Dr. Wright, the staunch Republican conservative that he was, made no mention of it either in sermon or prayer. I was puzzled and in emotional pain. The year at Princeton, at Immanuel Union, and the reality of urban problems had convinced me that the conservative politics of the Republican Party were not adequate for addressing the ills of the post-World War II world.

I loved the people of the Wilshire church. However, their pastor was controlling and non-relational. My task was to interpret the senior pastor to our students, care about them, and develop a program of support for the overall mission development for the church. He quickly became critical of me over small insignificant things. He wrote me notes pointing out my failures in not sweeping up the donut crumbs that the youth had left in the Women's Parlor.

He was the lead attorney for the pastor of First Church San Diego in his Presbytery trial. The pastor was accused of sexual misbehavior. Wright believed the Presbytery was seeking to remove him because he was a conservative. The truth was that he was a homosexual, been caught in his church office, and charged in the Presbytery court.

Wright told me he had hoped that I would be his successor at Wilshire. In other ways he was kind and wanted to be helpful, but I was in such inner turmoil in the mid 1960's that I probably did not give him a chance for our relationship to grow. However, it would have meant a lot to me if he had shown compassion for us.

During the fall, we began the process of adopting a child. We learned from tests that we might not be able to produce children and that we would need to adopt. My wife fully desired to do this. In January 1964 we received a ten-day old baby boy whom we named Arthur Jonathan Tankersley, or "Jon-Jon", after President Kennedy's son. Soon it was clear that my wife was deeply depressed. In the spring she told me she did not love me. When the baby was six months old, she returned him to the adoption agency without telling me. I thought I was going to die with grief. I called Dr. Harry Rosenthal, my Jewish psychologist. He provided the insight and empathy I needed. Before long, my wife moved out and I resigned from the church in despair.

Attorney Floyd Norris, an elder at the Wilshire Church, offered me a job in his law office and became a father figure to me. His son Floyd, "Chip", Norris, was in my high school youth group. Floyd and Martha owned a garage on Bunker Hill in downtown L.A. and he represented many of the poor people who lived on the Hill as the Community Redevelopment Agency was seeking to take their old Victorian houses by eminent domain. Clearly, it was the intention of the city leadership to develop Bunker Hill as the center of the cultural life of L.A. Later, this was the intention of Eli Broad, the entrepreneur, as he used his wealth to promote Bunker Hill as the center of L.A. downtown culture. I remember that the law said that the valuations of the houses were to be determined by the present use and not the intended use by the city. Mr. Norris saw this as a form of injustice. The courts were the only hope of the poor residents of Bunker Hill.

My experience of working with Floyd in his law office over a couple of years was not just a helpful transition for me, but the beginning of an expanded vision for life in the City of L.A. Floyd could be gruff and eccentric, as could Martha, but I loved them. I have always believed that God sent them into my life to save and to sustain me through those very dark times of grief. Floyd's counsels were words of wisdom that I sought to follow. At the top of his list was that I should be very careful not to have any connection with another woman because the chances were that my ex-wife would one day accuse me of adultery. I followed his advice, and it was wise. Only later would I see and understand what Floyd meant. Years later she called me in Laguna Beach and threatened to report me to Presbytery and to accuse me of infidelity. It was bazaar and sad. Of course, there were no grounds for such a charge. Clearly, she was deeply disturbed.

When he finally sold his garage on Bunker Hill to CRA and paid off the Spreckels Building at 7th and Hill, Floyd also paid off my car loan of $600. When Floyd and Martha died, years apart, I was asked to do their memorial services at Forest Lawn in Glendale. I did so with great gratitude for their loving me. Floyd could be tough, but he also had a compassionate and generous heart. Their son, "Chip" later in life became a major business writer for the New York Times.

My life and ministry seemed over that fall of 1964. I will never forget being alone in worship at Pasadena Presbyterian Church on

Thanksgiving Sunday of 1964 listening to Dr. Ganse Little reading Psalm 126 to commemorate the first anniversary of the President's death. In part the Psalmist prayed,

"Restore our fortunes, O Lord, like the watercourses in the Negeb. May those who sow in tears reap with shouts of joy. Those who go out weeping, bearing the seed for sowing, shall come home with shouts of joy, carrying their sheaves." (Psalm 126:4–6.)

It was comforting to me to realize that the faith of the church might yet be of comfort to me. Obviously, this was my prayer for my own tears of sorrow as well as our nation's grief.

The big issue for California in the election of 1964 was Proposition 14. The California Realtors Association had presented a Constitutional Amendment to nullify the Rumford Fair Housing Act that required home and property owners to sell or to lease to any person regardless of race or ethnic origin. Front and center were the big issues of "property rights". The political battle pitted conservatives against liberals.

Since WWII there had been large migrations of African Americans from the South into Los Angeles. Veterans from the war were returning and could not find housing that they could afford, or which would be leased or sold to them. Restrictive covenants were part of many bank loan applications. African Americans, Latinos, Asians, and the poor experienced segregated housing and were faced with living in racial and economic ghettos.

The expanding African American population threatened the Wilshire District of L.A. The Wilshire Church was seeking to minister to L.A. and Hollywood high school students. Property rights were a central issue for the white property owners of the wealthy Wilshire District of L.A. who were members of our church. I experienced firsthand the power of "property rights" in conflict with the "civil rights" of fellow citizens. Tensions were building as residential segregation and police misbehavior and mistreatment of "blacks" were being reported. There was a wave of demographic change moving in Los Angeles. The population South of Olympic Blvd was black and was threatening to cross over Wilshire Blvd and move north and west. The social and economic impact would have been major for the Wilshire Country Club property owners. To have a black family move into your neighborhood could lead to falling property values and for the homogeneity of the all-white areas of the city to be threatened. White flight would occur, and neighborhoods would deteriorate. Whites would move to the suburbs. Churches across America would be forced to deal with this urban change and their survival would be in doubt.

In August 1965 the Watts Riots occurred and South – Central L.A. exploded. Many lives were lost and an area of L.A., the size of Manhattan, NYC, was burned and looted by angry, frustrated, and oppressed blacks. Justice had been denied. Troops were called in and the city appeared as a war zone. By that time, I had separated from Wilshire Church and was living in Pasadena. During the riots my Dad came to visit in deep concern for me in the light of what was happening in L.A.

Of course, the Presbyterian Church was active in recommending a "No" vote on Proposition 14. Civil rights were more important than Property rights, it was argued. The prophet's visions of social justice were being betrayed by the white membership of the church. This position of the larger church infuriated Presbyterian California property owners who wanted their freedoms protected in the California Constitution. Proposition 14 was overwhelmingly passed in the election and property rights prevailed over civil rights.

During this time the Civil Rights and Voting Rights bills were passed in the Congress and signed by President Lyndon Johnson. When the President signed these bills, he realized he was losing the southern voting block for the Democratic Party. Later, Richard Nixon and the Republican Party would exploit this tension with their southern strategy to win election as President in 1968. This was an exacerbation of major economic and political polarizations in the U.S., which are still being lived out in our culture and history.

Race has continued to haunt the soul of America and we are paying for America's "Original Sin" of slavery. Ultimately, the U.S. Supreme Court declared that Proposition 14 was unconstitutional. Nevertheless, the issues of race, economics, and legal jurisprudence were revealed as national problems, which are still in play in American society. I watched this play out as an assistant pastor in a congregation that felt threatened by these issues. I kept my mouth shut, but I realized there were not only political and economic ideologies and legal doctrines up for grabs, but also biblical/theological teachings that needed to be brought into dialogue with this national debate.

In fact, the Christian churches, Catholic and Protestant, had struggled with the issues of race, property, and social justice from the early years of the Republic. I had seen the results of racial discrimination firsthand. I grew up in Texas within a segregated City. Plessey v. Ferguson from 1896 was the rule: "separate but equal". Blacks and Latino's lived on their side of Amarillo and whites on the other side. Mexicans went to the public schools, but African Americans had a separate school system.

On July 25, 2020, the *L.A. Times* ran an article by Hailey Branson-Potts about a thirty-nine-year-old man in Amarillo whose business was selling President Trump posters and politically offensive Covid 19 masks on Interstate 40 just outside the city. This was Highway 66 as I was growing up. His place of business was adjacent to the Cadillac Ranch near the Interstate. My high school friend, Stanley Marsh III, a wealthy, eccentric, and spoiled kid, had planted ten Cadillac cars nose down beside U.S. 66 to get some attention, to make a statement. For some reason this captured media attention and the Ranch was written up in the national media. My 50th class reunion at AHS was partially held at Marsh's ranch house. He was finally convicted of pedophilia and sentenced to prison. He died not to long afterwards. His escapades around Amarillo were well known.

The owner of the mobile Trump themed business sells the masks even though he refuses to wear a mask. The store owner is a cynical father of 9 children. He desires to make money and mocks those who purchase the masks to protect their own health and the health of others. His right-wing ideology allows him to thumb his nose and to use his middle finger to flick off the liberal elite whom he despises. The L.A. Times writer said, "Don Caple won't wear a mask. He doesn't think they actually stop the spread of the novel coronavirus, and he's pretty sure mask mandates are a 'communistic move' to see how much people are willing to give up their freedom."[1]

In reading the Times article I was reminded of how powerful paranoid ideologies may be in our lives. I would find it difficult to return to live in this culture in which I spent my life up to age 20. I have been saved from its prejudices and yet wounded by the injustices I observed. There are many fine people in Texas and many fine churches. Of the seven PCUSA churches in Amarillo, five of them left the denomination because of its liberal theology and practices. I am amused by a recent Facebook post of a former pastor of our Presbytery. He was observing that he now lives in a divided culture between red and blue folks. He wonders if there is room for normal people like himself. He wistfully suggested that he would like to move to Texas for the next year, until the 2020 election would be completed. I owe a lot to Texas, but I am glad that I live in

---

1. *L.A. Times, A Section*, June 25, 2020, 1.

California where red and blue identities may more easily live side by side with some degree of mutual tolerance.

Chapter 7

The Highways from La Canada to Laguna Beach

1963 – 1972

Divorce and Recovery

WITHOUT HARRY ROSENTHAL AND FLOYD Norris, I may not have emotionally survived in the last months of 1964 and 1965. Divorce was the last thing I could ever have imagined might happen to me. I had told myself that I would not allow this to happen to me. I did not know where my ex-wife was. I deeply cared for her but, I knew I had been unable to make her happy. She was gone and I was devastated. I thought my life was over. I moved to Alhambra and later to Pasadena to a second story apartment over an old garage on Euclid St., near the center of the city. I was in hiding, burdened with emotional pain, feeling humiliated by circumstances that I did not understand. I thought my ministry was over. I daily commuted to downtown L.A. at 5th and Spring and later to 7th and Hill to work in Floyd's law office.

Soon I visited Dr. David Hubbard, my Westmont College mentor. He had become President at Fuller Theological Seminary. He knew my ex-wife. He tried to connect with her. I'm not sure if he got an address for her. She did not respond. David recommended that I visit with Gary Demarest who was just beginning at La Canada Presbyterian Church as their new pastor. I did so and was welcomed into the church. Gary had experienced an early divorce after 10 years of marriage. His first wife had engaged in repeated infidelities and finally they agreed to end the marriage. God used Gary and Marilee Demarest and the La Canada Presbyterian Church people to resurrect and to restore my life.

During that time, I began to consult with a sub-committee of the Presbytery Committee on Ministerial Relations. They tried to reach her. They were unsuccessful. Finally, after Gary had invited me to become a temporary part-time visitation assistant pastor at La Canada, in January 1966, the Presbytery passed a motion that I was to remain in good standing as pastor even though I had suffered a failed marriage. I filed for divorce on the grounds of "Willful Desertion". Floyd Norris represented me. It was granted in early 1966. It was the beginning of a new life.

It was in those early months in La Canada that I learned via Gary that a woman from the Wilshire Church had called him and shared with him the affair that my ex-wife was having with her husband. He had been the chairperson of the committee that called me to the position at Wilshire. He was a man old enough to be her father. He had the reputation, I later learned, of being a likeable political lobbyist in Sacramento, and a known womanizer. How was I to know? One night in a blinding rainstorm, after Gary had shared this information with me, I went to their house in the Wilshire District of L.A. to confront him. His wife came to the door, refused my entrance, and showed me on her doorstep letters my ex had written to her husband suggesting that he could lie to his wife as she had done to me. I was crushed as I read them. Several years later a Fuller Seminary friend of mine from Amarillo told me in a letter that he and his wife had known of her other affairs while we were students. Again, I was troubled and felt betrayed. As it turned out, both of our wives were having extra-marital affairs. Across the years we commiserated as fellow Presbyterian pastors from the same hometown.

The point was that she had disappeared from my life, and I felt rejected, ruined, and deeply disappointed. It was a public humiliation. Wisdom required me to let it go and to move forward with my life. Rather than seeking revenge I needed to come to acceptance of what had happened, to move forward, to forgive her and myself and to deal with whatever I may or may not have done that contributed to the failure. This was tough medicine, and it required all the spiritual discipline I could muster, along with many hours of psychological counseling.

Many a Saturday night I would get into my VW bug and drive around L.A. and Hollywood alone to calm my sorrow and loneliness. I could not seek comfort in another relationship until the divorce was granted and I was set free legally and spiritually by the grace of God.

Dr. George P. Smith and Claremont Graduate School

I considered going to law school. I enrolled in night classes at California State University in Los Angeles in political science to test my interest in law. I thrashed around seeking to find a way into a new future. I met Dr. George P. Smith a Ph.D. in Government from Claremont Graduate School. We became friends. At the end of his course in Anglo-American Legal History he told me that I had the kind of mind suited for a Ph.D. in Government rather than law school. He inquired if I would help him write a book on American Constitutional jurisprudence. I was flattered. We began to read together Arnold Brecht's new book on Political Theory. I drove to his house in Claremont on Sunday evenings, and we took the book apart over several months. Brecht, Professor at the New School in NYC, introduced me to the history of philosophical and political theory and I came alive in a new way. The subject matter was thrilling for me.

I began to discover myself as a man with gifts. It was like I had been in a locked room totally focused on training for ministry from high school through college and seminary. Now a possible new future opened for me. I gained confidence in my intellectual and relational gifts. George saw me as a bright young theologian who was helping him to grow and to reflect on the reality of his life. We smoked cigars and pipes. We enjoyed fine scotch. He was a hell-raiser, a political party fundraiser, and a Korean War Vet. He had been captured in North Korea, wounded in his leg, which had never healed, and which later turned malignant. Years later George died from his wound. He was brilliant and fun. I loved George. He worked to get me accepted into the Ph.D. program in Government at Claremont. I'll never forget receiving the acceptance letter on a cold rainy night in Pasadena. The relief and hope I felt were palpable. I might have a future.

Gary Demarest and the La Canada Presbyterian Church

But what kind of future would it be? I was travelling on two roads. The La Canada Presbyterian Church was giving to me a new vision for pastoral ministry. It was a grace filled congregation that accepted me and affirmed my gifts. With approval from Presbytery, after three years I was called to be a full time Associate Pastor working in pastoral ministries with adults, leading the Bethel Bible Study program, developing an evangelism calling program that immediately bore fruit in new members, and sharing in general pastoral work. Gary taught me to embrace my humanity, to laugh again, and to affirm myself. I will be forever thankful for his friendship. He has been an older brother to me.

During that time Gary asked me to attend an Evangelism Explosion seminar at College Hill Presbyterian Church in Cincinnati, Ohio. There I came to know Jerry Kirk and R.C. Sproul. I brought the program back to La Canada and it was highly successful. Robert Munger was now teaching at Fuller Seminary, and we joined with Glendale and Burbank Presbyterian Churches to sponsor a national conference on evangelism. Nearly 200 pastors came from around America to participate in this training program. This was one of the truly exciting times of my life. I was doing what I had felt called to do from earlier years. While in Cincinnati I led a team of three on a home visit with a family who had visited College Hill Church. I presented the gospel message as simply as I could and invited the young man college student and his girlfriend to confess faith in Christ. They both said, "Yes"; we prayed; and I was filled with joy. We returned to the church to debrief, and everyone was excited by the response God had given to us.

It was such a spiritual blessing to work with Bob Munger, one of the gifted pastors in the history of the PCUSA. Together with Ed Danks, and Bob Whitaker, the evangelism seminar inspired many pastors to use the program in their church's outreach visitations. Dr. Munger invited me to share my experience with the gathered 200 pastors at the Burbank Church banquet. I was walking on air. It seemed my life had come full circle.

Marriage to Katherine Jeanne Hoppe: September 9, 1967

The best turn in my life and blessing from God came when I was introduced to Kay Hoppe. In March of 1966, shortly after my divorce was final, I met Katherine Jeanne Hoppe on a blind date made possible by two couples from the Wilshire Church. Sue Hughes was a social worker with Kay for L.A. County. Van and Sue Hughes, and Ruth and Aaron Wilterding, thought Kay and I had much in common. Both couples knew me well from Wilshire and Kay from her social work position in L.A. County. They proved to be good friends. During the months following my separation and aloneness, Aron and Ruth would have me over on many evenings for dinner and human community. It was a time of adjustment to single life. They arranged for the blind date. I called Kay and she gave directions to her apartment in South Pasadena. When she opened the door and I saw her I was smitten. She was a beautiful redhead with psychological and theological interests. She also read Paul Tillich. That night we went to dinner at Dino's on Colorado Blvd. We discussed theology and then Van took us on a tour of Cal Tech where he was a Ph.D. student in Physics. Kay saved the wine bottle from that first date.

Thankfully, Dr. Rosenthal helped me to face my fears. I invited Kay into my group therapy and the group confronted me with the truth that my passion and future would be with Kay. After a short breakup, I turned back to Kay. She invited me to Christmas Eve dinner with her family in South Pasadena and I knew I was home with a woman I loved with passion, and she loved me. It had been a precarious time for me, but the LORD saw me through it, and we fell in love.

We married on September 9, 1967, at La Canada Presbyterian Church. Gary Demarest and Marv Hiles married us. As I write we have completed 52 years of marriage. She has been a God blessed miracle in my life. I am so grateful for her love and support all these years. Through her I have learned many things about being a man who loves a woman and who allows a woman to love him. Years later she earned a Master of Arts in Psychology at California State University in Fullerton, and later a Master of Divinity at Fuller Seminary. She has been exactly what I needed and has stood with me in the highs and lows of parenting and pastoral ministry.

In 1969 we began the process of adopting a child through L.A. County. I was afraid due to my experience, but we moved forward. The County approved us. This was in the years before the abortion laws changed under Governor Ronald Reagan. The wait was only nine months for an infant.

First Trip to Europe

In June of 1969 Kay and I went to Europe for a month. This was a reward we gave to ourselves right after I had passed my doctoral qualifying exams at Claremont Graduate School. We joined the London Society, purchased two $139 charter plane round trip tickets to London, and we were on our way. Our plan was to do Europe on $5 a day. At the end of the month, we had spent one thousand dollars. By the time the plane was flying over Denver, we had each enjoyed enough liquor to be sick. Smoking was allowed and the 250 passengers on the expanded DC-8 were smoking and drinking up a storm. Finally, we landed in London and a great holiday was begun. We found a cheap room near the train station and did a quick tour of the city. Then we caught an overnight ferry across the English Channel, landed in Holland, picked up our pre-purchased VW Bug in Amsterdam and took off south through the Netherlands, to Germany, to Switzerland, over the Alps, to Italy, to Florence and to Rome. We toured the Vatican and the City of Rome. The exposure to St. Peter's Basilica was awe-inspiring. Then it was around the Italian and French coastlines. Ultimately, we went west to Barcelona, Spain.

Kay caught the flu in Barcelona; the doctor came to the hotel and gave her some medicine; I put her in the back seat of the VW, and we took off for Geneva. After 700 miles of driving, we arrived in the city of the Reformation and enjoyed seeing Calvin's St. Peter's Church and the chapel where John Knox had preached. We visited the World Council of Church's Center and the John Knox Retreat Center. As it happened, Pope Paul the Sixth visited and held an open-air mass that was televised. A pope had not visited Geneva from before Calvin's 16th century.

Then we drove to Lucerne where we rendezvoused with a La Canada couple, had dinner, marched in a parade to another restaurant, drank beer, ate apple strudel, and smoked cigars to top off the evening. The next day we took the tram up Mt. Pilatus and the party continued with fine chocolate. From there it was on to Paris, France, where we arrived at five p.m. on Friday afternoon. The Bug had a flat tire across the street from Napoleon's Tomb. We did Paris, went up the Eiffel Tower, visited the Louvre Museum, celebrated Notre Dame Cathedral, returned to Amsterdam, shipped the car back to Southern California, flew to London and were once again on the charter back to L.A. What a wonderful trip together. I drove over 4500 miles during those 28 days.

Adoption of Jeffrey Jarrell Tankersley: 1969

In early November we were advised that a ten-week – old baby boy was available for us. We had purchased a home in Glendale and were preparing the nest. Talk about excitement! When we walked into the room of the Adoption Agency, and they brought him in to us and placed him in a crib, he looked up at me with bright blue eyes while sucking on his fingers. Immediately, I knew we were dealing with a formed human being with a mind of his own and that he did not know what to make of us. We put him into the new '69 Chevrolet and brought him home. That evening Gary and Marilee Demarest, Aron and Ruth Wilterding, and Ken and Elizabeth Kalina with their baby David came over and it was a great celebration of thanksgiving.

That same day, November 25, 1969, my grandmother, Layla Jane Sparkman, was laid to rest at 82 years old in Lubbock, Texas. She had a surgery on her colon and died of a heart attack while in the hospital. I felt badly about not being in Lubbock for her service, but my mom and her family understood. Grandma would have wanted me to attend to our new baby.

Jeffrey Jarrell Tankersley became our son. He was born September 16, 1969, in Los Angeles. I handled the adoption papers and process. Six months after he came to us, we went into the judge's chambers in Pasadena and the judge made the adoption legal. That day was one of the special days of our lives. Little could I have imagined how much my life would change with joy, love, and anticipatory anxiety! We both really desired to be good parents, but we had a lot of growing to do. Being parents has been a major source of spiritual growth for us each.

Jeff became our legal heir and we promised to accept the stewardship responsibility of shepherding his life and soul into adult maturity. We both loved him and desired only the best for him. Gary Demarest, the pastor of LCPC, baptized Jeff and David Kalina the same Sunday morning. Jeff shouted, laughed, and cried out during the baptism. Gary said to the congregation that he clearly had the call to be a preacher. The journey of parenthood with all its joys, struggles, opportunities, and obligations have played out with laughter, tears, and fulfillment of our love for each other and for him. We have always told him of his adoption and have been willing to help him process his family of origin issues, but he has never seemed to desire to know a lot more than the information provided by L.A. County Adoption Agency. We have prayed for his birth mother and father through the years and hoped his birth mother made peace with her decision. She would be very proud of the man he has become.

Bible Lands Study Tour: 1971

When Jeff was two, Bob Latta and I completed teaching the year – long Bethel Bible Study Series group of 21 whom we were preparing to teach in the La Canada congregational phase. That year was one of the great years of my life. As a group we decided to take the 21 to the lands of the Bible. We started in Rome, went to Athens, on to Tel Aviv and the Holy Land. Then we went to Izmir, Turkey, to Pergamum, and on to Berlin, Germany. It was 1971. In Berlin I discovered the Pergamum Museum and Satan's altar taken from Turkey by German archeologists. The Museum also had the Ishtar Gates from ancient Babylon. What a treat.

    The problem and blessing for us was that we had to leave two-year-old Jeff with Toni and Howard Brooks who also had a two-year-old adopted son. Our anxieties and fears were almost paralyzing. We knew we could trust them. But we questioned: how would he respond? Would he feel abandoned? Would he forget us or love the Brook's more than us? What if something were to happen to him or to us? I remember taking my tape recorder into the backyard of our house in Glendale and dictating my affirmations of love for him so that someday he might hear my voice even though he likely would not understand. We were anxious throughout the trip. We had conflict between the two of us, but we made it through. I remember one night in our room at the National Palace Hotel in Jerusalem, a Palestinian hotel, we argued and listened to Palestinian music from the street below. It was haunting. What an amazing experience!

    It was a wonderful trip, and it did what we had hoped. Our Bethel teachers were ready to teach. We enrolled around 250 of our adult members to take the yearlong course. It began to raise the biblical literacy of our congregation. I had used my Bible teaching gifts to train the laity of the church to teach others. We had launched a revolution in the life and mission of LCPC. Thankfully, we returned, picked Jeff up, and went home. He was quiet on the way home, but he seemed to recover, and life went on.

Ph.D. in Government: Claremont Graduate School, 1971

In 1971 I finished the Ph.D. at Claremont in Public Law, Political Theory, American Government, and Urban Studies. That spring the degree was awarded at Claremont. My Dad and his girlfriend Lillie attended the graduation, and we went to dinner afterwards at the Magic Lantern. As I was walking across the stage to receive the degree, I could hear young Jeff calling out to me, "Mama, Mama". It was so funny. The only disappointment that day was that they ran out of Ph.D. hoods before I received mine. By that time, I was just happy to have completed the program. Later I purchased the Claremont Graduate School Ph.D. hood for myself. In the springtime the La Canada Church held a huge celebration at the Glendale Civic Center. During that evening they presented me with a make believe grey doctoral robe with all kinds of symbols attached that spoke of their love for me. It was a very affirming experience. I was filled with joy. My life was working. Years later Jeff wore that grey robe on Halloween.

Adjunct Faculty at CSULA: Civil Rights, Protests, Angela Davis

I was a part-time adjunct faculty teacher at California State Los Angeles in the Political Science department. I taught American Constitutional Law, Jurisprudence, American and California Government, and several graduate seminars. It was in the stimulating days of the Civil Rights movement and the Vietnam War. I became something of a chaplain at the university and a pastor in La Canada helping families struggle with issues of war and peace. Social justice became a passion for me while I was doing the work of a pastor and reprocessing my theological world view to embrace a two – legged gospel of personal and social salvation.

The middle years of the 1960's were filled with social protests much of which originated at American universities and in the Black Church. It seemed to me that the university was becoming the moral conscience of the nation and that the church was so deeply implicated in the culture of racism and warfare that it was paralyzed.

The national church General Assembly engaged the issues of race and peacemaking, but the local churches were threatened. Along the way, a committee of G.A. made a $10,000.00 contribution to the Angela Davis Legal Defense Fund. She was the black U.C.L.A. professor who was an avowed member of the American Communist Party. She was a loud voice for social justice and for the critique of American democracy and its capitalistic economy. During the protests in and around San Francisco she accompanied a group of terrorists who went into the courthouse and shot a judge during a trial. She was arrested and put on trial. It appeared that the Presbyterian Church was coming to her aid in the legal defense fund.

There was not a white community of America that was not angered by her acts, by her Communist political philosophy, and her unpatriotic and terrorist acts. When churches across the USA learned that a committee of our General Assembly had contributed to her legal defense and sided with her cause for justice, it was assumed that the liberal national church had violated the trust of conservative white Presbyterians and their churches. She symbolized all that was threatening America in the tumultuous 1960's.

The truth was that a small committee of G.A., without the knowledge or approval of the larger G.A., had made this contribution. When G.A. met, it censured the action of the committee for this gift. A group of black Presbyterian leaders raised $10 thousand dollars and returned it to the original fund from which the gift was made. But the damage had been done. People resigned from their congregations. They withheld financial gifts. The Presbyterian Church and white America were in protest.

One evening we organized a meeting with the La Canada membership for the purpose of listening to their rage and concerns. Gary moderated the meeting. I listened. I had never heard such anger and public protest. I was worried that the jammed packed meeting might turn against the pastors of the church. Gary did a great job of listening and responding. The angry boil was lanced and the next day I went to work writing a position paper for the session. To save our church's connection with the UPCUSA, I argued that the session needed to designate its mission funds and to give only to those causes in which we had trust. The paper was approved by session and presented to the congregation. By that time, it seemed the membership trusted us enough to move forward. But the national church, and even our local church hemorrhaged with lost members and diminished financial giving. I am still very ambivalent about the session letter I wrote, yet, at the time my priority was to facilitate the congregation's peace and trust in its leadership. Gary's allowing me to work on that paper for the session was a demonstration to me of his excellent leadership in ministry.

The Spirituality of the Church and the Social Gospel

La Canada was contiguous with northwest Pasadena and its mainly black population. Between the two cities, the Rose Bowl and JPL provided a buffer. I guessed that all white La Canada/Flintridge citizens were anxious about the black population moving across the invisible boundary line. White flight had brought many Pasadena residents into La Canada/Flintridge seeking security and homogeneity. In fact, some faculty from Fuller Seminary argued that church growth was dependent upon likeness and common skin-color. The church that set at the center of La Canada was enlightened and mission oriented, if the blacks stayed on their side of the Arroyo, at least that was what some of us suspected.

The Angela Davis contribution planted the seeds of mistrust in the heart of the local churches. It seemed that each year as the G.A. met there was another motion or action passed that reinforced the perception of the liberal agenda of the national leadership of the Presbyterian Church. It was joked that each time the G.A. met that the demons of hell celebrated.

At the time I did not fully realize that the Southern Presbyterian Church had developed a theology of separation and a spiritual gospel disconnected from the social and political demands of God's salvation. James Henley Thornwell had developed a doctrine of the church called "the Spirituality of the Church".

The church's mission was to promote the spirituality of the Christian faith without reference to the struggles of the world. Souls were to be saved for the sake of their going to heaven upon death. The church had no calling to speak prophetically to the ills of human society and a culture which was fallen and enslaved by the "principalities and powers and the rulers of this present darkness". The church's mission was to comfort its members, to build up spiritual identity, to teach the Bible, and to worship God. Believing and receiving the gift of eternal life in heaven was everything.

At the time Max Rafferty the California State School Superintendent was running for the U.S. Senate from California. He was a conservative Republican. He was from La Canada. He argued during social protest over race and other matters that it was time that the "preachers returned to their sanctuaries and pulpit's and to leave the affairs of the world to the politicians". His was the voice of "White Christianity" in much of America.

What was needed, I had come to believe, was a holistic gospel, a two-legged gospel of personal and social salvation. I had been informed by the need to rescue souls from hell through faith in Christ, but not a vision of social justice and righteousness revealed in the Bible. This was a painful awakening to the truth of the New Creation, the New Age of the rule and reign of God.

The Church: Racism, War, and Social Justice

I had grown up in the segregated world of northwest Texas. I had thought little about blacks going to the back of the public bus while whites rode in the front of the bus. There were colored waiting rooms in bus stations. Colored drinking fountains were in many places. Blacks could not sit at the Woolworth Lunch Counter. My city segregated blacks and Hispanics from whites. African Americans had their own school systems separate from whites. The south was living out Plessy v. Ferguson's, "separate but equal doctrine".

The only Negroes I knew worked in my dad's bakery along with Hispanics. I liked them and they seemed to like me. They teased me about sexual matters and behaviors. We worked and laughed together. In some ways my dad demonstrated an enlightened understanding of the workplace. One New Year's Day all his employees worked to complete an order. Dad cooked lunch for us all in the bakery ovens. When it came time to eat, the blacks filled their plates and went to a separate room to eat by themselves. My Dad would not let them do that. He brought them into the room with the other employees and we ate at the same table. This was enlightened theology, even though I doubt my dad would have understood that. He simply had a sense of fairness and equality in work. If we worked together, we could eat together. I was proud of my dad that day.

The 60's revealed to me amid the racial riots that rocked the nation that my dad was afraid of Negroes and Mexicans. He always slept with a gun under his pillow and drove with a pistol in his car. When Watts was burning in the 1960's he would come to check up on me in Pasadena. He cared for me, and I was deeply touched by his concern.

There was great social and racial unrest in America in the 1960's. The Kerner Commission validated some of the reasons. While I was taking courses at California State University in L.A., one of my fellow graduate students was a young man from a small town in the Panhandle of

North Texas, a town not far from Amarillo. We were about the same age. After class one evening we spoke in the parking lot, and he shared that his dad had been pastor of a Negro Southern Baptist Church in that town. He said he grew up listening to his dad preach anti-Semitic sermons blaming the problems of the world on the Jews. He wept as he shared. His Dad was simply passing on the racial attitudes of the larger white culture. Since he was oppressed by whites, "why not pass it on to hated Jews"? White superiority and the class structure needed to establish itself in the hierarchy of southern class culture.

Without my realizing it, the world and family in which I grew up formed racist attitudes within me and certainly anxieties and fears. I did not think much about it until I moved to California to finish college and to go to seminary. Amazingly, I grew up with an unexamined conscience about social and political issues. The 1960's brought these issues to my awareness. I remember the Eisenhower/Nixon years of the 1950's. Except for the Korean War it seemed an idyllic time of harmony, prosperity, and peace. I watched the political conventions of 1956 on television and came away assuming I was a Republican. Their convention seemed so much more civil. The Democratic Convention seemed deeply conflicted. I was still too young to vote, but my Grandmother Layla Jane Sparkman, loved Eisenhower and his wife Mamie. I was not aware if my parents ever voted. The Texas Poll Tax discouraged many from voting and of course that was its purpose.

I did not know how to respond as a white Christian to the Civil Rights movement of the late 50's and 1960's led by Dr. Martin Luther King, Jr. His preaching convicted me. His *"Letter from a Birmingham Jail"* was a rebuke to southern white preachers who counseled him to go slowly, that the nation could not handle a major social revolution. He was speaking to many of us. I wanted to join in his movement, but I was careful. Somehow, I understood that the churches I might serve would not appreciate bold action on my part, yet I knew that King was prophetic and was speaking truth to power.

1968 was a difficult year in America. In early April Kay and I were on a short vacation in San Francisco when we heard on the television that Martin King Jr. had been assassinated in Memphis, Tennessee. His mission had expanded, from the race issue to the war in Vietnam, and to economic welfare of the black men who collected the trash of Memphis. I was concerned with this transition. On Thanksgiving Sunday 1968 I preached in La Canada and asked: "How Can We Give Thanks in a Year

Like 1968?" The sermon was based on Luke 18 and the story of the self-centered Pharisee and the repentant tax collector. It was entitled, *"Two Attitudes Toward Thanksgiving"*.

In April King was killed by a lone gunman in Memphis. Bobby Kennedy had sought to calm the restless black crowds that evening. He reminded them that he too had lost a brother, a President, to an assassin's bullet in Dallas. It was an election year and the war in Vietnam and Civil Rights were front and center. Our major cities were burning. Our university campuses were filled with protests. Students were troubled by unrest and anger.

Eugene McCarthy joined the Democratic primary race against President Johnson. When he nearly won an early primary, Robert Kennedy joined the race, and Johnson soon announced that he would not run again. He retired to his Texas ranch and died at the age of 64. In the June 1968 primary I voted for Robert Kennedy. Late that June night I switched off the TV coverage of Kennedy's victory speech only to learn the next morning that he had been killed in the kitchen of the Ambassador Hotel in L.A. by Sirhan Sirhan. What a tragedy! Violence and death roamed the streets of America and Southeast Asia.

Along with race relations, the 1960's were troubled by America's engagement in Vietnam. Slowly but surely, from President Eisenhower to President Kennedy, to President Johnson, and to President Nixon, American troops were increased to face the suggested monolithic threat of Communism in the world. The leadership of our nation had embraced a domino theory of the threat to America from Russia and China. Push the first domino over and the rest of the dominoes would fall. Better to stop the spread of Communism in Korea and in Southeast Asia than to confront the peril on the shores of North America or Europe!

The church, communism, the War in Vietnam: 1968

It is helpful to remember the 1950's anti-communist fears. These were the fearful days of the early Cold War. Senator Joseph McCarthy believed that Russian communists had infiltrated every part of American life. He publicly charged many loyal Americans, in every part of national life, to be communists. He saw communists under every bush. There was an Anti-Communist Christian Crusade led by Fred Swartz. Together with the John Birch Society they were searching for communists. The pastor at the First Methodist Pasadena Church, Dr. Morgan Edwards, told our Claremont Seminary graduate seminar about being followed and having his phone tapped by Birchers who were seeking to prove that he was a communist sympathizer. Many pastors in mainline churches were watched and listened to, in order to prove they were dangers to American religious and political life. McCarthy was a paranoid alcoholic, whose public hearings were finally rejected by leading Republicans and Democrats. Even President Eisenhower had to appease him because the anti-communistic movement was so strong.

At one point in the 1960's five hundred thousand American military were stationed in Vietnam. From Kennedy, to Johnson, to Nixon, each President promised the U.S. was winning the war, but objective observers knew that we were losing. Finally, over fifty thousand American troops died and many more were maimed. In the process, the people of the U.S. became deeply divided over the Vietnamese War.

I was teaching at the university and the war was a major issue among the students. I was a part of the dialogue about the war. In the La Canada parish there was a family with two sons. One son was pro-war and the other anti-war. One son had done two tours in Vietnam and loved it as he flew in helicopters shooting into the jungles. The other son was seeking a C.O. classification and asked me to write a letter for him to his draft board supporting his spiritual claims against the violence of war. The family was in deep conflict. I sought to reconcile the two sons and their parents and to be a mediator, a peacemaker. All the while, I publicly remained neutral for the sake of my ministry with all sides. Gradually, I turned against the war as I realized that the U.S. government was lying about why we entered the war and about our winning or losing.

The Pentagon Papers, illegally released by Daniel Ellsberg, uncovered what the CIA knew. The Washington Post and the N.Y. Times began to publish them, proving that from Kennedy, to Johnson, to Nixon, the Presidents knew that America and South Vietnam were losing to the North. Many believed that political wisdom required American leadership to face up to their cover up and to withdraw from the battle. Yet, no President wanted to be in office and to be blamed for losing a war for which the nation had shed much blood and spent much of its national treasure. As a result, thousands of innocent people in Laos, Cambodia, North and South Vietnam perished in bombings, battles, and the spraying of Agent Orange to defoliate the jungles. Many American soldiers became drug addicted. Many were maimed and came home emotionally and spiritually wounded. The Veterans did not receive a hero's welcome as they came home from Vietnam. It was an angry and sad time that left deep scars in the soul of America.

The 1968 Democratic Convention erupted, and riots flowed into the streets and parks of Chicago. Nixon promised to end the war; that he knew how to end the war; but could not publicly reveal how he would end it. He was elected. His appeal to the Silent Majority, and promise to end the war, won the day. Behind the scenes, Nixon escalated the war and lied about it. Each President believed that increased military power could win and end the war. Together with the Civil Rights movement, the riots in our city streets and campuses, and the Vietnam War debacle, it was a tumultuous time to be a pastor.

General Assemblies of the United Presbyterian Church USA were taking positions against the war, calling for the ending of bombing, and for peacemaking between North and South Vietnam. This war changed America and our political parties. Some argued that a counterculture was created, and it represented the *"Greening of America"*. (Note Charles Reich's death in June 2019, LA Times Obituary June 25, 2019.) In 1975 the North Vietnamese armies overran the South. The last American forces were removed, and the war was over. Ultimately, the Wall commemorating the lost lives of American soldiers who died in Nam was built in D.C. I have never seen the Wall without weeping and again feeling the pain of the nation in my own heart. The name of one of my high school friends, a graduate of West Point, is on the wall.

After my Thanksgiving 1968 sermon as I greeted people at the front door of the La Canada church, one man asked if I were a member of the *John Birch Society*. Another asked if I were a member of the *Communist Party*. In seeking to be prophetic, I knew I was in trouble. We were all in trouble in that tumultuous year of 1968. I was caught in the middle seeking to preach the Word and at the same time to connect the message of the Word with our time and place. Of course, I was not a member of the John Birch Society or of the Communist Party.

While I was a student at Fuller Seminary (1959–62) there had been a Christian Heritage lecture established by a wealthy conservative donor. The first speaker had been Robert Welch, the leader of the Birch Society. His presentations were filled with fearmongering and divisive assertions. By the end of the week my fellow students were standing and confronting him while he spoke. The attendance dropped too almost nothing. I was embarrassed. He had spoken as a patriotic American only to sound like an enemy of our political order and perhaps a Communist himself. I was not a member of the John Birch Society. The man's comments to me were hurtful. Looking back, I can understand better why my sermon critics had such a response to me.

Sometimes the biblical message can call us to repentance, sting us, trouble us, and make us angry. Yet, I knew that I was a loyal patriot who loved his country. I was a young Associate Pastor seeking to find my way into the soul of my country and into the heart of the Word of God for my people. It was shocking for me to be asked that question. Years later, the movie, *"Forest Gump"* summed up the tensions of this period of American history.

How was one to preach in 1968? As I look back more than 50 years later, I think our people needed not only prophetic truth, but also God's comfort. Throughout my years in pastoral ministry, I have struggled with this tension. It was the tension between "the hermeneutic of prophetic critique and the hermeneutic of consolation". The biblical word to Israel contained each. The Gospel's contained each. God knows that we vulnerable human's need both. I need both. Every preacher worth anything must live in this tension, listen, pray, and faithfully respond with the message the Spirit has stirred within his or her heart for the occasion. If one is in the ministry in conflicted seasons of a nation's life suffering may occur because of faithfulness and obedience to God's Word.

It is interesting that our culture continues to seek understanding and healing for the wounds of the Vietnam period of our nation's history. One the movies nominated for the Academy Award for 2020 sought to interpret the 1968 trial of the Chicago Seven. The movie probed the racism and violent distortions of the truth of that summer season. The trial of the seven did not serve the cause of justice and reconciliation. The judge was later removed as incompetent and for failing to serve the requirements of justice. The movie focused on the prejudice of the judge and the conflicted testimony of government representatives. To be sure, the seven protestors and their followers in that crazy summer of 1968 brought much suffering upon themselves. Indeed, it was a time in which the events of our nation's history and the polarization of our political parties caused many persons, groups, and religious denominations to lose their way in the chaos.

The Confession of 1967: Reconciliation

During the 1960's, the General Assembly was seeking to either revise the Westminster Catechism or to prepare a new Confession relevant for this season of the church's life and mission. Many of the theological tensions that had afflicted the larger church in the first half of the 20th century again came to light when the first proposals for a new Confession emerged. After much study and debate, a section on the Bible was added to the new Confession of 1967. The conservatives were assured that Presbyterians were not moving away from the authority of the Scriptures as the written Word of God. *Presbyterians United for Biblical Concerns* pressed the larger church to present a high view of the nature, life, death and resurrection of Jesus, the living Word of God; but also, for a high view of the Scriptures of Old and New Testaments as the written Word of God inspired by the Holy Spirit but also bearing the imprint of their human authors.

Clearly, it seemed that the statement on the Bible moved the church away from the battles of the first quarter of the 20th century between the fundamentalists and the modernists. But the Presbyterian Controversy over the Bible and the Bible's understanding of God's salvation story has remained until today. C-67 affirmed,

> "God's word is spoken to his church today where the Scriptures are faithfully preached and attentively read in dependence on the illumination of the Holy Spirit and with readiness to receive their truth and direction."
>
> The theme of C-67 was reconciliation. The God of Israel had acted in the history of Israel and in the life, death, and resurrection of Jesus Christ for the sake of reconciling all people to God and to one another, in whatever nation. (2 Corinthians 5:16–21)
>
> "All this is from God, who reconciled us to himself through Christ, and has given us the ministry of reconciliation; that is, in Christ God was reconciling the world to himself, not counting their trespasses against them, and entrusting the message of reconciliation to us.
>
> So, we are ambassadors for Christ, since God is making his appeal through us; we entreat you on behalf of Christ, be reconciled to God." [1]

---

1. *Confession of* 1967, *The Book of Confessions*, sections 9.27 to 9.30.

Through the grace of our Lord Jesus Christ, the love of God the Father, and the communion of the Holy Spirit, the New Creation had already arrived. The churches mission was to make disciples and as the people of God to advance the kingdom of God among all people, healing the human heart, transforming the human mind, reconciling relationships, and of sharing the good news of God's love and justice for all humanity in the power of the one triune God.

The Confession of 1967 called Presbyterians to work for reconciliation in human society. Indeed, the 20th century had been violent, with major wars and massive human suffering. Social movements called for justice and social righteousness. Christians were called to be peacemakers seeking to bring the races together. In a world filled with enemies, conflicts, and violence, the church was to seek peace, God's shalom, God's reconciliation, forgiveness among people and nations. With the advent of nuclear warfare, it was imperative that the church be an agent of healing love and spiritual renewal. The future of planet earth depended upon God's reconciling power manifest in the people of God and witnessed to in the mission of the church.

Likewise, the divisions between the rich and poor threatened all humanity. Poverty causes war. There could be no peace without justice. Therefore, the church was called to follow in the way of Jesus who fed the hungry, who healed the blind, who set the slaves free, and inaugurated the Year of Jubilee in which humanity would live within the reality of the kingdom of God. This was the reconciling mission of Christ's church.

The 20th century had seen anarchy in human sexual relationships. The family needed reconciled. Persons were called to live with self-respect and the proper use of power in all relationships. With the advent of antibiotics and conception technology sexual anarchy had grown in male-female relationships. The misuse of freedom had wrecked the family. All relationships were called to new commitment both in and out of marriage.

The Confession of 1967 gave direction to me in developing a biblical theology that set me free from Scottish common-sense philosophy and the Princeton Theology of B.B. Warfield and J.G. Machen. This was especially important to me being a graduate of Fuller Seminary whose founding purpose was to reclaim the theology of the Old Princeton. What the Confession did for me was to set me free to surrender to the authority and inspiration of the Bible as the source of Reformed theology in the way of John Calvin. This Confession placed Jesus Christ my Savior and

LORD at the center of the Bible's witness. The mission of working for the healing of the world's ills, injustices, abuses of power, and social, racial divisions, became a compelling passion and motivating force in my life.

CHAPTER 8

The Highways to Laguna Beach and the Laguna Presbyterian Church

1972-2018

AFTER SIX AND A HALF years at the La Canada Church I felt it was time for me to make myself open for a new call. This was not an easy decision. I loved being on the staff with Gary Demarest, Bob Latta, Marv Hiles, Ken Kalina, and others. But people in the La Canada Church were beginning to encourage me to make myself available for a position of leadership, regular preaching, and teaching. Gradually, I did that and interviewed with several congregations. The PNC from Laguna Beach visited La Canada to hear me preach and to attend the evangelism conference. Kay and I visited Laguna Beach. We knew it was a beautiful beachside community and artist colony. It was also known for "sex, drugs, and rock n 'roll". New Age religion, sexual acting out, war opposition protests, a large population of gays and lesbians, the well - known Festival of the Arts, the reputation of Timothy Leary who was busted in the city, and rock concerts in Laguna Canyon made me question if any church could survive in the midst of this cultural chaos? It was a call to a church with a building, a budget, a pre-school, and a fragmented congregation that had suffered its own internal conflicts. Traditional churches were not all that popular. The city was in disrepair and physically and spiritually troubled at the end of the 60's. Yet, there was also a highly stable, traditional demographic in the city.

The congregation issued a call to me on June 4, 1972. I did my sermon as a candidate for the position. I waited in the pastor's study for the results of the vote of the congregation. Ed Hinds came up the stairs to the office to report on the meeting. The first words he spoke to me as he opened the door were, "Jerry, I am sorry". My heart nearly fell through the floor. Thankfully, he went on to say that he was sorry that he had been unable to see me after church since he was counting ballots. He shared that the vote of the congregation was strong in support of me, and I accepted the call. Thus, began the transition from La Canada to Laguna Beach. It was a move of sixty miles and the longest move Kay had ever made. I was 35 and she was 31.

On Mother's Day in the late 1960's Kay and I had lunch in Laguna Beach while driving through from San Diego on our way back to La Canada. The city was jammed with runaway kids and bumper to bumper cars. I said to Kay that this was the last place I would ever want to live. Little did I know that I would be called to be pastor of the local Presbyterian Church at the heart of the city!

Laguna Beach 1972 to 1983: Personal and Pastoral Challenges

Soon after we arrived to begin a new calling, Kay's Dad, Walter Hoppe, died in Northern California. I was installed as pastor on September 10, 1972. Walter and my mother-in-law were present. Walter died in late September and was buried at Forest Lawn, Glendale. Kay's mother moved to Laguna Hills and into a mobile home. Augusta Jeanne Hoppe joined the Laguna Church and thus began a pilgrimage of dealing with Jeanne in our family and in the church. For the most part it worked out. When in anger toward me she resigned from the church I kept her letter of resignation from the church in my file and never presented it to the session. The relationship smoothed out, but I had known when Kay and I married that her mom could be problematic for Kay and for me. Overall, I was glad to have her nearby. It was good for Kay and for Jeff. Families have conflicts and everyone gets involved. So, it was for me. I grew to love Jeanne and I think she loved me and always brought a unique perspective to our family. Not long after our conflict she invited me to dinner at her place and we calmly reconciled and moved forward. When she passed in

1977, I felt deep grief. Kay's brother Ed, at the time a zealous Mormon, did the graveside service at Forest Lawn.

After a few months in Laguna Beach Kay found a house in the Top of the World neighborhood. We bought the house from the owner. The price tag was twice what we had paid in Glendale on Santa Barbara St. We have lived on Bonn Dr. since January 1973. The house sits on the rim of the wilderness area that was known as the Moulton Ranch. We could hear cows mooing below us. Saddleback Mountain sits at the center of the northeast view from our living room and bedroom. In those years there was one line of lights that connected in Mission Viejo. We have loved the wild beauty and the buffer around the backside of Laguna Beach. The hills were filled with coyotes, bobcats, deer, raccoons, and all kinds of hawks and other birds. I always felt the eastward view functioned as a reminder that there was a larger world before us and that we were not to be captured or limited by the beautiful coastline of South Orange County.

Truly, moving to Laguna Beach was like returning to the "cradle of creation", a phrase I picked up from the movie, *"The Night of the Iguana"*. As I watched the rainclouds roll from the west and move inland from the blue Pacific and over our hills it was as if we had arrived where anyone would desire to stay over a lifetime. In fact, I have listened to many share the stories of their discovery of Laguna Beach and then to decide to move to this place to spend the rest of their years. Living in the Pasadena area had become more and more stressful with the air pollution. There were days in October in which the smog was so thick you could smell it. It would blot out the mountains from our view and make it painful for me to breathe. To play golf in the mornings of a smoggy day meant spending the afternoon with pain in my lungs seeking to recover.

For me living in Laguna Beach could become a dangerous attachment that might limit my understanding of the larger world that beckoned to me from the north, the west, the south, and the east. I did not understand why I had been called to this place and to this church. All I knew was that I had an inner peace and assurance that the mystery of the calling was in God's hands. There was peace in my soul about the call. I was afraid to commit to Laguna out of fear that it might bind me and make it difficult for me to consider any other call. This became partially true for me. When Kay and I were considering the call and interviewing with the PNC, while driving down PCH south of Corona del Mar, I said to her that we needed to bracket out the beauty and stay focused on whether or not the church desired to do the mission of God or if it was made up of people at ease in Paradise wanting nothing more than to be comfortable, insulated, and to have their lifestyles affirmed.

The Challenge of Ambition

I confess that when I arrived a part of me was climbing the ladder of upward mobility that within 10 years would lead me to a larger, more significant church. This was spiritually immature thinking on my part, but for an ambitious young pastor this fantasy claimed my imagination and planted the seeds of inner restlessness and anxiety within my soul. I had come from a church of nearly 2000 members, and which had national recognition. Over the years I have seen pastors arrive in new churches only to immediately begin looking for the next move. This destroys a pastor's soul and the trust of the congregation. The result is that the same ministry is repeated every 5 to 7 years in a new place. Personal and community growth may be limited.

Early in my Laguna Beach ministry a follower of Robert Schuller's sent me to his *Institute for Successful Church Leadership*. Charles Strong assured me that if I would go to the Institute and learn the principles of Successful Church Leadership that in quick – time I would double my salary in Laguna. Schuller argued that a pastor ought to begin a new ministry with the commitment of spending the rest of his or her life in that place. I questioned that! I had to tell Charles that I was not Robert Schuller, even though I could embrace much of what he said. Truly, he was a phenomenon in Orange County and around the world. Little could I foresee that I would ultimately watch the demise of the Chrystal Cathedral and its transition to becoming the center of the Orange County Diocese of the Roman Catholic Church.

One of the lay leaders of the Laguna Beach church had come from First Church Phoenix. In its day it had been one of the large and well – known congregations in the country. One day after church Oren Arnold came to me and said his old church was looking for a new senior pastor. He flattered me by saying I was too big for Laguna Beach. He wanted to recommend me to the PNC of Phoenix. I felt it was a test to determine my commitment to Laguna. From the mouth of my respected friend, the tempter was making the same suggestion that he had made to Jesus in the wilderness. (Matthew 4 and Luke 4) I was just getting started. I loved Oren, but I would not bite on his proposal.

This manifestation of pride and expression of human sin is common among pastors. We dress it up in spiritual and biblical language to justify it. The first disciples were in competition with each other to become the greatest and to have privileged positions at Jesus' Table. Even to the Last Supper in which Jesus broke the bread and poured the cup and instituted this Sacrament, the twelve whispered at the Passover Table their inner mixed competitiveness as to which of them was the greatest. Luke 22 clarified that Jesus knew all about this. The devil had tempted him in the desert in Luke 4 to desire to rule over the kingdoms of this world with all their power and glory. Jesus told his disciples that Satan had demanded to sift all of them like wheat. Jesus said that he had prayed for them and that after they had turned back after their fall that they were to strengthen one another.

Peter said he would never turn away from Jesus. Jesus warned him that he was about to fall away. Thankfully, Jesus modeled the way of downward mobility, of suffering, of death, of the way of the cross. (Philippians 2:5–11) He taught the twelve what it meant to be servants of God and to follow him. He washed their feet. He performed the humble task of the household slave. (John 13) (See Henri Nouwen's, *In the Name of Jesus*) Of course, we preachers of the gospel know all about this. It makes us uneasy and stirs our conflicted understandings of what it means to be professionals of the church and disciples of Christ at the same time. Have we been called to climb the ladder of professional success, or have we been called to bear the cross? Can we do both?

Without fully understanding this tension within myself I threw myself into being the new pastor of Community Presbyterian Church. I was installed by the Presbytery of Los Ranchos on September 10, 1972. Before I realized what was happening two years into my Laguna Beach ministry, a large central California Church's Pastor's Nominating Committee met me after the service as I was greeting people and asked if I would consider becoming their pastor. I was flattered, but also perplexed that they might think I would leave Laguna Beach after my first two years. It was easy for me to say "no".

In the late 1970's another of my senior friends came to me with the proposal that he place my name with the PNC of First Church Omaha. He had written a letter already to the retiring pastor of the Omaha church. I was a little embarrassed. He puffed me up by saying I ought to be the next pastor of Fourth Church in Chicago. Bill and Dorothy Thompson wintered in Laguna Beach each year. We would frequently go to Sunday brunch with them. Bill was a pastor, a professor, a psychologist, a philosopher, a poet, and a politician. He took a liking to me, shared his poems about Nebraska, and continually affirmed me. I loved him. Soon he told me that his son in law was Warren Buffet, the famous wealthy entrepreneur. At that point, I barely recognized the Buffet name. In simple innocence my aging friend and I became good friends. We were invited to family gatherings at the Buffet Laguna Beach home. When Bill passed in Omaha the family invited me to come and do his memorial. I was unable to do so. Years later this friendship and pastoral relationship would prove a blessing for Laguna Presbyterian Church.

The Challenge of Leadership

Already I was sensing that the call to Laguna Beach would not be a slam-dunk short-term miracle. In September 1972 I started; attendance was good, and enthusiasm was building. A month later the beach congregation moved into its yearly cycle of post summer relaxing, travelling, and seemingly dismissing the need for church attendance. The summer *Art Festivals and the Pageant of the Master* was over. The tourists went home, and church attendance dwindled. I began to ask myself if I had come to Laguna Beach to build a church or to bury one. Thankfully, by Thanksgiving the people were returning, and the holiday season was beautiful.

Throughout the fall, the winter, and the spring of my first year, I conducted home meetings organized by the deacons to introduce myself. It was good. One of my primary tasks was to build trust between me and the members of the congregation. As in most churches there were tensions between the conservatives and the liberals, between the group that had protested the last Director of Christian Education and those who supported the Director of the Preschool. The chairman of the PNC that called me was married to the Preschool Director. I needed to build bridges of truth and love to both sides of the conflict.

The session approved budget for 1973 was $158, 000. $77,000 would come from Preschool income. $76,000 would be received from congregational giving. It was clear that the Pre-School was leading the church into the future and that pulling these two sides together would be a challenge. It would take time. All I knew to do was to trust God and to preach the Word of God. Leadership meant listening to all voices and loving the people. I found both sides of the conflict delightful. The breach began to heal as trust developed.

In December of 1972 we held our first Session Retreat at Wylie Woods. I learned that the elders did not know the purpose of the church. The next year I led the session in a study of the Six Great Ends of the Church from the Book of Order. It was fun and eye opening. Gradually, we began to get a vision of what God had in mind for the mission of the Presbyterian Church in Laguna Beach.

In 1974 and 1979 we conducted Mission Studies. They were led by the Presbytery of Los Ranchos. New mission statements were adopted; goals and objectives were developed, and the membership had a renewed biblical-theological vision of where the Holy Spirit was guiding our church. It was an exciting time. Attendance and giving were gradually increasing. We were on the way. One of the first things we had to do was take an honest look at the membership statistics. When I arrived, the church had 955 members on its rolls. Many of them had disappeared and were no longer active. Within the first two years we reduced the membership to 700. The number was now honest, but a blow to my ego. Within two years I had eliminated 250 members, but this is what we had to work with. I wondered how low the membership numbers might drop before we turned it around. Or could we turn it around? I was going to be either a great success or a miserable failure!

The Challenge of Stress

Our family doctor, Dr. Robert Ralston, was wonderful to us. He cared about us and saw us regularly at his office. My first year I had one bad cold after another! Our son, Jeff, a three-year-old, was enrolled in the Pre-School. He was treated like royalty. He brought home all the sicknesses showing up in the school. I caught them all. Dr. Ralston told me I needed to begin exercising to build my resistance and to deal with stress. I did so. I started slowly. I could not run a mile. Gradually, I increased the laps at the high school track. I played tennis with church friends. I worked in the yard, planted roses, and tried to keep the weeds cut on our hillside. My health prospered and I made it through a very stressful time of transition and change.

It was evident that a population explosion was spreading across the valley below our house. In the forty years plus, we have lived on Top of the World, we have watched the ranch lands paved with concrete, houses, roads, colleges, shopping and business malls, and new cities with people. At times I have had nightmares about a tidal wave of development rolling in across the valley and swamping Top of the World, thus ruining our view and changing the pastoral environment. We are grateful for the establishment of the Laguna Coast Wilderness Park on the backside of Laguna Beach. That wilderness buffer has stopped the advancing development and razing of our coastal hills. On the dedication day for the Wilderness Park, I was invited to give the prayer. Laguna Beach celebrated the new park.

The Challenge of National Politics

Often, we watched as Air Force One carried President Nixon to the El Toro Marine Airbase and to the Western White House in San Clemente. It was an exciting time. In the 1972 election Nixon had been reelected by a land slide over George McGovern. Tragically, the Nixon White House engineered the break in at the National Democratic Party's office in the Watergate building in D.C. For the following two years, investigations led to the effort to impeach President Nixon. Finally, the smoking gun Oval Office tape was released, and it proved Nixon had been lying about the Watergate break in and was responsible for a cover up. The abuse of power and unconstitutional actions demanded a public accounting. Clearly, he would be convicted in the Senate and removed from office. Before they did that he resigned in August 1974. Our family was on vacation with Mike and Barbara Ross in New Mexico. Mike is my childhood friend and Barbara is Kay's cousin. We introduced them and I married them. On their 50th anniversary they called us from a dinner party. Mike asked, "Do you remember what you did to us?" Of course, while doing the wedding in the presence of both families, I blubbered all the way through.

I listened on my car radio to Nixon's resignation speech. I had met him at the wedding of Robert Finch's daughter, a member of the La Canada Church. He was personable and wanted to know about me and my experience at Princeton Seminary. His political problems were heartbreaking. In his last two years the political pressures were great. I sought to watch my words from the pulpit about the growing political division in the church and nation. However, I wrote a letter to our congressman, Andrew Henshaw, asking him to vote in the House of Representatives to impeach Nixon. I had been teaching a graduate seminar at CSULA on the constitutional processes for impeachment. In the spring of 1974, Henshaw's representative called and invited me to say a prayer at the Balboa Bay Club at a fundraiser for the congressman. Kay and I drove up in our aging VW Bug in a line of Cadillac's and Lincoln's. I was embarrassed. I knew Henshaw was seeking to co-opt me with a recognition. He was reelected, but it was revealed that he had committed crimes when he was the Orange County Tax Assessor. In 1976 he was defeated by Robert Badham.

Nixon left office in 1974 under a cloud of disgrace. But for two years we watched him come and go from El Toro to the Western White House. The White House Press Corp was housed in Laguna Beach at the Surf and Sand Hotel. A few times I ran on the high school track with Dan Rather and others. I came to know large contributors to the Republican Party. We were invited to attend a Disneyland Hotel dinner at which VP Gerald Ford spoke shortly before he became President after Nixon's resignation. Watergate deeply divided America. Nixon proved to be a liar. The Republicans had great difficulty in accepting this truth. I felt I had a front row seat to the political drama of the 1970's. His impeachment and resignation poisoned the American political system. The two major political parties have sought revenge ever since.

After some time in retirement in San Clemente, Nixon sold the Western White House and moved to New York City. The owner of Roger's Gardens in Newport Beach, a wealthy businessman and owner of Allergan Pharmaceutical, who lived in Laguna Beach, purchased the San Clemente residence for himself and his family. I married one of his daughters in Laguna Beach and the wedding reception was at the San Clemente estate. While there the owner led a small group of us on a tour of the Western White House and into the rooms where Nixon had hosted the Soviet Union leadership. The owner shared with me that once on a gardening visit to the residence while Nixon was still living there that the shamed ex-president called him into his bedroom. He found the room darkened with Nixon in bed, drunk, deeply depressed, and weeping. He asked him, "what am I going to do with the rest of my life?" Later at Monarch Beach, David Frost interviewed Nixon about his life, his successes, and downfall. I felt we were living at the center of the world's attention.

In 1976 Jimmy Carter defeated Gerald Ford to become the next President. President Ford, Nixon's Vice-President, had pardoned Nixon to end the nation's long nightmare. The pardon probably cost Ford the election in 1976. Jimmy Carter promised to never lie to the American people. He was and still is a good man, a Baptist layman who carried his Christian faith into the White House. His four years as President were trying times for America. The Iranian Hostage crisis and the oil embargo led to economic recession, increased inflation, high interest rates, and deep dissatisfaction among Americans. The Soviet Union invaded Afghanistan and in protest President Carter withdrew the U.S. Olympic Team from the Moscow Olympics in 1980. Carter was perceived as a good man, but incompetent in leading the nation.

In the mid-1970's the church held a big dinner and evening program at the Irvine Bowl. It was an evangelistic outreach. Our speaker was Jimmy Carter's sister, Ruth Carter Stapleton. We had a lovely evening with her. She was travelling the country, speaking in churches, and probably exploiting her brother's position as President of the United States. But even before that time she had been a recognized speaker on the church circuit. We felt honored to have her with us, although her honorarium was significant. Nevertheless, the evening helped build momentum for our church.

The following year we hosted Donn Moomaw, Pastor of Bel Air Presbyterian Church. Donn, the UCLA football hero, drew a big crowd at the Irvine Bowl and the evening was a success. This too built enthusiasm for our church. It was a great evangelistic outreach and it put us on the local map as a church where spiritual excitement was growing. Donn was Ronald Reagan's pastor in Bel Air. It was years later that Donn was accused of sexual misconduct with women and forced to resign the pastorate after 29 years. He was later restored to the ministry by Pacific Presbytery. He was a man with great charisma and a gifted evangelist. We have seen each other from time to time across the years and warmly greeted each other.

The following year we held an event on the corner of 2nd and Forest in the church front yard. We had a Texas barbeque, and I wore my cowboy hat and boots and preached from a platform to the city of Laguna Beach. It was interesting. We closed 2nd Ave. People gathered and we made a stir at the heart of the city. We were doing everything we could to get the attention of the city without public embarrassment.

I remember rationed gasoline supplies and increased prices during the Carter presidency. I would rise early in the mornings, go down Park Ave. in my white VW Bug and wait in line to fill my tank for the week. Ronald Reagan defeated Carter in the 1980 election. He promised that it would once again be morning in America. He cut taxes and adopted a "supply side" "trickle down" economic ideology. George H. W. Bush called it "Voodoo Economics". Let the rich get richer and the benefits would trickle down to the middle class and to the poor. Just before his inauguration in January 1981 the American hostages were released in Iran. By 1982 the economy was recovering, and political hope was born anew. Reagan was perceived as competent and charming. His election thrilled California Republicans, some of whom were members of our congregation.

The Challenge of the Bluebird Canyon Landslide

In the mid 70's I attended a *Bethel Series* meeting of pastors in Madison, Wisconsin. While in a beautiful retreat center one of the pastor's asked if I was from Laguna Beach. I affirmed his question. He said he had heard on TV that morning that the city had slide into the Pacific Ocean. I thought he was teasing. Soon I discovered that my new city, or at least the Bluebird Canyon part of it had slide and destroyed many houses. The city was in crisis. I called Kay and she confirmed that Top of the World and downtown were fine. When I arrived home Neil Purcell, one of our police leaders, drove me in his police car through the devastation. Some of our church members lost their houses. No one had been killed, but some had close calls. This was the beginning of a series of natural disasters that would threaten the city over our years in Laguna Beach. Since our house was built on a hillside, we were worried about the stability of the soil below us.

The Challenge of Property and Upward Mobility

We were swept up in the housing boom in Laguna Beach. Houses were appreciating so rapidly that many were selling and buying larger houses in hopes of flipping the houses to make big profits. We made an offer on a house with an ocean view contingent on selling our house for more than double what we paid and this within the first decade of being in Laguna. Thankfully, elder Chuck Smith helped us to see this would not help our ministry. We decided to stay put and to turn away from the visible signs of upward mobility that were so tempting. We loved our house on Top of the World. Kay got a real estate license, and the run was on, but it soon stalled for us when she realized she did not have the disposition to sell houses in Mission Viejo. We were both struggling with inner restlessness and desires for economic success that could have destroyed us if we had not come to our senses. Some of our members could not believe what we had to pay for our house on TOW. Looking back, it was the best investment we ever made.

The Challenge and Blessing of Former Pastors

I advocated new mission studies every five years to help keep our congregation on track. There were large church dinners in local hotels to build morale in the congregation. At the first one in Laguna Hills, we invited former Pastors Ray Brahams and Dallas Turner. They came and I was delighted to show the pastoral continuity in the pictures we took together. They were both special gifts to Laguna Beach. Ray had been pastor from 1925 to 1949, through the Great Depression, World War 11, and the post-war adjustments. He led in building the new sanctuary in 1928. Early in my ministry he came to the pastor's study that he designed with local architects. They modeled the office after a room in a valley ranch house. At the dedication of the new sanctuary in 1928 the small group of 31 members celebrated that they had built large enough to seat the entire community.

During his visit Ray said that when he graduated from Princeton Seminary in 1925 that Clarence McCartney, pastor at First Church Pittsburg, offered him a position as an assistant pastor with the promise that after three years he would place him in one of the largest pulpits in the country. He told the well - known Pittsburg pastor "thanks, but no thanks, I am going to Laguna Beach, California." So, he arrived when Laguna was a seaside village. From 1925 to 1949 the Laguna Church grew from about 30 to 750 members. Ray Brahams was called as pastor by First Church Boulder, Colorado, in 1949. In Boulder he experienced an emotional breakdown. He recovered and returned to Southern California. He was a wonderful man. He finished his ministry as an assistant pastor of visitation at St. Andrews in Newport Beach. It was there that his wife Ellen died. Later he remarried a woman named Grace whom he had known from years before. Grace was with me in 1971 on my first Holy Land Tour. At Ray's memorial she told me that Ray had received God's great healing. I will never forget those comments.

Anna Hills, the famous Laguna Beach artist and community leader painted a small picture of the sanctuary building for its dedication celebration in 1928. Anna and her sister Nellie were both members of the church. She did the small oil painting of the new church for the Brahams' family. Upon my 15th anniversary as pastor of LPC, Hap Brahams, the pastor in La Jolla, and Ray's son, was invited to speak. In doing so he presented me with the small, treasured painting. Years later an artist in our church took a picture of it and painted it larger. Many purchased prints.

Dallas Turner was pastor from 1950 to 1971. He grew the church from 750 to over a thousand members. This was in the hay day of church growth in Southern California. The Presbytery of Los Angeles could not build new churches fast enough to meet the needs of the expanding suburbs. The 60's were traumatic for the Laguna church and the city. American society was ripping apart over Civil Rights, the Vietnam War, run away young people, the Counter-Culture, drugs, sex, rock 'n roll, peace, and other social justice challenges. Dallas was a special gentleman who had to face challenges that seemed irresolvable. Both Ray and Dallas were deeply beloved. I never felt they interfered with my leadership. Following my call to Laguna, Dallas sent me a letter at LCPC. He congratulated me and shared that his years in Laguna Beach were the happiest years of his life and that he hoped this would be true for me as well. After his wife Virginia died, I married Dallas to Bunny Neece, his Laguna secretary and my first secretary. She was a saint. They moved to Walnut Creek, and he passed at nearly 100 years old. Bunny is now deceased.

The Challenge of Church Staff

Throughout the summer of 1972 as we were preparing to move, members of Laguna Church sent us beautiful postcards with pictures of the city and coastline to welcome us as their new pastor. The spirit of hospitality was evident.

During the 70's I knew I had first to rebuild the people of the congregation, to renew a biblical vision, to make disciples, and to win new members. Slowly, new members came. Throughout the 70's there was an influx of newly retired, highly successful people who still had energy and understood how to build organizations. They were mature church leaders. They formed a new fellowship group, the Clippers, and it rapidly grew along with a younger family group, the Becomers. The staff was formed.

Mark Snelling came as a student intern from Fuller Seminary. We funded his seminary education from the Carson Trust Fund that had been created for this purpose. He received credit at Fuller Seminary for his years with us. We called Art Chartier to be an assistant pastor. Al Hjerpe was the part-time retired pastor on our staff. Chuck and Betty Smith helped us form a youth group. Craig Williams came as a college student from St. Andrews to help with music and we were off and running. Slowly but surely, the ark of Community Presbyterian Church began to turn and gain new direction and vitality. I was greatly encouraged.

Kay was involved in women's ministries. She and other women from LPC attended the National Presbyterian Women's Conference at Purdue University and came home fired up by a call to ministry. The Bible teacher was Dr. James A. Sanders from Union Seminary in NYC. He taught on the Gospel of Luke. I listened to the tapes and knew his approach to Scripture was what I needed and desired. How excited I was when he came to Claremont School of Theology and Graduate School to teach Old and New Testaments and to develop the Ancient Biblical Manuscript Library. The church had received a $5,000.00 memorial gift from the Philips Estate designated for a pastor's continuing education. I asked the session to designate it for my doctoral studies at Claremont. They did so and I began another Ph.D. program in Christian Interpretation, biblical studies and preaching. I was thrilled.

The Challenge of Church Property: Restore the Splendor

The 1970s through 1983 were filled with excitement and growth in every way. The people came together. We launched our first building program to maintain the church buildings that were in great need. Our retired business executives were happy, and I was caught up in every dimension of pastoral experience. After ten years I felt I was just beginning in Laguna Beach. The good news was that the restoring of some of the church buildings only cost around $1.5 million dollars. At the end of the project in which we built a new fellowship hall we were still debt free. Elder John Bulleit, recently retired from Caterpillar Inc., led the committee, with Marvin Drew taking a major stewardship responsibility for launching the project. These men and their wives became very dear to me, and we worked closely together. With architects Storm Case and Frank Morris, the restoration project succeeded. A big part of the Restoration program was the building of a new fellowship hall, which in the mid 90's was named *TANKERSLEY HALL* upon my 25th anniversary.

I preached a series of sermons based on the prophecies of Haggai in the Old Testament. The theme that emerged for the campaign was "Restore the Splendor". We sent invitations to an all – church banquet at the Marriot Hotel in Newport Beach. However, we failed to carefully proofread the invitation. It was mailed with an invitation to the "Restore the Spendor" dinner. After all our careful work I felt we might have destroyed the momentum at the beginning of the fundraising by this misprint. I knew that some would be offended who had lost their sense of humor. I did not know whether to laugh or to cry. Thankfully, most of our congregation laughed. It was during this time that we changed the name of Community Presbyterian Church to Laguna Presbyterian Church.

The words of Haggai questioned the self-centered values of Israel in building their own houses but allowing the house of God to fall into ruin. It was time for them to rebuild the house of God in Jerusalem. The people's self-centeredness had brought destructive consequences upon their prosperity. The City of Laguna Beach and its neighborhoods were undergoing much physical restoration. Haggai spoke a word from God to us.

> "Take courage, says the LORD; work, for I am with you, says the LORD of hosts. My spirit abides among you; do not fear. For thus says the LORD of hosts; Once again, in a little while, I will shake the heavens and the earth and the sea and the dry lands; and I will shake all the nations, so that the treasure of all nations shall come, and I will fill this house with splendor, says the LORD of hosts. The silver is mine, and the gold is mine, says the LORD of hosts. The latter splendor of this house shall be greater than the former, says the LORD of hosts; and in this place I will give prosperity." (Haggai 2:4–9)

This was a major part of the work to which the LORD had called me. Yes, to rebuild this people and iconic church building at the center of the South Coast of Orange County for the purpose of our being a lighthouse of the gospel to the ends of the earth. One of my concerns was that the church property in a highly secular city might become a parking lot, an artist gallery, a restaurant, or even a private residence. God forbids! God's plan was to grow God's people, to empower God's people, and to use this people and city for the sake of building the kingdom of God. This was the mission of God, and I was determined to be faithful to this calling.

Near the end of this restoration program a large church from the State of Washington pleaded for me to become their next pastor. I did not have an inner peace about this. Their entire committee came to Laguna, and we spent Sunday afternoon in conversation with them. They were very attractive folks. Kay, Jeff, and I went to Washington to visit. It was beautiful and filled with potential. When approaching the Seattle-Tacoma airport we flew low over Mt. St. Helens. When we arrived back home, I was deeply conflicted and called the chair of the committee and told them I could not leave Laguna Beach. I was just getting started. It was a temptation and would have been a challenging call. One of my older seminary classmates whom I had always admired, had just been called to another congregation. I was happy to be seen as a good follow up for him. But I could not do it. I am so thankful that after 10 years in Laguna Beach that I stayed. It was a flirtation and an ego boost at a time when, if I had not been happy, I could have moved.

The Challenge of Presbytery Leadership

Los Ranchos Presbytery engaged me on its Presbytery and Congregational Development Committee. A subcommittee of PCD was New Church Development. I was chair of that committee. Constitutionally, it was the Presbytery's responsibility to begin new churches. Soon we discovered that St. Andrews Church in Newport Beach was planning to plant a new church in Irvine where the orange groves were being removed and a huge development project was beginning that would be known as the Village of Woodbridge. Their plan was to send one of their pastors to be the organizer of the NCD. Complaints from surrounding presbytery churches began to be heard.

We responded. We told St. Andrews they could not plant a new church by themselves. I pulled together representatives from surrounding churches and we began to act on behalf of the Presbytery of Los Ranchos. This proved to be an exciting project. Together with the General Assembly, the Synod, and the Presbytery we pulled the resources together, purchased land from the Irvine Company, (3 acres for $50 thousand an acre) drew up a development plan, and called Ben Patterson to become the new church developer. The goal was to plant a new Presbyterian Church in one of the fastest growing communities in America. People came together with the new pastor and support group and the new church began in a school. After a few years we chartered the new church in 1978, named the Irvine Presbyterian Church, and it began to grow. I moderated the chartering and installing process of elders, deacons, and pastor on behalf of the Presbytery. The larger church celebrated. This was the work of evangelism and new church development and it excited me.

In 1977 I was elected a Presbytery commissioner to the General Assembly meeting in Philadelphia. It was during that meeting that I was reconnected with Dr. Frances Pritchard who was the pastor who baptized me, my sister Kay, and my dad. I was around 10 years old when I was baptized at First Presbyterian Church in Amarillo, Texas. The larger church began to come into focus for me as I saw the organization behind the international and national ministries of the United Presbyterian Church in the USA. It was an inspiration to be a part of this governing process for which I had been ordained to the ministry. Some have said that the 1950's through the early 1980's were the golden years of the UPCUSA.

Dr. Morgan Odell, retired from the Presidency of Lewis and Clark College and a leader in the Laguna Beach church, proposed me for membership in Chi Alpha, a support group of pastors in the Synod of Southern California that met at Pasadena Presbyterian Church for the purpose of sharing and study. We went on retreat to Santa Barbara First. The subject was suffering. Honestly, I confessed, I had never suffered because I was a pastor. I asked them for clarification. They must have seen me as very naïve and inexperienced, and I was. I was only beginning to realize what a lifetime of being a pastor would open for me. I would come to experience the depths of the human condition, which would be revealed in my own experience. In the words of Eugene Peterson, it was to begin a *Long Obedience in the Same Direction*.

The Challenge of Suffering and Evil

Dr. Odell was a highly educated man and progressive in every way. He had been the President of Lewis and Clark College and I respected him. I did not want him to think of me as a fundamentalist. When I preached on the novel and the 1973 movie *The Exorcist* about the hostile influence of the devil in human life, he was offended and chastised me for being backward in theological interpretation. He told me that the only Word from God that Sunday was my pastoral prayer in which I spoke of God's love. I was wounded, and I knew that many were struggling with the subject, the movie, and the possible influence of spiritual evil in their lives or the lives of their children. I believed that the evil one often comes to us disguised as an angel of light even in a beautiful place like Laguna Beach. Indeed, the devil desires nothing more than to tempt us and to destroy the effectiveness and mission of Christ's church in the world. Nevertheless, we were not to be afraid because Christ had conquered the world through his death and resurrection. The Holy Spirit would indwell us and empower us to overcome.

C.S. Lewis had written about this in *The Screwtape Letters*. Lewis had first had the idea of writing these letters while in church in 1940. It was unclear to me how any pastor could avoid the subject in Scripture and the mission of Christ in liberating so many from bondage to the powers of sin and death. Lewis had fought in WWI and had seen the destruction of Europe and the evils of war. In 1940 he was once again watching violence erupt in Europe with the threat of totalitarian leaders who were intent on dominating the world. The older liberal progressive church had failed to face up to the human condition and the powers of evil. Joseph Loconte, in his book, *A Hobbit a Wardrobe and a Great War*, argued that WWI destroyed the myth of progress that had been nurtured in the pre-war period. Liberalism was shattered and neo-orthodoxy with its more biblical interpretation of the human condition found expression in the writings of Karl Barth, Emil Brunner, Paul Tillich, and Reinhold Niebuhr.

As a young pastor I did not want to give to the devil more than his due. The powers of the kingdom of God had landed and enemy occupied territory was being liberated by the gospel message. C.S. Lewis' *Mere Christianity* confronted this subject with straightforward biblical truth about what it is that we are up against as Christians in the world.

Lewis had shaped my theology in deep ways. In *Mere Christianity* Lewis argued that we live on planet earth in "enemy occupied territory". There has been a rebellion in this part of the cosmos, which has been captured and empowered by the devil. This has not destroyed the sovereignty of God. The Bible does not support a dualistic worldview, even though it skirts close to this philosophical view. The prince of this present darkness still has power, but there has been a divine invasion by the true King, the Lord Jesus Christ. He has acted to liberate planet earth through his life, death, resurrection presence, and power. God has won and will win. Therefore, the final liberation of humanity from its bondage to sin, death, and to all that holds us in fear is promised and will surely be revealed in the New Creation in which the principalities and powers will be redeemed, and the creation restored. Lewis and J.R.R. Tolkien, both who had seen the horrors of war trenches and the dehumanization of humanity, in their writings, wrote "true myths" that addressed the fallenness of the world and of the hope of restoration of freedom and peace.

In the introduction to *The Screwtape Letters,* Lewis cautioned that we must not take the devil too seriously. Likewise, we ought not to dismiss him as the source of human prideful rebellion. The best way to deal with the devil is with ridicule and humor. It would be a mistake for the Christian to see the devil under every bush. Indeed, this is God's beautiful creation, and it is still beautiful. The orders of creation give the potential for life to be good and just, but not perfect. Human life and history need liberating and transforming. This is the work of the kingdom of God's love and justice. The liberating powers of God's mercy, peace, justice, and love are central to God's mission through the church.

A very attractive family came to our church. They had a daughter who was our son's age and in the same grade in elementary school. Both husband and wife were very committed Christians who seemed to have it all together. They were from an Assembly of God-Pentecostal-Presbyterian understanding of the Holy Spirit, prayer, and the reality of Satan. People were drawn to them. One day their eight-year-old daughter was riding her bicycle around a corner near her house and was hit by a car at a blind intersection. She suffered major brain trauma. That evening people from Christian churches around Orange County gathered at the hospital to pray as she was operated on by the neurosurgeon.

The girl lived, but a portion of her brain had to be removed. The parents insisted that her brain would be restored and that she would be raised up and totally healed by the power of God and the prayers of the people. No one was comfortable in the prayer circle if they simply prayed for God's will to be done. The mother believed the accident occurred because she had failed to bind Satan in her morning prayers. Thus, years of re-patterning by friends, neighbors, and church members was launched. The beautiful little girl was not restored. The questions of theodicy became central for me.

As their pastor I felt uneasy about the theology of prayer that was being advocated. The theodicy questions came home to me in my pastoral leadership. How could a good God allow something like this to happen? If he did not answer the prayers maybe he was not good? If the prayers were not answered, then perhaps God was not powerful enough to do anything about it. Another option was that the prayers simply did not have the faith necessary to bring the miracle of healing to the girl and her family. I was deeply troubled and longing to be a good and faithful pastor.

This was a family that had roots in several South Orange County churches. In the aftermath of this suffering the Men's Group of St. Andrews Presbyterian Church invited me to lead their yearly retreat in response to this family's suffering. On the one hand I believed in the power of prayer and that God was able to do anything God might choose. I desired to hold this family, to be their pastor, to comfort them, but I could not embrace the signs and wonders theology. I knew that bad things happen to good people and that things like this happen all the time and God does not intervene. Rather, we are left to live with suffering and mystery while seeking to trust the God of healing love.

Finally, the multi-year experience drove me back into psychotherapy with Dr. Harry Rosenthal, my Jewish friend who had walked with me through the suffering and pain of my first marriage. He was a committed Jewish man who loved me and allowed me to struggle with this Job type story in the context of my parish. He taught me biblical theology at the existential level. He was a man who loved the State of Israel and who allowed me to argue with him about the condition of the Palestinian people. The Holocaust was a real-life experience for the Jewish people and for him. I remain grateful to God for him. He helped me deal with this crisis of faith and doubt. He suggested that the suffering parents would one day have emotional breakdowns if they did not come to terms with the mystery of their daughter's accident and surrender to the way of not – knowing – yet trusting.

After several years the parents sued the city and received a large settlement that allowed them to care for their daughter until her death at around 30 years of age. There was no miraculous intervention, but rather a sobering silence and learning to live with unanswered questions and prayers. The family left our church, moved out of the community, and I am sure suffered for all those years and still do. The interesting thing was they would visit our church from time to time. When I retired, they came to my retirement celebration and made it clear to me in personal comment that I had been a good pastor and that the church had comforted them. I truly appreciated their affirmation. We had all grown through this unwanted experience of shared suffering. I am still amazed at all the prayers, tears, laughter, and fellowship we had as believers in God's providence and mysterious ways. The woman who drove the car around the blind corner and hit our little girl was deeply grieved. She and her family also moved away from the city and that neighborhood. It was an accident for which the city was held liable for not trimming the bushes on the corner of the street, thus blocking the drivers view at the corner.

Through all this our church members grew spiritually and struggled with reality in the light of biblical faith. Many came to realize that pain awakens us to the deeper questions about life and love and calls us to pray in the depths for the faith of Psalm 23 and 46. Romans 8:28 became reality for my faith. In *The Problem of Pain*, C.S. Lewis argued that God shouts into our ears as if through a megaphone by means of pain. By this means he awakens us to our mortality and our need for God's help. I do not understand this, and I wish it were not so, but I have discovered that it is pain of one kind or another that has led me to surrender my personal autonomy and false self-sufficiency.

Malcolm Muggeridge, in a famous quote listed on Google, testified,

> "Indeed, I can say with complete truthfulness that everything I have learned in my seventy-five years in this world, everything that has truly enhanced and enlightened my existence, has been through affliction and not through happiness, whether pursued or attained. In other words, if it ever were to be possible to eliminate affliction from our earthly existence by means of some drug or other medical mumbo jumbo, as Aldous Huxley envisaged in *Brave New World*, the result would not be to make life delectable, but to make it too banal and trivial to be endurable. This, of course, is what the Cross signifies. And it is the Cross, more than anything else, that has called me inexorably to Christ."[1]

Of course, this is a mystery to me, but one that I accept. I do not seek suffering, nor would I suggest to anyone else that their affliction was caused by God or by the devil, but there is mystery here. The good news is that affliction causes us to trust God and to pray for help and deliverance. (Please note Romans 8, 1 Corinthians 1 and 2 Corinthians 12.) The LORD has become totally identified with the suffering of the world by taking it upon himself. Therefore, God's grace has become sufficient for all those who experience affliction.

---

1. Muggeridge, Google.com. quote.

1983–1999: A Pastor's Challenges in Laguna Beach

New Age Religion and the Occult

During my earlier years in Laguna Beach, I realized that a pastor needed to be careful in subjects he addressed. People in the larger community were listening and could be critical. Each month I wrote a short essay in our church newsletter. I used the opportunity to address issues in both church and community.

On one occasion I received an invitation, as did many of our members, to attend a fundraiser for the Laguna Playhouse. This is and has been and continues to be, a major institution for the arts in our city. Many of our church members had season tickets for the excellent productions. Apparently, the planning committee, made up of some of the movers and shakers of Laguna Beach, had decided to develop a program presented by representatives of the occult: fortune tellers, tarot card readers, palm readers, psychics, mediums, channelers of spirits, astrologers, and representatives of other magic arts and New Age devotees. The event was to be held at Moss Point at the estate of Constance Morthland, a recognized leader in the city and an Episcopalian.

I decided to write one of my church newsletters essays on the biblical view of the occult. I warned our members about the role of the spirits and of Shirley McClain type religion. I questioned whether Christians ought to be financially supportive of such fundraising. I had no conversation with anyone about the event and certainly did not suggest that the event be cancelled. I was simply seeking to teach our members about these manifestations of Old and New Age religion in our city.

A couple of weeks later I picked up the morning L.A. Times to discover that the fundraiser had been canceled because of the meddling of a local pastor in Laguna Beach, namely me, pastor of the Community Presbyterian Church. All hell broke loose in the media. The Times carried a series of articles and letters related to the event and my overstepping of my pastoral boundaries in seeking to use my influence to cancel the fundraiser. I received letters and phone calls threatening me with death and calling into question my enlightenment, my education, and position in Laguna Beach. I was frightened for my family since some of the calls came to me at home and were menacing. It was not unlike what the Apostle Paul experienced in Philippi (Acts 16) and Ephesus (Acts 19:11–20). The threats continued throughout the summer. I was told that some of the wives of members of our local Rotary Club were the leaders in the fundraiser and were enraged by my newsletter. I also was a member of Rotary and appreciated that relationship and wanted to stay involved. Their husbands ceased speaking to me at our Friday luncheons. I felt it necessary to stand during the meeting and publicly state that I had nothing to do with cancelling the fundraiser. Other than that, I remained silent and did not seek to address the issue except in my Sunday preaching during that summer.

I was amazed at how supportive the members of our church were of me. There seemed to be a consensus that I had touched a nerve in the community and that I had acted within my pastoral responsibility. But no one defended me in the newspapers. Finally, near the end of the summer the pastor of the Little Church by the Sea wrote a letter to the Times defending me. I appreciated the public support even though I had not personally spoken with anyone seeking to interfere with the Playhouse's right to fundraise in any way they might choose. My co-dependent people pleasing personality suffered during the whole affair. The truth was that I came to realize that the response to me in the media of Southern California was revealing of the inner spirituality of our culture and of the spiritual warfare Christians will face when the "principalities and powers, and the rulers of this age" are threatened. (2 Corinthians 4:1–12; Ephesians 6:10–20)

It is ironic that the Saturday, July 13, 2019, L.A. Times, featured a major article by Jessica Roy, entitled, *"Spiritual Quest: Millennials are turning from organized religion, toward crystals and meditation"*. The article was about the loss of interest in Southern California culture in organized, traditional churches. The growing rate of "none's", or those with no interest in orthodox, institutional churches, are still being drawn to spirituality and the ancient ways of paganism. The focus on Old Age/New Age manifestations in "psychics, astrologers, mediums, channelers of spirits, and other expressions of the occult now have a resurgence of interest." Palm readers, psychics, astrologers, and other New Age representatives have set up shop in a store in a mall across from LPC and in other places within the city. The marketplace of Laguna Beach is not unlike the agora of first century Corinth or Ephesus.

Even more interesting is the mixture of cultural narcissism with these ancient pagan practices. If it feels good, do it. If it works for you, then go deeper. Self-autonomy and self-interest are everything. When I arrived in Laguna Beach, New Age religion was everywhere and still

Laguna Beach And The Laguna Presbyterian Church

is. Once again, with the loss of interest in Christian Churches, or other expressions of religion, ancient pagan practices are moving out of what seemed narrow confines. Having jettisoned traditional religious institutions for one reason or another, spiritual hunger and thirst have not gone away. As always, humans create gods, religions, and spiritualities over which they have control.

In the 70's the Hare Krishna's came to Laguna Beach. A defunct Christian Church was secretly purchased by the Krishna's to be converted into a temple. In their Indian clothing and with their music they marched through the streets of Laguna Beach. One could hear their drums beating and their parade chanting Hare Krishna on Forest Ave on Sunday mornings as they carried their idol through the center city to remind us that they had come to town. They sent their prayer warriors to sit on the front lawn of Laguna Beach Community Presbyterian Church to ask their god to give our property and church buildings to them. Before long they sent their members out of costume to be in our worship and to confront me in argumentation after our worship service. It was an amazing experience of being evangelized in our own space by another religion. There were many of my Sunday pastoral prayers that were prayed with the background of Hara Krishna music and dancing outside the windows of our sanctuary on Forest Ave.

They are still in our city but much quieter. As they began to grow silent another group came to town. They were the Rajneesh, the orange clothed people of an Indian guru named Bhagwan Shree Rajneesh. They came and took over the Church of Religious Science at the corner of Laguna Canyon Rd. and El Toro Rd. In the State of Oregon, they took over the political system of an entire town. The minister of our local Church of Religious Science had gone on a spiritual journey to India and been converted to a follower of the cult's leader. He returned and sought to convert his church members to the cult. Other Rajneesh came to the city and joined the church. Their numbers grew and soon they outnumbered the aging religious science members. In a congregational meeting they voted to give the church buildings to the followers of this Indian cult.

This made me thankful that the Presbyterian Church has a Polity and Constitution that clarifies the ownership of church property. The takeover of a Presbytery Church property could not have occurred without the approval of Presbytery. The Book of Order of the PCUSA states that a local church holds its property in trust for the mission of the larger denomination. I could not have imagined this issue would become front and center in the first decade of the 21st century in the PCUSA. More on this later!

These orange folks used drugs and engaged in public sex. A couple came to live in the house on the corner of our home just above our house's long driveway. On one occasion we saw the nude couple having sex on their outdoor baloney overlooking our house. I told them to please go inside. We were saying goodbye to relatives from Colorado. There were children playing in our driveway. The neighbor on the other side of the street reported that he often watched them in the nude before the street facing windows having sex to entertain their Mountain View neighbors.

These folks would also parade through the streets of Laguna Beach. Finally, the cult leader was busted in Oregon at his ranch and returned to India where he died. The Rajneesh property in Laguna Beach was sold to a preschool that has prospered. These religions caused a lot of stress and strain for the city.

The Challenges of Local Politics

Early in our time in Laguna Beach the City dropped the prohibition of beach nudity. I do not remember the reason. The Council held a public hearing about this, and I spoke before the Council and the T.V. cameras in support of a new ordinance against nudity on our family public beaches for which the city is well known. Kay and I often enjoyed taking our little boy to Heisler Park Beach for a picnic. On one occasion a group of young women arrived and settled near us. Before we knew it, they had each removed the tops of their bikinis and were moving around on their blanket, standing up, eating their food, and causing a few eyes to pop. I was amused. I tried not to stare, but our five-year-old boy was transfixed by what he watched. A look of surprise captured his face. We had to interpret, as much as we could, what was happening.

I am not a prude, but it was clear to me what might happen on our beaches if nudity were allowed. Famous artists have painted the human body. Art museums post these paintings, and we celebrate their works. I wondered if any other pastor in America had to face such issues and decide what pastoral responsibility might require. I went to the public hearing and asked the City Council to pass an ordinance forbidding nudity on the beaches of our city. Amazingly, they did just that.

When I arrived in Laguna, I heard the gossip about our former pastor's beautiful daughter who had been photographed nude in Israel and whose picture was sold to Playboy Magazine and printed. This was the quiet embarrassed gossip and laughter in the barbershops of Laguna. I can only imagine what the pastor's family thought about this. We never spoke about it, but I am sure it was a source of public embarrassment for the parents. Most pastors have concerns about what their children may do to bring public ridicule toward the church or ourselves. The truth is we are all humans, and we do things in our lives that come back to haunt us. While we may be wounded by family behaviors, including our own, we must always stand with love and support for our children. Being graceful with understanding that we are all sinners seeking to find our way to adult maturity are foundational for life in the family and community.

In 1980 I was asked to join the Board of Trustees of South Coast Medical Center in Laguna Beach. Along with the new school superintendent I accepted. It was an amazing experience to discover how hospitals operate financially through their Boards. Constance Morthland came to my church office to recruit me for the Board. I was honored. My style of leadership was to openly invite the participation of my church session and for us together to make personnel and budget decisions for the church. I carried that style with me on to the hospital leadership team.

Before long I discovered that the hospital administrator had a different style. He and a small group made leadership decisions and brought them to the larger board for ratification. Apparently, they had determined to terminate an important member of the medical staff. When we were asked to support the decision, I asked questions. From that moment it became clear to me that I had violated the boards norms of behavior.

The terminated member of the staff sued the hospital, and I was called to be a witness to the board's actions. I realized I was in trouble. I was deposed by the employee's attorney. The hospital attorney was there for me. I really did not know any of the details that had gone into the decision to terminate. I think the hospital won the suit and all was well for me. Thankfully, when the next three – year term came up I was not invited to re-up for a new three – year term. It was a learning experience, and it satisfied my ego to have my portrait hanging in the hallway of the hospital for three years, but I was glad to be given a way off the board. I felt I had been a political appointment for the sake of the hospital's support in the larger community. I carried a sense of failure for some time afterwards, even though I had some insight into the politics. I discovered that hospital administrators, city managers, and school superintendents have short tenures in most communities. Indeed, the turnovers in Laguna Beach have been frequent.

Pastor's Covenant Group

When I arrived in Laguna one of my commitments was to form a covenant support group. I asked several pastors to covenant to support my leadership and to grow in friendship. At my installation they affirmed they would. When John Huffman was called to pastor St. Andrews in Newport Beach, Ken Kalina, pastor at PCOM, and I, invited him to join with us. He did so. Our group has seen members come and go. We have walked with each other through transitions, pastoral changes, failures, divorces, remarriages, and church crises. None of us would have made it to retirement without the prayer support and the friendships forged in this group. Two have died, but we still meet half a day each month for sharing, prayer, and lunch.

Ken Kalina was my fellow associate at La Canada Presbyterian Church. We often played tennis and fellowshipped together. We have been good friends through mutual challenges for our families and church's. He has been the source of good humor and shared ministry at PCOM in Mission Viejo and other Presbytery churches. Gary Demarest baptized his son David with our son Jeff at La Canada when they were both six months old. They were born a month apart in 1969. Ken chose to travel to Columbus, Ohio, to support me in my bid for Moderator of the 214th G.A. of the PCUSA. He and Bill Flanagan, along with David Dolan saw me through that stressful time. I will write more about this later in the memoirs.

When Bill Flanagan died from prostate cancer there was deep grief. He had been an associate pastor at St. Andrews. What a dear friend. We greatly miss him. Flan nominated me to Los Ranchos Presbytery to stand for moderator of the G.A. in 2002. He went to Columbus, Ohio, to walk with me through that process. He and Ken had been on staff together at First Presbyterian Church in Colorado Springs. Flan led the first LPC Men's Retreat on the Book of Jonah. When Flan died, Ken Kalina was one of the speakers. When we buried Flan's ashes it was Ken who placed them in the ground as the group looked on.

Laguna Beach And The Laguna Presbyterian Church

On the day we buried Flan's ashes, Dennis Tarr, long – time friend from Princeton Seminary, pointed us to the sky to see the rainbow on a clear day among the broken clouds. Dennis has moved in and out of the group as he has done various interim pastorates. He, Flan, and John were at Princeton Seminary during the same years. Dennis's first wife, Sandy, and my first wife taught in the same school district and we had become social friends.

When Ben Patterson was called to be the organizing pastor of Irvine Presbyterian Church, he also joined our group. What good times we had. The group went to the High Sierra's to ride horses to a lake for a couple of days. We rented an R.V. and journeyed up US 395. Along the way we bought new black cowboy hats. We will never forget that journey. After ten years, Ben received a new call to a church in New Jersey. Later he became chaplain at Hope College and then Westmont College.

When Jim Farley was called to San Clemente Presbyterian Church, he joined our group. We all really liked Jim and tried to encourage him in his leadership at the church. After several years he and his wife divorced and he received a call from a church in Hot Springs, Arkansas.

Michael Wenning was pastor at Geneva Presbyterian Church and later at Bel Air Presbyterian Church. Michael was my friend and colleague in ministry in Laguna Hills. He asked me to speak at his retirement party from Bel Air Church. I felt I did not do him justice because by the time I was supposed to be the keynote speaker, everything had already been said in praise of Michael. Nevertheless, I was honored that he asked me to speak. He and Freda hailed from South Africa, and he was a gifted preacher/pastor. When he passed away, the grief was profound. I did his graveside service in El Toro. It was a dark, cold, rainy day. I wept through the entire service with his family right in front of me. My heart was breaking. I had lost a dear friend and colleague.

Dick Todd joined our group when he was called to be an associate pastor at St. Andrews. He and John had been friends in their Pittsburg days. Dick is a remarkable and gifted pastor and has been a prayerful support for each of us in our group. In recent years he lost Bev, his wife, and their son John. We are grateful for his affirming friendship and service to God's kingdom. Dick is a prayer warrior and we have celebrated his being with us.

Roberta Hestenes, my friend from seminary days at Fuller, has been a special addition to the all – male group. She pastored at La Canada after my days there. She became president at Eastern College, worldwide representative for World Vision, pastor at Solana Beach Presbyterian Church, and of course on the faculty of Fuller Seminary. She was in our group during her time at Solana Beach and recently in retirement has joined us again.

John Huffman and I have been close friends since he arrived from Pittsburg in 1978. We bonded and have been there for each other through great joy, success, grief, and struggle with the PCUSA over matters of human sexuality, Israel/ Palestine, and schism of congregations from the PCUSA. John has provided outstanding leadership for the PCUSA by serving in many capacities. When John and Anne's daughter, Suzanne, died shortly after her graduation from Princeton University, her memorial service was held at LPC. John and I have travelled together to Scotland for study leaves, on a special C.S. Lewis Study Tour on the Sea Cloud Two, to Israel, and through the Panama Canal on the Sea Cloud. We have sought to comfort each other on long telephone calls late at night. Often, we have been together for lunches and other occasions. When he stood for moderator of the G.A. in 1991 in Baltimore, I was his campaign manager. He had to withdraw at the Assembly because of his daughter's illness. In 2002 he suggested my name to the Presbyterian Coalition group to stand for moderator of G.A. Then he arrived in Columbus the day after the election and was with me the rest of the week. John has been an encouraging brother for me for over 40 years. I was one of the speakers for him at his retirement party and he spoke for me at mine. More on some of our shared experiences later in the memoirs!

My Work Week Rhythm

Over 46 years I developed a work week rhythm that sustained my soul and my preaching ministry. On Mondays I studied next week's biblical texts. I led Bible studies on Tuesday and Wednesday mornings. The women gathered on Tuesday. Men and women met on Wednesday mornings. These were wonderful times of fellowship and biblical interpretation. Always there was much sharing and laughter, sometimes tears. We prayed and discussed the history and the meaning of our texts considering our new contexts. I loved these times. They spiritually nurtured my soul. Throughout the week I was in prayerful dialogue with texts, their contexts, and the people who would listen to me on Sunday mornings.

It took several years to develop this rhythm. For 30 years Mitzi Interlandi and Ellen Wright were our worship music leaders. They were greatly beloved by our congregation. Upon their retirements new organist and choral leaders joined us. Each made their unique contributions to the life of LPC. Finally, we were able to effectively coordinate all the gifts of our worship staff and to face the fact that we needed to allocate a larger portion of our church budget for worship. By the mid-80's we were well on our way to a creative shared worship leadership team anchored in our Reformed, contemporary vision of liturgy. I came to believe that the vital worship life of the congregation was the center of mission development and the training of disciples. But it took much patience and hard work to grow our team and our vision. Many of my work hours came to focus on Sunday mornings. It was a spiritual high for me to watch this happen weekly over years of gradual growth.

On Wednesday mornings I would leave the Bible class and meet with the Session's Worship Committee to plan the following Sunday's worship liturgy built around the study's texts and discussions. Beth Pinney was of great help in making this transition from study to worship. Over many years she has been a colleague developing the integrity of our Reformed liturgy with both art, order, praise, confession, praise band leadership, and relational wholeness. Beth became a candidate for the pastoral ministry and is now ready to be ordained when she receives a call. In July 2021 she will become the Designated Associate Pastor of LPC and be ordained. Thankfully, the LORD has kept her with us for years. Lorna Cohen and Kathy Sizer supported both me and Beth with their devotion and interest in worship as divine drama in dialogue with our history in community. Others elders joined us for these conversations. Linda White, our Chancel Choir leader, also brought the great music of the church's history into dialogue with God's Word. Sunday morning worship with Word and Sacrament, music, prayer, praise, confession, and preparation for service caused the life of LPC to be prepared for the sake of God's mission in the world. For me this was the beating heart of our congregation and helped us to build the highways to Zion in our disciple's hearts.

The Theology of Grace: Luke 15

The pastor lives with a unique tension in his or her life. I learned that my life in ministry was a gift that came from the love of God that mercifully accepted and forgave me. I had faced public humiliation in my early ministry and sought to grow to acceptance and forgiveness. Not only that! I desired to walk in the way of the LORD and to not cause anyone to stumble because of any misbehavior on my part. There was a growing desire within me to manifest the mind of Christ and to be a person on the way of transformation. The Presbytery of Los Angeles had mediated God's grace to me and gave my life back to me. I was restored like any other repentant sinner who comes to his knees in confession seeking a restored life and place in the community of faith. (Galatians 6:1–10; 1 Timothy 1:12–17)

Before I retired a lady from my youth group at Wilshire Presbyterian Church in the 1960's came to see me. I had been close to her and to her family. She lives in Northern California, and we had not communicated since the mid-1960's. She said that with my quick departure from the Wilshire Church she had not had opportunity to say goodbye to me. She needed to hear from me what had happened at Wilshire Church in L.A. She had heard the rumors about my wife's affair with the elder in the church and been hurt. She had baby sat for us and needed to have some questions answered. These questions and the church's secretive behavior had caused her to carry the burden for over 50 years. Over lunch I realized how the brokenness within a pastor's family can impact a young member of a church. When we parted, she gave me a hug and said "goodbye". I shared my spiritual journey with her, and she seemed to be at peace. She also had married, had children, divorced, and remarried. Her older brother and his wife had helped introduce me to Kay. I really desired to lift the burden from her heart and to thank her for being my friend and for seeking me out.

I have loved the Parable of the Prodigal Son. (Luke 15) The son who had rebelled against his father and wished him dead took his portion of his dad's estate and went to the far country where he blew it all and ended up feeding pigs. At last, he came to himself and remembered how good he had it at home as the son of his father. He decided to return home seeking a job on his father's farm, not thinking he could ever be accepted again as a son. The father welcomed him home and restored him to the family. He threw a party and invited the whole community. The fatted calf was prepared; the invitations were sent; the royal robe of Sonship was placed upon the broken boy. There was singing and dancing. The father exclaimed, "This son of mine who was dead is alive; he was lost, but now is found."

The elder son refused to come in from the field. He resented his younger brother who had consumed a big portion of the estate. He had seen his father's suffering and grief. How could the father be so profligate in welcoming the boy home? But then the father went out to plead with the elder son to come to the party. "This brother of yours was lost but now is found; he was dead but is now alive." "We must celebrate!"

This is grace; God's unconditional acceptance of us just as we are without one plea. The elder brother's judgment was that his father's behavior seemed like a form of divine injustice. But it is this grace that makes life possible for each of us. By grace alone we live. I have always wanted to err on the side of grace rather than justice. George Smith said to me, "give me mercy and not justice". Who of us can stand before the throne of the righteous judge? This is not "cheap grace" but the "dear and costly grace of God" which acts to restore us.

Rembrandt painted the *Return of the Prodigal.* (Luke 15) Henri Nouwen interpreted the parable in his book. He sat for hours before the painting in the Hermitage Museum in St. Petersburg, Russia, and interpreted each detail. More on this later! I have had a print of the painting hanging in my church office and at home. It still warms my heart and moves me to tears. I am the father and the younger son. I am the father and the elder brother. Rembrandt captured God's story and good news. He captured the reconciliation and joy we have all received and for which our Father prays. This is the good news of the gospel presented from Genesis to Revelation.

In one of my final study leaves Kay and I took a Princess Cruise around the Baltic Sea. We did this because I wanted to go through the Hermitage Museum in St. Petersburg, Russia. Kay and I stood in front of the famous Rembrandt painting and were spellbound. The huge room had several Rembrandt's paintings. In 1969 we had seen some of his paintings in the Amsterdam Museum. I bought another print of the painting. It was of much higher quality than the one I had previously purchased online. Now I have two framed prints of this artists work that have inspired many across the years. The new one hangs in the entry of our home as a reminder of the overflowing grace of the father's heart who welcomes the sinner home and sees with compassion the brokenness of the human heart. This is the source of all forgiveness and new life and the painting captured what I believe is the central theme of the Bible: "God's grace is at work in and through human sinfulness."

I have tried to live by this gospel truth of the grace of God, but I have found it difficult at times when circumstances required discipline and community responsibility. The difference between Tough Love and Cheap Love is difficult to work out in one's life.

Laguna Beach High School employed a part-time coach for its football team. The coach chosen was a former NFL player. He was highly successful as a player and as our high school coach. The problem was that he was arrested a couple of times for the possession of cocaine. It was written up in the L.A. Times. The School Board refused to terminate him as a bad influence for Laguna Beach youth. It was rumored that the coach was having an affair with one of the school board members. It was the gossip in my gym where I did aerobics and lifted weights. The coach and the school board member were often seen in the gym working out together. Boundaries were being violated. I wrote a letter to the editor of the Times calling for understanding and rehabilitation of the African American football star and coach. My letter sounded like cheap grace when it was incorrectly printed in the newspaper. I was arguing that I would rather err on the side of grace than be judgmental and moralistic. People complained.

I wrote another letter to the Times, and they printed my correction. They admitted they had failed to print the first letter in its fullness. I breathed a sigh of relief. Then I publicly supported the recall of members of the School Board for failing to act to discipline the coach. Again, I felt exposed in the community about an issue that was important, but which troubled my soul and left me open for criticism in the city. Often, I worked out at the gym with the coach and the school board member. There were times in which I was afraid the coach might punch me out to protest my public stand. I think we ended as mutually tolerant. Not long ago the former coach died.

Sex in the City

As we arrived in Laguna Beach it was as if we had a front row seat to the American Sexual Revolution. Some would say that sexual behaviors have been consistent throughout history. The Bible is full of stories about sexual behaviors that have moved beyond the boundaries of the moral law of God. At the center of biblical morality has been the call to "fidelity and chastity" and a challenge to separate from the immoral examples of people who have mixed religion and sex for the purpose of fertility or pleasure. Covenant faithfulness within the marriage of one man and one woman has been at the heart of a traditional Christian understanding of life together.

Lust is one of the seven deadly sins and rebellion against God has often been accompanied by sexual acting out in abusive use of the other. Combining self-centeredness, narcissism, alcohol, drugs, and the pursuit of sexual pleasure have led to suffering and scars upon the soul. I grew up in the 1950s when Hugh Heffner was first leading the sexual revolution with his Playboy Magazine and philosophy. According to his sex philosophy he argued that religious and moralistic prudery were what kept people in bondage and unhappiness. Sexual desire and freedom were to be explored and sought after within and without marriage. Gratification of the flesh would lead to happiness and self-actualization.

Indeed, every teenage boy was excited by this possibility. The walls of my Texas Tech dormitory rooms were papered by Playboy centerfolds. These pictures were objects with the power to stir the lustful fantasies of young men caught up in suggestions they did not understand and which I knew were not emotionally healthy for me to look upon.

Ironically, in Laguna Beach one of my elders took me to his barber who happened to have been a Playboy centerfold. On one occasion I went to her home where she lived with her husband. I walked through the house on my way to the place where she was giving haircuts and saw in her bedroom the wall sized Playboy centerfold picture taken in Laguna Beach at Eschbach's Flower shop a block from the church. It was beautiful. She was beautiful. She styled my hair and moved me from having the wet look to that of the dry look. When I walked down the church isle the following Sunday there was an audible gasp. Something about the pastor had changed. I could not reveal who had brought about the new dry look.

The barber was a lovely person, but I knew I could not stop for long in front of the huge picture in her bedroom. I could tell she was proud of it, but it was dangerous for me. Indeed, one could walk down the streets of Laguna Beach in the summertime or at Main Beach boardwalk and see almost as much. One day I was walking with one of my pastor friends toward the beach at noontime. We passed a gorgeous young woman in a bikini. He whispered to me, "I just fell in love again." We laughed. He had fallen into lust.

When I made a public commitment to follow Christ, I began to memorize Scripture. Sexual lust was not invented in Laguna Beach. Sexual desire has a long history. Ask King David and Solomon. The Navigators Bible memory program helped me in many ways. The first memory verses were from Psalm 119:9, 11, and 1 Corinthians 10:13. Keeping my mind centered on these truths helped me overcome many temptations. But that was not the end of the battle with my inner life. This is something that has been a lifetime discipline in seeking the mind of Jesus Christ with the effort to see the other through the eyes of Christ, not as a thing to be used for my own pleasure, but as a person to be valued and celebrated. I am sure that I repressed many lustful desires. These desires were figments of my imagination and if acted upon could have led to the objectification of others as "things" or "its" and not as persons to be honored with respect. Keeping myself faithful has been a lifetime discipline. I may not have acted out my fantasies, but I have surely committed adultery in my heart and mind. I remember what trauma it was when President Carter confessed in Playboy Magazine that he had lusted. How far we have come in what seemed acceptable for a candidate for the office of President of the United States.

Over the years I have come to have gratitude for my sexual desires. It is a real gift to see a beautiful woman or handsome man and to give thanks for the gifts of creation and for the ability to appreciate God given attractions placed in our bodies by virtue of the Creator's will. If we were not drawn to each other where would humanity be? Some have said this is part of what it means to be created in the image of God and for fellowship in community. But like all of creations gifts we turn them into ends in themselves, which we worship and serve. In doing this we lose our way, become idolatrous, and fall into deeper levels of depravity. (Romans 1) So we are seduced in the name of freedom into escalating passions that promise happiness when fulfilled, but end in guilt, shame, grief, suffering, haunting memories, and the destruction of life and relationships.

When I became a Christian and was walking in the Spirit, I felt these issues would be solved, that all my problems would go away and that finding the right girl to marry and with whom to have sex would bring true joy to my life. And of course, that has proven true in many ways for me. Yet, the world system of selling everything with sex and promoting happiness through sexual freedom and open marriage has scarred many persons and relationships.

In later years I participated in a 12 Step spiritual recovery program for co-dependents, who were destroying their lives by seeking to control others and who enabled the addictions of those whom they loved. As a recovering co-dependent, as a man in his 50s, in one large meeting I listened to several women share the destructive impact of sex and alcohol in their lives. It seemed that there was not a woman in the room who had not had a sexually transmitted disease. These were beautiful, intelligent, and accomplished women whom I admired and respected. Within our hedonistic culture that celebrates freedom and pleasure, almost all of us have surrendered ourselves to what promised fulfillment, but which has yielded the sour grapes of spiritual and physical broken-ness. It was the first time I understood that I needed compassion for myself and for all the others who had struggled, suffered, failed, and sought for love in the intimacies of life. Indeed, it was a sobering exposure to the truth of what might happen because of a promiscuous lifestyle.

As I write, our culture and politics are caught up in the "Me-Too" revelations. Central to the feminist complaint has been the witness by women that many men in the business/political environment, and even within the church, have harassed them. Not a week goes by that some famous man is not accused of making propositions to a woman for sex. Many a giant of politics, of business, of Hollywood, of the arts, and indeed of the church, have been accused and publicly humiliated by these disclosures. It seems that power and sexual acting out are connected. The more money and power persons have the more likely sexual abuse will occur.

I would argue that women living in patriarchal societies have frequently been treated as things for male sexual gratification and for the assertion of power. Too frequently women have used sex to manipulate men. In graduate school at Claremont one of my government professors said that our society is filled with "orgasm collectors". Diverse sexual partners have led to deeper relational loneliness. Healthy persons discover that lifelong sexual fidelity is the requirement for fruitful, happy living.

President John Kennedy became known for his sexual affairs. Even though the media did not report on his behaviors, later research revealed that the President was a sex addict as are many people. Our culture became known for "drugs, sex, and rock 'n roll". C-67 witnessed to the "sexual anarchy" of the 1960's and that the church had a calling to help men and women find the way to reconciliation and relational wholeness. It seems that we have not been successful in this mission.

President Clinton was well known for his sexual indiscretions. He was impeached because of his sexual affair in the Oval Office of the White House with his intern. He lied about it, but he was caught. Many believed that Hillary ought to have divorced him. After all, this was not the first time he was in violation of his marriage vows.

President Trump boasted that he could grab a woman's genitals and fondle her without her objection because he was handsome, wealthy, and powerful. This is but one manifestation of how some men think. The "Me Too" movement is seeking to hold men accountable for their attitudes and behaviors in relation to the opposite sex. Indeed, when the future President of the U.S. must cover up his sex affair with a porn star many men in the country say, "right on". Such misbehavior no longer seems to disqualify a man from running for high office, not even the presidency of the U.S.

Christian men have been infected by this libertinism. The Promise Keeper's movement revealed that we have become a nation of Promise Breakers and need healing from false ideologies of sexual freedom. Pornography has become a trap and an addiction for many married men. Internet pornography has captured the hearts and minds of many men. Presbyterian pastors must now undergo sexual misconduct training every three years. If not, the Presbytery will be unable to buy liability insurance. Protestant and Catholic clergy have behaved in destructive ways with those who have trusted them. Hardly a day goes by that the media does not report on the sexual misbehavior of those entrusted to be faithful shepherds of the sheep. This has been the cause of great spiritual unrest within the larger church. When trust is destroyed the whole fellowship is poisoned. The Protestant and the Roman Catholic Churches have been required to forsake their denials about the failure of the clergy and to hold leaders accountable. Huge financial settlements against priests have driven Catholic dioceses into bankruptcies and public embarrassment.

The Scriptures that we read, study, and teach are clear about sexual morality. The 10 Commandments prohibit adultery and covetous behaviors. Sexual infidelity became a metaphor for the disobedience and unfaithfulness of Israel to their covenant with the LORD. King David's story of adultery with Bathsheba and the consequences of that sin for his family and the people of Israel revealed the judgment and grace of God for the fallen. (Psalm 51) King David and Solomon betrayed their theological convictions and introduced the worship of gods that were no gods. They corrupted the hearts of their families and the larger community. Infidelities led to violence and chaos. Israel was weakened by idolatry.

Jesus was not married, but he understood the will of God regarding sexual faithfulness. In the Sermon on the Mount Jesus said,

"You have heard that it was said, 'You shall not commit adultery.' But I say to you that everyone who looks at a woman with lust has already committed adultery with her in his heart." (Matthew 5:27–28)

I believe that Jesus understood that sexual attitudes and behaviors come from deep within the human soul and mind. The tempter's suggestions seem to have access to these dimensions of our inner fantasies. Jesus taught, "It is what comes out of a person that defiles. For it is from within, from the human heart, that evil intentions come, fornication, theft, murder, adultery, avarice, wickedness, deceit, licentiousness, envy, slander, pride, folly. All these evil things come from within, and they defile a person." Mark 7:20–23.

The interesting reality was that Jesus had great compassion for those who knew they were broken and enslaved by the power of sexual sin. He welcomed prostitutes into his presence. He had compassion for them. He forgave them. He was harsh toward judgmental men who wanted to publicly expose them and reject them. Jesus called hypocrites to repentance. (Luke 7:36–50)

In John 4 Jesus encountered a woman at Jacob's well and promised her living, spiritual water. She was probably a prostitute. She came to faith in him and witnessed to her village. In John 8 religious leaders brought a woman to Jesus in the Temple who had been caught in the act of adultery. They wanted to see if Jesus would uphold the Law of Moses about stoning such a woman. He said that anyone who was without sin could throw the first stone at her. Slowly, the woman's accusers walked away smitten by the truth of Jesus' words. As she stood before him, he said to her, "Neither do I condemn you. Go your way, and from now on do not sin again." John 8:1–11

The Apostle Paul, while not married, was concerned about the immorality of the Greco-Roman world. In his lists of the works of the flesh he included such sins as "fornication, adultery, lust, greed, anger, murder, envy, strife, deceit, etc. (See Romans 1: 18–32; Galatians 5:19–21; Colossians 3:5–11; 1 Thessalonians 4:1–8)

Paul knew that many converts to the faith had come out of broken sexual experiences. He wrote to the Corinthians,

> "Do you not know that wrongdoers will not inherit the kingdom of God? Do not be deceived! Fornicators, idolaters, adulterers, male prostitutes, sodomites, thieves, the greedy, drunkards, revilers, robbers – none of these will inherit the kingdom of God. And this is what some of you used to be. But you were washed, you were sanctified, you were justified in the name of the Lord Jesus Christ and the Spirit of our God." (1 Corinthians 6:9–11)

Those baptized into Jesus Christ received the Spirit of Christ. They were called to abide in Christ and his Word so that they would bear the fruit of the Spirit. Over a lifetime of walking in the grace and truth of the gospel they would be transformed from the inside out and be given the mind of Christ. What was in his mind? Was it not love for God and for one's neighbors? Was it not to see and to treat others as persons loved by God and created in the image of God? Was it not to see with compassion oneself and other broken and wounded sinners in need of forgiveness and healing?

The fruits of the Spirit are: "love, joy, peace, patience, kindness, generosity, faithfulness, gentleness, and self-control. There is no law against such things. And those who belong to Christ Jesus have crucified the flesh with its passions and desires. If we live by the Spirit, let us also be guided by the Spirit." (Galatians 5:22–26)

The Church and Homosexuality

Growing up in northwest Texas about the only sexual issue of which I was aware was heterosexual in nature. Same-sex attraction and behavior were beyond the pale of my understanding and experience. I was so preoccupied with controlling my own sexual temptations that I had little thought for fellow humans who had inner conflicts about same sex attractions. I think I assumed that same-sex attractions and behaviors were chosen and sinful. I embraced the traditional view that male and female homosexuality were not God's will and therefore not acceptable. I could point to several Old and New Testament texts that revealed God's intentions within creation and called all humans to healing. I assumed that spiritual transformation would over time set one free from desires, attractions, and behaviors inconsistent with God's will. I did not hate homosexuals, nor fear them, and the Christian church, I believed, was called to help lead all people out of sexual confusion, anarchy, and toward disciplined, faithful living.

I was concerned about ministry with homosexuals in Laguna Beach. It was widely understood that Laguna Beach was an artist colony with a large population of gays and lesbians. Some argued that at least 30% of the population was gay. I wondered if there were same-sex persons, couples, and families in the church membership. In my early days of playing tennis with an older male leader in our church he warned me never to preach on homosexuality. Apparently, the culture of the city and the church had embraced tolerance and lived with some acceptance of those who practiced their freedoms in ways contradictory to traditional understandings. So why stir up an unnecessary conflict and disturb the status quo?

However, one could not avoid the issue in Laguna Beach. Throughout the 70's, on weekends I saw large black limousines moving through the city. They were filled with young gay men being transported to sex parties at mansions on our hillsides. There were gay bars. Gay tourists and residents frequented the bars. Not only was the liberty of the 60's being pursued by straight men and women, but also by the gay community. Unlike the bath houses of San Francisco, Laguna's Gay community seemed to be far more subdued. The Little Shrimp Restaurant and Bar and the Boom-Boom Room were well known as pickup places for visiting gays. At one time there was a bath house on Main Beach, along with a gay nightclub. The police department had come to an acceptance of gay behavior on weekends at local beaches and private residences. It was rumored that the police had promised not to harass the gay community. Most of the churches had come to the quiet acceptance of sexual behaviors and identities that were not the norms of traditional communities.

In the 1970's the issue of civil rights for homosexuals was emerging in both American culture and church. The 1969 Stonewall Inn riots in New York City had set off a gay civil rights protest across the country. Around 1976 the Presbytery of New York City asked the General Assembly of the United Presbyterian Church for "definitive guidance" on the question of whether or not a presbytery, or congregation, could ordain to the gospel ministry "avowed practicing homosexuals" who had graduated from seminary and fulfilled all their ordination requirements. The G.A. appointed a Task Force to study the issue from biblical, theological, ethical, political, ecclesiastical, and scientific findings about the origin and practice of homosexuality and then to give "definitive guidance" to the Presbytery and to the larger church family.

I was an observer at the 1978 G.A. in San Diego, Ca. when the report and recommendations were presented. The Task Force report stirred the interest of the larger church about homosexuality. It was a comprehensive report that concluded that there were four or five different points of view within the UPCUSA. Presbyterians were diverse; they read Scripture differently. We practiced different hermeneutical approaches to Scripture, but there was room within the church family for a diversity of conviction and behavior about responsible homosexuality.

The report argued that sexual identity is not chosen by persons, but that we are each born with a sexual identity which we live into and which we may consider to be God given and good. The Old Testament texts that seemed to address homosexuality were expressions of a pre-scientific worldview and could not possibly address our modern scientific discoveries about sexual orientation and behavior. More Light could be given to the church. On top of it all, Jesus never said anything about homosexuality. The Apostle Paul was addressing exploitive and abusive forms of sexuality, oftentimes connected with pagan religious rites. Straights and gays could live responsibly with self-affirmation. Full civil rights were to be extended to all. Same-gender marriage needed to be allowed and affirmed. Therefore, for responsible Christian homosexuals there was no prohibition against their sexual identity and that presbyteries and congregations ought to seriously evaluate each candidate and approve them for ordination, whether straight or gay, if justice-love was at the heart of the behavior.

Tensions were high in San Diego at the 1978 G.A. Suddenly the issue of sex and ordination were before the church in powerful ways. Many straight friends asked me why this issue was even before the larger church? Was it not clear that homosexual behavior was unacceptable to society? Clearly, much of the church would not approve of ordaining persons whose lifestyles were considered by the Bible to be sinful. Therefore, a minority report emerged from the G.A. committee charged with responding to the Task Force Majority Report. The well – known pastor of the church in Burlingame, Ca., Tom Gillespie, wrote the minority report together with a few others. He had earned his Ph.D. in New Testament from Claremont School of Theology while pastoring the Presbyterian Church in Garden Grove. Tom was later to become President at Princeton Theological Seminary. He was the Chairperson of the Candidates Committee of Los Angeles Presbytery when I was brought under care. We all held him in high regard. My friend John Huffman was a commissioner to the 1978 G.A. from the Presbytery of Pittsburg and was assigned to help write a minority report that was later approved by G.A.

What emerged was a minority report that replaced the majority report. It was overwhelmingly approved by the G.A. It argued that while "avowed practicing homosexuals" were to be welcomed into the membership of the church, they could not be ordained as either teaching or ruling elders or deacons. Why? Because both Old and New Testaments taught that homosexual behavior was sinful. One might have a homosexual orientation and, if celibate, be ordained. To endorse what the Bible called sin would betray our confessional, biblical tradition. Civil rights for homosexuals were to be supported by the church, but those ordained to the gospel ministry were to maintain a life of "fidelity and chastity" within the covenant of marriage between one man and one woman or in singleness. This standard was written into the Book of Order by the G.A. of 1997. At the same time, homophobia among believers was denounced. The issue seemed settled.

I remember sitting and listening carefully in San Diego. The tension was thick. What was launched was a 30+ year study, debate, and argument over the church's understanding of human sexuality and homosexuality. This issue held the larger church in deep anxiety, fear, anger, and hope. I will come back to this later in these memoires.

AIDS

In the early 80's a gay man's disease began to appear. It was HIV, a virus for which there was no cure at the time. Once one was infected with the HIV virus it was terminal. The virus would destroy the body's immune system. The virus was spread by the sexual practices of gay men and through blood transfusions. Laguna Beach was one of the epicenters of the spread. It began when an Air Canada steward visited Laguna, had sex with some local gays in the gay bar scene and the virus was released into the gay community of Laguna Beach. (See Randy Shilts, *And the Band Played On, Politics, People, and the AIDS Epidemic*.) Shilts was a journalist who later died of AIDS. He wrote this early definitive history of AIDS in America. His book helped my understanding of the disease and its spread. Those who suffered with HIV were thought of by many as lepers to be ostracized from social contact.

AIDS hit home in the membership of Laguna Presbyterian Church. A very handsome and accomplished man with a partner with whom he lived was diagnosed as HIV positive. On one occasion when his partner was absent, he had sex with another man at a gay party. He was infected with the virus. He was humiliated and in great anxiety and fear. The HIV virus took over, destroyed his immune system, and killed him. We all loved this man and we grieved deeply. I did his funeral.

Soon another heterosexual church member, a married man, received a blood transfusion with tainted blood. He died of AIDS. I did his funeral.

A young doctor came to town. He was a strong fundamentalist type who seemed to have a great future as he began his practice in the city. He joined our church. He spoke to our deacons about AIDS. We did not know he had AIDS. He thought he had been healed and was in remission. He was trying to stay closeted. But the virus caught up with him. He was deeply grieved. He was gay and had engaged in gay sex while in medical school. He shared with me that he believed gay attraction was a demonic delusion of lust. He told me that another doctor in town was a warlock and engaged in Satanic practices. I knew the doctor and considered him to be a good man and leader in our community. The younger gay doctor began to show signs of dementia. He had needed surgery and the surgeon had enquired about his sexual identity. The doctor told him he needed to affirm his gay identity and make peace with it. Up to that time he had been able to repress his desires for a while. As a patient in the hospital his lusts and temptations emerged like a storm in his soul. He was hanging on for dear life. He returned to his parent's home in another city. He was forced to close his practice and soon died. His parents were in deep grief. They were faithful Christians who cared for their son in his final days. I did his memorial service. He had asked me to preach the gospel to those gathered. I did my best. I did not reveal that he was gay. Most people present knew. He was a believer who was with the Lord, but all of us who loved him suffered for him and with his parents.

One night I received a telephone call from a man in Florida asking me about a friend of his who was a leader in the Laguna Beach business community. The businessman had AIDS. His Florida friend who had called told me that homosexuality was a delusion and he wanted me to call his friend to account and seek to minister to him. It was too late.

Parents from back East began to show up in Laguna Beach to discover for the first time that their sons were gay and sick with AIDS. They visited with me. I visited their sons in the hospitals. It was almost too much to see their son's bodies covered with black tumors.

Gay partners found themselves caring for each other. A seminary friend of mine with whom I had studied Greek as a fellow student was now a pastor. He shared that his son developed AIDS and that his partner moved into their home where his son was cared for until he died. He shared that the devotion his son and partner had to each other was remarkable. Others in the community delivered food and medicines. The compassion and caring of some of these healthy partners was an inspiration. San Francisco and Laguna Beach, California, seemed to be at the center of this epidemic. Yet, it was growing worldwide. Our President Ronald Reagan did not want to speak of AIDS. He and others were in denial about this modern plague for which there was no cure.

Our local ministerial association tried to respond. We were losing the leadership of the gay community in the city. Many of these men were bright, loving, and accomplished leaders who had become agents of a deadly sickness that was wreaking havoc in the gay community, but also upon us all. We organized an AIDS Memorial Service for all the victims. I floated the idea that we could have the service in our church sanctuary. One of the dearest men in the church who was on the Pastor's Nominating Committee that called me to Laguna begged me not to allow the AIDS Memorial Service in our church. I realized how fearful and prejudiced even good people could be. We held the service at another church, and it went well. Not many came, but all those present had personal friends who were either sick or who had already died.

I was in an awkward place. On the one hand I thought of myself as a Christ-centered, evangelical, Presbyterian pastor who had a mandate to uphold the truth of the Bible in the church and in the public square. On the other hand, the compassion of Christ was in my heart as I came to know real life persons and families who were suffering. I was learning about life, suffering, and untimely death.

I arranged for several parents in our church with homosexual children to meet with me for an evening of dialogue. The large living room was filled with suffering family members. I listened to the cries of people who I loved and for whom I was their pastor. Some were deeply conflicted and alienated from their children or siblings. Others had made peace within their families. Sexual identity or behavior was no longer an issue. I did not want to hurt any of them. I wanted their children to feel welcomed in our church. I sensed anger toward me from some of those present. I was not about to publicly out or humiliate any of them. I was aware that many of our young people were already sexually active as unmarried heterosexuals. The landmines were everywhere for a young pastor.

By the mid 1980's Laguna Beach had elected its first gay mayor. Robert Gentry was a professor and assistant dean at UCI. After one of my public pastoral letters about homosexuality, AIDS, and the Christian Church, he contacted me and invited me to lunch at the faculty club at the university. We met over lunch, and he proceeded to lecture me about human sexuality and what it had been like for him as a gay man growing up in the church in the upper mid-west. He said being gay was the last thing he would have ever chosen. It had cost him much pain and suffering. But he had made peace with his identity and had come out as a gay man. Life had improved for him in being out.

Bob made it clear to me that he would never walk through the door of our church if we regarded his identity and behavior to be sinful. His homosexuality had allowed him to bring love into his life. I respected that.

As mayor he acted to be helpful. He had the City Council appoint an AIDS Education Task Force to reach out to the citizens of Laguna Beach, to our public schools, churches, and clubs to interpret and to educate about AIDS. He asked if I would represent the church community on the Task Force. I willingly did that. In the process I came to know many in the gay community of Laguna Beach. They were respectful of me and I of them. We worked together for the good of the city. For the mayor the silver bullet for healing was education in how to have safe sex.

Over time I learned that Bob's gay partner died of AIDS. Several years later, in October 1993, when the city nearly burned down, Gentry lost two houses and walked into the Laguna Presbyterian Church seeking help in that time of emergency. Our church became the center of the Fire Relief. Twenty of our church members lost their houses. Our Fellowship Hall and Youth Center were filled with clothing, food, and counseling. Our lay people responded quickly, and we were able to help rebuild people, houses, and community spirit. It was a dark time and a deep depression set in upon the city by Christmas time as we sought to recover from an experience that had touched us all. I will write more about this later.

From 1978 on I did my best to become informed on human sexuality and marriage. The approach to Scripture that helped me was this:

Even though Jesus did not speak specifically about homosexuality one could not read the Gospels without understanding that he was a traditional Jew who believed that humanity was fallen from what God intended life to be. In Mark 10 he responded to questions about divorce and what God's law required. He quoted from Genesis 1:27 and 2:24 that in the beginning God created humans as male and female. "For this reason, a man shall leave his father and mother and be joined to his wife, and the two shall become one flesh. So, they are no longer two, but one flesh. Therefore, what God had joined together, let no one separate." Mark 10:2–9

In quoting this passage it troubles me. I know my quoting this passage causes the skin on some to crawl. This text has been used by Christians to beat up on gays and lesbians. God forbid that this biblical truth be simply applied to the sexually fallen. The manifestations of sin are systemic and touch every aspect of human personality and behavior. There was a time when a divorced person could not be ordained in the PC(USA). Jack Rogers wrote, "that if the church changed its mind on divorce, it might well change its mind on homosexuality and become inclusive."

The Apostle Paul went on to teach that Jews and Gentiles were both fallen. "All have sinned and fallen short of the glory of God. There is no one who is righteous, no not one." (Romans 3 and 6). The proof of God's amazing love was that while we were sinners, Christ died for us. (Romans 5:8). In Ephesians 2:8 Paul argued that God's grace came to us while we were spiritually dead. If it were not for God's costly grace, none of us would have escaped spiritual darkness by ourselves. God did for us what we could not do for ourselves. Because of the sacrifice of the life of Jesus his blood has made atonement for our sins and through faith we have been set free to live in love and justice. (Luke 18:9–14)

If all Christians were forgiven sinners, why not practicing homosexuals. But the Bible does not name sexual orientation as sinful, but good. Was not the church required to affirm the birth identities of same-sex persons and couples as consistent with the will of God? After all, these were consenting adults. Irresponsible homosexual behavior would be sinful. Married same-sex relationships were to be affirmed.

Sometime in the early 80's a couple of gay men came to my church office. They were students at UCI and leaders in the Gay Christian group. They were inviting me to be a panelist at their gathering at the university to present and to dialogue on these issues. As it turned out I was the only traditional religious leader present. The experience was painful to me because I was in the minority of one. Deep in my personality I wanted to be accepted as an intelligent person and in tune with science and higher education. After all, I had earned a Ph.D. at Claremont Graduate School. I was not a dummy. I could be wrong, but I cared enough to bear honest witness about my convictions.

It called to mind the evangelism visit I led to a home in La Canada. I was an associate pastor at the La Canada Presbyterian Church. One evening I led three of us to visit a family that had visited our church worship. The father of the household turned out to be a scientist at JPL. He was a Ph.D. from Harvard. He had not visited our church but someone in his family had. Things went well until I made the gospel presentation using the outline I had received from College Hill Presbyterian Church in Cincinnati, Ohio. He looked across the room at me and said that when he was a graduate student at Harvard, they had a place for people like me: the mental health hospital. Well, we wrapped up the visit quickly and departed.

When I related the experience to Dr. David Hubbard, President of Fuller Theological Seminary, he said "Jerry, you should have told him you had an earned Ph.D. from Claremont." But I could not do that. It would have seemed arrogant on my part, and I needed to accept his response to me and to realize I was an unannounced visitor in his home and had offended him.

The sense of vulnerability and embarrassment that I experienced that evening was what I felt at UCI. The young gay men had been making a case for how one could interpret Scripture through the lens of justice-love to embrace gay Christians in the church. Their case was made even as it was to be made in several Presbyterian churches and General Assemblies. I intend to come back to this discussion later.

One cannot write the modern history of the PCUSA without reflecting on human sexuality, sexual behavior both straight and gay, family, and marriage. The deeper issue is the Gospel of God and its power to heal, to transform, and to shape the mind of Christ within human personality, family, and community. For nearly 40 years the Presbyterian family has become fractured and angered by the conflicts about these matters. Pastoral insensitivity by both conservative and progressive factions within the church have led to schism and weakening of the mission of God through us.

Up to this point I had not fully understood the internal dynamic of a gay or lesbian person. I had not adequately struggled with a gay Christian's dilemma in coming to self-affirmation. Could it be that the scriptures of the Old and New Testaments could be faithfully interpreted in ways that might bring more light to the human condition? Was it necessary to jettison traditional interpretations of scripture to live with compassion, affirmation, and acceptance of persons who thought differently about these matters? Could a gay person be a faithful, Bible believing Christian, and lead a responsible sexual existence without a burden of shame and guilt? Or was the mystery of sexual identity locked within the human genome and that could never be changed? These were some of the issues that continued to haunt me as I taught and preached the Biblical message about the love and truth of God and the power of human brokenness, along with the human need to love and to be loved within the intimacy of marriage.

This conflict and conversation were rippling through other churches in our Presbytery. In one church, that I helped the Presbytery organize, there was a group of parents with gay or lesbian children who felt rejected and outed by their pastor. They were leaving their church, and some came to Laguna Beach. One couple was Mike and Debbie Regele. One of their twin daughters had shared with them that she was a lesbian. Mike and Debbie are deeply committed Christians. Mike is an ordained Presbyterian pastor who has been a blessing to the Presbytery over the years. It did not matter to them that their daughter was gay. The result was that Mike did an intensive study on the Bible and Science regarding human sexual identity and behavior.

His book on the subject was published. In it he shared his journey with this issue. *Science, Scripture, and Same-Sex Love.* Abingdon Press. 2014. He asked me to write an affirmation for the book to be published on the inside cover. I did so. Here is what I wrote,

> "Mike Regele writes about human sexuality humbly, graciously, simply, and wisely as husband, father, Presbyterian pastor, social commentator, and friend. His book is stimulating not only for an academic but also for pastors and persons in the pew. He helps us to listen, to think, and to speak about deeply held convictions in the spirit of a civility that builds others, affirms differences of opinions, and leads to reconciliation between conservatives and progressives within the church. Through serious Bible study, theological/scientific reflection, personal experience with

others and church debate, he has come to strong convictions about Christian sexual ethics and the power of God's love to heal the brokenness of our lives. His is a voice that we need at this table of our continuing dialogue as we seek to promote the 'peace, unity, and purity of the church.'"

I was touched by his acknowledgment of me and LPC. He wrote,

"The two-year period in which this book was written became a tumultuous time for my wife and me. We found ourselves outside our church of nearly thirty years. But two colleagues in ministry came alongside me (us), providing encouragement, wisdom, and a listening ear. Jerry Tankersley, pastor of Laguna Presbyterian Church, was someone I had known for thirty years but only at a distance. We don't even agree on everything I have written. But when I reached out to him, he opened his schedule and let me bare my heart in total safety. He has become a dear friend."[2]

As Christians who believe in the authority of Scripture, the Lordship of Jesus Christ, and the fellowship and mission of the church, it is inevitable that we have different ways of reading Scripture and Science in their interrelatedness. What matters is that we are brothers and sisters in Christ. I could hear Mike and Debbie's cry of love for Christ and their daughter. They desired their children to have loving, lifelong relationships and commitments that would affirm their identity as good and faithful, but also as dearly beloved and accepted in their family and in the church. As a parent I value this parental love.

In this writing I have shared my own hermeneutic struggles with Scripture and our Confessional tradition in the light of scientific discoveries. Wherever we come out on various issues, the final norm for our life together must be the truth, the love, the justice, and the grace of our Lord Jesus Christ as we seek to walk in the Spirit.

Gay persons are human and are beloved by God. We are called to love one another as God has loved us in all our mystery and brokenness. I now trust that the Lord can do what only the Lord can do, and that is shape our minds and hearts in the spirituality of the kingdom of God. In the meantime, let us make room for everyone and center ourselves in our journey toward the City of God. May the highways to Zion run through each of our hearts as we journey together toward the New Jerusalem.

---

2. Regele, *Science, Scripture, and Same-Sex*, xvi

Who knows, we may all be right or wrong in our interpretations of the Christian life? We may yet come to full acceptance of same-gender marriage as one of the ways we learn to live in faithfulness and devotion to Christ and to one another. I want to be open to the truth of full trust in the goodness, the love, and the power of God to make us all whole. But this journey will not be easy. It will lead us through the depths of human emotion and the heights of vision. It will open us to pain and suffering, as well as profound acceptance and joy.

Hermeneutics

When I arrived in Laguna Beach, I carried the blessings of my education at Fuller and Princeton Theological Seminaries. Also, I had been deeply impacted by my doctoral studies at Claremont Graduate School. In doing these memoirs I am writing my own intellectual history. Especially is this true regarding the interpretation of texts, the meaning of words, and the impact of new historical contexts for their interpretation. In working with George P. Smith on Arnold Brecht's, *Political Theory*, I discovered I was on a journey in the theory of knowledge in the pursuit of ultimate reality. That search continued in the selection of my dissertation subject. The project was entitled *A Metaethical Analysis of American Theories of Jurisprudence*. The finished product was approved by faculty readers: R.G. Ross, Gerry Jordan, and George Blair. The degree was awarded in 1971. The dissertation was placed in the Claremont Graduate School Library.

In the introduction I wrote,

> "This work represents an attempt to analyze American theories of jurisprudence (mechanical, functional, and realist) from the point of view of metaethical theory. Metaethics can be distinguished from normative ethics. One who is interested in normative ethics is searching for the 'true' foundation of morality. He seeks to discover the general principles of morality to which all men must appeal if they are to give sound reasons for their moral evaluations and prescriptions. . . .
>
> Metaethics does not make moral statements. It makes statements about moral statements. There is one central question which a metaethical approach tries to determine. Is the adoption of a given moral principle the expression of subjective commitment, or, can a principle or its denial be shown to be objectively true, and if so, how?

According to Felix Oppenheim, there are two metaethical problems:
What is the meaning of value words such as 'good, preferable' and moral terms such as 'right and duty'?
What is the logic of moral discourse? Are moral principles objectively either true or false? If they are, by what method can such principles be justified?" pp. 1–6

Mechanical Theory

What I carried with me from La Canada to Laguna Beach was this metaethical model in approaching authoritative texts in new contexts. The mechanistic reading of the U.S. Constitution and the application of the law assumed that a judge had the responsibility of finding the facts of a case, classifying the facts according to certain pre-existing legal categories, selecting the rule, principle or standard applicable to the relations involved, and applying the decision or judgment. "The judge is committed to administer justice in accordance with the fixed rules which could be applied by a mechanical process of logical reasoning to a given state of facts and made to produce an inevitable result. The meanings of these legal rules are fixed and do not change over time."[3]

Without my fully realizing it, this was little more than the 19th and early 20th century Princeton Seminary approach to reading the Scriptures of the Old and New Testaments. Taught by Baconian assumptions about facts combined with Scottish Common-Sense Philosophy, the preacher was tasked with interpreting biblical texts in the light of their authoritative, logical assumptions. The original copies of the biblical texts were without error and therefore, statements of objective truth. These truths (encapsulated in history and in words) were to be taught to disciples and to be used to guide the life and mission of the church.

As the U.S. Constitution had been adopted by the sovereign people of the United States in 1789, so the church had received the objective revelation of truth and justice in the Spirit inspired original texts of the Bible. These texts were to be applied in new contexts among the nations by those who were the inheritors of the tradition. Any rational preacher was called to this faithful way of knowing and applying the received biblical truth to the human condition. This was Propositional Theology.

3. Tankersley, *Metaethical Analysis*, 37.

The Westminster Confession of the 17th century was looked to as the Princeton tradition's understanding of the authority of Scripture. Yet the theologians of 19th century Princeton moved more in the direction of Protestant Scholasticism than toward John Calvin's 16th century teaching in his *Institutes of the Christian Religion*. Calvin taught that the authority of Scripture was in the witness of the Holy Spirit through the words of prophets and apostles. This is what the writers of the Westminster Confession affirmed. In the Book of Confessions, chapter 6.001-10 of the PCUSA it was confessed:

> "The authority of the Holy Scripture, for which it ought to be believed and obeyed, dependeth not upon the testimony of any man or church, but wholly upon God (who is truth itself), the author thereof; and therefore it is to be received, because it is the Word of God...our full persuasion and assurance of the infallible truth and divine authority thereof, is from the inward work of the Holy Spirit, bearing witness by and with the Word in our hearts.
>
> We acknowledge the inward illumination of the Spirit of God to be necessary for the saving understanding of such things as are revealed in the Word.
>
> All things in Scripture are not alike plain in themselves, nor alike clear unto all; yet those things which are necessary to be known, believed, and observed, for salvation are so clearly propounded and opened in some place of Scripture or other, that not only the learned, but the unlearned, in a due use of the ordinary means, may attain unto a sufficient understanding of them.
>
> The infallible rule of interpretation of Scripture, is the Scripture itself."[4]

Of course, the mechanistic reading of the Constitution does not assume the illumination of the Holy Spirit. Some Christians have believed the U.S. Constitution was divinely inspired, but the framers would not have endorsed this understanding. Rather, they saw the document as the political and legal ground norm for the judicial system and for the branches of the U.S. government. The application of reason and logic to the 1789 Constitution would guide wise, rational judges in maintaining the order of American life. To be sure, they assumed some form of "higher law" or "natural law" was embedded in the words of the Constitution.

---

4. Book of Confessions, Westminster, Pp 122-123

Through reason, a Supreme Court Justice would read the law and apply it to new fact situations. This was to do justice.

My dissertation analyzed Marbury v. Madison (1803) and the Dred Scott v. Sanford (1857) as examples of the Mechanistic, Traditional approach of American jurisprudence. This jurisprudential theory continues to be taught in law schools. Knowing the legal precedent and upholding the Constitution in the light of the Framers original intentions still informs our legal history. The original intent of the Framers narrowly restricts the thinking of many when it comes to judicial accountability.

In the Dred Scott 1857 Supreme Court case Chief Justice Roger Taney declared that since African slaves were defined as property in the Constitution of 1789, in the future they would always be property. This was the original intent of the Framers. Reformed preachers read and assumed that the writers of Scripture accepted slavery as God's order, so in all generations of preachers that truth was to be maintained.

This reading of Scripture and Constitution led to the perpetuation of the institution of slavery and justification of segregation after the Civil War. Southern Presbyterians justified support of the institution of slavery based on this reading of Scripture and the U.S. Constitution.

A number of New Deal legislative acts in the Great Depression years of the 1930's were declared unconstitutional based on the intent of the Framers. This way of reading texts is still central to issues of abortion and Civil Rights in our own time. It is central to the debate about gender identity and human sexuality. It has led to schism in the PCUSA in the 1920s and 1930s, as well as in the first quarter of the 21st century.

The Sociological-Functional Theory of American Jurisprudence

Sociological jurisprudence arose as a reaction to the mechanical theory.

> "Its major emphasis is that law ought to be significantly related to the rest of society. Law is a social institution. Rather than a logical development from assumed first principles, law expands itself through a series of adjustments to new empirical situations. This understanding of law sees law as a mechanism whereby society resolves its problems.
>
> These assumptions are made:
>> The universe is dynamic, changing, and relative. Society is dynamic. Clashing groups are held in dynamic equilibrium. History is relativistic and changing. One cannot read the U.S.

Constitution in 1970 and take it to mean the same as it did in 1787. At the root of this theory is the philosophy of pragmatism, which assumes that justice must be tested by its impact upon society.

The judge must take a creative, responsible role in the process of developing good law. He cannot abdicate his responsibility as did the mechanist judges. He makes law just like legislatures. Maintaining social stability in the light of needed change is vital for a judge. General security and well-being over time were foundational."[5] See U.S. v Butler and Brown v. Board of Education.

The preacher must interpret a biblical text in the light of new scientific, sociological, and historical discovery. Our understandings of the cosmos and of human nature require new readings of ancient texts. Harry Emerson Fosdick's famous sermon, *"Shall the Fundamentalists Win?"* makes a case for a church that has room for both old and new interpretations of biblical texts. Unity and diversity must be tolerated in any church where there are different ways of reading texts to address changed circumstances or to provide more – light upon human need. The arguments between the Fundamentalists and the Modernists of the 20th century presuppose that within any church ancient texts will be read and heard through conflicting eyes, ears, and hearts. Unless this is tolerated there cannot be "peace, unity, and purity" within the church.

The preacher has been called to a vocation of interpreting biblical texts in the light of a growing tradition of interpretation. In the final analysis the Holy Spirit is needed to bring illumination to the preacher's heart and soul allowing for a relevant message to be proclaimed, for a Word from God for the life of one who has stood in the presence of God and listened to receive a healing, transforming Word of God for a church living through changing times. Therefore, part of a preachers calling is to know the meaning of biblical words in their literary, historical contexts and history of interpretation, but also to apply that tradition to the personal, cultural, political, social, and spiritual needs of both the soul of the person and the soul of society. Without the help of the Spirit no preacher is adequate for this calling.

Ian Pitt-Watson, professor of Preaching at Fuller Seminary, argued that the preacher, in preparation for preaching, must do exegesis on both

---

5. Tankersley, *Metaethical Analysis*, 87.

the text and the new context. Only in this way will a Word from God be addressed to the life of the believer or the church fellowship.

Legal Realism in American Jurisprudence

There are law interpreters in this post-modern world who assert that law is constantly in a state of flux. It is moving and changing because it is the creation of legislatures and judges. For justice to be done an interpreter must read the legal precedent with the power of rational imagination. Law is what legislatures, presidents, and judges do. Law is not an end in itself. It must serve the needs of society. Stability and change are needs of any social and legal system. But objective truth does not exist. Words have different meanings over time. Therefore, there is no way of knowing ultimate reality as anything other than subjective assumptions and opinions that may work for a time, but which will change given the need to create a system that provides workable justice.

One may see that from mechanical, to sociological, to realist worldviews we have moved from theistic, to agnostic, to atheistic (skeptical) knowledge of ultimate reality. This is the world in which interpreters of texts live. The key is open-mindedness and humility before ever changing situations. Prior principles, precedents, assumptions, and truths will not allow for ultimate justice or moral guidance. In the 1960's this worldview undergirded *"Situational Ethics"*. The resultant ambiguity led to confusion and the search for certainty that continues both in legal systems and in theological/spiritual guidance.

Peter Enns wrote the book, *The Sin of Certainty, Why God Desires Our Trust More Than Our 'Correct' Beliefs*. The book narrates his personal journey to struggle with the tensions humbly and graciously between "faith and doubt", "certainty and uncertainty". I would place him in the Sociological/Realist camp, rather than the "Propositional, Mechanical" way of dealing with texts. He believes in the authority of Scripture but sees Scriptures of Old and New Testaments to be telling the story of the mighty acts of the God, but who seems at time to be absent or silent when it comes to resolving all the issues with which we interpreters struggle on the way to revelation inspired knowledge. His journey led to his dismissal from Westminster Theological Seminary in Philadelphia that still is committed to the theory of knowledge espoused by J. Gresham Machin who left Princeton Seminary over these issues in the early 1930's.

Laguna Beach And The Laguna Presbyterian Church

With these intellectual tensions within me, I began to teach and to preach the Bible in Laguna Beach. I needed help and more education. When the opportunity came for me to enroll in a new Ph.D. program at the Claremont School of Theology and to study with James A. Sanders and others, I jumped at the opportunity. It was a Ph.D. in Christian Interpretation, which I ultimately translated into a Doctor of Ministry degree. When I graduated in 1983, I was presented the *President's Award for Academic Excellence*. Given my history this was especially meaningful to me and allowed me to apply what I had learned into the 21st century as pastor of Laguna Presbyterian Church. My life cannot be understood without appreciating my quest for theoretical/practical knowledge and wisdom. What I learned along the way has informed my personal life, my spiritual growth, and pastoral experience. I have drawn from each of these theories of knowledge and revelation as I have sought to be faithful to the authority of Scripture and the illumination of the Holy Spirit as reflected in the Book of Confessions of the PCUSA. I hope to unpack some of this in my Laguna Beach story covering nearly 50 years.

"He Set His Face": Preaching the Christian Deuteronomy, Luke 9:51-18:14

"When the days drew near for him to be taken up, he set his face to go to Jerusalem."

LUKE 9:51

My program at Claremont was a gift from God to me. It took over five years of classes and dissertation work to complete the degree. It began as a Ph.D. in Christian Interpretation, but I finally realized that being a full - time pastor would not allow me time to finish up the Ph.D. Therefore, I converted the degree program to a Doctor of Ministry. It was a good decision. I did not want to neglect my duties as a pastor of a thriving congregation.

One of the courses I took was on the Gospel of Luke. James Sanders and David Tiede, the Lutheran scholar, led the graduate seminar. What I discovered in Luke/Acts was Luke's brilliant "theocentric hermeneutic". For Luke, God was the subject and God was on the move in creation and history. In Jesus of Nazareth the bearer of the Old Covenant promises had come to set his people free, to rescue and to save. Baptized by John the Baptist in the Jordan River, Jesus began his public ministry in the power of the Holy Spirit. His ministry was launched in his hometown synagogue in Nazareth.

On the Sabbath day Jesus, as was his custom, was with his people in worship. He was invited to read the assigned texts of the day from Isaiah 61 and 58. He read,

"The Spirit of the Lord is upon me, because he has anointed me to bring good news to the poor. He has sent me to proclaim release to the captives and recovery of sight to the blind, to let the oppressed go free, to proclaim the year of the Lord's favor." Luke 4:18

Jesus rolled up the scroll, sat down, and with all eyes in the synagogue upon him, gave his sermon:

"Today this scripture has been fulfilled in your hearing." Luke 4:21

The congregation spoke well of him. Their hometown boy, the son of Mary and Joseph, had proven to be eloquent. But then they whispered among themselves, "Is this not the son of ole Joe and Mary?"

Immediately, Jesus knew they did not believe what he had said. He had identified himself as the fulfillment of their Scripture. He was their Messiah. They were neutral witnesses on the way to being negative eyewitnesses to this mighty act of God. Therefore, Jesus told them two more stories from their scriptures. He spoke of Gentiles getting the blessings of God rather than the ancient Jews. He caused his friends to consider the truth that if they would not accept him as their Messiah, then they too could miss out on the blessings of the kingdom of God present in the life, the words, and the mission of Jesus.

Indeed, Jesus's people longed to see Isaiah's promised vision fulfilled in their own time and within their own elect community. The anointed one would proclaim "good news" to the oppressed and poor Jews of Israel. He would set them free from their bondage to the hated Romans. The blind would receive sight; the oppressed would go free. The Messiah would inaugurate the Year of Jubilee of which Leviticus 25 and Deuteronomy 15 had written. This was the year when debts would be canceled, slaves set free, lands restored with joy proclaimed at the reversal of the fortunes of the people of Israel.

What if their Messiah Jesus could not be believed? What if Israel was spiritually blinded to the in-breaking of the New Moses who had come to set the people free in a New Exodus from the powers of sin and death? What if Jubilee was being proclaimed and the people who had nurtured this hope missed its arrival?

The hometown synagogue experienced in their guts the anguish of being left out and of another people receiving what belonged only to them. Quickly they concluded that Jesus was a false prophet who was threatening the election of the Jewish community. Deuteronomy 13 instructed the Jewish religious community on how to deal with false prophets who threatened to lead them into idolatry in the worship of gods that were no gods. Put the false prophet to death for the sake of maintaining biblical truth and sound orthodoxy! Therefore, in righteous indignation the hometown synagogue filled with rage rose to take Jesus by force to drag him to the precipice of the mountain in Nazareth to cast him to his death.

In reading the story from Luke 4 we might conclude how faithless and corrupt these Jews were. Without realizing what they were doing they were killing the Christ out of spiritual blindness. Gentile believers might say that God rejected his people because of their rejection of Jesus. Indeed, many Christians across the centuries have advocated this anti-Semitic prejudice.

But, if we read this text honestly, with humility, with humor, and by means of the biblical hermeneutic that invites us by means of dynamic analogy to identify with Jesus' hometown synagogue, we too may feel the anger they felt in wanting to push Jesus out of their lives. This approach to Luke/Acts might be the only way to escape our own anti-Semitic assumptions.

Scholars have argued that Luke 4 was "programmatic" for the entire Gospel of Luke/Acts. How would the Jewish people respond to Jesus? "Their Messiah/A False Prophet?" Jesus' words were heard as a "prophetic critique" rather than a "constitutive" word of grace for the community. Therefore, those who heard Jesus' words through the eyes of faith might hear "judgment" or "grace". This accounted for the different responses that Jesus and his disciples received along the Way of God's mission.

As a young pastor reading the scriptures through Luke's eyes, I realized that when people heard the message of the Kingdom, they might become angry and that this might lead them to reject me and the message that I proclaimed. After all, my people were wealthy Americans who perceived their nation state to be an exceptional people and the recipient of God's blessings. Dare I call into question their election as God's New Israel? Was it not the better part of wisdom to proclaim a message of comforting grace and to affirm American/Presbyterian positions of privilege, power, and prosperity? A doctrine of personal spiritual salvation might be the least dangerous message. What if that comforting "cheap grace" was only half of the truth that Jesus lived and taught? Do any of us really want a "prophetic critique" of our political and religious identities and ways of living? This was the challenge before me as I sought to honestly apply the Gospels to myself and to my people from 1980 forward.

I did a series of sermons on Luke in 1982 using hermeneutical questions suggested by Sanders. I selected the Central Section of Luke's Gospel that runs from 9:51 to 19:27. Sanders' thesis was that Luke wrote a Christian Deuteronomy. The model for Jesus' journey to Jerusalem was Deuteronomy 1–26. This part of Deuteronomy purports to have been Moses' instructions to Israel after their 40 - year journey out of Egypt to Mt. Sinai and arrival at the gates of the Promised Land. It was a long sermon, if you will, on what it would take for Israel to choose life and to inherit the blessings of God's promises.

On the plains of Moab, Moses the elder leader of this rebellious people, gave his instructions and call to faithfulness to the Covenant Law received at Mt. Horeb or Mt. Sinai. At Mt. Nebo, in the modern state of Jordan, Moses was allowed to see into the Promised Land from south to north. It was a spectacular view over the Jordan Valley all the way to Mt. Hermon on a clear day.

My first visit to Mt. Nebo was in 1980. I had led a small group of 16, first to Cairo and then to Amman, Jordan. It was a cheap trip with Wholesale Tours International. They later went bankrupt, and their service was not good. They did not have our tickets to me until we departed from LAX. We stopped in Germany to see the Passion Play in Oberammergau. This was one of the best parts of the trip. The weather was good. Chuck Smith and I took an early morning jog through the iconic German village. The Passion Play was deeply moving. At the end of the day Chuck and I joined Joe Andrus in a pub. He left early and later we found him wandering the streets, after too many brews, searching for his hotel. After we got him home, we found our way to our dwelling.

When we left Munich, I was left in the airport as the plane was leaving the gate. I had been searching for a lady's passport. They boarded her without a passport and did not tell me. She said she had packed it in her luggage. Thankfully, they discovered me, stopped the plane on the runway and took me to it in a special small trolley. It was an amazing experience to approach the airliner on the runway with its door being opened for my embarking. Tour leader and group got reconnected with great anxiety on my part as we left for Cairo. I will never forget the conversation I had with the Egyptian Muslim engineer as we flew to Egypt. When we passed over Cairo at sunset, I got my first view of the pyramids as they cast shadows across the desert. What joy and excitement I felt!

The hotel in Cairo was subpar, but it worked. The light and sound show at the Great Sphinx and Giza pyramids was wonderful. There Chuck Smith and I saw Gary and Marilee Demarest from La Canada. That was a treat. When we left Cairo, we went to the Egyptian Airline's gate to discover a line of Egyptian workers waiting to board with us. The airline put our American group on board the plane in the front section and then boarded the very poor working – class Egyptians in the rear of the plane. I will not reflect on my theology or spirituality at this point, but in that moment, I appreciated the airlines sensitivity to our group of older Americans. We flew over Lebanon, turned southeast, and descended into Jordan. Our hotel in Amman, on the outskirts of the capital, was modest, but adequate. The next day we visited Petra, rode horses into the ancient city, and on the return to Amman visited Mt. Nebo.

As I investigated the Jordan Valley from Nebo, I read Deuteronomy 34 to the group. I was identifying with Moses. He had led the people for 40 years, seen many hardships, been the Spirit empowered, faithful leader always facing enemies within his camp of nomads on their way into a land promised to their ancestors. I was tired.

As I read, I began to weep. It did not seem fair of the Lord to prohibit Moses from entering the Promised Land toward which they had journeyed through challenging times of testing and resistance. In a moment of frustration and self-aggrandizement, Moses had made it appear that he was Israel's savior and not the LORD. He suffered the consequences. I had also made mistakes. Leadership has heavy responsibilities. I blubbered before my people. The Deuteronomy 34 story of Moses' dying and being buried by God so that no one knew where his body was buried caused me to wonder if I might have the same destiny, i.e., after many years of service not being allowed to enter the Promised Land.

Surely, Hebrews 11 ended with this commentary about the Old Testament heroes of faith, including Abraham and Moses. None of them inherited the Promise toward which they traveled. They saw the City of God, their true homeland, from a distance. They were tempted to turn back to Egypt. Their call was to do the will of God and to endure. They were exhorted to hold fast their Confession of Faith; to keep their eyes on Jesus who was the pioneer and perfecter of their faith; who for the joy set before him endured the cross and entered his Father's rest. The heroes of faith were part of God's plan of blessing that would not be complete without future generations of saints.

After weeping at Mt. Nebo, I have never desired to preach on Deuteronomy 34 out of my own insecurity, anxiety, and fear, that on my final day in Laguna Beach, a new Joshua will be waiting in the wings to replace me to complete the spiritual journey with God's people. In recent years I have learned the truthfulness of this anxiety. The text has haunted me, and I have been drawn to its truth over many years. It was a reminder to me that all leaders die still waiting to experience the fullness of God's kingdom. That awareness has drawn me to Psalm 90 with its exhortation to number my days that I may apply my heart to wisdom.

Moses had a day of assumption, of being taken up by God into the fullness of God's Sabbath rest. In fact, some have argued that the Travel Narrative of Luke's Gospel was modeled after Deuteronomy and the Assumption of Moses. "Using this Midrashic methodology, Luke wrote a Christian Deuteronomy presenting Jesus as the 'prophet like Moses', Dt. 18:15. He did this in order to challenge the doctrine of election then current in the religious establishment."[6] *Preaching the Christian Deuteronomy*, my unpublished D.Min. Project, Claremont School of Theology Library.

James Sanders tells us why such prophets as Jesus were never acceptable in their own country. He wrote,

> "No prophet, that is, no true prophet of the Elijah, Amos, Isaiah, Jeremiah type is *dektos* by his own countrymen precisely because his message always must bear in it a divine challenge to Israel's covenantal self – understanding in any generation. In other words, a true prophet of the prophet-martyr tradition cannot be *dektos* at home precisely because of his hermeneutics."[7]

Those reading Luke's Gospel who knew these ancient stories and, whose eyes had been opened, would immediately perceive that Jesus was the New Moses setting his face in prophetic style to prepare his followers for his departure, his lifting up in Jerusalem, through his death upon the

---

6. Tankersley, *Preaching the Christian Deuteronomy*, 51–52.

7. Sanders, "*From Isaiah to Luke 4*", *Christianity, Judaism, and Other Greco-Roman Cults*, 99.

cross, his Easter Sunday resurrection, and his ascension to enter heaven on clouds of glory to sit at the right hand of his Father as sovereign LORD.

Therefore, Luke's schema interpreted Jesus' New Exodus journey up to Jerusalem into the fulfillment of God's salvation story. Along the way, from Galilee to Judea, Jesus instructed his disciples about their journey in preparation for their mission from Jerusalem to Judea, to Samaria, and to the ends of the earth to bear witness to the truthfulness of what they had seen and heard along the way of their long obedience.

In a profound sense, the journey of God's mission, of God's story, would not end with the death, resurrection, and ascension of Jesus. Through these spiritually formed disciples the good news of what God in Christ had done, and what God was still doing, would reach the nations through the apostolic witness of those whose eyes had been opened to see, whose ears had been opened to hear, and whose minds had been opened to understand and to trust the mighty acts of God.

Luke's Gospel was brilliantly written under the inspiration of the Greek Old Testament and the illumination of the Holy Spirit. In the Prologue of the Gospel, one long sentence, stated his purpose:

> "Since many have undertaken to set down an orderly account of the events that have been fulfilled among us, just as they were handed on to us by those who from the beginning were eyewitnesses and servants of the word, I too decided, after investigating everything carefully from the very first, to write an orderly account for you, most excellent Theophilus, so that you may know the truth concerning the things about which you have been instructed." (Luke 1:1–4)

Luke was both a historian and a theologian. He was a teacher of the faith, a man of prayer, and the Word of God. His eyes and ears had been opened to believe and to obey. He was an investigator and interpreter of reality through the lens of Scripture as illumined by the Holy Spirit. Clearly, Luke saw himself as the writer of Scripture, which God was giving to his people to encourage them upon their dangerous travels through the Greco-Roman world. Some argued that he wrote Luke/Acts as a defense for the Apostle Paul as he faced his judges in Rome seeking to prove that Jesus and his church were not a danger for Roman law and order. This may well be true. But in the fullest sense Luke wrote the lengthy Luke/Acts to shape and to form the lives of the first century disciples who were the members of the new congregations that had gathered in response to Peter and Paul's witness to Jesus Christ and now were on the Way with the living LORD.

Each follower of Jesus is a Theophilus, "a friend of God", who needs to know the truthfulness of what happened and what continues to happen as persons and groups respond to the good news in every generation up to the present and surely into the future. Acts 1 continued the story with the focus on Peter and Paul and the advance of the kingdom beyond Jewish boundaries and into Gentile territory with all the challenges that would entail as a new covenant community was being formed made up of believing Jews and Gentiles.

It was no accident that Luke wrote his narrative by anchoring it in the Old Testament story of salvation. "Eyewitnesses and servants of the word" believed that the truth to be told began in the creation stories of Genesis 1 and 2. Luke 1 and 2 narrated another Abraham and Sarah story in the relationship of an old and barren couple who had been patiently enduring without the blessing of a promised child. Zachariah was married to Elizabeth. When the old priest heard the angel Gabriel's promise of a coming child who would prepare the way for God's Messiah, he could not believe. Therefore, he was not allowed to speak for nine months. He was not able to make sense of the angel's proclamation. It was not until John the Baptist was born that Zachariah's mouth was opened and he was transformed from being a neutral eyewitness into a positive eyewitness to the mighty acts of God. Like Abraham and Sarah, Zachariah doubted and laughed at the strange possibility that God might be doing a new thing in history and that his own journey of faith was a part of the truth.

The Virgin Mary became a positive eyewitness when Gabriel visited her. She had her questions, but she was ready to believe the impossible. Believing Genesis 18:14, "Nothing was too hard for the LORD," she answered, "Here am I, the servant of the LORD; let it be with me according to your Word." (Luke 1:18) Both Mary and Elizabeth were positive eyewitnesses to the in-breaking of God's powerful word in their lives. Mary sang about it using Hannah's Song from 1 Samuel 2 upon the birth of Samuel. Elizabeth's womb carried the embryo of John the Baptist and that embryo leaped with joy when Mary and her unborn child came into her presence. God was on the move! Who could understand how and why these things were happening? With God all things were possible! These things were the fulfillment of Biblical promises. Yet, how does one trust such news? By the end of Luke 2, angels, shepherds, old and young, male and female, were singing about what they had seen and heard.

When the baby Jesus was brought by his parents into the Temple on the 8th day Simeon took the child into his arms and cried,

> "Master, now you are dismissing your servant in peace, according to your word; for my eyes have seen your salvation, which you have prepared in the presence of all peoples, a light for revelation to the Gentiles and for glory to your people Israel."(Luke 2:28–32)

Luke marshaled positive, neutral, and negative eyewitnesses to the mighty acts of God.

The positive eyewitnesses were the most unlikely folks. They were young and old, male and female, unborn babies, outcasts and sinners, angels and shepherds, stones beside the road, the poor and the sick, the demons and the possessed, and others with no standing in Israel or Rome.

The negative eyewitnesses were the religious leaders of Israel, Pharisees and Sadducees, priests, the wealthy, the healthy, and the holders of privilege and power. They considered themselves to be the elect of God. They were the ones most threatened by a person and a message that had the power to turn the world upside down and to reverse their fortunes. Some negative eyewitnesses were transformed into positive eyewitnesses. Among them was Saul of Tarsus, who became Paul the Apostle. In Acts 26, Paul witnessed to King Agrippa that in his vision of the resurrected LORD on the road to Damascus, the LORD had opened his eyes and ears to the truth. Through that encounter, he received a new hermeneutic. The LORD said to him,

> "I am Jesus whom you are persecuting. But get up and stand on your feet; for I have appeared to you for this purpose, to appoint you to serve and testify to the things in which you have seen me and to those in which I will appear to you. I will rescue you from your people and from the Gentiles—to whom I am sending you to open their eyes so that they may turn from darkness to light and from the power of Satan to God, so that they may receive forgiveness of sins and a place among those who are sanctified by faith in me."(Acts 26"12–18)

The neutral eyewitnesses were the disciples, the followers of Jesus, who had seen and heard Jesus from the beginning, been drawn to him thinking he was the Messiah, and who thought they would be enthroned with Jesus when he arrived in Jerusalem to rule as Israel's king. The 12 expected they would sit to his left and to his right and rule in the kingdom of God. The Romans would be thrown out of the Holy City and every sinful person or group would be removed. At last, the true greatness of the 12 would be manifest. They had backed the right political candidate and would be rewarded. They fought among themselves as to which of them was the greatest. They were so much like us.

Repeatedly along the Way, Jesus sought to prepare his followers for what would happen to him when they arrived in Jerusalem.

> "He took the twelve aside and said to them, 'See, we are going up to Jerusalem, and everything that is written about the Son of Man by the prophets will be accomplished. For he will be handed over to the Gentiles; and he will be mocked and insulted and spat upon. After they have flogged him, they will kill him, and on the third day he will rise again.' But they understood nothing about all these things; in fact, what he said was hidden from them, and they did not grasp what was said." (Luke 18:31–34)

James Sanders taught that we must identify with these neutral eyewitnesses, as well as the negative and positive witnesses. By means of *dynamic analogy* we experience the puzzlement, the spiritual blindness, and restless expectation of those who encountered Jesus along the way of his journey up to Jerusalem. Who of us has not been on the glory road with Jesus expecting to be honored, to become wealthy, and to have positions of privilege, power, and prestige?

In Luke 24, on Easter Sunday evening, two disciples were returning home to Emmaus discussing all the things that had happened with Jesus in Jerusalem over the past week. Along the Way, a stranger who they did not recognize, joined them. The stranger asked about these things they were discussing. They were stunned that the stranger did not know about the rejection, the trial, the crucifixion, the death, and the reported resurrection of Jesus of Nazareth. The stranger responded to the facts of the story:

> "Oh, how foolish you are, and how slow of heart to believe all that the prophets have declared! Was it not necessary that the Messiah should suffer these things and then enter into his glory?" "And beginning with Moses and all the prophets, he interpreted (*hermeneutics*) to them the things about himself in all the scriptures." (Luke 24:13–27)

It was after this teaching that the stranger joined the two disciples for dinner in their home. At the table the stranger took the bread, blessed it, and gave it to them.

> "Then their eyes were opened, and they recognized him; and he vanished from their sight. They said to each other, 'Were not our hearts burning within us while he was talking to us on the road, while he was opening the scriptures to us?'" (Luke 24:28–35)

For Luke the key to faith was the power of the resurrected Jesus whose presence on the Way interpreted the scriptures, opened the scriptures, and their eyes, ears, and minds. In the mysterious presence of the living LORD, in both Word and Sacrament (or Table), their eyes, ears, and minds were opened to believe the truthfulness of the good news of God's story.

Later that Sunday evening in the Upper Room Jesus showed them his hands and feet.

> "Why are you frightened, and why do doubts arise in your hearts? Look at my hands and feet; see that it is I. Touch me and see; for a ghost does not have flesh and bones as you see that I have." "While in their joy they were disbelieving and still wondering, he said to them, 'Have you anything here to eat?'"
>
> "These are my words that I spoke to you while I was still with you—that everything written about me in the law of Moses, the prophets, and the psalms must be fulfilled."
>
> "Then he opened their minds to understand the scriptures, and said to them, 'Thus it is written, that the Messiah is to suffer and to rise from the dead on the third day, and that repentance and forgiveness of sins is to be proclaimed in his name to all nations, beginning from Jerusalem. You are witnesses of these things. And see, I am sending upon you what my father promised, so stay here in the city until you have been clothed with power from on high." (Luke 24:36–49)

From 1983 to 1999 in Laguna Beach

On September 5, 1982, Laguna Presbyterian Church presented me with a framed plaque that read:

> "Laguna Presbyterian Church
> lovingly celebrates with

152   A Pastor's Highways on the Way to the New Jerusalem

> Jerry Tankersley
> the completion of his first
> decade of meaningful ministry
> as its Pastor
> September 5, 1982
> 'He set his face to go to Jerusalem.' (Luke 9:51)

It was amazing for me to realize that I had completed ten very formative years for the church as well as for me and my family. Karen Stony had done the plaque's calligraphy with such care and beauty. The plaque hung over – looking my desk at the church for the next 36 years. My friend John Huffman, when I told him about the theme verse from Luke 9:51, asked if I did not understand that Jesus' journey to Jerusalem led to his suffering and death. Of course, I knew this, and this verse and all that it might mean for my future ministry and life haunted me.

Along the way the Clippers Fellowship Group adopted a project of redecorating the pastor's office while I was away on vacation. When I first arrived at the church office there was a large Persian Rug that covered the floor of the large room. I loved it. One day a woman came to the office and said she had arranged to pick up the rug to move it to L.A. I told her I thought it was the church's rug. "No", she said, "it was on loan to the previous pastor." We contacted Dallas Turner and he confirmed it was a loan for the pastor's study. When it was removed the large room seemed empty, the furniture looked old, the lighting was totally inadequate, and the desk looked used for many years. The removal revealed how little care the church had given to the space dedicated for the pastor's study. What a surprise when I returned from my vacation to face the empty looking room. Two new Persian carpets had been purchased from Pashgian's Rug store in Pasadena. There was new furniture; the room was painted. There was new lighting. The floors had been grooved and resurfaced. The new leather chair behind the new desk was beautiful. Chuck Reeves told me he hoped I wore it out. I was touched.

The restored office and ten-year plaque were tokens of affirmation and represented the bonding of pastor and people. It was a witness to a relationship of love that lasted for the next thirty plus years. The two rugs are just as beautiful as the day they were placed in the study. I am deeply grateful to God for this partnership in ministry. The pastoral relationship was turning into a long journey in the same place. My way up to Jerusalem seemed like a more pleasant journey than I had anticipated, but more was to be revealed. In the remaining parts of this memoir, I want to explore the mystery of longevity, growth, maturity, failure, success, adventure, and mission to the ends of the earth.

Playtime: Hiking the Grand Canyon, High Sierra Hikes, and Hawaii

Those early years were not all work and no play. There were summer and winter trips to Mammoth, for hiking and skiing. There was the awesome hike the family made with the Brooks family of La Canada. We started in the early morning from the north rim of the Grand Canyon. We hoped to make it to the Colorado River before it was too hot. Mind you, it was in the middle of June. It was a 14-mile hike to Phantom Ranch passing from 8 thousand feet above sea level to 2500 feet at the river. We moved through several geological zones. All the while the temperatures were rising. By mid-morning Kay was suffering heat stroke and vomiting. That afternoon we tried to cool her body in the stream. That night we slept beside the trail. She was sick. We could hear airplanes flying above the Canyon throughout the night. I prayed for deliverance. Some fellow in running gear passed us on his way to the south rim in one day, a twenty-two-mile run in terrible heat. I was with Kay. The two eleven-year-old boys had made it to Phantom Ranch and reported us lost. Howard Brooks was going to meet us half – way after descending the south rim. He had not made it. Toni and her daughter had also slept beside the trail closer to the ranch.

Early the next morning in the cool of the day, Kay and I broke camp. She was feeling better. We walked down the trail not knowing how far we were from the river. It was dark we could barely see the trail before us. Thankfully, we met the Ranger who was seeking us. At last, we arrived and were all reunited. We were able to purchase breakfast from the kitchen of the famous restaurant. We camped another night and soaked ourselves in the cold water of the stream running to the river. That evening we had a wonderful dinner meal in the restaurant. The next morning, we crossed the river and ascended to the Indian Springs Campground where we spent another night. The following morning, we came up out of the canyon at about 8:30 a.m. I will never forget the sense of accomplishment. We had hiked the Grand Canyon! All twenty-two miles of it! What an experience! I would have given anything for a helicopter to fly us out, but the ranger said "No". "You got yourself into the Canyon, now you have to get yourself out." It was a good lesson.

This experience launched several High Sierra hikes with Dick and Carol Maxwell. They were Boy Scout Leaders and real out-door people. These were long summer hikes of around 50 miles beginning at around 9 thousand feet and going up and down over peaks and passes at 13 thousand feet. Over several days we toughened up. These were exhilarating hikes seeing beauty, animals, and other things we would never have seen if we had not risked. Jeff was with us, sometimes resisting, but after getting started we could not keep up with him. The Beam family joined us with their son, Jeff. Jerry Immel, Jr. came along on one hike and carried cans of sardine for his food. He began to smell like sardines as he carried the empty sardine cans back to our trailhead. At one stop a bear approached Kay. She dropped her pack and ran. Dick drove the bear away and she did not lose her food. Lightning bounced off the rocks. It hailed and rained. The High Sierra Camps out of Yosemite were spectacular. The Five Lakes hike over Black Rock Pass led to encounters with huge bears. Glacier Pass with its melting glacier was awe-inspiring. There were times I was not sure I would survive. The Rae Lake Loop of 45 miles was breathtaking. As we descended to the trailhead parking lot all I could fantasize about was a huge cheeseburger with fries topped off with a cold mug of beer. One summer I hiked with Dick and Carol from Red's Meadow, near Mammoth Mountain, over the Donohue Pass and 13 miles down into Yosemite at Tuolumne Meadows. At the end of that march, we heard the news that Saddam Hussein of Iraq had invaded Kuwait and had taken it over.

I came back from these hikes in better shape than ever. Thankfully, I had been training with running and low impact aerobics at the local gym. Now, I wish I could do it again, but there is no way my eighty – year-old body could manage it.

A family in the church owned a condo on Waikiki Beach in Honolulu. For three summers they sent the three of us for two weeks at their place. What a gift. Carlyle and Georgia Dennis and their children and grandchildren became special friends. Carlyle and some other men in the church paid for me to preach on KWAV radio on Sunday mornings. Their promotion of me meant a great deal to me.

Jeff loved playing with the other children at the Oahu Hilton Hawaiian Village beach. On one of those visits I performed a wedding for Pat MacMillan of the La Canada Church at the historic Congregational

Church in Honolulu. Before the wedding, she and her fiancé took us on a harbor cruise with dinner and drinks. Kay and Jeff danced on the boat. These were very happy times of celebration.

On another occasion a member of the church invited us to stay at his condo on Maui. Three families of us enjoyed seeing the island. One of the families had moved from Laguna Beach to Maui and owned a 12 – acre ranch. They entertained us and treated us as royalty. Jeff had a great time going down the Seven Falls or Pools with the other kids. The other two families moved away from Laguna Beach, but over the years I have done their weddings and baptized their babies. This is what pastoral ministry may be like.

In 1984 I led a Reformation Tour through Germany, Switzerland, England, and Scotland. Included in the trip was the Passion Play and a short cruise on the Rhine River. In Berlin we moved through Check Point Charlie into East Berlin. Members of the Berlin Fellowship met with us and took us to church. What a contrast between east and west. When the East German police came onto our bus with huge German Shepherds to check our passports it was frightening. We looked over the Berlin Wall and saw where many had died trying to escape to freedom in the West. Jeff did not want to go on the trip, but now he looks back upon it and would like to do it again. He loved the castles on the Rhine, but there were too many cathedral visits for him. I loved teaching about Luther, Calvin, and Knox in the places of their lives.

Family Restlessness

Bill and Tallie Parrish drove Kay and I to my Claremont School of Theology graduation at the First Methodist Church of Claremont in the spring of 1983. We had become dear friends during our first ten years in Laguna. They were neighbors. They had raised three children and gathered great wisdom in the process. In the early 80's we barely realized how much their counsel would come to mean to us and how important it was for us as parents of our now adolescent son graduating from TOW Elementary School and moving into the 7th and 8th grades at Thurston Middle School. It was a major transition. That transition launched us into a new and challenging season of seeking to be faithful parents loving each other and our son Jeff.

Kay had her personal restlessness during those years. She had completed an MA at California State University in Fullerton. Her work was in Psychology. She had done well and was invited to read her research paper at a national conference. I was very proud of her. But what next? She began a Master of Divinity degree at Fuller Seminary in Pasadena. That meant commuting several days a week for 4 years. Again, she did well and graduated in 4 years with her M.Div. But those 4 years added stress into our family. I did not handle it well. Then she began a Ph.D. program in Clinical Psychology at a nearby university. I had my own preoccupations with the church. Jeff showed signs of depression and anger. Exhaustion and conflicted feelings were growing.

Not only had I been working on my degree at Claremont, but I had been pastoring a church that was waking up, engaging scripture through the Bethel Bible Study program, and working with a committee to address the needs of the church's campus buildings. I had to help raise $1.5 million dollars for the Restoration Project. I had lots of help, but the stress was significant. We were exploring every aspect of opportunity we could. At the same time, I tried to coach Little League and Boy's Club basketball with Jeff's teams. We had a lot going on. Youth sports added stressful tensions to my life. We were burning the candle on both ends. I fear that Jeff may have thought he was being neglected in our rush for personal and family fulfilment. I was working with a lot of anxiety wanting to be a perfect pastor, husband, and father.

Jeff began to act like many of the adolescents his age. He wanted to do things his way. He acted out at school. We were called in to the counselor's office. It was recommended that we might think about some counseling for him and our family. That was very threatening to me. I had already given myself to many years of psychotherapy. Yet, this was my beloved son and I wanted nothing more than to love him and to be loved by him. I did not want to fail in my marriage or my parenting. I loved Kay.

There were many dangers in the larger culture. Alcohol, drugs, sex, partying, the beach environment, youth rebellion, restlessness, self-actualization, ambition, upward mobility, depression, anxiety, and fear captured our attention. I had all the ingredients of co-dependency in my soul. I was trying to control the church, my wife, my son, and myself. I was in an emotional meltdown.

Gradually, Kay and I began to be aware that we needed to attend to what was happening between the three of us. We had soul and relational work to do, and it required us to slow down, to be available, to listen, to speak, to share, and to find ways of being together that brought relief from the pressures and produced new joy.

In the eighth grade we removed Jeff from Thurston for a few months and enrolled him in a school that would provide an enriched curriculum, counseling, and loving discipline. We met a lot of parents going through the same thing with their children. It was the best of times and the worst of times. It was painful. It was suggested that I needed to go to Al-anon and to work the 12 Step recovery program for co-dependents. Jeff was the identified patient, but I got into treatment. I called my recovering AA friend, Lyn Wilder, and asked him to help me get into Al-anon. We went together to meetings and had frequent lunches to talk about the program. He and his wife Pam were participants in the church, and both were in the program. I am deeply grateful for my friendship with Lyn and Pam and later with Lyn and Danine, whom I married to Lyn after Pam's death. The more my co-dependency was addressed the better our family did and certainly the better Jeff did. After a few months he was back in the 8th grade at Thurston, playing on the Club Volleyball Team, and Kay and I were chaperoning his team at the nationals in San Jose, Ca., and later at UC Berkeley.

During this decade I began my journey of working the 12 Steps of A.A. as a member of Al-anon. It meant facing up to the fact that my life had become unmanageable, and I was powerless to fix myself or anyone else. That was a revelation. Dale Brunner's commentary on the Gospel of Matthew, chapter 5, suggested that the first beatitude of the Sermon on the Mount was "Blessed are the poor in spirit for theirs is the kingdom of God." Mt. 5:3, was another way of writing the First Step of the 12 Steps. Jesus' words in this sermon spoke to my spiritual condition. My life was unmanageable. I was experiencing powerlessness. I was poor in spirit. Our family was suffering. I was becoming aware that some church members and residents of Laguna Beach were closet alcoholics. Some kids were doing drugs. Cocaine was showing up among our youth. Many great parents were filled with anxiety, anger, and fear. The High School was aware of the issue and sponsored a parent program, which Kay and I attended. Several of our men at church formed a prayer group to support each other and to pray for our children. These were times of self-disclosure and deep sharing. We held our children and our families in prayer. We pleaded for God's protection and guidance. We asked for wisdom.

I had been afraid for other church members to see me at an Al-anon meeting. But then I surrendered to the truth that I needed a deeper relationship with my higher power, namely God. I came to believe that there was a power greater than me who could restore me to sanity. Indeed, I was insane, troubled to admit it, but slowly finding spiritual freedom in becoming identified with the weaknesses and sufferings that I saw in others.

I began to turn my life and my will over to the care of God as I understood him. It was like a huge burden had been cut from my back. There was a God, and it was not I! Daily I surrendered the control of my life, of my family, and of my church, to God. This led to a serious and searching moral inventory of my own life to see what I was contributing to the problems of my wife and son. I got a sponsor; I did my 5th Step sharing and continued this new pathway to spiritual healing and community. Kay was on the same journey, and we encouraged each other.

Amazingly, my preaching and teaching became more vulnerable and relational. Many recovering alcoholics and co-dependents became my friends and connected with the church. This was one of the best things that ever happened to me and through me. My higher power was at work shaping and forming me to become the person and servant I needed to be. Pastoral opportunities expanded and our lives were blessed. Suffering had brought me to my knees. I began to pray in ways I never had. This was no longer an academic exercise. No, my soul, my family, and my church were on the line. I was learning to "Trust Anyway".

For me, it meant surrendering and detaching from those I loved for the sake of truly loving them and setting them free to become the persons God desired. The more this happened the better they did. I realized a good thing was happening and that I needed to stay put in Laguna Beach for the sake of my soul, my wife and son. I attended weekly Al-anon meetings for twenty years.

In the middle of this time a large Presbyterian Church in Northern California came to me and asked if I would consider becoming their new pastor. They were down to their last two candidates. I was honored to be considered as the next pastor following a man for whom I had great respect and appreciation. But I looked at the church and compared what was happening there and measured it with the potential of Laguna Beach and I realized my calling was to LPC.

I was in my mid-40's, and it might have been a good option for me without other considerations. But we were in the middle of it with Jeff and I could not move him from the place he loved for the sake of my own advancement, as questionable as that might have been. Basically, I closed the door when they wanted to speak with members at LPC about me to get references. I told them "No" and have never regretted it. I think they called the pastor they needed to have for their future.

In the middle of all this, we were at dinner with our dear friends, Byron and Donna, and they asked when I was moving to the church that had called them for a recommendation. I was so embarrassed. I discovered that interested churches have ways of finding out about a prospective pastor without the pastor being aware. Thankfully, it worked out and our friends understood and kept it to themselves.

Jeff graduated from Laguna Beach High School in the class of 1988. We were grateful. We thought he needed to get out of the beach environment of Laguna Beach with its unique culture and temptations. After speaking with a college admissions counselor, she identified Whitworth College in Spokane, Washington, as a likely school for him. He had been with us at Whitworth on a two - week Summer Institute of Theology when he was in elementary school and really enjoyed it. He was admitted in the fall of 1988, and we drove him to Spokane by way of Skyline Ranch in Telluride, Colorado. The three of us spent an enjoyable week at the Ranch eating great food, being with wonderful people, and hiking over the mountain passes. Then we were on our way to Spokane. We stayed with our pastor friends Dick and Darlene Gronhovd and checked Jeff into the dorm. When we arrived home without Jeff, I felt the pains of an empty nest. I knew it would come, but we were happy for him. Kay's mom, Jeanne Hoppe, left a small trust for Jeff's education. It paid for the first two years at Whitworth. Then we refinanced our house to pay for the last two years.

Jeff majored in Sociology at Whitworth. Several old friends of mine were on the faculty, Dale Brunner, Ron Frase, Don Liebert, Leonard Oakland, and others. Ron and Don took him under their wings. Jeff matured. He signed up for the semester abroad in Central America. After a month of language study in Guatemala, with Kay and Mary Cannon going along for the first month of language study, the students visited other countries and carried on a semester long travelling seminar on issues of historical, political, economic, and religious interest. We joined him in San Jose, Costa Rica, for a couple of days.

While in Costa Rica there was a huge Sunday morning earthquake. I thought our hotel would shake down. I was in the shower naked and wet. We then spent a week at a Pacific Resort and Jeff and his group continued their journey. Don Liebert wrote me a letter from Mexico sharing Jeff's giftedness with the street children. He had a way of moving into their world, identifying with them, and playing with them that was beyond anything Don had ever seen. Don and I were in seminary together at Fuller and at Princeton. I was grateful to receive his letter of affirmation for Jeff. Ron became a surrogate parent for Jeff at Whitworth. He looked after him and was there for him when he needed help.

Jeff played on the freshman basketball team. Kay and I went up to one of his basketball tournaments that first winter. And then in 1992 he graduated from Whitworth. We were there. Then he spent 7 months with Partners of Hope in Mexico City. We were grateful for Jeff's successes. He has taught elementary school in the Santa Ana District for several years, earned his Master's in Teaching from a local college, and has done a great job. In 2019–20 Jeff was named Teacher of the Year by his school. We are proud of him. More later about Jeff and Rachel.

Preaching in the Reagan Years

The 1980's were Ronald Reagan years for America. He promised that it would be "morning again in America". He was full of optimism and good cheer. He comforted the evangelical church in America. He was Governor of California for two terms. He was a Presbyterian Christian and member of our Bel Air Church. Donn Moomaw was his pastor. The Cold War was reaching a crescendo between the Soviet Union and the U.S.A. The accumulation of nuclear weapons by east and west nations caused massive peace protests in Europe and America.

When Reagan came to the White House in 1981, the country was in an economic recession with inflation growing so that housing loan interest rates were around 20%. Reagan came to office with what George H.W. Bush had called Voodoo Economics. This was a Supply Side theory that required the lowering of taxes for the wealthy, the cutting of government regulations on business, increased spending for defense, for missiles and atomic weapons, with the assumption that the increased wealth of the rich would "trickle down" to the middle class and the poor.

America was in major competition with the Soviet Union. The threat of nuclear war was real. The leadership of our congregation was strongly pro-Reagan. The economy began to boom. The stock market soared; interest rates were lowered, and many believed they were getting rich. The theme of the movie, *"Wall Street"*, "Greed Will Save America", was a compelling slogan for 1980's America.

During that time, I did a series of sermons on the Minor Prophets of the Old Testament, preaching one sermon on each of the 12 Minor Prophets. One stands out. The text was from Amos 7, *"Amos and Amaziah"*. Amos was called by God to travel from the Southern Kingdom of Judah to go to the central worship shrine in the Northern Kingdom at Bethel and to prophesy, to proclaim the Word of the LORD to Israel. Amos was a sheepherder who had received God's Word. The Northern Kingdom had become idolatrous at its central shrines of Dan and Bethel. The poor were being neglected and sold cheaply. There was no social justice in the land and King Jeroboam II had come under God's judgment.

Using the hermeneutic of prophetic critique and dynamic analogy, I preached,

> "Amaziah was a professional clergyman. He had worked for years in the ecclesiastical structure of his time, in his denomination, in his nation, and on behalf of King Jeroboam. He had risen through the ranks no doubt from a small parish, until at mid-life, he had finally arrived at the National Presbyterian Church in Washington D.C.
>
> For years he had worked to build up the nation. He had instructed his people to believe that the gods were with them as a nation in a special way. The northern kingdom, Israel, had arrived at a time of relative peace and prosperity. The mood of the people was one of optimism. Business was good on the surface. Religious interest was increasing. The National Church was packed every sabbath and this must have thrilled Amaziah. He was at ease in Zion and enjoying this renaissance of his nation's life.
>
> "Things were not perfect, of course. Human nature being what it is, you never have a completely just political or economic system. He reasoned that some people are going to lose all that they have and meet economic disaster. The little man, the small businessman, was always at a disadvantage when competing with the giant corporations. The elite of the nation were getting richer, and the poor were hurting. While it was sad that so many small farmers were losing their lands, Amaziah had learned to overlook these things, to desensitize his own soul and to go on celebrating the prosperity of the kingdom."
>
> "Amaziah was the kind of man who would have read last Saturday morning's L.A. Times article about the young couple

whose farm was being auctioned away in Ohio. Owing $400k, they had been unable to pay their mortgage and were losing their farm". Amaziah would have read the article and said, 'Oh, that's sad, but you can't do much about it. That's the way it is in this rough and tumble competitive world.'"

"There were merchants who cheated people in the streets. There were judges who were accepting bribes from the wealthy and deciding cases in their favor."

"The number one priority for King Jeroboam was building up the national defense even if it meant draining off the resources of the nation and leaving the poor ground into the dust."

"The poor you always have with you and these political, economic issues are too complex for a simple-minded prophet. Amaziah's job was to keep the king happy, to perpetuate the mood of ease and comfort and optimism. He was to keep the people busy with religious festivals, celebrating the blessings of the gods and preaching a gospel that guaranteed that the multiple deities were on their side. God would always bless his elect elite people."

"Amaziah trusted that some of the wealth and prosperity of the economic winners, who enjoyed their luxuries on the hillsides of Samaria, would ultimately trickle down to help the people of the land."

"But then Amos arrived from Judah, the Southern Kingdom. He had a word from the Lord. He proclaimed at the National Shrine in Bethel that the Lord had a special compassion and mercy for the poor. He had delivered his poor people from Egyptian slavery and planted them in the Promised Land. Therefore, he required his people to be a light to the nations, to demonstrate justice and righteousness."

"Amos saw what was happening in Israel. He saw an economic system in which the rich were getting richer, and the poor were getting poorer, and no one seemed to care. He saw a legal system that was corrupt. He saw a marketplace in which dishonest merchants cheated the poor. There were many homeless people sleeping in the streets of Bethel. He saw a religious establishment in Bethel that had domesticated the gods. He saw a church with a hole in its gospel. It was proclaimed by the religious establishment that personal salvation was God's interest. Leave the political, economic, and social system alone. The authorities managed the systems according to the laws of supply and demand."

"Amos proclaimed,

"That he had been sent to the White House in Washington D.C. to speak a word of judgment, of hope, and restoration. In the late 1960s and 70s several of my clergy friends were invited to the White House in Washington, D.C., to the East Room, to preach to the President of the United States, to his cabinet and to other invited guests. Apparently, the President had been hearing some embarrassing sermons out in the country. It was decided that it would be safer politically to draw up a list of trusted men of the cloth who would be invited to the White House and who would not embarrass the President and who would stick to personal, positive, comforting words at the center of God and country."

"I will never forget the ecclesiastical scrambling of all of us Amaziah's for such a prestigious invitation. Can you imagine having an opportunity to preach at the White House, in the East Room, and to return to one's congregation with pictures of one's important self with the most powerful person in the world? This was 'heady' business. If there was ever a bit of Amaziah in me, it came forth. 'LORD! That's my kind of calling.'"

"Amos would never have been invited to the White House, to Bethel, to Samaria. He had no standing, but he went and delivered the word of the LORD in such a powerful way that the land could not bear it. How often have we heard sermons that we could not bear?"

"In threat, anxiety and panic the pastor of the National Presbyterian Church ran to the President of the U.S. and reported, 'Amos has conspired against you at the center of Israel's political and religious capital.' King Jeroboam II rent his clothes and sent Amaziah back to Amos with these words,

'O seer, go, flee away to the land of Judah and eat bread there, and prophesy there, but never again prophesy at Bethel, for it is the king's sanctuary, and it is a temple of the kingdom.'" (King Jeroboam was apparently as insecure as President Trump is at the present. Loyalty to his reign meant everything.)

"The church and the nation desperately need to hear Amos' call for justice and social righteousness. Amos came as a troubling presence to all of us in the church and the nation who are at ease in Zion; to all of us who are comfortable with our wealth and our luxury on the hillsides of our city but who are unconcerned about the plight of the homeless poor and needy in our city and nation. Amos comes as a troubling presence to all of us who are excited by personal religion but who care little about the political and economic pain of our society. He comes as troubler to the church; to all of us whose gospel is personal and private, without social relevancy, to all of us who have made God the patron of our nation or our church and defined God as the servant of our needs. We either chase this Amos out of our lives as Amaziah did or we turn to Amos' God, the God of the covenant, in a new way. We either cry out 'crucify this Amos' or we bow before the LORD for whom he speaks and plead for mercy and forgiveness."

Amos summed up God's judgments upon Israel,

"The time is surely coming, says the Lord God, when I will send a famine on the land; not a famine of bread, or a thirst for water, but of hearing the words of the LORD. They shall wander from sea to sea, and from north to east; they shall run to and fro, seeking the word of the LORD, but they shall not find it." Amos 8:11–12

I was afraid to preach Amos' message. The following week I received a letter from a conservative member of our church suggesting that I did not understand American capitalism and that I ought not to dabble in politics or economics from the pulpit. Clearly, I had angered the man and called into question his worldview. In a minor way he was chasing me away from those who were at ease in Zion, who did not want to hear the truth of the LORD from an honest telling of the biblical story.

This was Jesus' trouble also. In his hometown synagogue of Nazareth his teaching of the Old Testament story called into question the election of those who were convinced they were God's elite people, who believed that the blessings of God would be for the in-crowd and not for those on the outside, the Gentiles. Who were the poor if not Israel? When God's final blessings were poured out, the members of the church would be blessed and not the outsiders. In Luke 4 Jesus saw that it was dangerous to proclaim a prophetic critique of the self-affirmed elect. It was his prophetic word as recorded in the Gospel's that led to his crucifixion and death upon the cross. The amazing truth was that in his suffering upon the cross in humble weakness and sacrifice that God's love poured forth into a rebellious world.

In Luke's Sermon on the Mount Jesus' said,

"Blessed are you who are poor, for yours is the kingdom of God . . . But woe to you who are rich, for you have received your consolation." (Luke 6:20–26)

Jesus proclaimed the gospel of the kingdom of God that revealed that the good news was that those who had suffered in this world would be lifted and comforted in the next. Their fortunes would be reversed. When the powerful rich heard Jesus' parable of the rich man and Lazarus in Luke 16:19–31, they were convinced that Jesus had it out for them. The poor beggar who had been at the rich man's front door and had not been seen or helped, died, and went to heaven into Abraham's bosom where he was comforted. Then the rich man died and went to hell. Across the chasm he saw Lazarus and pleaded with God to send Lazarus with a cup of water for him. But no!

> "Then send someone to warn my brother, the rich man cried."
> "No!" 'They have Moses and the prophets; they should listen to them. If they do not listen to Moses and the prophets, neither will they be convinced even if someone rises from the dead."

Those of us who are Amaziah's have become co-opted by the rich and powerful. We spiritualize Jesus' message and miss the point of what the kingdom of God is about. The preachers of the southern United States justified human slavery as God's will by this means. How does one function as an Amos in a church that has embraced God and country as one reality of capitalism as the Bible's blessed economic system, of a political and economic system that has little compassion for the poor, the weak, and the fleeing immigrants waiting at the gates to the land of security as we justify keeping them out of our country?

If you want to keep your job in a conservative Presbyterian Church in the USA, you dare not call into question the truthfulness of your people's spiritual identity, faithfulness, and morality? There are boundaries and one must build trust and gradually lead the people, even as the white clergy of Alabama counseled Martin Luther King, Jr. I have been grateful for the love, the patience and the tolerance of my congregation while listening to my efforts to be faithful to God as we have together sought to understand, to believe, and to be faithful to the truth of the Word proclaimed through my human insufficiency.

This weekend the New York Times carried the story of an Alabama Southern Baptist preacher, Chris Thomas, who sought to be a prophet on issues of race, poverty, and justice in his small community church. Gradually, with the Advent of Trump, the members had moved from being progressives in the Southern Baptist Convention to being threatened conservatives. A small group of conservatives warned him to stop preaching the social gospel from their pulpit. His sermon from Jesus', "Sermon on the Mount" had been seen as an attack on President Trump.

The warning group said of the Beatitudes, "Those are nice, but we don't have to live by them. It was like; 'You're criticizing our president. You're clearly doing this.'" From thereon, Thomas said, "my words were being measured." The result was that he was forced to resign as the church turned away from the fullness of the New Testament Gospel. *New York Times*, June 20, 2020, *"The Walls of the Church Couldn't Keep the Trump Era Out"*, By Nicholas Casey

On two session retreats I showed the movie *"Mass Appeal"*. Jack Lemon played the older Roman Catholic pastor/priest charged with teaching a young seminarian in training for ordination. This was fine if the young man towed the line in his radical social gospel. But he began to preach against the hypocrisy of the members of the church and their lack of compassion or understanding of the problems of the poor in relation to the rich. Many of the issues of the rich and the poor were addressed in the movie. Literally, the young man was driven from the church by the anger of the privileged establishment mob. He was accused of being gay, and the popular, alcoholic senior priest was pressed to remove the young man.

There were white Protestant pastors who marched in the Civil Rights protests in the 1960's. Some became "Freedom Riders" to the south. When their California church members heard of this back home, they were fired upon return. I was a young pastor in the days of the Civil Rights marches. I did not have the courage to publicly identify with them. I knew what would happen. Max Rafferty, the GOP candidate for the U.S. Senate from California argued that the priests and pastors of America needed to return to their sanctuaries and to get off the streets.

Becoming a prophet has a job description that includes potential persecution and suffering. Over the years I played it safe but tried to push the envelope with full understanding that church members were mature and immature. Nevertheless, if one accepts responsibility for teaching and preaching the scriptures of the Old and New Testaments, the big issues of life will emerge and challenge all of us seeking to live under the authority of the whole Bible and not just our favored canon passages. We dare not do what Thomas Jefferson did and work from a canon within the canon by cutting out the texts we do not accept, or which do not agree with our personal values. One well – known Presbyterian pastor of a large congregation advised his young interns to never preach from the Old Testament.

During Reagan's Presidency the Cold War became hot. There was a nuclear arms race. There were enough nuclear bombs and missiles between east and west that the planet could have been destroyed several times over. Our General Assembly approved a study document named, *Peacemaking: the Believers Calling*. Sessions were asked to affirm a *"Peacemaking Commitment"*. The City Council of Laguna Beach voted for the city to become a nuclear free zone. Many mocked the word "peace". Anti-Communism was rampant in America and within the evangelical church. Presbyterians were divided. *The Confession of 1967* affirmed,

> "God's reconciliation in Jesus Christ is the ground of the peace, justice, and freedom among nations which all powers of government are called to serve and defend. The church, in its own life, is called to practice the forgiveness of enemies and to commend to the nations as practical politics the search for cooperation and peace. This search requires that the nations pursue fresh and responsible relations across every line of conflict, even at risk to national security, to reduce areas of strife and to broaden international understanding. Reconciliation among nations becomes peculiarly urgent as countries develop nuclear, chemical, and biological weapons, diverting their manpower and resources from constructive uses and risking the annihilation of mankind. Although nations may serve God's purposes in history, the church which identifies the sovereignty of any one nation or any one way of life with the cause of God denies the Lordship of Christ and betrays its calling." [8]

This was a prophetic witness to a church and nation in Post – World War II America. 1945 had introduced the nations to the Atomic Age with the dropping of atom bombs on two Japanese cities for the sake of ending the war. President Truman argued that the bomb was necessary to avoid an invasion of mainland Japan. Hundreds of thousands of American lives would have been lost in the invasion. From that moment on the Nuclear Age had arrived and the arms race with the piling up of nuclear weapons began and grew. These weapons had the potential of destroying life on planet earth.

As a child I grew up in Amarillo, Texas. Not many miles away was the site in New Mexico where the first atomic bombs were developed and exploded. In my hometown was a plant called Pantex. Few of the citizens of our city knew that this was the place where all of America's nuclear

---

8. Book of Confessions, C-67, 9.45.

arsenal was assembled. We thought we were safe in the middle of the country in the flat farm and ranch lands. But with the advent of a nuclear war Amarillo would have been a primary target for the Soviets to hit. I remember the school drills of the 1950's when we were required to get under our school desks in case of an atomic attack. Looking back, in such an attack we would all have been annihilated.

The fruit of America's nuclear development has produced the by – products of nuclear waste that is buried in various places, and which will remain destructive of life for thousands of years. If the radiated materials leak from their underground storage containers, the water supplies of the western U.S. would be compromised. Already, the burial of the nation's nuclear waste from atomic bomb tests in the South Pacific in the Marshall Islands is being questioned. "The Dome", as it is called, is believed to be leaking and some are saying that an independent investigator needs to be appointed to determine the safety of the site.

In the 1960's a movie was made named *"Dr. Strangelove: Or How I Learned to Stop Worrying and to Love the Bomb."* It was a comedic satire of our anxiety and fear in the nuclear age. The political ideology of rightwing America was exposed as a form of craziness and paranoia. Who will ever forget the B-52 bombers sent on a false mission to the Soviet Union to drop their atom bombs on their pre-assigned targets not realizing they were releasing the Russian doomsday bomb scenario for planet earth? I showed this movie on a church session retreat only to have some of my staff and elders take offense. Nevertheless, in the 1980's the fear of nuclear annihilation was growing in the heart of America. Many were in denial of the danger. I felt it my responsibility to teach and to preach about this possibility. It was not a popular position to take in the presence of those whose souls had been blinded by a destructive patriotism that was unwilling to face the truth and who had been captured by fear of the Soviet Union.

Of course, the argument for "nuclear deterrence" was used to justify the proliferation of atomic weapons. Many argued that assured destruction for any nation that launched a nuclear attack was what guaranteed peace. Neo-orthodox theologian Reinhold Niebuhr was the father of Christian Realism. The assumption of this Christian worldview was that we live in a fallen world filled with evil and violence. Sin has led us to where we are. Sinful violence must be met with just acts of violence. WWII was a just war because freedom and civilization required that Hitler, the German armies, and Japanese Imperial expansion had to be stopped. Presbyterians have never been Pacifists. We have had a realistic view of what living in a sinful world requires. Nevertheless, the longing for world peace, for *Shalom*, healing, and reconciliation has found expression among many Christians, including Presbyterians.

President Reagan's strategy was to out – spend the Soviets in the competition to build missile systems and defenses for "Star Wars" in space and among nations of differing political and economic ideologies. It could be said that "fear" had driven this international competition. Woe unto any nation that was not prepared to face down nationalistic pride and to deter perceived dangers. After Ronald Reagan left office and George H.W. Bush was elected, in 1989, Soviet dominance began to collapse. Several of the eastern block of nations declared themselves for freedom from Soviet control. Nation after nation saw protests and walls fall. The Berlin Wall fell, and Germany was reunited. The Soviet Union became Russia. The U.S. had won the Cold War. Some declared that it was the end of political oppression in the world and the triumph of democracy. It was a giddy time in which the problems of making and maintaining peace in a violent world were changing. It was hoped that a "peace dividend" would help nations to address social needs.

At the end of *The Magicians Nephew*, C.S. Lewis had Aslan, the Christ-lion, in *The Chronicles of Narnia*, answer Polly's question about the "Deplorable Word" that the witch, the Empress Jadis, used to destroy the world of Charn. The word was a secret, but she used it to destroy her sister and Charn. Polly asked, "But we're not quite as bad as that world, are we, Aslan?"

> "'Not yet, Daughter of Eve,' he said. 'Not yet. But you are growing more like it. It is not certain that some wicked one of your race will not find out a secret as evil as the Deplorable Word and use it to destroy all living things. And soon, very soon, before you are an old man and an old woman, great nations in your world will be ruled by tyrants who care no more for joy and justice and mercy than the Empress Jadis. Let your world beware. That is the warning. Now for the command. As soon as you can, take from this uncle of yours his magic rings and bury them so that no one can use them again.'" [9]

JRR Tolkien's "ring of power" that threatened the peace of the hobbit's world had the same power to guarantee the triumph of evil and of

---

9. Lewis, *Magician's, Nephew*, 194.

anyone that possessed it. At the same time, the ring destroyed its possessor. That is why it had to be destroyed in the one place it could be destroyed. It was this ring that inspired the hobbit's journey to that place in the face of imminent danger. In the final moment, Frodo, who had been commissioned to destroy the ring of power, was overwhelmed by his desire to keep it to exercise its power. Clearly, both Tolkien and Lewis had been shaped by the evils of the 20th century with the rise of totalitarian empires and the violence they released upon civilization and freedom. Power has a seductive dimension which may only be overcome by the power of God's Word and Spirit.

My Dad's Struggles

As the Reagan years were coming to an end my dad was having major health problems. Earlier he had developed prostate cancer and was operated on at UCLA. That solved the prostate problem. His cardio-vascular system was being compromised by progressing diabetes. His eye's retinas were detaching. He developed glaucoma. By age 74 he had gone totally blind. Up to that time Dad had become a gift to many divorced or widowed women. He brought his girl friends to our home for dinner on many occasions. They loved to go dancing in the San Gabriel Valley where he lived in his small trailer. It was a hard time for him. His brother Clarence, "Bud", Tankersley died of cancer. Vivian, my aunt, came to California from Amarillo, Texas, from time to time, to care for her brothers and my grandmother.

Upon the death of their younger brother Fred in New Mexico, while I was a student at Princeton Seminary, my Aunt Vivian became a committed Christian and member of First Baptist Church in Amarillo, Texas. Uncle Fred had never found himself. When he was sober, he would do fine. One night in Albuquerque, N.M., while living with my parents, he participated in a gang fight and was killed by another man with a blow to his head with a tire iron. My Dad threatened to kill the man who hit him. He carried his pistol and stalked the man after he was released from jail. My Dad and Mom called me at Princeton to speak about the tragedy. Dad suggested that he must have done something bad to see his brother die in this way. I assured him that this was not an adequate explanation for what had happened to his brother.

Aunt Vivian was saved from the brokenness of her earlier life, married again, and became, with her husband, John Heket, a leading person in Amarillo and in her church. Vivian became a saint, and I was grateful for the help she gave my dad and many others. John owned Continental Trailways out of Amarillo and was a friend of Jim Lehrer of the PBS Newshour. Jim had Trailways Bus signs posted in his office. He got some of them from my uncle John Heket. In his autobiography Jim spoke of Uncle John as "Heket".

In his blindness I got Dad into Regent's Point in Irvine, but he did not like it. He could not function as a blind person who was also developing dementia. Earlier he received open heart surgery and a five - way bypass. The surgeon told me he had kidney impairment as well. Dad needed constant care and Vivian could not provide it, nor could I. He asked my mother to take him in and care for him in Lubbock. She was not able to do that. I told her not to try. The history of their life together precluded her trying, even though she still loved him in her enabling way. Dad had a girlfriend in Amarillo named Ruby. He asked her to take him in and professed his love for her. She was a good woman. I know they loved dancing together. I was grateful that she was willing to care for Dad in her Amarillo home. Her children liked Dad. I flew with him from LAX to Amarillo. He lived until the age of 77 with Ruby.

A few months before his death my wife and I, together with my sister Vivian Kay, visited Dad at Ruby's house in Amarillo. As the two Kay's comforted my dad in Ruby's living room, I walked outside on that cold northwest Texas late afternoon. The train tracks ran by at the end of the street a few blocks from where I had grown up on Austin Street. I was emotionally hurting. I knew the end was coming. My heart was breaking. I looked up at the cloudy sky with the sun shining through. My soul was comforted, and the peace of God flooded my spirit. I knew it would be ok. My wife came out to get me and said, "Go back into the house and kiss your father goodbye." I did so, but it was one of the hardest moments of my life.

That evening we drove back to Lubbock, 120 miles south of Amarillo. We drove the same highway we had taken hundreds of times in growing up. We got back to my mother's house. We were all upset. My sister lost control of her anger and grief, verbally attacked my wife Kay, stormed around the house, slammed doors, and frightened us. It was not unlike the fights between my mom and dad as we were growing up. Suddenly I was reliving it again. I do not know why she did this, but it was a common experience with my sister. She may have resented the affection my wife was showing to my dad.

My mother was caught in the middle and tried to make peace, but when we left the next morning, I was happy to be going. My mother lamented that I would probably never return, but that was not to be the case. Both Mom and my sister apologized later but the damage had been done to my wife's soul. I did not want her to be exposed to this behavior again. I returned for visits on many occasions over the years. On one occasion, my mom told me that my sister was jealous of me and of my life. For me this was tragic and sad. We had grown up together and been close friends all those years. For whatever reason, after four broken marriages she was unable to do the recovery work she needed to do and withdrew into herself and nurtured her resentments and angers. Her anger destroyed her marriages. She and my dad shared the same anger problem.

Dad went to be with Jesus on April 15, 1991. He was determined to be buried next to his brother Bud at Rose Hills in Southern California. His body was flown back to Rose Hills. He made me promise that I would make sure it was his body in the casket. That was hard for me to do. But I did it and left the viewing room.

I heard my Aunt Vivian lamenting and crying loudly over his casket. These were the cries that had frightened me at my Great Grandmother's funeral when I was a teenager. I hated this. It caused such anxiety and fear in me. Dad's body was taken to the gravesite where my two associates, Larry Coulter and Jeannie Thorndike, conducted the service. Many of our friends from Laguna Beach came to the service and it was such a comfort to us. These transitions have wrenched my soul across the years. I have driven away from many gravesides and wept all the way back to church. Several times my emotions have overwhelmed me at the grave, and I have apologized to others needing my comfort. By in large I learned to discipline my tears and make it through for the sake of crying in private.

Over the years since my dad's death, I have visited his and his brother's gravesite several times. I have found myself speaking with my dad and crying my eyes out. It has been like all the joys and sorrows of our life journey together poured out from the depths of my soul. I guess I had kept it all in and it needed to find expression. Grief is a powerful emotion. We experience many loses over a lifetime. If they are not grieved, we suffer for it.

When my Aunt Vivian died, I was unable to attend her memorial service. By telephone I spoke with her son, my cousin Dick. We both cried our eyes out long distance. She had meant so much to each of us. She was an amazing servant to her family. She prayed for their salvation. She cared in practical ways that I could not. God had done a great work in her heart.

Spiritual Formation

Thankfully, in the early 1980's Kay and I discovered the Stephens Ministry and attended their national seminar at UC Berkeley. Kay, my wife, was theologically trained with excellent pastoral-counseling gifts. Not only that but she had a spirit of compassion and caring. She took it upon herself to train a group of lay Stephen ministers to care about the needy in our LPC congregation. Built into that program was great wisdom in how to listen, to share, and to serve. I was a member of the first group she trained and together we had a very positive impact on the life of our church. After the first wave of Stephen's training, we moved the program to our Board of Deacon's who earlier had organized the congregation into parish units with equal numbers. We desired to build caring and compassion into the membership-fellowship of LPC. Gradually, it happened. Future associate pastors worked with the principles and wisdom of Stephen's as we taught the Deacons to care about members of their parish's.

In the 1980's we embraced the *Disciple* program of the United Methodist Church. My associate pastor and I went to the Disciple orientation, and we enrolled Laguna Presbyterian Church in the one – year study of both Old and New Testaments. I led one selected group and Jeannie Thorndike led the other. Not only was the biblical story reviewed, but also built into the program were spiritual disciplines and the discovery of spiritual gifts. The printed materials taught us, but also the video presentations done by outstanding scholars nurtured our understanding of Scripture with its applications. The first year ended in a retreat at Sierra Retreat Center in Malibu. After a year together in the Word and in Prayer, each member of the group was prayed over, and the larger group affirmed each other's spiritual gifts. It was a powerful time of sharing that was life transforming. When we launched the congregational phase of *Disciple,* Kay facilitated one of those groups in the Gospel of John and the Book of Revelation. Four years later the adult congregation had moved through the four years of Disciple's biblical training. Hundreds of our adult members, just as with the Bethel Bible Study program in the previous decades, had their biblical knowledge and spiritual life built up and empowered for mission. The result was that the congregation became biblically, spiritually, and missionally informed. Many small groups emerged out of this program.

By the late 80's and early 90's I had come to realize that my personal spiritual life was deepening. From my early days as a believer, I had read Scripture and prayed. Many of my prayers were centered on my personal needs and desires. If I had received all the things my prayers asked, I would have been a mess. But of course, God intends us to lift all the concerns of our lives to the heart of God. Jesus' disciples asked him to teach them how to pray. He had powerfully modeled the importance of prayer for his own life. What they received was the Lord's Prayer. (Matthew 6 and Luke 11) Paul the Apostle taught the Roman Christians that we often do not know how to pray. We do not have adequate words and we do not really know what the deep needs and desires of our lives are about. The good news is that the Holy Spirit is searching our hearts and minds and is lifting our prayers, for which we have no words, to the throne of God. (Romans 8:26–27)

On one occasion near the end of my Doctor of Ministry studies at Claremont, I was in James A. Sanders office in the Ancient Biblical Manuscript Library. We were speaking of the promises of God. He made a statement to me that I have never forgotten. He said that even if humans destroyed planet earth that God's promises would yet be fulfilled. I believe what he was saying was that *YAHWEH*, the LORD of Israel, the God and Father of our Lord Jesus Christ, the Creator, Redeemer, and Sustainer of all life, would faithfully transform the Old into the New Creation, that sin and death would be destroyed, with every tear wiped away, with God at the center of the New Heaven and New Earth. That vision of God's kingdom has made all the difference for me. (Revelation 21 and 22)

After 20 years of leading the Laguna Beach Presbyterian Church, the 12 Step program was also leading me into a deeper awareness of my need for a Higher Power daily, moment by moment. Spiritual practices and disciplines were now necessary. They were not just academic interests but were strongly related to my survival as a person, a pastor, a husband, a father, and a man charged with responsibility for many lives. My soul was hungry and thirsty for the living God. (Psalm 42:1–2; Psalm 63; Matthew 5:6) I understood as never before that I needed the Spirit of truth and the grace of God in my heart to sustain and to empower me for the longer journey of discipleship.

I learned that Eugene Peterson was leading a Doctor of Ministry seminar for Fuller Seminary at the Schuller Retreat Center in Mission Viejo. It was called "Spirituality and Ministry". During those two weeks Gene taught a large group of us to pray the prayer book of Israel and of Jesus, *the Book of Psalms*. I learned that Christian leaders and followers of Jesus needed a daily spiritual rule, a discipline of prayer and theological reflection.

The historic rule of many disciples of Jesus was each day to pray Psalms 1, 2, and 5, along with five psalms. In thirty days, one could pray the entire 150 Psalms and then begin anew. Then would come a systematic reading of the New Testament and other spiritual readings. Spiritual and theological reflection would flow from this dialogue and bring fruitfulness to Sunday worship. I have followed this rule since 1991. I am not sure how many times I have prayed through the Psalms, but many times.

Not always did I desire to do this. Many of the Psalms did not seem to address the needs of my soul, yet, as the years have passed the Spirit of God has blessed me with a deepening relationship with God through all the Psalms. Peterson said that the Psalmists were prayer masters. If one desired to learn to pray one would need to be enrolled in the School of Prayer, the Psalms.

Walter Brueggemann suggested that there are three types of psalms: Psalms of Orientation; Psalms of Disorientation, and Psalms of New Orientation.

Psalms of Orientation were prayed by the masters during times in which all was well with them in relationship with God and others. There was an equilibrium and the psalmist felt on solid ground. It was a time of shalom, peace, and well-being. Who of us does not long for these times? However, Brueggemann argued that these were not times of imaginative praying.

Psalms of Disorientation were prayed by the masters when life had lost its equilibrium. Perhaps the psalmist was ill or had lost a valued relationship. These were psalms prayed when the writer was in trouble and perhaps anguished with suffering and depression. Maybe they were prayed when the people of Israel were surrounded by their enemies and were filled with fear. The one who prayed was walking through a dark valley and his or her future or the future of Israel was being called into question. These prayers became exilic prayers of the people of Israel enslaved in Babylon. (Psalm 137) There were times of anger and grief when God seemed unresponsive to those who prayed, or life seemed unfair. Often the psalmist had failed or fallen into sin and the burdens of guilt and shame were heavy. In fact, the prayer masters of Israel were not afraid to pray every longing of their lives or the life of the people of Israel.

This reality gave me permission to pray the truth of my life and my experience. If the masters had done this, was it not okay for me to pray in this way? For me this was liberating and has given me courage to cry out. On the evening of 9-11-01, the people of Laguna Beach gathered in our sanctuary, and we prayed Psalm 46 in a moment in which America had been attacked by terrorists who crashed the airplanes into the World Trade Center towers. (More on this later)

God knows all about me and us from beginning to end. God searches for us and within us. Nothing may be hidden. Thankfully, the one who searches is good and knows the plans he has for us, to give us a future with hope. (Psalm 139, Jeremiah 29)

Psalms of New Orientation were prayed by the masters with thanksgiving for new beginnings, of the experience of forgiveness, restoration of faith, hope, and love.

One may find the footprints of the Scriptures in the life of Jesus. The Old Testament Scriptures, and especially the Psalms had shaped Jesus' identity and destiny. I believe Jesus had prayed the Psalms into his heart and mind. This has become my deepest desire, to be shaped and formed in my relationship with God through the prayers of Jesus that he learned at Joseph and Mary's knees, in his synagogue and in the Jerusalem Temple. All 150 Psalms have shaped the liturgy of both Israel and Church. Powerful worship and personal devotion have been inspired by the Psalms and of course, all are parts of the biblical canon. These Psalms have moved me to "pray without ceasing". Peace has come to my restless heart over and over and after 30 years of praying the Psalms daily I bear witness to the Holy Spirit's gift of a new mind, the mind of Christ. This is one of the great gifts of my life journey. I have not arrived at perfection, but I am on the way by the grace of God. (Philippians 3) It was no accident that Reformed Protestant worship life was informed by the Psalter of Israel and Jesus.

With the books of Peterson and Brueggemann a deepening desire has developed in my heart to know God and to bring my human, imperfect story into dialogue with the poetry and passions of the Psalmists. The Psalms began to capture my life at the Princeton Summer Institute of

Theology in 1990. James L. Mays, the author of the *Interpretation Commentary on the Psalms*, introduced us anew to the Psalter. Through it all, I have concluded that the Lord is more interested in what is happening in my heart, mind, and behavior than in what any geographical, professional move to satisfy my ego might inspire within me.

Remaining in Laguna Beach and being the pastor of Laguna Presbyterian Church for 46 years has allowed the Word and the Spirit of God to form the mind of Christ within me. It almost sounds haughty, if not arrogant, to write such a thing. The biblical narrative and literature of the Bible have opened my mind to be shaped and formed in the image of Christ. Is this not what the Apostle Paul promised in Romans 8 and 12, and in 1 and 2 Corinthians, Galatians, Ephesians, Colossians, and Philippians?

Learning to pray the Scriptures and the prayers of the Psalter have led to the transformation of my life from one degree of glory to another. (2 Corinthians 3:12–18) C.S. Lewis taught about the believer's daily work of getting up and dressing up like Christ. The promise is, he said, that we will one day look like him from the inside out. In the process we pretend to be "little Christ's", all the while knowing that we are not Christ. Of course, God is the one who is pretending. I did not know how necessary and how deep the transformation would be. I thought I might be in for a little cosmetic face lift, but no. The LORD was more interested in a complete remodel of my life. He was at work building up, tearing down, pushing out, and totally renewing my humanity. It has hurt, but also been necessary.[10]

I have been like Lewis's Eustace in *The Voyage of the Dawn Treader*. One morning Eustace awakened to discover that his inner foul spirit had become manifest as an external physical dragon. What was worse was that he could not strip the dragon scales from himself to rediscover his essential boy. One night the lion Aslan, the Christ figure in the Chronicles came to Eustace in his desperation and powerlessness with the word that He alone could strip the scales from the little dragon for Eustace to recover the human he was intended to be. The Lion plunged his claws deep into the layers of dragon skin and removed them, layer after layer, literally pealing him until all that was left was the small boy. At last, the little boy was restored. The Lion took him, bathed, and baptized him in a pool of water and his sore body was comforted and healed. Then the

---

10. Lewis, *Mere Christianity*, Book 4, Chapter 7.

Lion clothed him in new clothing and brought him to the community of friends who had been searching for him to continue their mission on the seas of Narnia seeking for lost seafarers.

After the stripping, Eustace was still the boy he had been. He could still be troublesome to his shipmates, but they were able to overlook his remaining imperfections because they could see that the healing had begun. This is the truth of the Church fellowship of justified and sanctified sinners. The journey of transformation has begun. We still struggle with the old self-centeredness of sin, yet we know that Christ won the victory for our salvation by his death upon the cross. Because he has been raised and is alive at the right hand of the Father, we are forgiven and filled with his Spirit. We are dying to sin from the moment of our baptism into Christ. Through walking in his Spirit and abiding in his Word, slowly, over a lifetime, the dragon skins of our enslaved humanity are being stripped from us. [11]

"Beloved, we are God's children now. What we will be has not yet been revealed. What we do know is this: when he is revealed, we will be like him, for we will see him as he is. And all who have this hope in him purify themselves, just as he is pure." (1 John 3:1–3)

We have already, through faith, been adopted into the family of Christ. To shift the metaphor, we have become citizens of the kingdom of God. The truth is that we live between the *"already and the not yet"* of the kingdom. During this interim journey from the earthly city to the City of God, we are coming to trust that one day we shall have arrived in the fullness of time at the celestial City of God where God dwells, where sin and death are no more and where every tear has been washed away, and where love will be perfect. Our baptism will be complete. Upon that arrival we will have received "new faces" and will have become "like Christ". We will clearly see the ultimate love of reality from which we have never been separated. What began in the Shadowlands will come to reality "further up and further in". (*The Last Battle*, C.S. Lewis; also, *The Great Divorce*)

Mission on Our Doorstep

In the 1980's the Lord brought Dr. John Chandler to be the executive pastor of the Presbytery of Los Ranchos. John was a church developer, and he came with a pastoral vision. He visited the pastors of the Presbytery

---

11. Lewis, *The Voyage of the Dawn Treader*, Book 5, Chapter 7, 99–113.

and allowed us to share our joys and our sorrows with him. He always wore a train engineer's Levi jacket and drove an old model car. During the 1980's he came with support and encouragement for me and helped me as a person, a pastor, and a spiritual father. On behalf of the Presbytery, he found Dr. Madison Hinchman, "Skip", a Ph.D. Social Worker from USC to help the struggling pastors of the Presbytery. Skip saved the lives and ministries of several our Presbytery pastors. When Skip unexpectedly died, his wife called, and during our grief we held a memorial service for him at LPC. John Chandler came and preached.

John brought a vision for evangelism and new church development to Los Ranchos. In one of the fastest growing parts of the U.S. our Presbytery had not established a new church for over a decade. John had added an associate executive, Tim Hart-Anderson, to work along with him and the Presbytery. They brought in Robert Worley from McCormick Seminary to study the area. In the process Dr. Worley met with me. He shared that Laguna Presbyterian Church's parish was an island. On the west was the Pacific Ocean and on the east were the coastal hills and greenbelt. The population growth was inland and there were only two roads into Laguna Beach from the growth area. He shared that our staff would need to work 2 to 3 times harder than any other staff just to maintain our church size of 700 members. This was discouraging for me and for us because we had an expansive vision of Laguna Niguel being in our parish. From that area we were already drawing new members. Worley was very affirming. He said that if he could move our staff inland to the population that we would build a congregation of 5000.

The truth was that God was bringing the world to our doorstep. The inland area was a vast mission field populated by diverse people from many ethnic backgrounds and religions. It was ripe for harvest. We needed new churches planted. And of course, Laguna Niguel was first on the list. I protested on the floor of Presbytery, but the new church was approved anyway. The Presbytery was asking for us to transfer some of our Niguel members to be charter members of the new church. Very soon I understood that all our South County parishes were overlapping and that people boundaries could not be easily maintained. Yet Laguna's future was being limited by geographical boundaries, but also by the demographics of the south coast. Our parish was not the Bible belt! It would require long-term relationship and trust building to make inroads into secular and materialistic lives. There was spiritual, New Age type interests, but the mainline churches in Laguna Beach were struggling. This was the challenge.

I made my peace with this. We supported the new church, transferred some of our members, and joined in helping to raise $10 million dollars for the needed new developments and redevelopments within Los Ranchos. Eventually, Laguna Church gave around $1 million dollars for this outreach. During this time, we helped staff several surrounding congregations. Vickie Orr, our Christian Educator who had graduated from Fuller, was called to be an associate pastor at Mission Viejo. Craig Williams, my associate, was called as the new church developer in Trabuco Canyon. Dee Hazen, our Adult Educator, joined the staff at Laguna Niguel and later at San Clemente Presbyterian. We were reaching beyond ourselves to address the mission challenge with our financial and people resources. All the while the Laguna Church continued to maintain and to prosper. This was an exciting time for me.

In 1990 I was elected Moderator of the Presbytery of Los Ranchos. During my Moderator time John Chandler retired and moved away. Tim Hart-Anderson went to San Francisco to pastor Old First Church. I served for a year and a half as Moderator. In 1991 John Huffman asked me to manage his standing for Moderator of the General Assembly meeting in Baltimore. Several of us went to Baltimore with John to support his effort. Sadly, during this time John's daughter was terminally ill and he needed to withdraw from the race. Again, the G.A. was confronted with a human sexuality report that advocated the ordination of homosexuals if they met all the requirements. A lengthy study was presented to the larger church. The debate on the floor of G.A. was intense and there was much conflict and pain. The recommendations of the report were not supported by the G.A.s vote and many of us felt the church had dodged another threat to our institutional/theological identity. But this issue was not to go away either for our church or for our nation.

The world was on our doorstep with all its challenges and there was a growing sense that the Presbyterian Church in the U.S.A. needed to affirm that *Theology Matters* and that our commitment to biblical authority would guide us into the truth, not only in areas like ordination, but in many other issues before our society. In 1993 the question of Reformed theology and the identity of the PCUSA rose to the surface in the Re-Imagining Conference in Minneapolis. Feminist theology was beginning to demand that the church rethink its biblical and theological vocabulary for the sake of more inclusive affirmations of the role of women in the life and mission of the church. The ecumenical conference spoke of God in feminine terms. "Sophia" and "milk and honey" terminology was lifted at the communion table and in the media as ways of thinking and speaking about God.

The PCUSA had little financial investment in the Re-Imagining Conference, but some of our national staff were involved in the leadership. The Presbyterian Layman publication that was always sniffing out apostacy in the PCUSA published troubling critiques and called into question our denominations commitment to our Confessional history. There was a huge uproar across the church.

Even in our own Presbytery, Jim Brown, the head of the PCUSA mission agency, had to confront a troubled meeting seeking to explain that "theology" still matters. Kay, my wife, had the courage to ask Jim a critical question at the Los Ranchos Presbytery gathering. She was deeply troubled by the language for God at the Minneapolis gathering. At the G.A. meeting in Albuquerque, N.M., Jim lost his job along with Mary Ann Lundy who had been a prime mover at the Re-imagining gathering. In Albuquerque my covenant group went to dinner at a restaurant to discuss what had occurred only to have Jim Brown and his support group seated a few booths away from us. We were embarrassed for him. Jim went on to pastor a church until retirement. I came to know his son in Laguna Beach when they came for pre-marital preparation. I invited Jim to officiate the wedding as he did later at the baptism of his grandchild

It is important for me to say that I fully support equal rights for women. Women bring special gifts to leadership within the church. Theologically, in Christ, male and female are reconciled and made one, each with specific gifts for the body of Christ. (Galatians 3:27–28; 1 Corinthians 12:12–13) In my experience, it has been the gifted women in the churches that I have served that have made the difference. It would trouble me to think of a church being led exclusively by men. Historically, women have been marginalized by patriarchal systems and cultural prejudices to keep them out of leadership. All we must do is to follow the example of Jesus in how he depended upon women and who was a liberator of women from bondage to male domination. However, the Re-imagining Conference was not helpful for serious theological/biblical study of roles of men and women in the church. It led to a painful time that further divided the church into camps of advocacy.

It played into the later controversy caused by a Presbyterian pastor's question in a sermon, "What's the Big Deal about Jesus?" Many tried to answer the question, as did I. Clearly the national church was building toward a major theological debate and possible schism. At St. Andrews in Newport Beach, Associate Pastor Bill Flanagan preached a powerful and popular sermon on Jesus and why Jesus remains a Big Deal for the Reformed tradition.

In 1992 I was elected from our Presbytery to be a commissioner to the G.A. in Milwaukee, Wisconsin. The big issue in that Assembly was abortion rights. A major study advocating freedom of choice had been presented and the G.A. approved it. Late one evening an effort was made by gay rights advocates to reverse the previous G.A.'s vote on ordination rights for gays and lesbians. It was late at night, and everyone was tired and unprepared to vote on such a divisive issue. The motion was almost approved. From that evening I realized that the PCUSA would continue to struggle with sexual identity and role issues until one side or the other had won a decisive vote. The lines were drawn, and the political battle was engaged that continued for the next decade plus. Once again it was conservatives versus liberals and the polarization in church and culture grew.

Of course, the media reported the conflicts in our national church and Presbyterian pastors had to interpret what had occurred. The tensions increased between the progressive and conservative groups within the larger church. These were still being played out in the first decade of the new millennium. (More later)

World Mission

When Jeanne Thorndike was called as our associate pastor, she brought the *"Discover the World"* program. The founder of DTW and his wife came and taught the curriculum that required an urban plunge into L.A. for the sake of raising our awareness of mission challenges to the church. Kay and I participated in this. It made a huge impact in our church.

Soon we explored a connection with Frank Alton's *Partner's in Hope* program in the poor parts of Mexico City. Kay and I joined others from our church in a visit with Frank and Judy Alton who had embraced Liberation Theology and were working among the poor of the city. Our consciousness was raised about the challenges of doing the mission of Christ among dear folks whom we grew to love. It was a life changing experience for which I was deeply grateful. One evening we were required to spend the night with a Mexican family. I had a cold and tried to get out of it. I was afraid. Frank asked me if I was afraid of allowing a poor family to care for me. And of course, this was true. I took the leap of faith. Kay and I visited, slept together on the family's couch, ate their food, and grew to love this family. After graduation from Whitworth College, our son Jeff lived for 7 months with this family.

While there we learned that Helen and Mark Pines' son, Tim, had been lost in a snow avalanche on Mt. Baldy. Mark never got over the loss of his son. He was my tennis partner and a committed Christian and elder in our church. From that time on I watched Mark be physically broken by his grief. I loved Mark and Helen and I shared their grief. Tim had been in our high school group; had graduated from Whitworth College, married, and had become the father of a son. His memorial service was at San Clemente Presbyterian Church where Tim and Becky were members.

Laguna Presbyterian Church sent several mission teams to work with the folks in the Ajusco of Mexico City. We helped to rebuild an orphanage. The church made it possible for our Mexican friends to visit us and other churches in our Presbytery. This was an enriching partnership and we have been grateful for it. We made lifetime friends with many and have enjoyed fellowship in our exchanges. To be sure we came back from Mexico seeing our community in new ways.

Later, Frank and Judy Alton returned to Southern California having done a wonderful mission work in Mexico. He was called to become the pastor of Immanuel Presbyterian Church in Los Angeles. He seemed a fit for this challenging post. His parents had been members of LPC, and we had formed strong family connections with Frank and his first wife. When his dad, John, died, I conducted his memorial service at LPC. To our surprise, Frank and Judy divorced. Later, he left Immanuel, and I learned that he had come out as gay and had a partner. Frank never spoke with me about this. It just happened. In the process he became an Episcopal priest and serves in Los Angeles. I am grateful that his rich life experience is being used in pastoral ministry. His mother transferred to Geneva Presbyterian Church in Laguna Hills. For reasons I do not understand people come and go through our lives. Friends disappear and we may be left with questions that will not be answered in this life. I still think of myself as Frank's friend. As I have felt on many occasions, life is difficult and who knows what is going on in any of our lives. Thank God that the LORD understands and will one day join us in joyful reunion.

In 1990 we read about the Romanian Orphanage crisis and the fall of the Marxist Romanian government in 1989. I received a call from Gary Dennis of the La Canada Presbyterian Church. He invited me to be a part of a mission discovery trip with representatives from six PCUSA congregations. They included Laguna Beach, La Canada, Danville Presbyterian in northern California, Christ Church Edina in Minnesota, Colonial in Kansas City, and Memorial Drive in Houston. As it turned out we traveled with World Vision personnel and representatives of the World Council of Churches.

In November 1991 we flew into Bucharest and on into Cluj, Transylvania, Romania. The L.A. Times and the Orange County Register covered our project as the six churches joined to help rebuild an orphanage in Cluj. In the process we visited Romanian Orthodox churches and Reformed Churches, along with their seminary. Many children had been warehoused in orphanages around Romania. The children had nurse maids but had not often been picked up or emotionally bonded. Their physical, intellectual, and emotional growth was stunted. We decided to send a delegation made up from our six churches to build a new playground for the children and to help rebuild parts of the building. Through our first group we carried computers and medical programs to give to the university medical school. They had not been allowed to receive post – World War II medical information from the West. One can imagine the blessing the information was for Romania. As we boarded the small Romanian airplane to travel to Cluj from Bucharest, I do not remember seat belts. The stewardess brought us each a small glass of whiskey which we downed before departure. Thankfully, we arrived in Cluj safely.

The cities we visited were unsafe for western travelers. We saw long bread lines. Not long before our visit to Bucharest, World Vision representatives were attacked outside our hotel, and one was killed. Political and economic oppression was evident. I walked through the restaurant in the hotel on a way to a meeting and saw beautiful women staring at me from their tables. I realized they were prostitutes seeking to make a deal. The Iron Curtain had fallen, and freedom was coming to the former Soviet Bloc of countries. The Communist dictator, Nicola Ceausescu, had been arrested and publicly executed a short time before our visit. In the Cluj hotel some of my clothes were stolen from my room.

After we completed our visit to Cluj and we left Bucharest, I had a terrible cold. It was in November 1991 and winter was in full force as we landed in Vienna, Austria. That evening our group walked the downtown part of Vienna and visited St. Stephens Cathedral while it was snowing. Later, we enjoyed a wonderful German dinner with large mugs of beer. I slept well that night. The next morning Gary Dennis and I were on our way to L.A. It seemed that God was opening doors for mission not only on our doorstep, but also in Mexico and Romania.

Panic Attack

It was in the springtime of 1991 that I was not feeling well driving from Skip Hinchman's office in El Toro. By the time I was in Laguna Hills my heart was beating rapidly and I felt faint. I thought I was having a heart attack and I drove myself to the emergency room of Saddleback Hospital. They took me in immediately and tried with Valium to relax me. It did not work. My heart continued to race. They knocked me out for an hour of sleep. When I awakened, my heart rate was normal. I put my clothes on and was introduced to a psychiatrist who said I had experienced a panic or anxiety attack. His first question for me was whether I had ever contemplated suicide. That frightened me. He said he thought I was mildly depressed and anxious. I had not had a heart attack, but my body was stressed out. I visited with this good doctor several times talking about my life.

He gave me Xanax and asked me to take some time off. I did a wedding on the following Saturday at the Five Crowns Restaurant in Corona del Mar. To make it through I took half tablets of Xanax and I stayed calm. Then Kay and I left for a couple of days in Palm Desert. I continued to have bouts of rapid heartbeats. It made me feel terrible. Anxiety and fear would overwhelm me. I could feel the pressure of cars bearing down on me in Laguna Canyon. Sunday mornings I had a small Xanax pill in my shirt pocket to take in an emergency. I went to my Al-anon group and shared what was going on with me. The following Sunday I shared with the congregation in my sermon about the panic attack. Many came up to me after the service to say they had experienced the same. That was comforting. The sharing relieved my anxiety and fear. Over time the symptoms diminished. The following summer we did one of our long back packs in the High Sierras. That was the best medicine of all.

All of this was brought on by family and church stresses. The largest Presbyterian Church in Lincoln, Nebraska, the capital of the State, the church to which the Governor belonged, was in pursuit of me to accept their call to become their pastor. The University of Nebraska was nearby. I could teach there and have a ministry with faculty and students. I almost accepted, but in the final analysis could not bring myself to do that, even though it was tempting. I had told myself that I would see Jeff through high school in Laguna Beach and then consider a move. Thankfully, after much prayer and reflection I knew I could not move at that time. I needed to relax and to surrender my life and my will to the care of God and stop trying to control my future. My life was in God's care. God was good and could be trusted to make it clear the plans he had for me. At that moment the place was Laguna Beach. The peace of God calmed me.

Presbytery International Mission Leadership

By this time the Presbytery of Los Ranchos had entered a partnership with the Protestant churches around Miraj, India, and the Wanless Mission Hospital there. Nearly 100 years before, Dr. Wanless had felt the call to minister in Miraj. When he arrived in Bombay, he met a departing missionary who told him that he might as well return to the United States since India was totally unreceptive to the Christian religion. Dr. Wanless pressed on and planted a medical mission in Miraj that developed into a major Christian hospital for that part of India.

It was time for the Presbytery's second mission team to travel to Miraj and to Sangli and to the Richardson Leprosy Hospital where we were building a village of houses for the families of recovering lepers. The Presbytery asked me to be the pastoral leader of the group along with Dick Grace, a ruling elder from Trinity Church in Santa Ana. We flew to Hong Kong and on to Bombay or Mumbai. I will never forget the night we arrived. As we were loading our bags on to the bus at the airport, a young boy who was crippled pleaded with us for money. The darkness and the poverty we saw in the streets on the way to our five - star hotel in Bombay were overwhelming. The hotel was hosting weddings of very wealthy families who drove up to the hotel in Rolls Royce's while people were lying in the streets outside suffering and dying in their poverty. The contrast between wealth and poverty had never been more visible, not even in Mexico City.

The next morning, we went to the train station in Bombay. It was raining heavily. Our group took cover under the arches of the station as a woman with a Cobra snake walked in front of us with the snake coming out from its basket. A controller was directing her from across the street and they were seeking to intimidate us to give. Dick Grace had a snake phobia and began to shout at the woman. Finally, she retreated, and we entered the train station. What we saw and smelled was almost sickening. People were lying in their own excrement in the lobby of the station. It was unbearable.

We were supposed to travel by train first class 300 miles to Miraj. But the first – class car had been canceled and we were placed in the lowest class section with open windows, smelly toilets nearby, with stops at every small city where maimed beggars stretched their faces and arms into our compartments seeking money. By the time we arrived in Miraj we were all undone. Our hosts greeted us at the Miraj train station, and we were bused to the Fletcher Mission Compound near the hospital. Archie and Hulda Fletcher had given their lives for the medical mission work in Wanless Hospital. They were now retired and living at the Presbyterian Retirement Center in Duarte, California. They came and met with our group before we left the U.S. They were people of great and humble faith and they had made a difference over many years. They had given the missionary retreat center near the hospital.

I had come to know of the work of Presbyterian missionaries in India through the visitation in Laguna Beach of Nancy Ramer. She, and her husband Robert, had founded the industrial trade school in Sangli, not far from Miraj. This was the place of the Richardson Leprosy Hospital. The Laguna Presbyterian Church had supported the development of the trade school and the ministry of the Ramer's. Bob Ramer had needed surgery and had it at the Wanless Hospital. The anesthesiologist had mistakenly placed a tube down his throat and Bob died on the operating table. Nancy had retired to Minnesota.

In visiting the hospital, I saw first-hand why no westerner would want to be a patient in that hospital. We saw blood and urine in the stairwells. The cleanliness of the hospital was far less than a western medical center. They treated every form of medical problem, from cobra bites to childbirth. They had an orthopedic unit and a psychiatric hospital. As we toured the hospital, we saw an aging cobalt radiation machine for the treatment of cancer. On the wall behind the machine was a painting with the resurrected Jesus Christ standing projecting the light of God's healing love through the radiation scope. I will never forget that painting and its witness to me of the source of healing power, Jesus Christ, the Light of the World.

At the Fletcher Mission Center, we slept under mosquito nets in bunk beds. At night the compound guards walked the property with their poles pounding the ground to scare off Cobra snakes. The kitchen help boiled our water each day and we took it to the work site. In three weeks, we added several rock houses to the village and dedicated them in the name of our Presbytery churches. Three were dedicated by LPC. It was hard work, but it was a life changing experience.

On two occasions we did field trips. One trip was led by Dr. Kalindi Thomas. She guided us as part of the hospitals outreach to surrounding villages. I learned that a high percentage of the citizens of India lived in these poverty – stricken villages. Their stoves were not ventilated, and the people breathed noxious fumes of smoke. Those fumes were causing lung diseases. Likewise, the people lived with their animals, with the waste of their cows. Health education and birth contraception were important parts of the education program. Childbirth kits were made available for the villagers. Medical care was provided for ill people. These visits were touching.

On another day we were taken to the large city of Kolhapur, India, to visit a Hindu Temple. This was a real religious cultural shock. Poor people were bringing gifts of food into the dark altar room where a Hindu priest wrapped in red was taking their offerings and placing them on the altar. In the darkness there was no sense of joy, but rather of fear. When we left, we visited the estate of a Maharaja from years before. It was a reminder of the divide between the rich and the poor. I was lucky to make the trip because I had come down with the monsoon flu. Several of us had contracted it and were running fevers. I had to go to bed for a couple of days and take antibiotics. Dr. Cherian Thomas visited me and assured me I would get well. There were two or three who were overwhelmed by culture shock and were unable to leave the mission compound. They too recovered.

One day we visited a wedding venue and enjoyed a wonderful Indian wedding feast. On one of the Sundays, I preached at a local church in Miraj and was translated to the congregation. On some afternoons we visited the huts and hovels of the families who were living next to the Richardson Leprosy Hospital. During our work breaks we would enter the hospital and have tea with their staff. We met some very special people.

Kalindi took several of us to downtown Sangli to visit a jewelry store. On the street outside the store, we saw a huge elephant being ridden down the street. I discovered that Indians highly value gold jewelry. It is a way of investing. I bought Kay a wedding necklace. She liked it very much.

Dr. Provakha Samson, who was the director of the Leprosy Hospital, taught us much about leprosy (Hansen's Disease). It can be healed with antibiotics. Sadly, healed lepers would return to work their fields. Walking in the soil they would contract the bacteria and need to be repeatedly treated. He shared that one of the great blessings of life would be in allowing a leper to touch you. He later went to work as the Director of the International Leprosy Mission organization.

One Sunday morning I was asked to preach in the hospital chapel. Dr. Samson chose the text from Luke 17. I read the text and then I was to interpret it to the recovering lepers seated on the floor around me. Dr. Samson interpreted my words. It was the story of ten lepers who were healed by Jesus. On their way to see the local priest they discovered themselves clean of the disease. They all rejoiced, but only one returned to give thanks to Jesus and he was a Samaritan, a foreigner.

At the end of the worship service the recovering lepers, small persons seated on the floor, crawled to me to touch me. I nearly came unglued with emotion. It was as if they were saying "thank you" for coming to us with the Word, with love and healing. I will never forget their gratitude. On another occasion we distributed rice we had purchased. The line to receive the rice ran around the block. The looks on their faces and the expressions of thanksgiving blessed me more than anything I could have ever given. It was a life transforming experience of gratitude expressed in the smiles and tears of those who received the food.

In preparation for the trip, I wrote a study guide entitled, *"The Journey to India"*. I built it around the central section of Luke's Gospel and the mission of God through Jesus. I had our team read the novel, *City of Joy*, that had been made into a movie. It was the story of a Catholic priest's mission to Calcutta, India. Over time and with much suffering he became bonded with the poor of the city and worked with Mother Theresa. The story of compassion, suffering, and the call of Christ was moving. Along with the novel I assigned Lesslie Newbigin's book, *The Gospel in a Pluralistic World*. Newbigin had given 40 years of his life to India as a United Church missionary from the UK. He was brilliant and his book stirred my deep interest in God's mission through Christ and the Church in a broken, pluralistic world. Daily I taught our group from the study guide. Newbigin summed up the need of the world and the call of Christ's church: "The world is still waiting to see a church that not only believes the gospel, but also lives it."

The sights, sounds, smells, and life of the people of India became real to our group. Thankfully, the group had a First – Class overnight train from Miraj to Bombay. I slept from time to time. The following Sunday I preached at the First Methodist Church of Bombay. It was an Independence Day Celebration. I was given a text to preach from and I preached from my heart to the dear people gathered during their nation's celebration. In Bombay we visited the Jain Temple, but also the outdoor cemetery where human corpses were placed in the open air in high places where huge birds would feed upon them until they were devoured.

On our return to the U.S., we spent two nights in Bangkok, Thailand. Our hotel was on the river and named the Shangri La. It was luxurious. We toured the city. On one evening Dick Grace and I rented a small taxi and went to the Red-Light district. Time Magazine had written of it in one of their magazines before we left home. It was an amazing experience. From foot boxing in open bars, to male and female prostitution, everything was for sale. On the street we were offered a visit to a brothel of young boys who were selling themselves to foreigners. It was sickening, yet it was an important experience for us to see.

Upon our return to Laguna Beach the first Sunday our group wore their Indian cloths purchased in Miraj. As it turned out Dr. Samson was visiting, and we had him to our home for lunch. What a special man of God who hosted us at the Richardson Leprosy Hospital and who witnessed to us of his faith in Christ. Not long after we returned, Bonnie Changstrom, a church member who recently died at age 97, presented me with a picture of a woman for whom we had built a house. The picture looks like a painting, and it hung for many years at the entrance of my church office. Now it is at the entrance of our home. It is an expression of Bonnie's faith, hope, and love, and of her love for God's mission in the world. I treasure the picture. I do not know the woman's name, but I know the sense of gratitude she had for the gift of a place for her family while at the hospital.

The Laguna Beach Fire

On October 27, 1993, Laguna Beach and surrounding communities were devastated by a fire blown by a hot, strong, Santa Ana wind. Most of the north end of Laguna Beach had to be evacuated. We packed three of our cars with everything we thought necessary from our home. I assumed that night that our neighborhood on Top of the World would be in ashes the next morning. On the evening of the fire, I left the church office in downtown Laguna Beach at 6 p.m. The houses on the hills above the church and Laguna's City Hall were beginning to explode. The dark smoke was funneling down onto Forest Ave. and blowing toward Main Beach. In our part of Orange County 400 houses were lost that evening.

Kay and I spent the night at Jeannie Thorndike's home in Laguna Niguel. The next morning, I was able to hitch a ride with a police officer into downtown Laguna Beach and then with Gary Unger riding in the back of his pickup truck as we moved through the neighborhoods that were in ashes.

A group of our leadership people from the church called a public meeting for the community in our church sanctuary. Quickly, with the leadership of Ed Sauls, John Moore, and many others, the city mobilized. Twenty of our church families had lost their homes. Our church facilities became the recovery center for the city. The Youth Center was filled with representatives of organizations who were there to meet with people in need. Fellowship Hall was filled with furniture and clothing. Local restaurants provided emergency food. All the churches in town rallied. From counseling, to clothing, to food, to housing, to money, provision was made for human need. It was an amazing display of compassion. Buddhists came from Monrovia to distribute checks for $300.00. The Salvation Army was there. Insurance groups were present. Local relators counseled those in search for a temporary place to live. This went on for weeks.

I had airline tickets to go to my mother's 80th birthday party in Lubbock, Texas. David Tomlinson, our Presbytery Executive, suggested I ought not to go because I was needed in Laguna Beach. Kay went to Lubbock to represent me at the birthday party. The Sunday morning after the fire the sanctuary was jammed. Television stations and newspaper reporters were present. My words were inadequate, but I was present. We were all present together and people were comforted in their fear and grief. Presbyterian Disaster Relief sent $10,000.00 to help people. World Vision sent money to us for the relief effort. We were now on the receiving end of mission.

By the first of December 1993 a pall of depression descended upon the City. I thought we would have a spiritual revival because of the church's leadership in the City's time of need. My aunt Vivian Heket from Amarillo, Texas, came for a visit. She was a comfort for us. Our house was safe. The neighborhood did not burn, but we were all in grief caused by the ruin of large parts of our city and the surrounding areas.

The Year of Africa

Soon after our return from India, Bill Flanagan, and I, with representatives of Trinity Church in Santa Ana, began to plan for the Presbytery's Africa mission. The PCUSA had designated 1994 as our denominations "Year of Africa". Los Ranchos was beginning a partnership with the Presbytery of Limuru just north of Nairobi, Kenya. Flan, Dave Tomlinson, our Presbytery Executive, and Dick Grace from Trinity in Santa Ana were to travel with a team of members from Los Ranchos churches to negotiate the partnership. I was a member of the team.

Our group stayed at the Serena Hotel in Nairobi. One Sunday I preached at the Bahiti Martyr's church where Jesse Kamau was pastor. At the time, Bernard Muindi was Moderator of the PCEA. He and Eunice, his wife, invited Flan, Kay, and I, to their home in Nairobi for dinner. It was a wonderful reunion of old seminary friends.

Our leadership group met with Limuru representatives at the Serena Hotel to negotiate the partnership. We listened to their perceived needs and how we might help them. Together we decided to finance water wells, help build schools, and orphanages. We met with World Vision leadership and considered working with them, but the Limuru people wanted to arrange the water drilling with another group. The search for water resulted in several productive wells. Water was provided for drinking, irrigation, and for selling. The result was that enough money was raised to build some new churches in Tanzania.

After a short visit to Massa Mari, we returned to Limuru. On Saturday evening Kay and I were guests of the Lari Parish. The large living room of the manse was filled with members of the Parish. Women provided food. The only light came from oil lamps. After dinner the women were invited to enter the living space for the evening conversation. Kay and I were the only two white people in the room. We were in the middle of Africa among very poor people who were fellow Presbyterians. During a time of questions and our answering we were asked interesting, personal, intimate questions about ourselves, our church, our family, and why we had only one son?

I grew up in West Texas in a racist culture in which a white man would not have crossed the cultural barrier to be on the other side of town. I confess I felt some anxiety and fear for the two of us. They had purchased a new mattress for us, but there was no running water. The next morning the women of the parish were in the backyard cooking breakfast on an open fire. Without a shower, I dressed in the suit I had brought and preached in the church with a bad cold. We made it through, but it was stressing. While there, the Presbyterian Women's Guild invited Kay to speak to them. She did a wonderful job, and I was very proud of her. After our return home, we learned that the pastor had been removed from the Lari parish because of sexual misconduct.

Early in our visit in Limuru our group met with a team of their Presbytery at a retreat center. We shared dinner in a large hall. Following the dinner time, Pastor Joseph Iteri, the moderator of their Presbytery, spoke to the group. He began by calling our attention to the opened beamed ceiling with a wooden cross hanging over us. He said that because of our history we could only be together in fellowship under the cross. At the cross of Jesus, he poured out his blood to make atonement for our sins and to reconcile us to God and to one another. I was deeply moved by his words. He was right. Dividing walls of hostility were broken down and we were incorporated into one body of Christ as brothers and sisters of Christ. We were black and white, but Jesus had made peace. Thus, was launched the new humanity indwelt by the Holy Spirit.

During the next fall Limuru sent a delegation to visit in Los Ranchos. Joseph stayed with us in our house. His parish was economically poor, and he was a humble man. He graciously accepted our wealth and shared with us the love of Christ. Their team visited most of the churches of our Presbytery. It was a great exchange of hospitality by members of one body of Christ.

Social and Political Challenges of the 1990's

After Iraq's invasion of Kuwait in 1991 President George H.W. Bush announced that he would not allow it to stand. Under his leadership the nation pulled together allies to join in a coalition to push the Iraqis out of Kuwait. In a short period of time the allied nations accomplished their goal. Americans watched via T.V. the missiles and bombs flying through the night skies of Iraq. Kay and Jeff were in Central America when the Persian Gulf War was launched. The evening of the invasion I was at Chuck and Martha Reeves home having dinner. The aircraft activity out of El Toro Marine Airbase increased. It was clear we were at war. Thankfully, President Bush chose not to go to Baghdad to remove Saddam. With the war won the allied armies were removed. Saddam had made a major mistake by invading Kuwait.

I was at the Baltimore G.A. in 1991 when the U.S. troops came home to Washington D.C. A huge military parade was held. Jim Farley and I drove to D.C. on the Sunday after the parade, and we saw the military equipment parked on the mall. It was impressive. A quick and successful attack had been waged and the troops were home. The President's popularity soared. No doubt, he assumed he would be reelected.

But soon the economy began to weaken, and people became worried. Bill Clinton won the Democratic nomination and argued that "it is the economy stupid". Clinton defeated Bush and soon the economy recovered. Bill and Hillary were popular. However, Bill Clinton had already been accused of sexual misconduct in Arkansas where he was governor. Apparently, the Clintons had developed many enemies in Arkansas. Several women charged him with sexual harassment and other crimes while governor of the State. Paula Jones and Jennifer Flowers were only two who gained notoriety. The Whitewater land deal in Arkansas was promoted by the Republicans as a scandal.

But then he had a sex affair with Monica Lewinsky in the White House. She was a White House intern who was seduced by the President's charisma. He lied about the affair and was proven to be a liar. All of this stirred the passions of the Republican Party, and they were determined to impeach Clinton. Kenneth Starr was appointed as a Special Prosecutor and his investigation covered every aspect of the President's personal and political life. Articles of Impeachment were approved by the House of Representatives and passed on to the Senate. After the Senate trial the President was acquitted. It was payback time for the Watergate scandal of Richard Nixon.

All of this captured the attention of a church that was mainly Republican. Sides were chosen and arguments developed between the left and the right. It impacted our national life and the fellowship of the church. Even our staff was divided over whether a sex affair and lying about it ought to be interpreted as "high crimes and misdemeanors", as the U.S. Constitution required for an impeachment?

Clinton was surely lacking in personal character. He publicly betrayed and humiliated his wife and daughter. He lied to the American people, but I did not think these personal sins rose to the level required by the Constitution for an impeachment. As I look back on the drama, I can see that this had a lot to do with the later "Me Too" movement in which women were determined to hold powerful men accountable for their secret sins and abuses of power. Every American institution, government, business, educational, or religious, have been shaken by the revelations of sexual misconduct on the part of powerful men.

These abuses of power have captured the prurient interests of the general population. Our movies and television programs have been filled with open sexual behaviors that many require to be entertained. The epidemic of pornography eats away at the human heart and mind. The Internet and social media have aggravated the problem. In the 1990's these new means of communication brought the sharing of information to the public and to business. The digital age made it easier for dishonesty and misbehavior to exact a toll on the human spirit.

Great benefits have come to the world with the advent of the internet, but human nature takes the gifts of the human mind and imagination and corrupts even the highest advances in science and technology. We ask, "Are personal integrity and honesty required in positions of authority and power?" A process of communal discernment seems necessary if the foundations of truth are not to be compromised.

Related to the above question was the undergirding issue of truth and falsehood. Are there binding norms required for civil society to which all people may agree, and to which be held accountable? Sexual misbehavior may be the least of a society's concerns when it comes to justice and social righteousness as proclaimed by the prophets of the Bible and which I believe necessary for the human community to flourish.

During this decade, the public was also fascinated by the murder of Nicole Brown Simpson, the wife of O.J. Simpson, the professional football player and actor. Nicole and her boyfriend were attacked by an unknown assailant outside of her residence in West L.A. Both were brutally killed in the darkness by a knife bearing person who caught them by surprise. O.J. Simpson was charged with the murder.

We knew O.J. and Nicole well in Laguna Beach. One of my friends told me that he had observed violent behavior between them at their house on Victoria Beach. O.J. was a USA football hero and Nicole a beautiful blonde. Both sides employed famous lawyers. The trial was televised. The nation was absorbed with the legal witnesses and the efforts to prove that Simpson had committed the crime. Legal questions; racism; parental rage; families; children; money, sex, and power, fanned the flames of popular passion. O.J. was acquitted. Everyone was amazed. Personally, I could not believe that O.J. would have killed his wife. Again, our church staff was divided in their opinions. Looking back, I am now convinced that O.J. in fact killed his estranged wife in a jealous rage over her seeing another man. The 90's were captivating on almost every score. The result was the destruction of public trust in the legal system and the impartiality of juries.

Woodstock 1999 represented the manifestation of the sexual misconduct of America's leaders and the nations uncivilized behaviors . Recently, Netflix has shown a movie reflecting the 1999 weekend music concert that drew literally thousands of mainly white young men and women. It was an effort to capture the spirit of the first 1960's Woodstock. It failed to do so. The multitudes were fanned into a hostile, angry, amoral "sex, drug's and rock 'n roll" orgy in which young women were molested, drugs and alcohol over consumed, and the language of the performers was sexually abusive and destructive of human well-being. It was shocking to watch the movie on T.V. and to see the moral devolution of which the Apostle Paul wrote in Romans 1.

1990's Study Leaves

My covenant brother John Huffman invited me to join him on two separate summertime two – week studies at St. Andrews, Scotland. In 1995 we stayed at Dean's Court at the University. Morning times were for reading. On my 60th birthday Gary Demarest had given me David Bosch's book, *Transforming Mission*. My goal was to read this excellent and lengthy book on the theology of mission. It was biblically and theologically transforming for me in my understanding of the mission of God through the church. Over the summer I made my way through the book. In the afternoons we played golf. The course at Crail was outstanding. As it happened, the British Open was played at St. Andrews during our 1995 time there. We got to follow world famous golfers for several days. It was a thrill. I was only with John for a week. Kay arrived and we took off for a week of driving around Scotland. The visit to Iona was inspirational. On this island Christianity was brought into the British Isles. Kay and I drove through the highlands, the Island of Skye, and around to Edinburgh. We boarded the train for London to visit with Peter and Vanessa Simpson. The UK was having a heatwave. Our London hotel had no air-conditioning. I thought we would melt.

In 1997 I joined John in Glasgow, Scotland. We immediately drove to the Troon Royal Course and caught an afternoon of the Open. Then it was on to St. Andrews for study and a round or two of golf on the New Course and at Crail. Dornoch was our destination where we stayed with the Mackenzie's in their fabulous estate. What a treat it was.

Holy Land Tours

In 1990 I led a large group of our church members to Athens and from there on a Greek Island cruise. We made stops at Athens, Ephesus, Patmos, and other islands. Then it was on to Cairo, Egypt. After two days in Cairo, we bused across the Sinai by the Way of the Sea. We were escorted by the Egyptian military in case we were attacked by terrorists. The Mediterranean Sea was beautiful as we drove across the sands of the desert. The lunch at a seaside hotel was excellent and we made it to Israel.

Annis, our Palestinian guide, met us at Rafah. He was my first guide in 1971. I had requested that he be our guide in 1990. Annis had owned a candle store in the old part of Jerusalem and had gathered fragments of the Dead Sea Scrolls from Arab contacts. The scrolls stirred his interest in the history of his land and in the work of archeology in recovering the past. He left his store and was educated to become a tour guide in the Holy Land. He met us at the Rafah crossing point. I was so glad to see him after 29 years.

Our hotel was the Seven Arches on the Mt. of Olives. Kay and I were given the front room overlooking the old city of Jerusalem. We looked right onto the Dome of the Rock, the ancient site of the Temple of *YAHWEH*, the place of worship that Jesus loved. In the middle of the night, we heard the calls to prayer from the mosque. The voice was heavenly and comforting. We awakened and were in a dream like state. What a blessing.

On the flight from Tel Aviv to Munich, Germany, and on to the Passion Play, the KLM crew allowed us to visit the pilots. Such a thing would never be allowed post 9/11/01. The Alps were beautiful as we passed over them. The trip was a great success. It allowed me to teach the Scriptures throughout Israel/Palestine. It was before the Separation Wall was built and groups could move smoothly from West to East.

In 1996 I led an Exodus trip that allowed us to follow the route of the Exodus story from Egypt into the Sinai and up to the famous mountain where Moses received the Ten Commandments. At Sinai our hotel was at the base of St. Catherine's Monastery. What a treat to see this world – famous place where important biblical manuscript discoveries were made, some of which are in the British Museum in London. The icons of the church were breathtaking. At their Getty Museum exhibit in L.A., we enjoyed them years later.

The crisis we had was in climbing Mt. Sinai. The geography of the surroundings of the mountain inspired awe within me. The sky was dark blue. A sense of mystery pervaded the air. We were on holy ground where Moses and the people of Israel had entered covenant relationship with the LORD. This was the place where the bush burned and was not consumed. At this bush the *LORD, YAHWEH*, called out to Moses to return to Egypt to be the agent of God's deliverance of his people from slavery. Our group worshiped at the base of the mountain on the *LORD'S DAY*. Inside the monastery we had seen the burning bush plant that had been identified as the type of bush that Moses would have seen. I still remember the green shirt I wore as I taught our group the story. Here heaven and earth overlapped and interconnected. It was cold at night but had warmed by mid-day. We were determined to climb to the peak. Often pilgrims ascended the mountain early in the morning to arrive before sunrise and from that vantage point to watch the sun rising in the east. It was a switchback trail that was slippery and straight up for the final 1000 steps. As we ascended the mountain we were passed by American G.I.'s running past us, skipping the trail all together.

Two members of my group were sisters named Helen and Louise. They came from a long line of fundamentalist Christians and had been Christian educators. They were in their 80's and unstable on their feet. Yet, they were in good shape for their age. The NAWAS guide advised me not to allow them to try the climb. They could easily fall, break a leg, and cause the whole group to be delayed. I told them they could not make the climb. Their anger toward me was severe, but everyone in the group agreed with me. It took them a long time to forgive me for denying to them this lifelong dream of climbing Mt. Sinai.

I have thought a lot about this over the years. I have wished that I had escorted them, carried them, and lifted them to see the peak. Yet, I still believe my decision was in their best interests. On church retreats I had seen them attempt hikes in the southern California mountains only to fall and to break bones. Nevertheless, they were angry with me, but they finally forgave me. I had had other experiences with them on my tours to Europe and Israel. In Athens at the airport Louise Adams had carried a paring knife in her backpack for peeling apples. The guards at the boarding gate saw the knife in her backpack on the imaging. She had to unpack everything and convince the guards that she was not a terrorist. We finally got on the plane but to everyone's frustration, including the Egyptian soccer team that was travelling with us to Cairo. They were waiting for Louise and me. As we entered the plane a member of the team was being resuscitated from the heat inside the cabin.

On another occasion at the Egyptian and Israeli border as we were going through the baggage ex-ray machine Louise turned backwards to remove her pack from her back and fell backwards unto the conveyor belt for the bags. She was heading into the powerful ex-ray machine on her back. The Egyptian soldiers were laughing so hard they could barely stop the belt and rescue her.

Once in Switzerland, in 1984, our group went to dinner in the hotel. Helen was not with us. She was late. We asked Louise about her roommate sister. She could not explain her tardiness. Louise went searching for her in their room. She discovered she had locked her sister in the room and taken the key to dinner. Helen had been screaming and was considering tying together the sheets from their bed to escape through the window. Over the years, there were all kinds of stories about these two sisters whom we all loved.

Teaching at Daystar University in the Summer of 1998

Africa captured my heart. A pastor friend of mine, Roger Anderson, who had organized the Edina Christ Presbyterian Church in Minnesota, upon his retirement had spent three years as a missionary in Kenya. He inspired me with tales about Kenya and the Christian mission. Especially, Roger spoke of Daystar University, a Christian institution developed for the training of African Christians. He encouraged me to go with him to

Kenya. I had met him at UCI in the summer of 1972 just as I was arriving in Laguna Beach.

After the Year of Africa partnership, I connected with Roger and Dottie, his wife, about the possibility of my teaching during a summer term at Daystar. Together we took a team of LPC members in the summer of 1998 to Nairobi for me to teach. They asked me to teach two short courses over a week's time: *"Communication and Intimacy in Marriage"* and *"The Politics of Jesus"*. The marriage course had 40 African students in it. I wrote a syllabus for the course, and we carried it with us. So also, I wrote a syllabus for "The Politics of Jesus" short course. Throughout 1998 I had worked on these papers, and they were well received.

The marriage course reviewed the syllabus but turned into a group interaction and personal sharing time. I opened my heart to them and shared my divorce and restoration journey. That sharing opened the door for honest dialogue and much laughter. The sexual behaviors in marriage in Kenya were interesting. By the end of the week, I felt very loved, and I hated to leave them. I learned about the issue of polygamy in Africa. One young woman asked me, "Why is it that men need so many women?" She had tears in her eyes, and it seemed that her question came from the heart of her life experience.

The *"Politics of Jesus"* and the relationship between Christians and the political powers was threatening. Nevertheless, the class was receptive, and I learned much in the process of preparing using the writing of John Yoder and Walter Wink to interpret the "principalities and powers".

On one of the Sundays, I preached at St. Andrews Presbyterian Church in Nairobi. This is the large Cathedral type church in the middle of the city. They were honoring the Women's Guides of the church. The women spoke in the packed sanctuary for two and a half hours. I had to get up and run to the rest room. I could not believe that the congregation would listen to me at two and three quarters an hour. But they did. I decided not to preach the sermon I had prepared. Rather I preached about the role of women in the Gospel of Luke.

On another Sunday I preached for my friend Bernard Muindi, and he translated me. It was a grand experience. I felt so humble and inadequate as I preached, yet so thankful for the LORD'S presence with me and the help Bernard gave. He had asked us to bring some communion ware for the five churches he pastored. We did so. It was quite an effort to carry the bags of the communion kits through the various check points of air travel. On the Sunday that I preached at Bernard's central church in Nyrie, other members of our team preached in the other four churches. Roger opened doors for us to visit mission projects in the slums of Nairobi. These were places that tourist did not see. They revealed the poverty and suffering of the people. Roger also introduced us to coffee plantations owned by white Kenyans. We had tea and fellowshipped in the living room of one of these wealthy persons. Roger's personality was well known in Kenya. He loved the people and they showed hospitality to our group.

LPC Affirmations in the 90's

On the 20th anniversary of my pastorate in Laguna Beach, the church hosted a special celebration and Texas BBQ. My mother and sister came from Texas in January 1994 for the event. In the early 1980's the church had an all-church talent show in Fellowship Hall. My associate Craig Williams, and friend Gil Orr, decided that we would do an Elvis impersonation. I rented an Elvis outfit; we formed a small band, and I sang several of my favorite Elvis songs. The church went wild. I have never seen such laughter and fun. In that moment I was branded as an Elvis impersonator.

When my performance became known in the Presbytery, the pastor's insisted that we do the act again at skit night of the Presbytery Pastors Retreat. Craig, Gil, and I performed. It was a riot. Vickie Orr and Lydia Sarandan bowed before me as I mopped my brow and gave them the kleenex. To say the least, I have never lived it down. On the same evening, John Huffman sang karioki style, Frank Sinatra's "I Did It My Way".

On John Huffman's 20th anniversary at St. Andrews, Anne Huffman talked me into doing the Elvis act in their Fellowship Hall. I'll never forget getting John and his congregation singing together, *"I'm Just a Hunk a Hunk of Burning Love"*. Kay told me that if I ever did that act again, she would divorce me. Indeed, it was fun, but it was embarrassing for her, I am sure. Nevertheless, fun for an exhibitionist pastor.

At the 1994 BBQ 20th anniversary the LPC congregation crowned me "The King". Several of my pastor friends roasted me and after each roast I was pressed to put on another item of an Elvis costume. Gary Demarest, John Huffman, Craig Williams, Jon Moore, Larry Coulter, Don Theis, Byron Beam, and Dee Hazen each spoke. It was called *"The Making of a King"*. At the end of the evening Gil and I sang together for the crowd as we did *"Lovesick Blues"* and then an Elvis tune to which Gil had written new words. My mother and sister were about to burst their girdles with laughter. My mom loved this kind of music. I used to sing country western songs as a kid sitting in a backyard tree on Monroe St. in Amarillo. I guess I grew up thinking I could sing. More than anything there was a bit of a ham inside me. In Fellowship Hall they had written my name, "Jerry" in shining lights upon the front wall.

My 25th anniversary caught me by surprise. We had a Friday night combined Session and Deacon dinner. After dinner we moved into the Church Parlor. Dave Tomlinson, our Presbytery Exe, was the speaker about spiritual gifts. As he spoke in the crowded room folks began to stir as he went off message speaking about me. Suddenly an Elvis impersonator walked into the room and the celebration began. By the end of the evening, he had me up singing with him some Elvis numbers. Great fun was had by all.

But that was just the beginning. The following Sunday morning I was ready to preach and began to climb into the pulpit when my associate, Jeannie Thorndike, interrupted me and told me to join my family on the front row. A new roast began as part of our worship. Byron Beam had written a poem and read it. Then he gave to me a framed enlarged picture of me in the High Sierra's with only my legs showing, with Kay sitting on top of me to appear that she had a man's hairy legs. In the process, Gus Altazzura, an elder, presented me with a wooden sign that was to say, "*TANKERSLEY HALL*". The session had voted to put my name on the Fellowship Hall as an honor and recognition of my 25 years of leading the church. I was overcome with emotion. This was touching. It was an affirmation that this people loved me and trusted me as their pastor. I feel highly honored to have my name on the building in downtown Laguna Beach. I told the congregation that I was not ready to retire.

Jerry and Kay Tankersley on the 100th anniversary of Laguna Presbyterian Church.
September 17, 2017

Chapter 9

The Highways to Louisville and beyond

2000 to 2018

These years were jam packed in surprising ways.

Y2K

They began with Y2K anxieties. There were some who feared that the world might come to an end and that there might be a catastrophe of some sort. A member of our church advocated that we store food in the basement of the church in case there was a meltdown. We did not give in to that kind of fear. We confessed that our history was part of a *grand metanarrative, a "Big Story"*, of the kingdom of God. Indeed, the promises of God will come to fulfilment. There will be a New Creation. What we need in the present is a sure confidence in the goodness of God.

A Family Wedding

2000 was a big year for our family. Jeff, our son, had met Rachel Rao, and fallen in love. They had met at Taco Tuesday in Laguna Beach and before long they were making plans for life together. We first met Rachel for dinner at a Laguna Beach restaurant. Indeed, she was beautiful, of Indian origin. Paul and Betsy Rao had immigrated to the U.S. from India when she was three months old. They were a Christian family, and we were grateful for her addition to our small family. We could see the love in Jeff's eyes for her. We fell in love with Rachel and her family. They hosted a dinner party at their rented Laguna Beach home. Most of those who were present were Indian members of their larger family. After a wonderful Indian dinner, they dressed Jeff and Rachel in Indian clothing and placed them at the center of the family circle. Each member present made an affirmation of them and then placed paint on their faces, arms, and hands. It was a truly moving experience to see beautiful Rachel and our handsome son so affirmed and loved. It was an answer to our prayers for him. They will soon celebrate their 20th wedding anniversary. We have two grandsons, Quinn Joseph, and Luke Zane.

On June 10, 2000, they were married at Laguna Presbyterian Church by my former associate, Craig Williams. We hosted the rehearsal dinner at our home. It was a great time. The wedding reception was at Tortilla Flats where they met. Kay and I danced and enjoyed the food with the Rao's and many of our friends. Watching Kay and Jeff dancing together was a supremely happy moment for me. We helped them with the honeymoon to Jamaica. Seeing them get launched as husband and wife was a special joy. We love them. Hard to believe they have now been married for 20 years and have two sons, Quinn, and Luke. One of my life's joys was to baptize both grandsons in Sunday morning worship services and to have Rachel's parents and brother Richard participate with us.

Prostate Cancer

In December 2000 I was diagnosed with Prostate Cancer. From my mid 40's, I had watched my PSA levels with yearly tests. I had periodic prostatitis, or infections in the gland. This caused the levels on the tests to go up and down. My Dad had developed the same disease and had radical surgery at UCLA. Other men in the larger family had the same issue. I was carefully monitoring my situation. By age 63, after three biopsies, the lab discovered two of the eight probs had cancer cells in them. I moved quickly and scheduled surgery with Dr. Paul Brower at Saddleback Hospital. I felt like a huge truck had run over me. The good news was that the pathologist said that it was an early detection in less than 5% of the prostate. The first PSA test six weeks after the surgery was 0. It has remained at that level since March 2001. The doctor finally pronounced me healed.

Wild Man Retreat with Father Richard Rohr

A few months after the surgery, Byron Beam and I attended Franciscan Richard Rohr's Male Initiation at Ghost Ranch, N.M. I will never forget that experience with around 300 men from all parts of the world. They were Catholic and Protestant believers seeking to deepen their spiritual maturity. Together we were renewing our baptismal vows. After much ritual and teaching by Father Rohr, I was amazed at the painful issues with which men deal and which they must grieve as loses in the process of living into the cruciform way of Jesus Christ. Deep father wounds were evident in many, with great anger and tears. The retreat came after a year of doing the Ignatian Prayer Exercises with a group of lawyers and judges in Orange Country. I am still grateful for the mystery of Christ in me, of dying to sin to live into the resurrection life of Jesus in the power of the Holy Spirit.

Byron and I travelled in his BMW and visited Mesa Verde National Park on the way home. We literally flew across Navajo country at way over the speed limit. It was fun, but at times frightening. Byron was an outstanding lawyer in Orange County, and I had great respect for him. He and Donna were students in my Bethel Bible class and were on their way in spiritual maturity. I loved them as dear friends. When they transferred to the Catholic Church, which was Donna's original church, I grieved. As spiritual directors they incorporated their knowledge of Scripture into service in the RCC. I married their daughter and baptized their grandchildren. We are still close friends in Christ.

91101

On September 11, 2001, the world was turned upside down by terrorist attacks in New York City, Washington D.C., and in Pennsylvania. It was Tuesday morning, and I was watching the T.V. news as I ate breakfast. I could not make sense of what I was seeing on T.V. The voice was coming from New York City, but the picture was from D.C. with the Pentagon on fire. The phone rang and Nancy Wade asked if I was watching the news. She filled me in on the horrible story of the commercial airliners being flown into the World Trade Center Towers in N.Y.C. I watched for a while and then realized that morning I had to teach my regular Women's Bible Study. I turned the T.V. off and went to my home office to do my morning prayers and scripture readings. That morning I journaled my initial thoughts and prayers:

"09/11/01—Major terrorist attack this morning on the U.S. Apparently, two airplanes hijacked and flown into the World Trade Center in NYC. One of the two towers have fallen. Must be hundreds killed. Pentagon building in D.C. attacked by another airliner. All air traffic in U.S. is grounded. White House evacuated. President Bush in Florida.

Well, the world has come to the U.S. It was inevitable. We are the great hated superpower that has been using its military technology to rule the world. The conflicts, hatreds, violence of the world, the lack of justice and peace in the Middle East, Balkans, Arab world, everywhere, has created a condition in which evil thrives.

All of this will set the agenda for the western world today and for many years. With the warfare in Palestine/Israel, and the U.S. involvement the world could be in for major terrorist retaliations."

On 09/13/01 I wrote, "I am depressed. My inner spirit is so caught up in the contradictions, pluralisms, ideologies, truths, and fanaticisms of humanity, and the divisions within the church, that I just want to escape, to get out of this world. How can God be used as a pretext for human evil?"

"Little time to prepare to preach for Sunday. LORD, help me. People must be feeling as I do. Drained! In pain. Anxious and Fearful. Troubled by the world in which we live."

"Brokenness is all around and within. We cannot protect ourselves from these attacks. Looks like 3000 people missing in NYC. Our world has changed. Our security gone. The mystery of evil is all around us. Violence lurks in the human heart. Yet, your Holy Spirit has come to dwell in your people's hearts. You empower us to love ourselves and one another."

On Sunday, 9/16/01: "Much emotion. People in grief. Church full. Angry. Nation deeply wounded by WTC building attack. I have anger in me. LORD, have mercy."

President George W. Bush proclaimed that we had heard from our enemies. Now they would hear from us. War was launched on Al Qaeda in Iraq and Afghanistan. Thus, began the longest war in American history. Many joined the military to pursue our enemies. The War on Terrorism has taken us into Iraq, Iran, Syria, Jordan, and Israel. It is still not over. The problems seem insurmountable. Terrorism has spread to the nations with bombings, knifings, poisonings, and threats of all kinds. From planes, to trains, to buses, to trucks, to shoes ready to explode, international travel has been altered. Refugee people from many nations have poured into Europe and the U.S. Chaos has touched almost all continents. The cost in human lives and national treasure is incalculable. LORD have mercy. Will justice and peace ever come to human history? The need for revenge multiplies with each threat or attack. The dark side of human nature has become manifest, not only in the 20th century, but also into the 21st century. The impact of this on the way the Western World lives its life has branded us. Surely, the fear of terrorism has divided us into political, economic, and religious camps. Polarization has grown and our angers have turned us against our newly defined enemies. The Sermon on the Mount has never been more relevant.

On a return trip from London to LAX in 2006, there was a plot to bomb several airliners over the North Atlantic. We waited in long lines in London to be cleared by security. In front of me was a young Palestinian man who had returned from the West Bank of the Jordan after his marriage. I laughed to myself about the irony of this. His Palestinian bride was not allowed to return to the U.S. with him. Once we landed at LAX the passengers and their baggage were unloaded and all bags had to be x-rayed. The wait in customs was 5 hours. Kay was waiting for me during that time and was longing to see me walk up through the tunnel to her. There was no cell phone access from our holding place. After 911 air travel would never be the same.

Since 91101 America has been at war. U.S. Foreign Policy has assumed that we had a moral responsibility to spread an American style of political, economic, and religious freedom and if necessary, impose democracy in the Middle East. Therefore, removing the Taliban and capturing Osama bin Laden became legitimate military goals. The result was that we found ourselves in the same quagmire that the Soviet Union confronted in their invasion of Afghanistan in 1980.

The Bush administration assumed that Saddam Hussein of Iraq was behind the Al Qaeda 911 attack. Saddam was considered a threat to western democracy. It was believed that he was developing weapons of mass destruction, i.e., atomic bombs and germ warfare capability. President George W. Bush and his Vice President Dick Cheney pushed for an invasion of Iraq to remove Saddam from power and to liberate the Iraqi people. In 2003 America invaded Iraq. This was W's opportunity to complete what his father refused to do in 1991, remove Saddam. Democracy was coming to the Middle East at the hands of American military power.

With "shock and awe" Saddam was removed, convicted, and hung after being found hiding underground. His statues were pulled over, his sons killed, and a deep divide was introduced into Iraq between the Sunni's and Shiite's. The Christian Church in Iraq was weakened. The tragedy for American foreign policy and intelligence was that after Iraq's defeat there were no atomic weapons found or chemical weapons of mass destruction. There was no evidence that Iraq was behind the 911 attacks. America's invasion of Iraq was a huge mistake for it led to the destabilization of the entire Middle East and brought even greater danger for our allies in Israel. But the damage had been done. In 2020 our leaders are still searching for a way to exit Afghanistan and Iraq without doing even greater harm.

Standing for Moderator of the 214TH General Assembly of the PCUSA

Early in January 2002 I received a telephone call from John Huffman, pastor of St. Andrews Presbyterian Church in Newport Beach, California. John and I had been friends and leaders within the Presbytery of Los Ranchos since 1978. He shared that the leadership of the Presbyterian Coalition, a conservative/evangelical advocacy group within the larger church had contacted him about standing for moderator of the 214th G.A. meeting in Columbus, Ohio, in June 2002. He shared that he could not do this but that a member of his church had told him that if he did not do it then she would stand. John suggested to the various leaders of the Coalition that I would be a good choice for them to consider.

I began to receive telephone calls from people like Jerry Andrews, Parker Williamson, and others, encouraging me to hear this as a call from God. I received several faxed letters for me to present to the session of LPC that very week. After session discussion, the session voted unanimously to support my standing and to do everything possible for me to succeed. I was overwhelmed that so many across the church would have such confidence in me to represent a large mainstream of evangelical witness within the denomination.

At the coming Presbytery meeting Bill Flanagan, associate pastor at St. Andrews, and another of my covenant group brothers, placed my name in nomination to be endorsed by the Presbytery of Los Ranchos. The vote was taken and only one of our commissioners was opposed.

Again, I was overwhelmed by the affirmation of my brothers and sisters with whom I had served for so many years. At the coming springtime Pastor's Retreat in Malibu, my friends gathered around me, had me kneel, laid hands on me, and prayed for me.

This was my first foray into church politics at the national level. It was a time of great conflict within the larger church. Two other pastors joined the race to become Moderator of the 214th G.A. Laird Stuart, pastor of Calvary Presbyterian in San Francisco was the first to announce his intentions. The other was Fahed Abul Akel, a Palestinian pastor from the Presbytery of Greater Atlanta. Both men were outstanding and represented different constituencies of the PCUSA. I would have to be interviewed with them before the 700 commissioners of the G.A. and be able to address the important issues before the church and our world. Then a vote would be taken to elect one of the three. Fahed was elected on the second ballot.

That springtime John Huffman and I attended the Confessing Church conference in Atlanta. John gave one of the sermons as did Parker Williamson, the editor of The Presbyterian Layman. John and Parker passionately preached and stirred the larger gathering. Laird, and Fahed were both present. The moderator of the 213th Assembly, Dr. Jack Rogers, was present. Very ugly things were said on the floor about Jack. I was embarrassed for Jack and for the PCUSA. Even though Jack had progressive convictions about human sexuality, he was a brother in Christ, who had served the evangelical and Reformed cause of the church with honor. I regret that he was not treated with civility at the gathering. There was anger in that gathering expressed toward the G.A.

The Peace, Unity, and Purity Task Force, Co-Chaired by Gary Demarest, my mentor, was meeting seeking to study the causes of unrest and conflict within the PCUSA. Mistrust was afflicting the church. Laird had been the leader of the Covenant Network, the progressive wing of the denomination, and was a bold and effective supporter of gay ordination and marriage. Fahed was a late entry into the race, and he was a powerful voice for justice in Israel/Palestine. He was well known in the southern part of the PCUSA.

Soon, Laird, Fahed, and I met with Cliff Kirkpatrick, the Stated Clerk of the G.A., and were introduced to each other. Becoming friends with Cliff and the other two was the beginning of a meaningful journey for me. Cliff was neutral and fair to the three of us with the reminder that only one of us would be elected. Jack Haberer, one of the Coalition leaders, joined me for a drink in Dallas after we attended a meeting of the Task Force on Peace, Unity, and Purity. He shared that he thought I was mature enough to handle it if I were not elected. The truth was that I had never entertained the idea of becoming involved in the national political life of the church. Therefore, I told him that I would not be badly disappointed. I only desired to not embarrass myself before the Assembly and to present myself for service in the larger church. I also hoped to be a uniting person to build up the church.

In contemplating my message to the G.A. I had a dream one night in which it came to me that Ephesians 1 and 2 contained the message the larger church needed to hear and to trust. "At the cross of Jesus, God acted in human history to accomplish God's plan and purpose to unite all things in heaven and on earth through the blood of Christ. Through Christ's death and resurrection, God's reconciling grace broke down dividing walls of hostility, thus making peace. There was no longer Jew or Gentile, slave or free, male or female, but in Christ the way had been opened for a new spiritual humanity to emerge." Therefore, the deep divisions and tribal barriers of the human race were already overcome in Jesus Christ our LORD and Savior. The church's calling was to live into this reconciliation, to be ambassadors of God's grace, and to call all people and nations to gather into one new family of beloved children of God united at the cross and empowered by the Holy Spirit to do God's mission."

The national church seemed divided on the questions of "who is Jesus?" "What is the truth of the gospel?" A fellow pastor had asked these questions at a national conference that deeply stirred the theological passions of the whole church: "what's the big deal about Jesus?" No central authority answered for the church. I wanted to answer in my statement before the G.A. The G.A.'s Theology and Worship unit had been working on a statement to be presented to the Assembly. It was named, *"Hope in the Lord Jesus Christ"*. Our Confessional Statements in the Book of Confessions were presented in summary form. Especially, the Apostles Creed and the Nicene Creed were, as well as the Reformation Creeds and Catechisms. I was deeply encouraged by the small booklet and theological statement of faith produced by Theology and Worship. When presented to the whole G.A., it was overwhelmingly approved.

It was our answer and reaffirmation that the one who was born in Bethlehem was the incarnate Son of God. This fully God and fully human, Jesus of Nazareth, in perfect obedience to the will of God his Father, bore the sins of humanity upon the cross, was bodily raised from the dead on the third day, and reconciled us to the Father and to one another. In the power of the Holy Spirit, the One triune God, launched the mission of God through the church to heal all nations.

After Fahed had been elected Moderator on the second ballot, Laird Stuart and I were asked to present a joint motion to the Assembly recommending this paragraph of the document:

> "Jesus Christ is the only Savior and Lord, and all people everywhere are called to place their faith, hope, and love in him. No one is saved by virtue of inherent goodness or admirable living, for 'by grace you have been saved through faith, and this is not your own doing; it is the gift of God' (Ephesians 2:8). No one is saved apart from God's gracious redemption in Jesus Christ. Yet we do not presume to limit the sovereign freedom of 'God our Savior, who desires everyone to be saved and to come to the knowledge of the truth' (1 Timothy 2:4). Thus, we neither restrict the grace of God to those who profess explicit faith in Christ nor assume that all people are saved regardless of faith. Grace, love, and communion belong to God, and are not ours to determine."
>
> "Paul, after a beautiful development of his thought, in Romans 10:17 at length concludes, 'So faith comes from hearing, and hearing from the Word of God by the preaching of Christ.' At the same time, we recognize that God can illuminate whom and when he will, even without the external ministry, for that is in his power (The Second Helvetic Confession, 5.006, 007). [1]

It was a positive and warming experience to stand with Laird before the Assembly to make this motion. It was overwhelmingly approved by the 214th G.A. Indeed, this document was the church's answer to the question, "What's the big deal about Jesus?" *Theology Matters*! The denomination was being accused of being apostate and more unitarian than trinitarian. As a church we were being challenged to stand up for our Reformed theological tradition in the spirit of truth, grace, and love.

Leading up to the G.A. the three candidates were invited by Pittsburg Theological Seminary to participate in a Moderator's Forum to which the student body was invited along with people from the Presbytery. We began that morning in the class on Presbyterian Polity. We each made opening statements and then answered questions from the

---

1. *Hope in The Lord Jesus Christ,* 11–12.

class. I remember telling the class of soon to be pastors that if they were going into the ministry as a profession then they ought to terminate their preparation and choose another way of making a living. I argued that unless they each had a divine call, they would be unable to endure the stresses of ministry in the new century. Apparently, after the three of us were dismissed from the class they took a vote as to who won. On the second ballot, I was told, I was elected by the class.

At lunch I was seated beside President Samuel Calian. As we were eating, he shared that he had been going over my prepared documents presented to the G.A. and had noticed that there was a gap in the dates of my service of nearly two years. He wanted me to account for what I was doing during that interlude. The years were 1964 – 1965. I took a deep breath and shared my experience of being ordained by the Presbytery of Los Angeles in the summer of 1963 to serve as an assistant pastor at the Wilshire Presbyterian Church in L.A. In 1964 my wife announced to me that she did not love me and left the marriage after five years. The result was a divorce which humiliated me and left me emotionally crushed and alone. I resigned my position at the church and began a new journey seeking to survive while working with an attorney from the Wilshire Church who offered me a position in his office. Sometime later, I was told that my wife had willfully deserted me in hopes of marrying the church elder who chaired the committee that invited me to become an assistant pastor. This was the last thing I ever expected to happen.

In the spring of 2002, I had asked a few my pastor friends if I ought to write about this life experience and how I was restored by the grace of the Presbytery. These were painful discussions. President Calian stunned me after I told him the story. He said I had to share the same story on the floor of the G.A. as a part of the public presentations. He argued that what the church needed was to rediscover the forgiving grace of God and the power of God to heal and to restore even broken pastors.

That afternoon in the forum, Sam Calian asked the three of us if we would speak about one formative experience in church ministry that had shaped and formed our persons and our understandings of ministry. I knew that he was setting me up to tell my story of God's grace of healing in my life. I did! It was a liberating experience. I was glad because I did not want the truth of my life to be exposed by anyone other than me. If it meant I would be rejected by the Assembly, so be it! My friends in Los Ranchos decided this was important for me to do. There could be no hiding of the truth of my life.

I had failed in this marriage in ways I did not fully understand, but the LORD did not abandon me. The LORD placed people in my life who helped me more fully understand the mystery of life together and how sometimes we fail. I had not been unfaithful to my marriage vows. Floyd Norris, the lawyer, became a father to me. David Hubbard, my professor mentor at Westmont College and now President at Fuller Theological Seminary introduced me to Gary Demarest who was just starting as pastor at La Canada Presbyterian Church. Gary had experienced a marriage failure in his earlier life and was restored and remarried. He understood and extended grace to me. Dr. George P. Smith, a new professor at California State University of L.A., encouraged me to help him write a book on legal philosophy, and Claremont Graduate School accepted me into their Ph.D. program in Government.

After a complete investigation by the Ministerial Relations Committee of the Presbytery of L.A., the committee presented a motion to the Presbytery that I was to continue in good standing with the Presbytery and continue the ministry to which the *LORD* had called me and for which I had worked so hard. That was a moment of grace for me mediated by the church. It was as if the church gave my life back to me. My heart swelled with gratitude for this mercy. After the Assembly in 2002, my college, Westmont College, asked me to tell the story in the Alumni bulletin. That experience was life affirming.

This experience of brokenness has followed me across the years. I have not backed away and tried to hide it. I was upfront with the PNC at the Laguna Church when they asked about it. I sensed that some were troubled by what I said. I just knew I had to be honest and allow the LORD to open or to close the door.

The morning after the election at G.A. in Columbus, Ohio, in 2002, John Huffman and I were walking together in the hallway of the Convention Center when we were encountered by an articulate African American man. He was sent by his Presbytery a year early to G.A. to observe in preparation for being a commissioner the next year. I tried to listen carefully to his criticism of me. He shared that he was ready to vote for me until I shared my divorce and restoration story. He went on and on. Finally, John nudged me and said "Jerry, you do not have to take this anymore." We walked away.

There was another time when a large university church was interested in me, and I had to tell my story to be honest. Their committee asked in an interview if there had ever been any brokenness in my life. It was an open door for me to witness to God's love in my life. Before long I received a letter of rejection from the committee with an invitation to call the Chair of the PNC. I did so. He shared that I was their leading candidate, but some on the committee, reflecting the theological commitments of many in the church, would be unable to accept a divorced pastor even though he had been remarried for nearly 30 years. I was hurt by that rejection. When I invited the President of Princeton Seminary to preach in Laguna Beach, our Presbytery Executive had already told him what had happened. Tom comforted me in my office by saying that "God saved you from a very troubled church in which there is little grace." I could understand their reticence since their former pastor had committed adultery and it had been a scandal.

Thus, it is with the brokenness of the PCUSA. Across the years I have been grateful that the grace of God has overflowed for me. In 2019 Kay and I celebrated 52 years of marriage. What a gift! She has been a major part of God's healing love in my life. She has made it possible for me to have a family life and to pastor at the same time. She travelled to Columbus, Ohio, to be with me in the nominating process. When I was not elected, as a large group of friends we went to a local bar for drinks. Later that night Kay arranged to return home the next morning. She was thankful that I was not elected because of the interruption it could have brought to our life. It was better for her to go home since the next days of my life were very busy at the G.A. When I attended the Committee to which I had been appointed, the moderator of the committee affirmed my attendance. She said that in the past other candidates who failed to be elected were so hurt that they left their assemblies. But I was there. There was never a thought about leaving. I was there to serve and to do my duty.

Later in the summer Kay and I booked a 10 – day cruise to Alaska. It was a needed rest. We flew to Vancouver, B.C., boarded the Princess ship, visited Anchorage, took the train past Mt. McKinley and through Denali National Park on to Fairbanks. At the mountain we enjoyed a helicopter flight up to the base of the peak on a clear day. It was a spectacular view of the mountain.

The members of LPC were sad that I was not elected moderator. Most were relieved that my service for the congregation would not be interrupted. At the July Presbytery meeting I received a standing ovation. An affirmation was expressed that I had well represented the Presbytery. I was grateful for this. Thus, was launched the next sixteen years of my ministry which were filled with ever increasing opportunities to serve the larger church in Louisville and beyond.

General Assembly Nominating Committee

In the fall 2002 I received a call from a representative of the Coalition Advocacy group asking if I would be willing to have my name presented to the G.A. to be the representative of the Synod of Southern California and Hawaii on the denomination's Nominating Committee. Our Synod was one of 16 Synods. The Moderator, Fahed Abul Akel, had authority to appoint me to be approved by the next Assembly in Denver. Later I was told that there were some in the Southern California Synod who did not want me appointed to the important committee that was charged with nominating members for all the committees of the G.A. My guess was that I had been pegged by some as a conservative who might not deal fairly with progressives who desired to serve on these committees. Nevertheless, my name was submitted by Fahed and I was elected by the 215th G.A. (2003) that met in Denver.

I served for five years on this national committee of representatives of the 16 Synods of the PCUSA. During my final year I was selected to be the Vice Chairman of the committee with a special charge of leading the worship of the 16 representatives of the national church as we periodically met. This was a special call to serve. I got to know well people I would have never known without this gift. Valarie Small, the GA staff person who worked with us, was married to Joe Small, the leader of the GA's Theology and Worship staff. Working with them proved to be a special gift. Each member of the GANC were wonderful persons, highly committed to the work of the national church. There was openness and fair-mindedness toward the names that came from across the church to serve on these national committees.

We met two or three times a year in cities like Denver, Philadelphia, San Antonio, Phoenix, Louisville, Richmond, and Atlanta. There were brief periods in which we saw nearby places of historical interest. We ate in some great restaurants, but basically, we worked in committee in the interest of appointing the best people the church had to lead its national and international missions. We attended the G.A. meetings in Denver, Richmond, Minneapolis, and Birmingham. I am grateful for this leadership opportunity. It gave me an appreciation for the talent that is in the national church.

Company of New Pastors

Sheldon Sorge of the G.A.'s Theology and Worship Committee was charged with overseeing the CNP's program. The program was for developing support groups for new pastors recently graduated from seminary. This was a program funded by the Lilly Foundation for the purpose of promoting the spiritual formation of young pastors as they were plunged into their callings as new pastors. The need was great. The statistics were alarming. A high percentage of newly ordained pastors had been leaving the pastoral ministry within five years. It was as if they were not spiritually mature enough to deal with parish life, with conflicts, with differences on church staffs, and stresses of the wider world.

I asked Candie Blankman, pastor of our Downey Church, to be a co-mentor with me. Thus, began a fruitful friendship in ministry. We led two five – year groups over 10 years. The program was based on the church's Reformed liturgy. We read many books, wrote papers, and met with our groups a couple of times a year for several days. I only wished that I had such a group in my early years in ministry. We experienced the fellowship and worship life of the church at the grass roots of personal and small group friendship. We were all transformed. Most of our fellow disciples came out of our years together as stronger persons and more fruitful pastors. The majority continues in church ministries. Our friendships are deep as fellow humans and disciples of Christ. Our reading of Scripture and study of our Book of Confessions continued our spiritual and theological experience of the grace and truth of the Gospel.

This has become a model for me of what the church ought to be in its discipleship programs. Over a number of years, I have continued to learn the importance of spiritual life planted deeply in the soil of the knowledge of God, the experience of God's love, nurtured by the written Word of God, filled with the Holy Spirit, and being sent for God's mission in the world. This is what the church is to be and to do.

National Presbyterian Pastors' Sabbaths

The six General Assembly Agencies were becoming aware of the high rate of pastoral burn out across the larger church. Therefore, together they funded an effort to call the pastoral leadership of the church to spiritual renewal. I was invited to be a leader in developing two of these Sabbath gatherings.

Our first pastoral leadership team came together at the Louisville Presbyterian Seminary. I think we were around 20 pastors, male, and female, from across the nation who planned and executed the gatherings. We chose the place after reviewing sites across the nation. Snowbird Ski Resort in Utah was the best deal. We advertised and the result was that 650 pastors and spouses came to the Utah mountains to listen to great preaching and teaching. Rest and inspiration were at the heart of the program. The text chosen was from Mark 6:30ff. After hard labors in ministry Jesus invited his 12 disciples to come apart for a while to rest and to renew in relationship with God and with one another. I wrote the basic study guide for this retreat based on the Mark 6 invitation. The group refined and edited my work, and we were off running. Some of the leadership names were Walter Brueggemann, Tony Campola, James Forbes, and Barbara Brown Taylor. I will never forget Forbes' evening message on pastoral ministry and its challenges. I was left weeping and open to God. Kay came to me and held me. It was one of those holy moments of my life and our life together.

Cliff Kirkpatrick, the G.A. Stated Clerk, asked if Laird Stuart and I would co-chair the next Sabbath event three years later. Laird and I stood for Moderator of the 214th G.A. We had become friends from 2002 on. Even though we were competing for the same office, the bonds of our personal friendship had grown. We had theological differences, but Jesus Christ was our Savior and LORD. Later he shared how painful it was for him in not being elected moderator of the G.A.

Again, a group of pastor leaders from across the church were selected to join us on the planning team. We struggled with a theme and finally settled on a text from Isaiah with the theme of Exile. (Isaiah 43:1-7) I wrote the study paper around the theme and the committee refined and edited my work and we were launched. This time the registration was slow in coming and the result was about half of the first event. Nevertheless, it was rewarding. The preachers and teachers were not as well known, but they were excellent. Names like Craig Barnes, Cynthia

Rigby, and others brought inspiration and wisdom to us. The G.A. had a financial deficit from the event but all in all we gave our best realizing that the larger church was moving into a time of growing conflict and schism. I felt affirmed when a pastor from the south said to me that Laird Stuart and I had done more than anyone in the denomination to promote the "peace, unity, and purity of the church." I was recently saddened to learn that Laird had died but died in the faith.

This is the sermon I preached immediately after the Sabbath Retreat.

S070806 Psalm 130

"PRAYING OUR PAIN IN HOPE"

"Help, God—the bottom has fallen out of my life! Master, hear my cry for help! Listen hard! Open your ears! Listen to my cries for mercy." *The Message*. Ps. 130:1

I. Praying Our Pain

Last week I was at the National Presbyterian Pastor's Sabbath Retreat in Utah. I have been co-moderator of the planning team for the past two years. I wrote the study guide for the retreat based on Isaiah 40. It was truly a wonderful event. 350 of our pastors from around the United States were present. The last evening in worship I shared my own spiritual renewal, and I asked the worshipping congregation whether or not their lives had been touched. Their hands went up and their applauses were loud in enthusiasm for what we had experienced together. Over and over, I heard in the hallways that pastors were returning to their parishes with new energy and hope.

But throughout the retreat there was the sharing of great suffering and pain. Presbyterian Disaster Assistance paid the way for our Gulf Coast pastors who had been impacted by Hurricane Katrina. A number of them had literally lost their homes and their church buildings in the depths of the floods in New Orleans. In one storm with winds and waves the waters filled their churches and their houses, displaced their congregations, and left them with nothing. One pastor's wife told of not knowing where their congregations might be or if they would ever return to New Orleans to help rebuild either church or city. The retreat's theme was "exile" and "new exodus". They were living it. They were crying to the heavens out of the depths. The bottom had fallen out of their lives. In the words of Psalm 69 they were praying their pain:

"Save me, O God, for the waters have come up to my neck. I sink in deep mire, where there is no foothold; I have come into deep waters, and the flood sweeps over me. I am weary with my crying; my throat is parched. My eyes grow dim with waiting for my God."

The psalmists prayed their anxiety, fear, suffering, pain, depression, sickness, sin, death, spiritual emptiness, yearning, and longing in the faith that there was One who listened and who heard the cries of his people. The psalms teach us how to pray our sorrows and our joys, our sufferings, and our thanksgivings.

Should we be surprised that Christians suffer pain? Eugene Peterson's chapter on Psalm 130 says that the Psalm teaches that "Suffering is real, and God is real. Suffering is a mark of our existential authenticity; God is proof of our essential and eternal humanity. We accept suffering; we believe in God. The acceptance and the belief both emerge out of those times when 'the bottom has fallen out' of our lives."[2]

One of our preachers, Craig Barnes, who is a professor at Pittsburgh Theological Seminary, reminded us of the suffering of the Apostle Paul. He told a story from his own Sunday school days. From all those years ago, he remembered the "flannel board" stories that his teacher told. The teacher would put the flannel on a board and then take the biblical character cut outs and attach them to the flannel. By means of static electricity the biblical characters would stick to the flannel and the teacher would tell the story.

Craig said he could still remember the cut out for the Apostle Paul. Over time the cut out of the Apostle had been wrinkled, discolored by fruit juice, and had had its head ripped off. However, the Apostle's head had somehow been reattached. Due to all the abuse of the years, the teacher had great difficulty in getting the Apostle to stick to the flannel. She had to continually apply the figure to the flannel and wave her hands over it to get it to stick. All of us who have ever been to Sunday school had a good laugh at the story.

Then Craig reminded us that this was the Apostle's dilemma in real life. Wherever he had preached he had faced opposition, beatings, stoning, sickness, danger, and suffering. His thorn in the flesh brought him low and made him dependent upon the very ones he was seeking to win to Christ. There were times when the Apostle was convinced that the sentence of death was upon him. Paul literally felt on many occasions that

---

2. Peterson, *Long Obedience*, 142.

the bottom had dropped out of his life and mission and that he would sink in the mire of the deeps. His life ended in prison in Rome where he was finally beheaded in Nero's persecutions in 64 A.D.

Craig shared the flannel board story in the light of our text from Isaiah 40's witness to the truth:

"All people are grass. The grass withers, the flower fades; but the word of our God will stand forever."

Therefore, he reminded us that we are grass that withers and flowers that fade. We are mortal. There is a God, and it is not us. That is good news. He suggested that some of us would like to post a sign for our congregations to read: "Keep Off the Grass!".

Some of our pain is institutional. The Christian Century magazine, (June 26, 2007), which many of us read, reported that the PC(USA) dropped another forty-six thousand members last year. In our nearly eleven thousand congregations our adult baptisms averaged less than one per church and child baptisms were just short of three per congregation. Not a formula for growth. The waters have come up to our necks in more ways than one and the leadership of the church carries its institutional anxiety and fear. There seems to be a sense that the bottom is dropping out for the mainline Christian church. In a time in which we are far more interested in debating human sexuality, ordination standards, and control of property, we have lost our passion for the mission of Christ in making disciples and doing evangelism. The truth is that the situation is bringing us to our knees and is calling us to repentance. We are at a turning point in which our cries for help for God to listen are ascending to the heavens.

II. Praying Our Hope

Out of the depths we pray to the One who sees, hears, speaks, and promises his presence and power. The Psalm promises that Israel's God is the God of steadfast love, and with him is great power to redeem. "It is he who will redeem Israel from all its iniquities." Ps. 130:7-8.

"If you, O Lord, should mark iniquities, Lord, who could stand? But there is forgiveness with you, so that you may be revered."

"I wait for the LORD, my soul waits, and in his Word, I hope. O Israel, hope in the LORD!" Ps. 130:3-4, 7.

This is the theology of hope. During praying our pain, we also pray our hope.

At the deepest levels of our prayers, we know that the LORD'S word of promise is of forgiveness. This is truly good news for saints and sinners, for we are all sinners. For surely, "all have sinned and fallen short of God's glory. There is no one who is righteous, no not one." (Romans 3.) This was the Apostle Paul's argument in his Letter to the Romans. At every moment of human existence, we are reminded that we are totally dependent upon the grace of God.

Our sins have separated us from God, but God has proven his love for us in that while we were still sinners, the Son of God died for us to reconcile us to God and to one another. God acted to build a bridge between himself and humanity. That bridge is the cross of Jesus, and we are invited to come back to fellowship with God by means of the blood of Christ.

In large measure, the waters that threaten to drown us are our sins. We need forgiveness, whether we know it or not. A few years ago, I was auditing a course at UCI on the novels of Ernest Hemmingway and William Faulkner. During that time one of you gave me a book of all of Hemmingway's short stories. One of them was entitled, "*The Capital of the World*".

The setting of the story was Madrid. Hemmingway wrote,

"Madrid is full of boys named Paco, and there is a Madrid joke about a father who came to Madrid and inserted an advertisement in the personal columns of El Liberal which said: 'PACO MEET ME AT HOTEL MONTANA NOON TUESDAY ALL IS FORGIVEN PAPA' and how a squadron of Guardia Civil or police had to be called out to disperse the eight hundred young men who answered the advertisement."[3]

On the way to Utah, I was reading Miroslav Volf's new book on forgiveness, entitled *Free of Charge, Giving and Forgiving in a Culture Stripped of Grace*. He opened his chapter on forgiveness with Hemmingway's story about Paco.

Volf wrote,

> "The joke is about the ubiquity of the name 'Paco' in Spain. But it works only because of the underlying longing of many to be forgiven, whether they are sons or daughters, mothers or fathers, friends, or colleagues. We desire forgiveness because we value relationships, and we know that relationships cannot be mended without forgiveness." [4]

The good news is that God is the Forgiver. This is the message that is at the heart of our Psalm. To be sure, we pray our pain and suffering. We pray the incompleteness of our lives. We are aware that we have not

---

3. Hemmingway, *Complete Short Stories*, The Finca Vigia Edition.
4. Volf, Free of Charge, 127.

loved God with the totality of our being, nor have we loved our neighbors as ourselves. We are a broken people. We pastors are wounded healers who carry the scars of our sins in our own lives. What this means is that we understand that we have contributed to the depths of our own pain and are partially responsible for the wreckage of both church and culture. Our greatest need is to hear a word of hope that will call us and empower us to turn to God and to others in confession. We turn in hopes that God's grace will restore us, heal us, and bring us together in fellowship with all those from whom we are separated.

For this we wait. For this we watch. For this we hope. Our longing is to see the fullness of God's salvation in the church and in the world for which Christ died. Sometimes we lose hope and conclude that our world is so messed up that it can never be mended. Yet, we experience ourselves as called to work for the healing of the world.

The truth is that every one of us is deeply wounded. We live in a broken and fallen world and there are many manifestations of the wreckage. In the 1970's it was the Catholic priest, Henri Nouwen, who spoke openly and honestly of his struggles to keep his head above the waters. He said that pastors and priests are but wounded healers. He had experienced many times in his life in which he felt he was going under the waters. He was afflicted with deep insecurities and struggled with depressions that were complicated by his loneliness.

He had an emotional breakdown and during that time he wrote a diary of the experience later published as *The Inner Voice of Love*. In his diary he challenged himself to live through his wounds. For him this meant living one's wounds from the heart and not just from the head. He believed then in a mysterious way, wounds would become a means toward both hope and healing.

Michael Ford's book on Nouwen entitled, *Wounded Prophet*, not only witnessed to Henri's struggles but also to those of J.B. Phillips, the British Bible translator, whose New Testament translations caused millions to hear the message with new relevance. Not many people knew that Phillips struggled with depression and perfectionism. "Phillip's ministry was worldwide. He guided many through the dark places of doubt and loss of faith. While he was doing this for others, he was himself powerfully afflicted by dark thoughts and mental pains. He knew anxiety and depression, from which there was only temporary release."[5]

---

5. Ford, *Wounded Prophet*, 51.

Nouwen loved the old legend in the Jewish Talmud of the question that came to Elijah about recognizing the Messiah. Elijah said to the questioner that you will find him sitting at the gates of the city. "How shall I know him?" "He is sitting among the poor, covered with wounds. The others unbind all their wounds at the same time and then bind them up again. But he unbinds one at a time and binds it up again, saying to himself, 'Perhaps I shall be needed: If so, I must always be ready so as not to delay for a moment.'"[6]

PCUSA Board of Pensions

Shortly after the first Pastor's Sabbath, the moderator of the group, Bill Forbes, a pastor from New Jersey, moved to the staff of the Board of Pensions. He asked if I would join a national tall steeple pastor's group to dialogue about the work of the Board. I told him I did not think of myself as a tall steeple pastor since our church only had 700 members and the assumption was that a tall steeple pastor would be the leader of a thousand – member plus congregation. He said he still wanted me in the group. I joined the group. It met two times a year in Philadelphia. I was grateful that Bill trusted me and felt I had something to contribute to the Board.

This proved to be a stimulating experience. I was introduced to several leaders in the PCUSA. We spoke of our concerns for the larger church given the divisions and different theological worldviews. We also were introduced to the work of the Board of Pensions that invests and manages the dues received from congregations on behalf of their pastors. It was encouraging that the Board was interested in listening to the grassroots concerns of our pastors.

The Board of Trustees for the Board of Pensions has done an excellent job investing its resources. It is probably the strongest Church Pension program of all denominations. It was developed to allow the servants of the church to retire with some well-being and dignity. All of us are grateful for the faithful stewardship of these assets.

---

6. Nouwen, *Wounded Healer,*

Presbyterian Divestment

The PCUSA was a strong supporter of the State of Israel when it was established in 1948. We have acknowledged that our spiritual roots are in the Jewish people. We have worked hard to guarantee that a Jewish Holocaust never happens again as it did in the 1930's and early 40's in Europe. We carry guilt for the long history of anti-Semitism among Christians.

But since the founding of the State of Israel we have had a growing concern for the Arab Palestinian people who were driven from their historic land in Palestine to settle the growing number of refugees from Europe. Historically, the Presbyterian mission outreach has been active among Arab people throughout the Middle East. We built schools, hospitals, and social welfare programs, along with Presbyterian churches. Therefore, when Palestinian Christians began crying out for justice, we supported their cry, since this was the cry of the prophets of Israel and of Jesus of Nazareth.

I responded to an email from a college student doing an internship at the Simon Wiesenthal Center in Los Angeles. He said his colleagues there questioned the PCUSA's divestment controversy. He asked me to explain.

> PC(USA) AND ISRAEL 2004
> By Dr. Jerry Tankersley
> Pastor, Laguna Presbyterian Church
> Dear - --,
> Thank you for the invitation to share my observations and concerns about the relationship between we Presbyterian Christians and our brothers and sisters who worship the God of Israel, whom we Gentiles have come to know through faith in Jesus Christ. In writing this, I am aware that the State of Israel is a nation among nations and that not all citizens of Israel are religiously connected. However, it does seem that the vast majority of American Jews, religious and non-religious, are united in their support of the State of Israel. My comments to you are written from the perspective of a Presbyterian Christian who values what Christians and Jews share. I am especially concerned that you communicate to the men and women of the Simon Wiesenthal Center my sincere affection, gratitude, and compassion in this time of tension between Presbyterians and Jews. I am committed to being a peacemaker and facilitator of a deepening interfaith dialogue among Christians, Jews, and Muslims.

I hope that you will direct your Jewish friends to the website of the PC(USA) and encourage them to carefully link to the posted materials that seek to interpret what the General Assemblies of our church have said over the past 50 years. It seems to me that our Assemblies have been straightforward, honest, and deeply committed to encouraging reconciliation, peace, and justice in the Middle East. Some within the Jewish community may not approve nor appreciate what has been written and affirmed, but it has been reasoned, intelligent, compassionate, and a reflection of our complex theological vision and love for all the people living in Israel/Palestine. Let me refer you to this link: www.pcusa.org/interfaith/assembly.htm The link will provide links to all the documents we have produced over several decades. Please take the time to read them.

I cannot speak for the members of my congregation. Nor can I speak for the General Assembly. We are a people of many different opinions on the various issues before the church currently. Our session has taken no formal position about Israel/Palestine. So far as I know, our presbytery has not taken a vote on any of the G.A. positions related to the State of Israel. The G.A. speaks to the church, but not for the church. The Constitution of the Presbyterian Church (USA) gives voice to our belief that, "God alone is Lord of the conscience, and hath left it free from the doctrines and commandments of men which are in anything contrary to his Word, or beside it, in matters of faith or worship." "Therefore, we consider the rights of private judgment, in all matters that respect religion, as universal and unalienable." Book of Order G-1.0300–01.

"That all Church power, whether exercised by the body in general or in the way of representation by delegated authority, is only ministerial and declarative; that is to say, that the Holy Scriptures are the only rule of faith and manners; that no Church governing body ought to pretend to make laws to bind the conscience in virtue of their own authority; and that all their decisions should be founded upon the revealed will of God. Now though it will easily be admitted that all synods and councils may err, through the frailty inseparable from humanity . . . ." Book of Order G-1.0307

Built into our Constitution is a commitment to leading the church with a democratic-representative polity, with dependence upon the illumination of the Word of God by the Holy Spirit. In humility, we regularly confess before God that we are sinners, that we may be wrong, that we may willfully fail, and that we must continually ask for God's forgiveness. History is filled with a long record of Christian failure, unfaithfulness, and outright sin in our relationships with the Jewish people.

We have attempted to speak truth to power, based on our understanding of God's call for truth, reconciliation, and justice. However, we also recognize that we are sinners, and that we may be wrong. We pray that God will continue to open our eyes to areas in which we have fallen short in our relationships with Jewish people, so that we might ask forgiveness. We also pray that, if we have correctly spoken the truth, that it will be heard and heeded.

Having said this, the PC(USA) has often had prophetic insights and truthful convictions about many issues. As we have come to know the will of God, we have courageously witnessed. Our witness has sometimes divided our own camp, stirred anger, and lost us members whose personal convictions were offended. In 1861 we divided over slavery in America. In the 1960's, the issues of civil rights, the war in Vietnam, and truth in government polarized us. Since the 1970's we have had major conflicts and tensions, as has the breadth of American society, over the issues of abortion, human sexuality, ordination, same sex marriages, race, the war on terrorism, the war in Iraq, and, increasingly, over positions taken on Israel/Palestine.

We have studied many issues, written position papers, made pronouncements, and largely been dismissed by the political, economic, and religious power brokers of American society. This is perplexing for those who feel they have something to contribute and who want to be taken seriously.

I stood for Moderator of the 214th General Assembly. The pastor elected as Moderator was an American Palestinian. Fahed Abul-Akel was from the Presbytery of Greater Atlanta. Partly, it was his moving faith story of what happened to his Galilean family in 1948 that moved the Assembly to endorse him as our Moderator. As a child he watched as his village and his friends were driven from their lands by the invading Jewish armies. Fahed's family were Christians, evangelized by Scottish Presbyterian missionaries. Like thousands of Palestinian Christians, he was displaced, came to America to finish his education, and now had a wonderful ministry with international students in Atlanta. His soul had been shaped by the love of God for both Jews and his own people. He incarnated the spirit of joy, love, and hope that I believed was at the heart of the PC(USA).

The following is a part of my letter that was printed in 2004 in the "Presbyterian Outlook."

1. Presbyterians have been and will continue to be some of Israel's best Christian friends. Israel's God is our God. Israel's book is our book. Like most western Christians, we bear the burden of history's guilt over the Jewish people. I have been to Israel four times, leading groups on study seminars. We have visited the Holocaust Memorial in Jerusalem. Many of us have visited the European death camps of the Third Reich. The Christian Church was mainly silent through this period of history. We repent of our silence. This is a source of profound grief for us and we are not about to replay that sin.

2. Our spiritual roots are in the Jewish people. We were engrafted onto the olive tree of Israel by faith in Jesus, to whom our Scriptures witness as Messiah, the Christ. Our Savior and Lord was a Jew, as were his first followers. Historically, the church has been made up of believing Jews and Gentiles. Israel's suffering is our suffering. We do not understand the mystery of this suffering. Somehow, we pray that it may be redemptive. We want nothing more than for the State of Israel to live within secure borders, with peace and justice, and with warm relations with her neighbors, the Palestinians. We believe that God is sovereign, and that God's covenant promises will, in God's time and way, come to fulfillment for all Israel. (Romans 9–11).

3. We have historic ties to Arab and non-Arab Christian Churches of the Middle East, including the Palestinian Christians. We have watched their struggle to survive, to grow a new nation on their own ancestral lands, to work for peace and justice. Only a few Christians remain in Israel/Palestine. They are being squeezed out of their homeland by the State of Israel, Israeli settlers, and by some Muslim elements in their society. We believe that a Holy Land, emptied of its Christians, will become a witness to man's inhumanity to man. As American Presbyterians we are not about to abandon either our Jewish friends or our Palestinian brothers and sisters. This places us in the middle, being torn, frustrated, grieved, hoping, and longing to see a new day of peace and prosperity in which Jews and Arabs will be living side by side.

4. If you have read our documents, you are aware that many of us are convinced that neither the Jews of Israel or the Jews of America, nor the Palestinians, have been listening to our passionate concerns. We have watched as the cycles of

violence and revenge have escalated. World Terrorism is, at least to some degree, the result of the inability of the Israelis and the Palestinians to work out their differences and to renounce violence. Therefore, the violence has spread and continues to threaten human life everywhere. On 9/11/01 it touched the United States. Peace must be won, not just with bombs, missiles, and armies, but by the hard work of negotiating differences, and by the assertion of the political will of all faiths and peoples. Our General Assembly has consistently called upon all Palestinians, whatever their faith, to renounce violence and terror against the State of Israel.

5. In frustration, the 216th G.A. voted to move toward a possible selective divestment in multi-national corporations doing business in or selling products used by the State of Israel to make war upon innocent Palestinians. Please note, the report will go to the Council of the G.A. next March 2005. If there are recommended actions, the next G.A. will review them in 2006. Before that happens there will be much study, dialogue, and many efforts made to spell out expectations from corporations before any economic divestment might be enacted. But the intent is serious, and the leaders of the world Jewish community need to hear the cry of their friends.

6. The separation wall, being built through the heartland of Israel/Palestine, will become an even greater problem for the world. "Though it is being built to promote security for Israel", it is going to hurt Israel and be a symbol of oppression. It will not make Israel safer. Better to use Israel's resources to build bridges for peace! The wall only enflames Israel's enemies with deeper resentment and gives to the citizens of Israel a false sense of security. The western world well remembers President Reagan's challenge concerning the Berlin Wall, "Tear Down This Wall!"

7. Your friends at Simon Wiesenthal must be aware of the Presbyterian ambivalence about evangelizing Jews. The very liberals who voted for selective divestment are the ones who are opposed to the messianic church in Philadelphia. It is presbyteries that start new churches. My guess is that Presbyterian messianic new church developments will be few around America and will not represent any threat to the Jewish identity or community. The greater weakness, and embarrassment, of the PC(USA) is that we do not know how to witness to our faith in ways that produce either Jewish or

Gentile Christian's converts. We are probably as awkward about this as are the Jews in spreading their faith. Israel's major concern ought to be its Protestant fundamentalist friends, Christian Zionists, who are prepared to uncritically endorse whatever Israel does, but for the goal of converting all Jews to Christianity.

Having said all of this, I do have to share with you my reaction to the Jewish response to our 216th G.A. Dennis Prager and the world Jewish media have written things about the Presbyterian Church (USA), that not only distort, but also reveal the writers have not carefully read our website documents. There have been efforts by the Jewish community to stir up strife among Presbyterian believers and to divide congregations. Efforts have been made to publicly persuade our members to leave our churches and to withdraw financial support. We have been called, "stupid, immoral, evil, anti-Semitic, liberal, unpatriotic, etc". These labels have about the same impact upon us as the words, "Christ killers", have upon the Jewish community. They call into question the progress we have made in understanding and interfaith dialogue and reveal what still lurks in the heart of our separation, and that is: lack of trust, lack of mutual respect, and hostility.

I would encourage the Jewish leadership to find a way to apologize to its Presbyterian friends who have sought to "speak the truth in love" to a nation that seems determined to have its ways whatever it may cost the world. We have heard the Jewish anger and public protest. Jews have heard our frustration and conviction. Now let us find ways to stay in dialogue and to cooperate in making peace and loving our enemies.

The stakes are too high for us to fail. We have too much in common for us to fail. Our knowledge of God and the rich spirituality of our traditions are desperately needed by an increasingly hopeless, polarized world. Please assure your Simon Wiesenthal friends that they have friends in the Presbyterian Church (USA).

In Covenant Love,
Dr. Jerry Tankersley
Pastor
Laguna Presbyterian Church, Laguna Beach, California

Not too long after this letter was written and published, I was invited to a gathering in Louisville at the Old Brown Hotel. The subject was Peacemaking in the Middle East. Several hundred from across the

U.S came to this informative session. I was invited to join in a panel discussion and addressed the question of Christian Zionism and its impact upon the membership of our churches. Books arguing a Dispensational, Christian Zionist, interpretation of Scripture and the importance of Israel in God's plan for the ages had influenced the laity of many Presbyterian Churches across the nation. Hal Lindsey's *Late Great Planet Earth*: Tim LaHay and Jerry Jenkins' multi-volume series called, *Left Behind*; presented Dispensational, Christian Zionist interpretations of Scripture and the second coming of Christ. The multi-volume story and movie led many of our people to think this was the truth of the Word of God in a modern story form. People loved these stories. The author's made millions of dollars from this project. One man, a former member of my church who had moved to another state told me that the Left Behind book scared him to death and led him to a spiritual conversion. "He did not want to be left behind".

It grieved me that we Presbyterians had so neglected our Reformed eschatology and failed to preach or to teach the inbreaking kingdom of God and the second coming of Jesus, that we had left our people unprepared to deal with the errors of Dispensational teachings. Many fundamentalist churches were jammed to listen to the distorted interpretations of the State of Israel. Political leaders uncritically embraced these 19th century theories that moved away from the central teachings of the Protestant Reformation. Reformed doctrines neglected have often led to cultic type teachings that have swayed the masses. (See the booklet, *Between Millennia, What Presbyterians Believe About the Coming of Christ*, published by the PCUSA in 2001 on behalf of the Office of Theology and Worship; Stephen Sizer, *Christian Zionism: Road map to Armageddon?* IVP Academic; UK, 2006)

During these years I sought to prepare the members of LPC to more fully understand the issues presented by Israel/Palestine. We sponsored a series of Sunday evening conversations with Palestinian and Jewish local citizens. I led these conversations. Across the street from LPC was an American Indian jewelry store. Ironically, it was owned by a Palestinian woman born in Bethlehem and who knew the story. She invited her Palestinian friends. They came from across Southern California. Mainly, they were Muslims. The first session we had a few Jews, but they fell away after the clash in the conversation. We met several times. Our Presbyterian church members were amazed at the intensity of feelings and arguments. It was all I could do to moderate the conversation, to be balanced, and to present some of the arguments I had made in 2004 in the Outlook response.

It could have been an explosive event. Somehow, we managed, made a lot of friends with American Arab Muslims, and threatened some local Jews. I was glad that we had hosted the discussion. But clearly, we were at the center of a controversial issue often avoided by pastors and churches.

My guess is that the vast majority of Southern California Presbyterians believe that the rise of the State of Israel after WWII was the fulfilment of Old Testament prophesies. The assumption was that after the suffering of the Holocaust that the western countries needed to support a homeland for the refugee Jews who had suffered so greatly. In fact, practices of the German Third Reich in attempting to murder every European Jew for the sake of allowing the Aryan race to flourish is one of history's low moments that ought to grieve the soul of all humanity. Anti-Semitism has afflicted the soul of America, even after WWII. There is great work to do. All of this, I believe, breaks the heart of God, and betrays the vision of justice and peace in all our traditions.

Nevertheless, one would have thought that a people who had suffered so many loses would have a heightened concern for the Palestinian people who were driven into captivity into refugee camps around the Middle East. The history of the State of Israel has demonstrated its continued desires to remove Palestinians from their historic lands for the sake of expanding the Jewish State. Many Jews of Israel strongly believe that God promised them this land and that they will never return it.

Rewriting the PCUSA Paper on the Relationship Between Christians and Jews.

In the early fall 2005 I received a call from Pastor Jay Rock who was the coordinator of the Office of Interfaith Relations of the G.A. He invited me to participate in a series of dialogues with other Presbyterian pastors and theologians, along with an equal number of American Jewish leaders who represented the various expressions of American Jewish religion. From 2005 to 2009 we met in dialogue at Princeton Theological Seminary, Columbia Theological Seminary in Georgia, at a retreat center near Swarthmore Pennsylvania, and finally back at Princeton Seminary.

At the fall 2005 meeting in October Jay Rock picked me up late at night at the Newark, N.J. airport. As we left the airport, we lost our way on the streets of Newark. It was not exactly a good time of day for two white guys to be circling around in an all-African American neighborhood. The Halloween season was in full force on the east coast. I remember walking the sidewalks of Princeton surrounded by fall colors and deep piles of leaves that crunched under my feet. Children were out trick or treating. It was an idyllic setting and brought back memories of my student year at the seminary.

This was our first introduction. The Jewish-Christian group reflected on the 1987 paper approved by a previous G.A. entitled, "The Relationship between Christians and Jews". The document contained seven major points that were the affirmations that Presbyterians believed foundational for interfaith dialogue. They were:

- a reaffirmation that the God who addresses both Christians and Jews is the same—the living and true God.
- a new understanding by the Church that its own identity is intimately related to the continuing identity of the Jewish people.
- a willingness to ponder with Jews the mystery of God's election of both Jews and Christians to be a light to the nations.
- an acknowledgement by Christians that Jews are in covenant relationship with God and the consideration of the implications of this reality for evangelism and witness.
- a determination by Christians to put an end to "the teaching of contempt for the Jews".
- a willingness to investigate the continuing significance of the promise of "land" and its associated obligations and to explore the implications for Christian theology.
- a readiness to act on the hope that we share with the Jews in God's promise of the peaceable kingdom.

PCUSA, Theology and Worship #7, "Christians and Jews: People of God", A Theological Understanding of The Relationship Between Christians and Jews", Louisville: 1987

The first dialogues we had were provocative to me. The question of "truth" was presented to the combined gathering? Our small groups discussed the question, "What is truth?". When the groups reported the results of their conversation, the Rabbis' responses were that there was no one true answer to this question. Reformed, Reconstructionist, and Conservative, gave post-modern answers: "truth is a matter of personal conviction, and those assertions or subjective preferences cannot be objectively proven to the satisfaction of others."

I was thankful that Pastor Joe Small answered for the Presbyterian delegation. For us truth was revealed in Jesus the Christ, "the way, the truth, and the life." John 14:6. For our confessional community truth was revealed in the person of Jesus Christ. John 1. "The law was given by Moses, grace and truth came through Jesus Christ," the Word of God incarnate.

What a way to begin our dialogue, I thought to myself. For me truth was a matter of revelation and not of reason or personal experience alone. Reason and experience were important, but openness to see, to hear, and to believe the Word of God in Scripture was foundational. Without this foundation we had no place to begin. We were all in need of the Spirit of Truth revealed in Jesus. We began and these conversations and papers were presented in the form of a book entitled, *Let Us Reason Together, Christians and Jews in Conversation.* Edited by Joseph D. Small\ Gilbert S. Rosenthal, Witherspoon Press, 2010

Our Jewish friends were gracious and hospitable. At each gathering they provided kosher food and it was delicious. At our last session at Princeton, it was clear that they had one unified conviction and that was the importance of the State of Israel. The conversation was passionate and heated. It was an awkward moment, but we each held our ground, expressed our love for the people of Israel, but called for the State of Israel to promote reconciliation and justice for all the people under their control.

Over four years and four conversations we made good friends. Especially, I grew to respect and to love Rabbi Gil Rosenthal. Across the years I have enjoyed Jewish friends with whom I have had conversations about life, faith, hope, and love. Jewish people have blessed me, and we have been mutually supportive.

At the end of the dialogues a new paper was written. I did not write the paper. I think Jay Rock, Joe Small, and Charles Wiley wrote the paper based on the deliberations. It was presented to the G.A. committee that was assigned to consider if it would be presented to the entire G.A. for approval. I wrote my response to the paper to Jay Rock. I warned that our Palestinian advocacy group would not be pleased with the results. It was too pro-Israel and not an adequate account of the dilemma of the Palestinian people. Fahed Abul Akel was a major antagonist against the paper. That is exactly what happened. Fahed's group of Palestinian supporters protested before the G.A. committee and the committee voted to reject the new paper.

Sometime after this I was invited by the Presbyterian Office at Fuller Theological Seminary to represent Fuller at the International Conference of Jews for Jesus that was meeting in San Francisco. At my own expense I flew up and spent the night at the hotel of the gathering. I think this larger gathering was pro-Zionist in its thinking. I brought copies of my 2004 Presbyterian Outlook article on Israel/Palestine, and the PCUSA. They wanted me to present the Presbyterian theology on the State of Israel. The response was very cool to me and almost hostile. But I was glad to have been exposed to this group of Jewish Christians who were involved in Messianic Churches. The mainstream American Jewish groups believed that the Messianic congregation founded in Philadelphia by the Presbytery of Philadelphia was dishonest and was seeking to present the Christian gospel under the guise of a Jewish synagogue.

Joining Hearts and Hands: PCUSA

This was an effort of the denomination to raise 40 million dollars for the purpose of New Church Development, Redevelopment, and mission personnel. Two of my friends in the Presbytery of Los Ranchos, Bill Saul and John Huffman, were on the national JHH's Task Force. I was asked to chair the Presbytery effort to raise $4.5 million dollars, $3.5 million for our Presbytery, and $1 million for the national church and its international mission. I wrote,

> "Joining Hearts and Hands: Los Ranchos goes to the very core of who we are as Presbyterians. Through this initiative, we can join as one, focusing our efforts on evangelism and mission. Working together we can make a profound difference—from starting new churches in our own neighborhoods, to expanding our ethnic ministries, to sending new mission workers into the field."

I visited almost every session of our Presbytery churches. Our Presbytery committee had set estimated goals for each of our churches. We hoped St. Andrews would give $1.5 million. They made this commitment and paid their pledge immediately. We asked Laguna Beach for $500,000. Since Laguna was just launching its major fund drive for the redevelopment of our campus, we believed we could provide leadership to the Presbytery and be a good faith support for my appeals to the other churches as I met with their church sessions.

Our session pledged the $500,000 as a witness to our own members to the importance of reaching beyond ourselves. I was very proud of them, even though not everyone in the church was strongly supportive. As it turned out in the long run, after we had given the $500,000, in order to succeed in paying off our $7 million mortgage, we asked the Presbytery to return $250,000 for the purpose of making our final payments. The Presbytery Trustees agreed to this over a ten-year period. I will return to the meaning of this return commitment later in the memoir.

When all was said and done, the Presbytery made its goal of $4.5 million, and we all rejoiced. It was a major accomplishment given the tensions within the denomination during those years.

C.S. Lewis

In 2004 John Huffman called and said he had been given an opportunity to join a tour with the C.S. Lewis Foundation led by Stan Mattson. It would begin in Belfast, Ireland, move to Dublin, join the Sea Cloud II for several days, and then motor up to Oxford, UK, to visit Lewis' home named "The Kilns". John's wife Anne was not interested so he invited me to join him. For years I had enjoyed the writings of C.S. Lewis, and in particular *Mere Christianity* and *The Chronicles of Narnia*. John and I joined the group at a greatly reduced cost. The Sea Cloud was a huge, luxury sailing ship with its own history. The group was made up of Lewis's devotees who were wealthy and could afford the high price of the tour. The theme was *The Voyage of the Dawn Treader*. Each evening on the Sea Cloud, Douglas Gresham, Lewis' stepson, read to us from chapters of the *Dawn Treader*. It was a sweet time. In Dublin I had opportunity to visit the National Museum of Art and Trinity University with its *Book of Kells*. As we boarded the Sea Cloud, I was touched by the bronze statues in the harbor depicting people leaving Ireland during the famine years.

We sailed across the Irish Sea to St. David in Wales. Our intention was to go to church at St. David where John Stott was preaching. By the time we arrived off the coast the tail end of Hurricane Charlie was approaching, and the captain warned us about trying to board the tender to disembark for St. David. Some did, but I did not. It was Sunday and the seas were rough. The Captain of the Sea Cloud was concerned about getting across the Channel that evening. Nevertheless, that afternoon we motored off to the next port of call in Ireland.

I was asked to say the opening prayer in the dining room that evening before the dinner. As I approached the dining room, I felt the waves of sea sickness overwhelm me. I needed to return to my room. I left word for Stan and returned to lie on my bed and to hang on for dear life. That night the full force of hurricane winds blew upon the sea. John came down to my room to check on me. He said thirty to fifty - foot waves were breaking over the bow of the ship. I had taken every sea - sick pill I could handle. If I was flat on my back my nausea did not lead me to vomit. John reported that the storm had cleared the dining room. Plates were flying. Wine bottles were being tossed across the room. People were getting sick and staggering to their rooms. I checked the manifest for the next port of call. It was Cork, Ireland, the last port of call for the *Titanic* on its maiden voyage across the North Atlantic in 1912. I knew the story of the great ship crashing into a submerged iceberg and sinking. This was no source of comfort for me.

I tried to sleep as I clung to my twin bed at the lower level of the Sea Cloud. I prayed and surrendered to what might happen. Sometime in the middle of the night we sailed under the leeward side of Ireland. Suddenly, the sea calmed, and we were safe from the hurricane. I went to sleep. The next morning, I learned that several on the Sea Cloud were very ill from seasickness.

That day we visited the Blarney Stone Castle built in the 15th century. Of course, we lay down on our backs to kiss the Blarney Stone by hanging into a bottomless, narrow hole. Thankfully, there was a guard who held each of us tight as we lowered our bodies into the open Castle hole. I purchased an Irish woolen hat in the gift store of the Castle and the group returned to the Sea Cloud to motor over night to islands off the coast of England where there was a tropical garden and walkways. On the way to the ship, we visited the famous Waterford Chrystal glass factory near Cork where we saw the famous glass pieces being manufactured. Indeed, it was a journey not unlike what Lewis described in the *Voyage of the Dawn Treader*. The magic of the land of Narnia was coming alive in my imagination.

At Plymouth, England, John departed for Scotland, and I went on with the group by bus across the Cotswold's, to Wells, into the Cathedral of Wells, to Bath where we walked around the Roman baths. Then it was on to Oxford. We stayed at the famous Randolph Hotel. Then we visited the sites around Oxford related to C.S. Lewis. Stan Mattson led the group to the Kilns and to the Headington Church of England where Lewis worshiped and where he was buried in the church's cemetery. One evening Walter Hooper, Lewis' editor, joined us for dinner. What a delight to be introduced to the one who had known Jack very well and had edited some of his writings and had become an expert on his stories and other writings.

On August 28, 2004, I sat alone in the Oxford pub named "The Eagle and the Child" or "The Bird and Baby" founded in 1650 A.D. I finished reading Lewis' *The Great Divorce*. I wrote at the beginning of the book, "Lewis and Tolkien and other 'Inklings' met regularly in this pub. I had lunch there on this date as a part of the C.S. Lewis Study Tour". I signed, "Jerry Tankersley".

Friendships may be fragile. Relationships may change, but grace and gratitude prevail over time. So, it was for Tolkien and Lewis. Humphrey Carpenter ended his book *The Inklings, C.S. Lewis, J.R.R. Tolkien, Charles Williams, and their friends*, with a quote from a letter Tolkien wrote to one of his children.

> "I am sorry that I have not answered your letters sooner; but Jack Lewis's death on the 22nd has preoccupied me. It is also involving me in some correspondence, as many people still regard me as one of his intimates. Alas! That ceased to be some ten years ago. We were separated first by the sudden apparition of Charles Williams, and then by his marriage. But we owed each a great debt to the other, and that tie, with the deep affection that it begot, remained. He was a great man of whom the cold-blooded official obituaries have only scraped the surface."[7]

One evening our group attended an outdoor Patriotic Concert at Blenheim Palace, not far from Oxford. Before the evening was over the orchestra and the choir performed the Church of England hymn with lyrics from William Blake's famous poem. There was magic in the night air as the audience stood on the green at Blenheim Palace under the stars. Maybe it was the magic of Oxford and C.S. Lewis. I was enchanted and reminded that in a mysterious way all our work in the world is to build the justice and peace of the New Jerusalem into our sin-sick world. The movie, *"Chariots of Fire"* had ended with this national anthem being sung. I had taken a literature course several years before and fallen in love

---

7. Carpenter, *The Inklings*, 252.

with British Romanticism, of which Blake was an early representative in his protest against the excesses of the Industrial Revolution. Blake's poem about *Jerusalem* had been put to music and had become a patriotic statement of love for England. The words of the poem were these:

> And did those feet in ancient time,
> Walk upon Englands mountains green:
> And was the holy Lamb of God,
> On Englands pleasant pastures seen!
> And did the Countenance Divine,
> Shine forth upon our clouded hills?
> And was Jerusalem builded here,
> Among these dark Satanic Mills?
> Bring me my Bow of burning gold:
> Bring me my Arrows of desire:
> Bring me my Spear: O clouds unfold:
> Bring me my Chariot of fire!
> I will not cease from Mental Fight,
> Nor shall my Sword sleep in my hand:
> Till we have built Jerusalem,
> In Englands green & pleasant Land.
> Beneath the poem Blake inscribed a quotation from the Bible:
> "Would to God that all the Lords people were Prophets"
> Numbers XI. Ch 29.v[8]

In 2006 I received a letter from David and Linda Roberson, members of the Laguna Presbyterian Church. The letter informed me that they had made a gift to the Lewis Foundation project of renewing the Kilns, the Oxford home of Lewis. They wanted Kay and I to know that the gift had been in honor of me their pastor and friend. The Orchard Garden would be dedicated in my honor by a wooden bench and bronze plate with my name on it. They expressed their hope that I would be able to take my family to the Kilns so that we might enjoy the dedication in the Orchard Garden. They asked what I would like engraved on the plate. I suggested they put their names on it, but they declined. I suggested that if my name were on the plate it should read, "By Grace Alone". I was overwhelmed by this honor. I suggested that we put a group together from the church and do a Lewis site tour that would retrace the tour group I was on in 2004 with John Huffman.

---

8. Quoted from Wikipedia.

This we did, except for the Sea Cloud II. I wrote a study Manuel that I used to teach the group. Kay joined David Dolan in London and they met us in Oxford. The next day we dedicated the bench in the Orchard Garden. The Garden reminded me of the garden in the *Chronicles* that seemed small on the outside, but once entered was larger than the outside world. My imagination was caught up in this dedication and it was a high moment of our life made possible by the Roberson family. I had married three of their children and baptized several of their nine grandchildren. Dave and Linda were both elders in our church. I loved them. He had co-chaired our building program and Linda had served on the planning team. I will write of our rebuilding the church sanctuary later in the memoirs.

Sadly, for us, in the following years they left the Laguna Church and returned to St. Andrews in Newport Beach. They had come to think that I was moving away from my Reformed theology and tradition, especially regarding ordination standards. This grieved them and me. I could not convince them otherwise. As the years passed Dave suffered from COPD and finally passed away. Linda asked me to conduct his service at St. Andrews. I gladly did so. There must have been a thousand people in attendance. I bore witness to the good things I knew about Dave and his service to the church of Christ. His convictions and passions were strong, and I had great respect for him. When I retired, Linda and her children and grandchildren attended my final service in June 2018. I hugged her as I walked out of the sanctuary knowing that for me and her the pain and love were real. This was one of those pastoral moments that I will never forget.

Shortly before Dave passed, he came to my church office with a framed picture of the old prophet Simeon holding the baby Jesus in his arms with tears running down his face. Simeon spoke these words of prophesy over Jesus,

> "Master, now you are dismissing your servant in peace, according to your word; for my eyes have seen your salvation, which you have prepared in the presence of all peoples, a light for revelation to the Gentiles and for glory to your people Israel."
>
> "Then Simeon blessed them and said to his mother Mary, 'This child is destined for the falling and the rising of many in Israel, and to be a sign that will be opposed so that the inner thoughts of many will be revealed—and a sword will pierce your own soul too.'" (Luke 2:29–35)

Dave told me that his new pastor at St. Andrews had shown this painting on the worship screen while preaching on the text from Luke. The Spirit spoke to Dave, he said, and affirmed that I was the Simeon in the text holding him and his family for many years and weeping over him. He asked that it hang in my church office as a reminder of their thanksgiving for me. Wow! I was stunned. The painting print was beautifully framed as fitting to hang in the Roberson home. It is now in my home office.

I am not sure what Dave meant by his interpretation of the picture. He did not remain in my office for long, but it seemed like an effort for a deep reconciliation and an affirmation of our wonderful, yet painful relationship. I treasure Dave's sentiments expressed to me. It has helped heal some of the pain he caused by leaving LPC under such circumstances. I look forward to glad heavenly reunion with him in the fulness of time.

Kay left the Lewis group and returned to L.A. I went with the group to Cambridge University to visit the college where Lewis taught in his final years. In Lewis' quarters where he lived during that time of his life, I had the privilege of reviewing some of his personal books from his library. One of them was a copy of Shakespeare's *Hamlet*. I was drawn to the notes he made in the margins and his observations inside the front cover. I felt like I was on holy ground and that I held in my hand's a personal item of my hero's work.

The group scattered after our time in Cambridge. On my way to Heathrow, I heard that a plot had been discovered to blow up airplanes flying from London to LAX. The strategy was to place explosives in small bottles of liquids that would not be detected by security. The lines at Heathrow were blocks long. I waited. At last, we boarded the flight, and all was well. But in L.A. the plane was not allowed to go through customs at the Bradley International Airport but was moved to another terminal. There we waited for five hours while our baggage was taken to the x-ray machines at another terminal. We were all fit to be tied after an eleven – hour flight, and then to be held waiting for baggage for five more hours. When I finally walked up the terminal tunnel, Kay was anxiously and thankfully waiting to pick me up. I was so happy to see her and to be at home.

Peace, Unity, and Purity Task Force Report

During the first decade of the new millennium, especially from 2003 to 2010, there was constant rumbling among many conservative churches across the denomination. Likewise, the Covenant Network churches, with their advocacy of gay ordination, continued to push for change in the standards adopted in 1997. Through the decade, the polarization grew. We were becoming a denomination of red, blue, and purple churches. The struggle for most pastors was in preserving the "peace, unity, and purity" of their congregations without alienating one side or another. Those of strong biblical/theological conviction of the left or the right were coming to view the other side with disdain. The talk of schism was in the air.

The PUP Task Force was made up of representatives of all parts of our denomination. They were charged with discerning God's will on issues of Christology, biblical authority and interpretation, ordination standards, and power. The central issues revolved around the haunting question of the ordination of avowed practicing homosexual persons by the judicatories of the denomination. What did Scripture say about human sexuality and how were Christians to live out their discipleship under the authority of the Bible and our Book of Confessions? What did we think about marriage? These questions increased the deepening divisions within the church. Was it possible to pastor a congregation with many in different camps on these emotional issues?

After the Report was published and presented to the G.A. there was a church wide effort to interpret in all our Presbyteries the results of the study and recommendations. During that time, San Francisco Theological Seminary and Fuller Theological Seminary hosted a joint interpretation for the Synod of Southern California and Hawaii. Members of the Task Force were present at the Pasadena Presbyterian Church for the interpretation. I had been invited to participate in the panel discussion consisting of the Seminary Presidents and members of the TF. When David Tomlinson introduced me for the panel, he was very complimentary. He had been the Executive of Los Ranchos and we had worked together in many ways as I had with our earlier executive, John Chandler. He shared that I was the one to whom the Presbytery had looked for wisdom and commitment to the mission of our churches. I was a trusted peacemaker within the body of Christ. This was what I had hoped to have affirmed about me in a diverse and divided church. My presentation followed:

THEOLOGICAL TASK FORCE REPORT:

The Highways To Louisville And Beyond

PEACE, UNITY, AND PURITY
"COME TO THE TABLE"
FULLER/SFTS DIALOGUE Pasadena Presbyterian Church

Invited Response by Dr. Jerry Tankersley, January 18, 2006
Pastor, Laguna Presbyterian Church, Laguna Beach, CA

"Thank you for inviting me to respond to the report of the Theological Task Force on Peace, Unity, and Purity. As I do so I am very much aware that we are engaged in a family dialogue and conflict. Some members of the Task Force I have known and loved for years. Some of my colleagues on the Task Force have nurtured my life in special ways. I have profound respect and love for them each. I wish to say "thank you" to the entire Task Force for their friendship and their willingness to serve and to risk becoming targets for those who disagree with the results of their report.

Let me say at the outset that whatever the outcome of the TF report, that I am committed to being in the PC(USA). This is the covenant community that has mediated to me the forgiveness of sins, called me to accountability, taught me the transforming gospel of Jesus Christ, and encouraged me to spiritually mature in humility, patience, the pursuit of biblical/theological truth, and in relationship with my brothers and sisters. How grateful I am for our covenant connection. Presbyterians have been a gift to America and to the world, and I believe we will continue to be, even during our conflicts. Therefore, the Task Force's recognition of our need for one another in our strengths and weaknesses, and with our diverse gifts, strikes a chord in my heart. This vision of commitment to the church was informed and inspired in my earlier years by the leadership and faculty of Fuller Seminary, as well as by others who have nurtured my love for the PC(USA).

Now, having said this, I want to make the following observations:

I celebrate the reports good news that God loves us, saves us, and empowers us to proclaim the gospel. These sections of the report need to be studied and embraced by the larger church. But I am deeply troubled by the statement beginning in line 521:

"The theological and biblical literature on human sexuality in general and same-gender sexuality is diverse, subtle, and complex. It could not readily be divided into the two categories-either approval or disapproval of same-gender relationships and practices."

But I ask, "does Scripture not clearly reveal the mind of Christ on the great issues of faith and life? How is it that we Presbyterians cannot now agree on whether Scripture has an authoritative Word to speak about God's intentions for human sexual behavior and faithfulness? Consider Romans 1, I Corinthians 6, and Ephesians 4:17–5:3. Read Richard Hays chapter on homosexuality in *The Moral Vision of the N.T.* referenced in the report's footnotes.

The report does witness against lasciviousness and calls for fidelity in all relationships. I am grateful for that. For nearly 30 years Presbyterians have studied and debated the biblical witness to God's intentions regarding human sexuality. The General Assembly's "Definitive Guidance" statement of 1978, reaffirmed in 1991 as an A.I., and written into the Book of Order in 1997 by a majority of our presbyteries, as G-6.0106b, has clearly stated that "those who are called to office in the church are to lead a life in obedience to Scripture and in conformity to the historic confessional standards of the church. Among these standards is the requirement to live either in fidelity within the covenant of marriage between a man and a woman, or chastity in singleness." This mandatory standard placed into our Constitution is consistent with what the Christian Church has believed for over 1900 years and with what our mission partners around the world believe. The Task Force Report's ambivalence about the Scripture's witness, if approved by the G.A., will, I believe, weaken our witness to biblical and confessional truth, confuse the church, and in a time of sexual anarchy, open us to ridicule in the eyes of the larger church and the world.

What is interesting is that the report's recommended A.I. of G-6.0108 would allow congregations and presbyteries to ordain practicing gay and lesbian persons if they declare their "freedom of conscience" violated by the national standard of G-6.0106b and, the ordaining body discerns that the departure is not one of the "essential tenets of the Reformed faith". To ask the G.A. to approve the suggested A.I. of G-6.0108 by-passes the presbyteries through an action of a majority of G.A. commissioners at one meeting. This is too important a matter to be trusted to the vote of one Assembly. I believe we may only "promote the peace, unity, and purity" of the church by relying on what will likely be a regular biennial debate and vote about amending the Constitution. Even if the Assembly approves the report, I see no evidence that the biennial debate will cease. Already there are 17 presbyteries requesting the G.A. that the standard be removed. Therefore, let the conflict rage and let us learn how to engage the issues with integrity, in the Spirit of Christ's truth and love, and with openness to the voice of the larger church through a majority of our presbyteries.

If the TF goal and appeal is to promote trust, recommendation #5 will only increase the lack of trust and fragmentation. I am the chairperson of our Presbytery's Joining Hearts and Hands campaign committee. I have visited many of our sessions and pastors from whom we need large pledges and have discovered that between the concerns for the TF and the issues of divestment/investment in Israel/Palestine, that many of our pastors and elders are not only lacking in trust but are outraged. If the G.A. approves the TFR as it stands, I believe our Presbytery's churches will remain in the denomination, but I fear with a growing indifference to G.A. appeals and participation. This will be tragic for a denomination that has been in a membership and mission decline for many years and needs spiritual and missional renewal."

The co-chair of the TF, Gary Demarest, my pastor-mentor, and friend of many years, responded to my presentation that in his earlier years he was one with my convictions and concerns, but over time as he matured in his thinking and pastoral experience, he had changed his mind. Gary had already made a presentation to a gathering of Presbyterians for Renewal at the Trinity Church in Santa Ana. My table at Trinity happened to also have Paul Jensen, Presbyterian laymen and lawyer, who had grown up in the Laguna Church, but which he left shortly after I had been called as its pastor. He made it clear that he hated me. Before Gary was introduced Paul commenced to insult me with language that was hurtful to everyone at the table, especially to me.

When Gary was introduced, but before he could begin his interpretation of the TF report, Paul Jensen jumped up and walked to the center of attention as everyone watched. He presented Gary with a large name tag with Benedict Arnold written upon it. He insisted that Gary had betrayed the conservative cause within the PCUSA. Gary handled the accusation with calm and made an excellent presentation.

After the Seminary Forum at PPC Gary asked permission for me to present my above statement immediately following his presentation on the floor of the Presbytery of Los Ranchos meeting Saturday at the Geneva Presbyterian Church in Laguna Hills. I also moderated the dialogue time after Presbytery in the Fellowship Hall. Repeatedly, I felt the need to support and to defend Gary from some of the hostile questions that came to him from some of our Presbytery commissioners. It was through this interchange that my conviction was confirmed that the Presbyterian Church USA needed to find a way to live together with mutual respect of our differences or we would fragment into a congregational system with walls dividing us.

Amending the Book of Order and Ordination Standards

With the acceptance of the PUP Task Force Report at the Birmingham General Assembly, the pressure mounted to change the Constitutional standards related to requirements for ordination within the PCUSA as regarding Teaching and Ruling Elders and Deacons. A following G.A. voted to approve G-2.0104b and sent it for approval by a majority of our Presbyteries. This time the required number of approvals were received, and the Book of Order was amended.

– 2.0104 Gifts and Qualifications

a. To those called to exercise special functions in the church—deacons, ruling elders, and teaching elders—God gives suitable gifts for their various duties. In addition to possessing the necessary gifts and abilities, those who undertake ministries should be persons of strong faith, dedicated discipleship, and love of Jesus Christ as Savior and Lord. Their manner of life should be a demonstration of the Christian gospel in

25 *Book of Order* 2011/2013
G-2.01–G-2.02 Form of Government G-2.0104a–G-2.0201

the church and in the world. They must have the approval of God's people and the concurring judgment of a council of the church.

b. Standards for ordained service reflect the church's desire to submit joyfully to the Lordship of Jesus Christ in all aspects of life (F-1.02). The council responsible for ordination and/or installation (G.2.0402; G-2.0607; G-3.0306) shall examine each candidate's calling, gifts, preparation, and suitability for the responsibilities of ordered ministry. The examination shall include, but not be limited to, a determination of the candidate's ability and commitment to fulfill all requirements as expressed in the constitutional questions for ordination and installation (W – 4.4003). Councils shall be guided by Scripture and the confessions in applying standards to individual candidates.

G-2.0105 Freedom of Conscience

> It is necessary to the integrity and health of the church that the persons who serve it in ordered ministries shall adhere to the essentials of the Reformed faith and polity as expressed in this Constitution. So far as may be possible without serious departure from these standards, without infringing on the rights and views of others, and without obstructing the constitutional governance of the church, freedom of conscience with respect to the interpretation of Scripture is to be maintained. It is to be recognized, however, that in the ordered ministries of the Presbyterian Church (U.S.A.), one chooses to exercise freedom of conscience within certain bounds. His or her conscience is captive to the Word of God as interpreted in the standards of the church so long as he or she continues to seek, or serve in, ordered ministry. The decision as to whether a person has departed from essentials of Reformed faith and polity is made initially by the individual concerned but ultimately becomes the responsibility of the council in which he or she is a member.

These amendments were passed by a majority of the PCUSA Presbyteries. In a later meeting of a G.A., marriage was redefined by a majority of Presbyteries and the Book of Order amended as follows:

W-4.06: The Covenant of Marriage
W-4.0601 : Christian Marriage

> In Baptism, each Christian is claimed in the covenant of God's faithful love. Marriage is a gift God has given to all humankind for the well-being of the entire human family. Marriage involves a unique commitment between two people, traditionally a man and a woman, to love and support each other for the rest of their lives. The sacrificial love that unites the couple sustains them as faithful and responsible members of the church and the wider community. In civil law, marriage is a contract that recognizes the rights and obligations of the married couple in society. In the Reformed tradition, marriage is also a covenant in which God has an active part, and which the community of faith publicly witnesses and acknowledges.

W-4.0602: Preparing for Marriage

> If they meet the requirements of the civil jurisdiction in which they intend to marry, a couple may request that a service of Christian marriage be conducted by a minister of the Word

and Sacrament† in the Presbyterian Church (U.S.A.), who is authorized, though not required, to act as an agent of the civil jurisdiction in recording the marriage contract. A couple requesting a service of Christian marriage shall receive instruction from the minister of the Word and Sacrament†, who may agree to the couple's request only if, in the judgment of the minister of the Word and Sacrament†, the couple demonstrate sufficient understanding of the nature of the marriage covenant and commitment to living their lives together according to its values. In making this decision, the minister of the Word and Sacrament† may seek the counsel of the session, which has authority to permit or deny the use of church property for a marriage service.

W-4.0601: 2 Helv. Conf. 5.245–5.251; West. Conf. 6.131–6.139. 106

Book of Order 2019/2021

W-4.06–W-4.07

Pastoral and Occasional Services W-4.0603–W-4.0703

W-4.0603: Order of Worship

The marriage service shall be conducted in a manner appropriate to this covenant and to the forms of Reformed worship, under the direction of the minister of the Word and Sacrament† and the supervision of the session (W-2.03). In a service of marriage, the couple marry each other by exchanging mutual promises. The minister of the Word and Sacrament† witnesses the couple's promises and pronounces God's blessing upon their union. The community of faith pledges to support the couple in upholding their promises; prayers may be offered for the couple, for the communities that support them, and for all who seek to live in faithfulness.

W-4.0604: Recognizing Civil Marriage

A service of worship recognizing a civil marriage and confirming it in the community of faith may be appropriate when requested by the couple. The service will be similar to the marriage service except that the statements made shall reflect the fact that the couple is already married to one another according to the laws of the civil jurisdiction.

W-4.0605: Nothing Shall Compel

> Nothing herein shall compel a minister of the Word and Sacrament† to perform nor compel a session to authorize the use of church property for a marriage service that the minister of the Word and Sacrament† or the session believes is contrary to the minister of the Word and Sacrament's† or the session's discernment of the Holy Spirit and their understanding of the Word of God.

With these amendments to the Book of Order the conservative advocacy groups within the denomination concluded that their causes had been lost and that the denomination's theological drift was complete. The issue now was more cultural norms than the biblical witness to the truth.

Many of our churches were deeply divided over the issues of ordination and marriage. LPC was asked to be a pilot church for the new marriage curriculum developed by Theology and Worship. I selected 20 of our members that were equally divided in their interpretations. It was almost too much for me to moderate. There were strong feelings on both sides. At the end of our dialogues, we continued to be good friends in Christ who saw reality through different eyes and hearts.

Open Door Building Program

In 2001 LPC projected in a mission study that we needed to address the condition of our church buildings. Partially, it was our growing understanding of the theology of worship that led us to see and to understand that the sanctuary building of 1928 had been physically neglected and needed restoration. It was an iconic building, one of the earliest buildings around which the village of Laguna Beach had developed from the early part of the 20th century. The church was chartered in 1917 and the sanctuary was built in 1928. At the time it was built large enough to seat all the citizens of Laguna Beach. The church had a membership of 31 persons in 1928. The sanctuary will now contain around 500. In 2002 it had the 1928 roof that was badly leaking in heavy rains. Downtown Laguna Beach was built on a flood plain. During heavy winter storms an underground river would flow beneath our sanctuary and flood the lower level of the sanctuary. Water damage was impacting all parts of the building. Retrofitting was required to address the earthquake problem.

The church had done a patchwork cosmetic job in the early 80's, but the structural issues remained unaddressed. The Restore the Splendor project cost about $1.5 million. John Bulleit, on behalf of the session, managed the project. John and Jean were dear friends and major supporters of the church. Jean had suffered from M.S. for many years. John cared for her in every way. He supported their adult children in their careers. He brought great business wisdom to the church. He was an arch conservative with a sharp mind. I was grateful for his leadership that brought the restoration project to completion with the church debt free.

But in the first decade of the new century, 2001 to 2017 the Build It for Him or The Open Door program cost would approach $15 million. I worked with the new committee of our church for the better part of a decade and a half. Dave Roberson and Rick Hume co-chaired the committee. Key members were Lorna Cohen, Linda Roberson, Rocky and Susan McGill, Kathy Sizer, Frank Morris, Beth Pinney, Gus Altuzarra, John Loomis (our architect), Storm Case (architect), Tom Magill, Katy Coffin, Robert Habiger (liturgical architect), and Steve and Peg Donner. This was an amazing group of gifted leaders and followers of Christ. Outside of a few tensions, we all worked together in such a way that whatever conflicts we may have had did not divide the group. Each of them loved Jesus and his church. We each had a heart for the mission of Laguna Presbyterian Church as a lighthouse of the gospel on the South Coast of Orange County.

I identified between 5 to 10 members and friends of our church who might have the capacity to give $1 million dollar gifts to the church. The identity, the mission, and future of our church in Laguna Beach was in question. In 1973 the church had an operating budget of $158 thousand, half of that supported by the Pre-school income. Could we now maintain the operating mission program budget that was approaching $2 million per year, and at the same time, respond to the crisis in our buildings? One evening at a Christmas cocktail party a woman came up to me and said she knew the future of Laguna Presbyterian Church. "It would become a parking lot", she said. "We would be unable to maintain the building over time." I had nightmares about it becoming an art gallery, museum, restaurant, or private residence. This was happening to churches across America. (See the L.A. Times of July 5, 2020, regarding the First Baptist Church in Venice, California)

I personally thought that if God did not move through my requests for multi-million – dollar gifts, that we would not succeed. With fear and trembling, I made appointments with potential key donors. Prayerfully, I outlined the need and asked if they would consider a large gift to the church. Over the next 15 years the church received 5 or 6 million – dollar plus gifts. These dear persons launched us into the congregational phase of fundraising. Storm Case, Dave Roberson, Rick Hume, and I met with multiple small groups throughout the parish. These were important interpretations of our plans and the likely costs. It would be difficult to imagine the pastoral impact these conversations had upon me and the success of this project. The weekly meetings of the Open – Door Committee were joyful times in which we planned, prayed over, and discussed every detail of what needed to happen. From 2004 to 2017 we maintained our operating budget and received what we needed to pay our rebuilding costs.

In 2007 the Presbytery and the Congregation approved a $7 million dollar line of credit. The evening that we met with the representative of the Lane Foundation he asked me to sign the document sealing his loan to the church for $7 million. I was almost in shock. He said he always had the pastor sign because it made it harder for the pastor to leave the church before the debt was paid in full. After we had all signed, he wrote out a check for $7 million and gave it to us. We had 10 years to pay it off at $73 thousand a month. Thus, began the final push in hopes that the congregation and friends of LPC would make it possible for the church to once again be debt free. By paying off the loan early we saved thousands of dollars of interest. The interest rate on the loan was 4.5%. To save interest expense, we made payments in advance.

At the beginning of 2017 we still owed $1 million. The 100th anniversary of our church was in the fall of 2017. Therefore, I visited with ten of our faithful givers and asked if they would each give $100 thousand dollars by the first of July. I did this with trepidation. We had all given sacrificially for over a decade. Kay and I had given sacrificially as well. I was laying my discipleship on the line. They all made it easy for me. They came through and we made the final payment and were debt free. What a blessing to celebrate with our congregation in September that the $7 million debt was repaid. The loan paper was burned at the Hotel Laguna Banquet. Through God's people the LORD had been faithful to his church's mission in Laguna Beach.

During the construction years the congregation moved into Tankersley Hall, the Fellowship Hall, to worship. We watched the deconstruction of the building up close. On the last Sunday before we moved into Tankersley Hall we took the old pews down and shipped them to a Catholic Church near New Orleans as a gift. Just as the building was down to its skeleton the Great Recession of 2008 hit the nation's economy.

It was surely the worst of times and the best of times to be caught in the middle of a huge building project. The miraculous thing was that the resources were faithfully provided. It was as if our people took delight in faithful stewardship of the church's special place on the South Coast of Orange County and within Laguna Beach. I think we all realized that we were building for the next 100 years seeking to pass on a heritage of faithfulness to the gospel and a place from which to advance the world mission of God.

In my first year of pastoral leadership in the year 1972–73, I began to wonder if I had been called to Laguna Beach to bury a church rather than to build one. All I knew to do was to preach and to teach the Word of God as faithfully as possible and to love my people in total dependence upon the LORD. I was greatly concerned about our Reformed tradition and my personal integrity. Little did I realize what the future held for me and the church. The temptations of money, sex, and power were ever present. It was a giant leap of faith to trust that God could use me as an instrument of his grace and peace for the sake of blessing our gold coast of Southern California. What was needed was a mission base with a Spirit filled people, walking with Christ, living the gospel, to make an impact on the persons and families of our parish. We desired to be a lighthouse of the gospel on the South Coast of Orange County.

In December 2010 the congregation re-entered the restored sanctuary to worship. We still had 10 years of paying on the mortgage. I shall never forget that morning. The sanctuary was filled. I walked out to the center of the chancel to give the morning welcome. My throat tightened and I could not speak. Tears ran from my eyes. I was emotionally overwhelmed by the Holy Spirit, by the beauty and theological integrity of our worship space, and by the smiling faces before me. Everything was new, yet its basic structure was the same. I recovered my composure. The people were shedding tears of joy. We were bonded in the presence of Jesus and of the Holy One who had blessed his people. After the first service on that date a check from one of our members was presented to me for $275,000.00. The gift compounded my thanksgiving for God's blessings. In July 2017 we made the last payment on the $7 million loan. The church was debt free.

Two years into my retirement as Kay and I watched the LPC 2020 Easter Service on – line from home it was the same vision of the Holy that Isaiah the prophet experienced in the Jerusalem Temple that moved me to weep with joy and grief. Once again, I could not speak. But I could feel with the depth of the Spirit's passion and the love of God. I was filled with such gratitude for God allowing me to be a part of this major work of inspiration and faithfulness. The imprint of that experience will forever rule in my heart and mind. When Gareth, the interim pastor, sang about the love of God with such Spirit filled excellence, I was connected to the ground of all being and to the meaning of my life and calling. I had not buried a church; I had, by God's grace, built a church for the glory of God.

I led a tour to Israel and to Rome in early May 2017. In Jerusalem at the Church of the Holy Sepulcher on Mt. Golgotha, inside the Church, I had an experience that was spiritually transforming. I got on my knees at the altar under the communion table on Golgotha. Then I placed my arm and hand into the hole of the rock that tradition says held the cross of Jesus. In that moment my world seemed overwhelmed by a swirling disorientation. It was as if the sufferings of Jesus came into focus as he bore the sins of the world in his own body. It was as if I was spiritually zapped by an electrical current. I quickly withdrew my hand and arm. There was mystery in this epiphany that made me aware that this was holy space. It was a profound experience of what I did not rationally understand, but which was real and surprising.

This must have been what Isaiah saw and experienced in the Jerusalem Temple in Isaiah 6 as he heard the word of God and saw the glory of the Holy One of Israel. He confessed his sinfulness and the sinfulness of his people, received forgiveness from the altar of the LORD'S presence, and heard the call to God's mission as a prophet to Israel. Perhaps this was Peter's experience in the boat with Jesus as he was invited by Jesus to cast his fishing nets into the deep of the Lake of Galilee. He pulled in so many fish that the boat began to sink. Peter fell before Jesus, confessed his sinfulness, and asked Jesus to depart. (Luke 5:1–11) When Peter and the other disciples returned to shore with two boats filled with fish, they heard Jesus' call. He said to them, "Do not be afraid; from now on you will be catching people." "When they had brought their boats to shore, they left everything and followed him."

The group then moved to the Holy Sepulcher on the lower floor of the Church. While standing in a long line waiting to enter the encased traditional site, the sun's huge circular beam shined through the dome of the church and illumined the entrance to the tomb. It was awe-inspiring. Ed Sauls and I entered the tomb together, knelt and prayed for a few moments as we rested our arms on the marble slab where the body of Jesus had been placed. As we exited the tomb, I remembered Father James

Martin's experience. As a well-known Jesuit priest and professor, on his first visit to the Holy Land, he walked from the Sepulcher to the side wall of the church and felt compelled to sit and reflect for a couple of hours. What became clear to him was that this was not the Church of the Holy Sepulcher but the Church of the Resurrected LORD. He wrote his personal witness in his book about his Pilgrimage to Israel. At the cross and at the tomb he also had an epiphany, and it shook the foundations of his perception of reality and his own call to ministry. "Jesus of Nazareth was not a dead hero, but he was the living LORD of Life".[9]

I have been inclined to dismiss such mystical experiences as irrational and emotional hysteria. Propositional certainty and rational truth had always been important to me, and they still are important. My Jerusalem experience was mystical, and I could not deny it. I recalled Frederick Buechner's story about parking his car beside the highway near where he lived in a time of great anxiety and fear related to his daughter's anorexia. As he cried out to God a car passed him slowly enough for him to see and to read the license plate. It had one word on the plate, and it was the word he most needed to hear: "TRUST". Intuitively and spiritually, he saw and heard the comforting message to "trust" the sovereign presence, power, and providence of God. Peace came to his soul. Years later he wrote about this experience and of a man who was the "Trust Officer" at the local bank who had read his article and brought him the license plate. Buechner still has this relic of faith on his home bookshelf. He asked, "What do you call a moment like that? Something to laugh off as the kind of joke life plays us every once in a while? The word of God? I am willing to believe that maybe it was something of both, but for me it was an epiphany." [10]

I wrote in an unpublished paper for a seminar I presented at a Synod of Southern California Conference on Mission and Stewardship, February 3, 1996,

> "The subject of Christian spirituality and discipleship is personal and corporate. We live out our faith in community. Our personal stories cannot be separated from the life of the community. The church, when it is as God intended, ought to be a safe, trusting environment in which we honestly tell our stories and bring encouragement to one another. Why are we afraid to

---

9. Martin, *Jesus A Pilgrimage*, chapters 21 and 22.
10. Frederick Buechner, *Telling Secrets*, 49–50.

.share our spiritual pilgrimage and to witness to how we have seen God at work in our lives?"

I have tried to live this pastoral wisdom in my life and ministry, but it has never been easy for me. I will tell someone else's story, but my own encounters with the Holy and mysterious have been threatening to tell, but also powerful in other lives as I have risked telling my secrets.

Several years ago, a group of 8 Presbyterian Pastors gathered at St. Josephs Spiritual Development Center with Dr. Dallas Willard of USC. I had read several of his books and been encouraged in faith and commitment. We were discussing Philippians 4 in which the Apostle Paul exhorted the believers to rejoice always. "Have no anxiety about anything, but in prayer and supplication, with thanksgiving let your requests be made known to God. And the peace of God which surpasses all understanding, will guard you hearts and your minds in Christ Jesus." Philippians 4:4–7.

I shared with the group that often when I pray my anxiety's I become afraid that I will come unglued in some form of spiritual meltdown. Dallas said to me, "What better place to have a meltdown than in prayer before the LORD?" His words were wise and gave to me permission to pray the inner struggles of my soul. In effect, he was saying that Paul and Peter received this understanding of prayer in praying the Psalms. So often the Psalmists courageously prayed whatever was going on in their lives. The Lord was present, and the Lord listened. Peace came to the souls of those who prayed in times of disorientation. This is my testimony as well. On another occasion as I was going into the hospital for surgery, I was afraid. I listened again to a sermon Dallas gave at a gathering in Houston that Kay and I attended. He spoke about death and that we ought not to be afraid of dying. I reread his teaching on death and dying in *The Divine Conspiracy*. It was so comforting for me. Dallas died of cancer a couple of years ago. I know he died in peace with trust in the goodness of our Sovereign Lord Jesus Christ.

Peacemaking, the Believers Calling

Fostering Peace Through the Abrahamic Religions:
   the Promise and The Pitfalls
   February 7–9, 2010, Basel, Switzerland
   Report by Dr. Jerry Tankersley, Pastor, Laguna Presbyterian Church

On Tuesday morning, September 11, 2001, the world changed for me and, I believe for all Americans. While having breakfast I turned on the television news only to see the reports of the airliner crashes into the World Trade Center Twin Towers in New York City and into the Pentagon in Washington D.C. There was also news of another crash in Pennsylvania. Soon telephone calls began to arrive at my home from members of our congregation asking if I were watching the news. It was early morning on the West Coast, and I quickly moved to my home office for my morning scripture readings, prayers, and journaling. That morning, I noted in my journal that our world would never be the same.

It soon became clear that approximately 19 Sunni radical Islamic terrorists, inspired by Osama bin Laden and Al Qaeda, had commandeered several airliners, and flown them into their targets. Thousands of innocent American citizens, as well as citizens of many other countries and members of different religions were murdered in this evil act.

Later that evening our church sanctuary was filled as the community spontaneously came together in grief to turn to God and to one another for comfort and reassurance in our time of need. We read from the Psalms of the Old Testament and from Romans 8 in the New Testament. We prayed for understanding, meaning, and comfort for our stunned, grieving nation and world that found it almost impossible to believe that any religious group could have plotted and carried out such an attack upon innocent men, women, and children. Perhaps the greatest puzzlement was how such an evil act could have occurred on American soil. We thought we were immune to such acts.

Most of us understood that the governments of the western world would be required to seek justice and to stop further terrorist plots and attacks. National and inter-national self-defense demanded such a response. Soon a western alliance of nations, led by the United States, took the battle to Afghanistan and to the training camps of bin Laden. There was broad support for this just war of self-defense. It was generally recognized that the attacks upon America were an assault upon the wealthy, materialistic, immoral, western, secular, and modern world that was perceived by radicalized groups within Islam as a threat to the spiritual and moral foundations of the Islamic religion. Quickly, the Taliban were removed from control of Afghanistan. Bin Laden was nearly captured, and it appeared that the foreign fighters who shared his distorted view of the world were on the run and would be unable for a long time to mount another attack upon the west.

The Highways To Louisville And Beyond

In August 1991, Saddam Hussein sent his Iraqi armies to war in Kuwait to recover land that, he claimed, belonged to Iraq. The first Gulf War invading armies stopped short of Baghdad and the removal of the dictator, whom the U.S. had supported in Iraq's long war with Iran.

In 2003 the United States, with several friendly nations, launched a war upon Iraq for the purpose of removing Saddam Hussein and his political party from control of that nation. A case was made that Iraq was a staging ground for Islamic extremists and that Saddam was seeking weapons of mass destruction, both nuclear and chemical, for the purpose of attacking Israel, Europe, and the United States. In fact, the Israelis had bombed a nuclear plant in Iraq for the purpose of eliminating the danger of a nuclear armed Iraq. It was known that he had committed acts of genocide by gassing the Kurds in the northern part of Iraq.

The Bush administration had adopted a policy of preemptive war for the purpose of national self-defense and the peace and order of the world. As the last remaining superpower from the Cold War years, it was asserted that the United States had a political and moral obligation to maintain the peace and order of the civilized world and to use its high – tech military to defend the political, economic, and religious well-being of the nations.

As a pastor of the Presbyterian Church (USA), a Protestant Christian denomination that has been at the center of all the events of American history since the founding of the nation, I have believed it was a vital part of my pastoral calling to provide theological reflection for our people in matters of biblical interpretation and spiritual formation related to war and peace, justice, and injustice. Presbyterians have not been pacifists, even though we have many pacifist members. We have provided chaplains for our military and our members have served in all the wars fought by our nation. We regularly pray for the young men and women who serve in our country's armed forces. In general, we have believed in the separation of church and state and have believed we had the responsibility to support the policies and programs endorsed by our political leaders. By in large we have embraced a traditional reading of Romans 13.

On the other hand, we have also believed in the sovereignty of God over the nations and that political leaders have a divine calling to pursue peace and justice according to God's will revealed in Scripture for all people (Psalm 72; Jeremiah 6 & 7; Isaiah 2:4; 9:5–6). What this has meant is that Presbyterians have from time to time been in patriotic tension with the social norms, economic practices, and the political decisions of American society and government. This has led, at times, to conflict within the denomination as we have sought to support the civil authority while fulfilling our calling from God to be "peacemakers". (Matthew 5:9). Presbyterian Christians do not want to be insensitive or blind to the things that make for peace. With Jesus we have often wept over Jerusalem and the capitals of the nations that have not known the things that make for peace. (Luke 19:41–44)

There has been a continuous ferment in the Presbyterian, Reformed Protestant family, as we have sought to discern, to articulate, and to live into God's vision for human life on planet earth, while being steadfast patriots and servants of our national interests and international well-being. In a conflict of loyalty to nation or to the kingdom of God we have committed ourselves in our creedal statements to faithfulness to God's kingdom above any earthly allegiance. In our Confession of 1967, our church affirmed this faith commitment:

> "God's reconciliation in Jesus Christ is the ground of the justice, and freedom among nations which all powers of government are called to serve and defend. The church, in its own life, is called to practice the forgiveness of enemies and to commend to the nations as practical politics the search for cooperation and peace. This search requires that nations pursue fresh and responsible relations across every line of conflict, even at risk to national security, to reduce areas of strife and to broaden international understanding. Reconciliation among nations becomes peculiarly urgent as countries develop nuclear, chemical, and biological weapons, diverting their manpower and resources from constructive uses and risking the annihilation of mankind. Although nations may serve God's purposes in history, the church which identifies the sovereignty of any one nation or any one way of life with the cause of God denies the Lordship of Christ and betrays its calling."[11]

It was the General Assembly's endorsement of this Confession in 1967 and its prophetic application to America's war in Vietnam that brought discord to the PCUSA. It is important to remember that in the

---

11. *Confession of 1967, Book of Confessions*, 9.45.

PCUSA polity and Constitution that the General Assembly is given authority *to speak to* the whole church on spiritual, social, political, and economic issues. *It does not speak for the whole church.* Presbyterians honor freedom of conscience within the limits of God's Word and Spirit. Therefore, the G.A. cannot bind the conscience of all 2.4 million Presbyterians in its social/political pronouncements.

As a pastor, I am called to faithfully proclaim and to teach the Word of God as I prayerfully discern the Word within the boundaries of historic Reformed hermeneutical principles. Those who listen reserve the right to either agree or to disagree with me. I hope the members of my church take me seriously and I believe they do, but I do not expect them always to agree with their preacher. Nor do I want them to move to another church where they think they will agree with everything that comes from higher authority or from the local pulpit. The truth is that that is never the case, either within or without our denomination. We are a diverse fellowship of believers who bear with one another for the sake of our life together and are reformed and always being reformed by God's Word and Spirit. (Book of Order, chapters 1to 6)

My interest in peacemaking intensified when I was asked to stand for Moderator of the 214th General Assembly of the PCUSA in 2002. I knew that I would be asked this question: "where was God on 9/11/01 and how do we interpret that historic day in our national experience?" The question was asked. In answer, I pointed to the cross of the First Presbyterian Church of New York City that stood above the wreckage of the Twin Towers. Where was God on that day? God was identified with the human suffering caused by that act of terror and grieving with the world over man's inhumanity to man. 9/11 was another witness to God's grief over a world often committed to redemptive violence in the name of politics and religion. Deep down 9/11 was a manifestation of the line of sin that runs through every human heart, culture, or political system, and which may only be healed by the presence and power of the God of love and peace at work in the life of God's people.

We believe that there are good and ethical people among all people and religions and that the grace of the One God cannot be contained or controlled by any religion or political order. The 214th General Assembly (2002) endorsed the statement entitled, *Hope in The Lord Jesus Christ*. Within this faith affirmation there was a very important paragraph lifted for special affirmation by the Assembly. It read,

"Jesus Christ is the only Savior and Lord, and all people everywhere are called to place their faith, hope, and love in him. No one is saved by virtue of inherent goodness or admirable living, for "by grace you have been saved through faith, and this is not your own doing; it is the gift of God" (Ephesians 2:8). No one is saved apart from God's gracious redemption in Jesus Christ. Yet we do not presume to limit the sovereign freedom of "God our Savior, who desires everyone to be saved and to come to the knowledge of the truth" (1 Timothy 2:4). Thus, we neither restrict the grace of God to those who profess explicit faith in Christ nor assume that all people are saved regardless of faith. Grace, love, and communion belong to God, and are not ours to determine."[12]

The Assembly in 2002 was committed to advocating peace in the Middle East, especially peace between the Israelis and the Palestinians. It was perceived, and I think generally accepted, that the lack of peace in the Holy Land had contributed to the hostility between Jews, Christians, and Muslims. As a denomination we have been for sixty plus years strong supporters of a national homeland for the Jewish people. As were most Americans, we were deeply affected by the Jewish Holocaust of the 1930's and 40's in Europe in which six million innocent Jewish men, women, and children were murdered by the evil acts of Hitler's Third Reich simply because they were Jews. We became steadfast friends of the Jewish State of Israel from its inception and have supported the U.S. efforts to guarantee its well-being in a surrounding world often characterized by anti-Semitism and hatred of the Jewish people.

I suspect that American Christianity in the minds of many in the Middle East is linked to American foreign policy and that we are suspected of supporting new crusades against Muslim nations on behalf of Israel. This is a tragic perception. The truth is that Presbyterians have mission partnerships with Arab Christians throughout the Middle East. Palestinian Christians have lived in Palestine for two thousand years. There were Arabs present on the Day of Pentecost in Acts 2. Arab Christians and churches have been important parts of the Middle East and we value our fellowship and partnership with them.

This has led several General Assemblies to advocate peace between Arabs and Jews and for a two – state solution in the Holy Land. We believe in and advocate justice for our Palestinian sisters and brothers in Jerusalem, the West Bank of the Jordan River, and the Gaza Strip. We

---

12. Office of Theology and Worship, *Hope in the Lord*, 47.

have sought to hold the secular government of Israel accountable to international standards of justice. And we have also called upon all the people of the Middle East, whether they be Jewish, Christian, or Muslim, to renounce terrorism against one another for the sake of peace and prosperity in their lands. We are aware that there will be no perfect settlement for either side of the Holy Land conflict. Both Jews and Arabs live out of narrative stories that conflict with the others defining story. Nevertheless, Presbyterians have called and continue to call Jews, Christians, and Muslims, all children of Abraham, to be reconciled and to come to the table of peace for the sake of healing the world.

As Presbyterian Christians we believe that we have been adopted into Abraham's family through faith in Jesus, the Jewish Messiah. We have been engrafted into the olive tree of Old Testament Israel and have become heirs and joint heirs of God's covenant promises made to Abraham and to his family. There is still a lively conversation among Jews and Christians about the Old and New Covenants, but it is a dialogue of respect and mutual affirmation. Increasingly, we have renounced supercessionism, while embracing both Jews and Muslims as members of Abraham's family, along with us. We believe that all people have been reconciled by God in the death of Jesus upon the cross and his resurrection from the dead. Through his blood God broke down dividing walls of hostility, made peace, and incorporated us into one new humanity and spiritual temple for the indwelling presence of the living LORD. (See Romans 9 to 11; Galatians 3-4; Ephesians 1-2; Hebrews 8) What this means is that by God's grace the followers of Jesus have been brought into a peaceful fellowship with all of Abraham's spiritual children. As Presbyterians we are called to live into this gift of peace from God.

For the past five years I have participated with a team of Presbyterian pastors and theologians in dialogues with American Jewish leaders in hopes of healing some of our conflicts and misunderstandings of each other. We have discussed issues of truth, scriptural authority, evangelism, the theology of land, and issues of justice. It has been a family conversation with much good friendship developed, but also continuing flare ups between those who must learn to live in friendship with those who have much in common, but much also that makes them different. We recognize that there will not be perfect peace within Abraham's family until the fullness of God's kingdom comes. The result has been a deepened spiritual and intellectual awareness of what unites us, but also of what still divides us. With all of this, we affirm that we are persons and peoples created in the image of God and that we share a common humanity. We live on the same planet. We can choose peace or war. If we choose war, we have the potential to destroy one another and this beautiful planet. God forbid that we fail in our stewardship responsibility.

I recommend Michael Oren's book, *Power, Faith, and Fantasy*. He is a first-rate scholar who traces America's involvement in the Middle East from 1776 to the present. At present he is Israel's Ambassador to the United States. (2009 to 2013) I think he presents a fascinating story of which most Americans are not aware.

The Basel Interfaith Dialogue

For the sake of privacy, I will not name the persons who came together in Basel and who represented their Jewish, Muslim, and Christian religions. I share a word of thanks from Professor Robert Destro of The Catholic University of America.

"Let me begin, with a word of thanks to PRIO, which has so generously supported our Abrahamic Dialogues, and to Mofid University, and all of the learned scholars, clergy, and experts with whom we have been so privileged to work in this effort since 2002."

The dialogue was organized by The International Peace Research Institute, Oslo (PRIO); The Columbus School of Law of The Catholic University of America, Washington, D.C.; and Mofid University, Qom, Iran.

My name was recommended to the organizers by Dr. John Huffman and the invitation came to me in December 2009 and provided an opportunity for me to attend the National Prayer Breakfast in Washington, D.C. and then to travel on to Basel with others of the U.S. delegation. The dialogue was held at the Grand Hotel Les Trois Rois that overlooks the Rhine River. All expenses from Washington, D.C. back to Los Angeles were paid by PRIO. Approximately 26 attended.

Professor Destro reminded us of the Vatican's encouragement for these dialogues and of the mission of The Catholic University of America in promoting this creative engagement. He quoted the words of Pope Gregory VII, who in 1076, wrote in a letter to al-Nasir, the ruler of the North African nation now named Algeria:

"Almighty God, who wishes that all should be saved, and none lost, approves nothing in so much that after loving Him, one should love his fellow man, and that one should not do to others, what one does not want done to oneself. You and we know this charity to ourselves especially because we believe in and confess one God, admittedly, in a different way, and daily praise and venerate him, the creator of the world and the ruler of this world."[13]

The dialogue was divided into five sessions. They were as follows:
Session 1: Role of Religious Leaders in Peacemaking.
Session 2: Foundations of Peace in the Abrahamic Faiths.
Session 3: Peacemaking.
Session 4: The Places of War in Religions of Peace.
Session 5: Abrahamic Cooperation and the Road Ahead.

Session One: Role of Religious Leaders in Peacemaking.

Two papers were presented, one by a Jewish scholar and the other by a Shiite Muslim leader. They focused on the importance of the spirit and the process of reconciliation between conflicting parties and the roles religious leaders may play as mediators. In the one case the emphasis was upon a group's elders and in the other the important role of the religious leader in resolving conflicts among the sects and among others outside a particular sect, i.e., Shiites and Sunnis.

What seemed especially important to me was the priority of reconciliation within Islam. Reconciliation is seen as a priority over war. (And if they incline toward peace, then you too incline towards it, and put your trust in Allah. Indeed, He is the All-hearing, the All-knowing.) *surat anfal* v. 61

It has been reported from the Prophets that whoever becomes a mediator between people for reconcilement, and at least between two people, the Angels of God will eternally send benediction on him. (*Namazi*, p. 309)

It has also been stated in this tradition that whenever you stand face to face to your enemy, do not be the first to start fighting and do not be the first to begin war. (*Majlist*)

What seemed important to me as a Protestant American Christian pastor was the concern, I heard from both a Jew and a Muslim concerning the priority of peacemaking and reconciliation. Clearly, in both traditions there was an understanding that peacemakers, reconcilers, or

---

13. Presentation paper Professor Destro.

mediators, are gifts of God for the purpose of resolving conflicts in the larger society and among members of one's own sect.

Biblical Christianity shares the same priorities. Jesus said,

"Love your enemies, do good to those who hate you, bless those who curse you, and pray for those who abuse you. Do to others as you would have them do to you. Love your enemies, do good, and lend, expecting nothing in return. Your reward will be great, and you will be children of the Most High; for he is kind to the ungrateful and the wicked. Be merciful, just as your father is merciful." (Luke 6)

The Apostle Paul believed that he had received the ministry of reconciliation. He identified himself as an "ambassador of Christ".

"All this is from God, who reconciled us to himself through Christ, and has given us the ministry of reconciliation; that is, in Christ God was reconciling the world to himself . . . So, we are ambassadors for Christ, since God is making his appeal through us; we entreat you on behalf of Christ, be reconciled to God." (2 Corinthians 5:16–21)

Since Christians have been reconciled to God by the grace of God's forgiveness in Jesus Christ, we are called to forgive one another and to become reconciled within the body of Christ, the church. We, therefore, carry the spirit of reconciliation into all our relationships both within and without the fellowship of the church. We seek to translate love into social justice.

I noted to the group that one of the great needs all religious groups share is the spiritual formation of its leaders in the vision and spirit of peace. Education will play a role. Religious wisdom will shape a leader's mind. Life experience and proven maturity in resolving conflicts within family and community will be important. Disciplined and law informed behavior will guide. Scripture and Tradition will provide precedent. But beyond these priorities will be the training in Godliness and righteousness. Christians speak of having the mind or the Spirit of Christ. The mind of Christ will flow from the leaders abiding in Christ, allowing his Word to shape and to form attitudes, behaviors, and priorities. (John 15) The fruits of the Spirit, (love, joy, peace, patience, gentleness, kindness, faithfulness, generosity, and self-control, (Galatians 5) will be manifest in the leader's life.

Within both Catholic and Protestant leaders this need has been recognized. The connection between the priest/pastor's heart and his or her speech from lectern and pulpit will be decisive in the work of reconciliation. What I heard from our Muslim friends was the same awareness.

We cannot preach and teach hatred from the church, temple, or Muslim place of worship and expect our people not to reflect our anger and prejudices. If the leader is lacking in spiritual integrity, then the body, sect, or community in which the work of peacemaking is enacted will suffer from lack of trust, unresolved conflict, and continued controversies.

In recent years I have become more interested in WWI. This war was primarily Christians against Christians in the name of God. The other side was defined as enemy and worthy to be destroyed by those who believed God was on their side. All forms of the Christian church, but primarily Protestant and Lutheran, beat the war drums from their pulpits and stirred the war passions of their congregations. Patriotic duty was interpreted as participation in a Holy War against the other side. The trenches on both sides were filled with the bodies of dead Christians. On one Christmas Eve early in the war, the Christians came out of their trenches to sing Christmas carols together. That experience of mutually shared joy and peace soon reverted to hostile killings of the other side. This is one of the tragic events of world history. WWI sowed the seeds that allowed Adolph Hitler to come to power in Germany and for the Japanese Empire to launch WWII.

Jewish, Christian, and Muslim nations have not lived up to their highest ideas. From synagogues, to churches, to mosques, to temples and cathedrals, the word of warfare has sounded forth in times of national anxiety, fear, and religious-racial bigotry. The nations of the earth stand under the judgement of Almighty God. LORD have mercy. The 20th century was the most violent in the history of the world. Millions of lives were destroyed, and national treasures exhausted. The great need for reconciliation and for taking risks for the sake of peace remain the number one challenge for nations and underscore the importance of this Abrahamic effort toward that end.

Session Two: Foundations of Peace in the Abrahamic Faiths.

In Basel we heard three excellent presentations from the perspectives of Shiite Islam, Jewish, and Christian thought. Since 9/11 many Americans have become suspicious of all Muslims, whatever sect. In fact, in the mainstream of American culture there is little understanding of or appreciation of Islamic religion and culture. The result is racial profiling and religious discrimination on the part of many frightened citizens who see all Muslims as terrorists. Educated people know this is not true, but still, even within the church we have work to do in helping our people deal with their fears and to broaden their knowledge of both Jews and Muslims.

The Shiite scholar asserted,

"In Islam, peace is a fundamental and deeply rooted principle that relates to the nature of Islam as well as Islam's general view about the world and man's life.

The entire world has an essential unity and solidarity. A divine wisdom rules the world. All human families have a common origin.

There is a movement in the world toward a single divine goal, perfection.

Ethics is the goal of religious teaching.

The Koran explicitly repudiates warmongering. God extinguishes the fire of war. The Koran invites us to peace and an irenic way of life. It calls for peaceful coexistence. It condemns any kind of assault, aggression, and injustice. It negates all sorts of racial, national, and physical inequality. The fundamental attitude of the Koran is one of decent behavior towards fellow humans, even if they belong to the infidels, provided they also adhere to the principles of peaceful coexistence. The Koran disapproves applying any sort of coercion in making others accept the religion of Islam.

The prophet of Islam was a person of character and integrity. All his wars were defensive in nature."

The presenter quoted the commentary of *"Al-Mizan"*:

"When Islam has the choice, it does not start a war; rather, it is the enemy that stalemates the Muslims so much and puts them into such difficulties that they are forced to use war. But even then, Islam holds the conduct of war must be an honorable one.

Destruction, setting fire, acts of injustice, shutting down the water supplies of the enemy, and the killing of women and children are *haram* and forbidden. One must treat them decently and in a friendly manner, even though they are full of hatred and hostility towards the Muslims . . .

The missiles that the Germans fired on London during WWII that resulted in the destruction of buildings and the killing of women, children, and innocent citizens, as well as the bombing of German towns by the Allied forces and the use of the nuclear weapon against Japan by the US are all actions that are not in harmony with the teachings of Islam. God only knows what future destruction will be brought upon mankind by the new weapons like the nuclear missiles and hydrogen bomb in case of a third world war." [14]

The Jewish scholar asserted that monotheism is the foundation of all three Abrahamic religions. Judaism asserts that nature is not God because the God of Hebrew Scripture transcends nature and interacts with human history. The great goal of human history is the creation of a society of justice and peace. The prophets called for this. (Isaiah 2 and Micah 4; Isaiah 9 and 11). Therefore, hatred among nations is not God's will. The prophet Amos said there could be no peace without justice. The Jewish religion aligns itself with the poor and the powerless for the sake of lifting them up. The vision of the Year of Jubilee, of new beginnings, of the release of slaves, the cancellation of debts, the return to lands, and the entry into Sabbath rest are called for in Leviticus 25, Deuteronomy 15, and Isaiah 61. The forgiveness of sins and the making of atonement were central to Israel's life. With the coming of the Messiah there will be a New Covenant and a New Creation in which ancient wrongs will be healed, Israel restored to her Promised Land, and justice and righteousness, with peace will prevail. The knowledge of the LORD, the Holy One of Israel will fill the earth. This vision of God's will languish in both sacred and secular spheres of all nations.

The Roman Catholic Christian priest and theologian asserted that "all Christians believe that the message which God sends in Jesus Christ is one of peace. All Christians believe that peace is the origin and the goal of all Creation." "The kingdom of God's peace is coming even though we do not know the day or year of its coming. It will be a kingdom of justice and peace."

"Jesus saw himself as inaugurating the Kingdom of God, a Kingdom of Justice and Peace. The context of the Passion Narratives is one of Jesus' non-resistance to evil. The overall message of the N.T. is one of non-violence and peace. For the first three centuries after Jesus' life on earth, the church was primarily pacifistic. Christians did not serve in the Roman army."

"From the 4th century on till the 20th century Christian theology and practice gradually changed. The church inherited the Roman Empire and barbarians were a threat to Roman rule and Christian faith. Saint Augustine, in *The City of God*, argued for the just war and articulated its requirements. Thomas Aquinas advanced Augustine's thoughts on the

---

14. *Al-Tabataba'l, Hussain, Al-Mizan, vol. 4, 164.*

just war. There was the *jus ad bellum*, the right to go to war, the *jus in bello*, the rights which must be respected during a war, and the *jus post bellum*, the rights to be respected after a war is won. The criteria for a just war, developed in the Middle Ages, were agreed upon. They were these:

A just cause.

War is the last resort.

The war is declared by a proper authority which has

The right intention.

There is a reasonable chance of success and

The end is proportional to the means used.

In the 20th century there have been serious challenges to *Just War Theory*. The century was the most violent century in the history of humankind. Millions of people were killed in the two World Wars. Events such as the Jewish Holocaust, the fire-bombing of Dresden, and the dropping of the atomic bombs on Japan caused many to question if modern warfare, with weapons of mass destruction eliminated the very possibility of a modern war being just."

The Roman Catholic Church has become more cautious in its evaluation of the criteria of Just War theory. "Both Pope John Paul 11 and the present Pope Benedict XVI have made it clear that they do not think the invasion of Iraq is a just war. Some Protestant Churches in the U.S. and elsewhere have come to the same conclusion. There is increasing doubt that modern warfare can ever meet the criteria of a just war." With the emergence of strong peace churches, it is now possible to discern a trajectory towards pacifism within the RCC.

Sessions 3 and 4: Peacemaking and the Place of War in Religions of Peace.

After 9/11 one of the authors to whom I have paid close attention is Jean Bethke Elshtain. Her book entitled, *Just War Against Terror, The Burden of American Power in a Violent World* was a passionate defense of Just War theory and of the American government's response in Afghanistan and Iraq in 2003. Professor Elshtain was scheduled to be with us in Basel as one of the presenters. At the last moment she had to cancel, but provided a paper written for the American University International Law Review. It was entitled, *"Just War and Humanitarian Intervention"*. Her paper was presented and interpreted by one of the participants who did an excellent job of both presenting the paper and critiquing it from the pacifist perspective of John Howard Yoder.

Professor Elshtain writes out of an Augustinian Just War position and does it powerfully. She has expressed profound admiration for the Christian Realism of Reinhold Niebuhr. Niebuhr was likely the outstanding American Protestant theologian of the 20th century. Niebuhr took evil in history seriously and argued WW11 was a just war against the evils of the Third Reich. When President Obama accepted the Nobel Peace prize in Oslo, he reflected Niebuhr's influence on his own thinking regarding war and peace. The President's words were quoted by our presenter, and they are worth repeating.

> "We must begin by acknowledging the hard truth that we will not eradicate violent conflict in our lifetimes. There will be times when nations—acting individually or in concert-will find the use of force not only necessary but morally justified.
>
> I make this statement mindful of what Martin Luther King said in this same ceremony years ago— 'Violence never brings permanent peace. It solves no social problem: it merely creates new and more complicated ones.' As someone who stands here as a direct consequence of Dr. King's life's work, I am living testimony to the moral force of non-violence. I know there is nothing weak – nothing passive – nothing naïve – in the creed and lives of Gandhi and King.
>
> But as a head of state sworn to protect and defend my nation, I cannot be guided by their examples alone. I face the world as it is and cannot stand idle in the face of threats to the American people. For make no mistake: evil does exist in the world. A non-violent movement could not have halted Hitler's armies. Negotiations cannot convince al Qaeda's leaders to lay down their arms. To say that force is sometimes necessary is not a call to cynicism—it is recognition of history; the imperfections of man and the limits of reason." [15]

I believe the representatives of Abrahamic religions need to attend more closely to the question of evil and how spiritual evil may be overcome on earth. It has been helpful for me, as a Christian pastor, to engage the New Testament understanding of the "principalities and powers" of which the Apostle Paul wrote in Ephesians 6 and Colossian 2 by means of literature and fairytale. I refer to the writings of C.S. Lewis, the Oxford University interpreter of *Mere Christianity*. In *The Chronicles of*

---

15. President Obama, quoted in unpublished paper.

Narnia, The Lion, The Witch, and the Wardrobe, Lewis told the story of four English children, who were playing a game of hide and seek. They found themselves passing through a door inside a wardrobe and entering a new land called Narnia. In Narnia they discovered an alternative world in which it was always winter, and Christmas never came. The sun did not shine; the sky was always overcast, Father Christmas had not been seen for years, and spring never came. This frozen land was ruled over by a wicked witch. Her rule was totalitarian. If the citizens of Narnia did not obey her every command, she would touch them with her magic wand and turn them into stone statues. She claimed that she was the ultimate ruler of Narnia, and her rule was ruthless. There was no freedom or joy in the land of Narnia.

There was an ancient story about the true Sovereign of Narnia who might come someday to rescue this oppressed realm. The witch said that conjecture was simply an illusion. She was the true Sovereign of Narnia. The residents of Narnia longed for the day of Aslan's coming. This was their hope. One of the four children who had entered Narnia betrayed the other three human children to the witch, and reported to her the rumor that Aslan, the true Sovereign of Narnia, was on the move. Sure enough, there had been a sighting of Father Christmas; a spring thaw was beginning; the witch was panicked. The Liberator was on his way.

There was deep magic written into the fabric of Narnia. A traitor could only be set free from death by the death of an innocent one. Aslan, the Christ figure, a huge, innocent, golden lion, came to rescue the traitor. Aslan was the true Sovereign of Narnia, but he could only save the human traitor by dying. So, Aslan chose voluntarily to lay down his life for the traitor. The witch killed him at the stone table to appease the deep magic of Narnia. But three days later, Aslan came back to life. What the witch did not know was that there was a deeper magic written into Narnia' ancient past, before the dawn of time, that once the innocent one died, that time would begin to run backward, and history would be reversed. Therefore, Aslan lived; the witch was defeated, routed by her own treachery, and the citizens of Narnia were liberated from bondage. Springtime and summer blossomed.

This was a story written for children, but it communicates a keen insight into the spirituality of what Lewis called, "enemy occupied territory", or planet earth.

The writings of John Howard Yoder, *The Politics of Jesus*, and Walter Wink, *Naming the Powers; and Engaging the Powers;* have had a profound impact upon my theological reflections about making peace in a world where we must take evil seriously.

Both Yoder and Wink provide a model for interpreting the reality of the world. They make three points about the "principalities and powers".

1. The Powers are created by God and are good.
2. The Powers are Fallen.
3. The Powers will be Redeemed.

The structures of reality were created by God. They are the structures, institutions, and rulers that God the Creator ordained for the well-being of humanity. They are, "human traditions, the course of earthly life conditioned by the heavenly bodies, morality, fixed religious and ethical rules, the administration of justice and the ordering of the state." They are the state, politics, class, social struggle, national interest, public opinion, accepted morality, the ideas of decency, and of democracy." They are "the place of the clan or the tribe among peoples, the respect for ancestors and the family, the manifold moral tradition and codes of which moral life is full . . . the powers of race, class, state and Volk."[16]

Wink suggests, "These powers are the necessary social structures of human life, and it is not a matter of indifference to God that they exist. God made them. Humanity is not possible apart from its social institutions. They are accountable to the Creator if they fail to serve God's purpose."[17]

The tragedy is that the Powers are fallen. They have rebelled, inspired by the invisible spirit of rebellion that rules the world as we now experience it. Clearly, this is another way of speaking of the Satan, or the devil, or the wicked witch. "The powers claimed for themselves an absolute value. They thereby enslaved man and his history. To what is man enslaved? Precisely to those values and structures which are necessary to life and society, but which have claimed the status of idols and succeeded in making men serve them as if they were of absolute value." [18]

Wink wrote, "the doctrine of the Fall affirms the radicality of evil. Evil is within us and among us, but much of that can be

---

16. Yoder, *Politics of Jesus*, 145.
17. Wink, *Engaging the Powers*, 66–67.
18. Yoder, *Politics of Jesus*, 144.

raised to consciousness and transformed. We are speaking now of a deeper evil—a layer of sludge beneath the murky waters that can be characterized only as a hellish hatred of light, of truth, of kindness and compassion, a brute lust for annihilation. It is the sedimentation of thousands of years of human choices for evil that has precipitated Satan as the spirituality of evil. Call it what you will, it is real."[19]

"Evil is not our essence. God intended us for better things. Fallenness does not touch our essence, but it characterizes our existence. No one can escape it. The fall does not mean that everything we do is evil, vain, or hopeless, but merely that it is all ambiguous, tainted with egocentricity, subject to deflection from its divine goal, capable of being co-opted toward other ends."[20]

The good news is that the Powers will be redeemed and have been saved. Through the life, death, and resurrection of Jesus, symbolized by the cross, God has acted to redeem this "enemy occupied territory" by an act of self-sacrificing love that has unmasked the "principalities and powers", revealed their idolatrous, self-serving claims, and brought liberation to planet earth.

The Christian church is called, along with all other freedom seeking, peacemaking people, to put on the whole armor of God, described in Ephesians 6 for the sake of transforming the "principalities and powers" and for the healing of human life.

I would add that the Bible's eschatological insight is very important for this peacemaking work. Presbyterian Reformed Christians believe that in Jesus the Kingdom of God has "already" come but is "not yet" present in the fullness of its power. The decisive victory over the powers of evil was won at the cross, but the fullness of the kingdom will only be experienced in the New Creation at the end of this age.

Therefore, in the present we live "between the times". In this time there is still warfare. The spirituality of evil still wreaks havoc in human nature and among the nations. High walls of ignorance, hostility, and hatred keep us divided. "Might makes right" still masquerades as the ultimate wisdom of the world. Love is crucified over and over. Self-sacrificing, servant love seems like foolishness. Sin and death still rule the world as Abraham's family waits and works for the kingdom.

---

19. Wink, *Engaging the Powers*, 69.
20. Wink, *Engaging the Powers*, 72–73.

But we do not despair or surrender to evil in the present. We continue to live by the promise of blessing to the nations given by God to our Father Abraham. In ways that remain mysterious to us we reach out to members of the family for dialogue in the hope that we may make a difference in this global City. To that end we continue to pray and to work. "What does the Lord require of us but to do justice, to love kindness, and to walk humbly with our God." (Micah 6:8.)

Till the kingdom comes in the fullness of the New Creation, in humility we own our own fallenness and ambivalence about the things that make for peace. I desire to be a faithful follower of Jesus Christ, the Prince of Peace. I renounce the way of violence for the sake of justice and peace. I commit myself to the ethic of peace, perfection, and love. Nevertheless, I confess, along with other Christians, that I am constitutionally more at home with the Just War tradition and St. Augustine than I am with Yoder or Wink. Professor Ehlstain and President Obama have spoken of the dilemma the children of Abraham face as they continue to live in a threatening, nationalistic, and competitive world in which the powers of evil still seek to have their ways, in our hearts and minds. Nevertheless, I am willing to risk, to reach beyond myself, to encourage dialogue for understanding, and to advocate for patience and diplomacy. I reaffirm the hope of the good news which Abraham's family continues to embrace, that at long last we may, together, make our way to the source and center of blessing.

By Dr. Jerry Tankersley, Pastor, Laguna Presbyterian Church

The Confession of Belhar

Joe Small, head of Theology and Worship of the General Assembly, invited me to join a Task Force to study and to make recommendations to the General Assembly about adding this South African Reformed Confession to our Book of Confessions, Part I of the Constitution of the PCUSA. To amend the Book of Confessions is a long process of study, discussion, approval, and Presbytery votes. It takes two thirds of our presbyteries to vote in favor of amending. It only takes a majority of the presbyteries to amend the Book of Order, Part II of the Constitution.

I felt honored to join this first Task Force made up of seminary professors and pastors. I had always desired to contribute to the American struggle with race, reconciliation, and justice. Thus, was begun a multi-year process. The results were disappointing. The presbytery two-thirds majority vote was not achieved in the first go around.

A new Task Force was appointed by a new Assembly, and I was invited to join again. Cliff Kirkpatrick, former Stated Clerk of the G.A. and now professor at Louisville Theological Seminary was the chair of the new Task Force. As I had done on the previous TF, I made major contributions to the paper making a case for why we needed the Confession added to our Constitution. The second time around I jumped in to write the case for Belhar. The final product belonged to the TF, but my work was the foundational paper. Sadly, when presented to the G.A. committee considering the Confession, the paper making the case was rejected, but the Confession was presented to the G.A. and finally approved by two-thirds of the Presbyteries.

For the Ecclesio website I wrote this case for Belhar:

WHY THE CONFESSION OF BELHAR?
By Dr. Jerry Tankersley, Pastor
Laguna Presbyterian Church

"The congregations of the Presbyterian Church (USA) are blessed to have a Book of Confessions as the first part of our Constitution. The Book represents a rich spiritual tradition that has nurtured and inspired many people. The eleven Creeds, Confessions, Declaration, and Catechisms represented the vision of Reformed believers witnessing to their faith in various times and places as the church struggled to be faithful to God's grace in Jesus Christ as revealed in the Scriptures.

The eleven documents affirmed the great Protestant watchwords, "grace alone, faith alone, Scripture alone". None of the eleven said everything that might have been said about the grace and truth of God at work to rescue a fallen world from its bondage to the powers of sin and death. But when read together in dialogue with the Scriptures of the Old and New Testaments, in dependence upon the illumination of the Holy Spirit, the church has been Reformed and always in the process of being Reformed.

The Confession of Belhar from the black Reformed Church of South Africa deserves to be included in our Book of Confessions. We need to have the Confession of Belhar in our confessional tradition. It was written by one part of the South African Reformed family for the sake of reforming the larger South African church. It emerged in a time of the evil of apartheid in which the churches of South Africa were divided along racial lines. That division was justified by an interpretation of the Bible as allowing racial separation and segregation, even at the Lord's Table. The larger Reformed Christian world saw that theology and practice as heretical and in violation of the grace and truth of God's character and intent. The church's stance on race was used to validate the racial divisions of the nation. There was no prophetic word calling the nation to reconciliation, unity, and justice. The Confession of Belhar called church and culture to repentance.

The Christian churches of the United States have lived and witnessed in the context of a history of racism that has uniquely formed our church, our national life, and culture. I believe that no person or citizen of our country has escaped the spiritual, cultural, political, and economic consequences of the scarring caused by the enslavement of Africans. Africans were captured against their wills, sold, and bought as chattel, separated from native lands and families, and defined as partial persons and citizens under the U.S. Constitution. With the loss of compromise between north and south in the mid-1800's, the Presbyterian Church divided with the outbreak of the Civil War. We fought a war in which 750 thousands of our fellow citizens died. The War ended, but the problems of racial hatred, segregation, discrimination, and the efforts to deny civil rights to the strangers among us continue to this day.

The PC (USA) is still racially divided. Both church and nation are in denial and in great need of pursuing Martin Luther King, Jr's biblically inspired vision of a just and racially harmonious society. The Book of Confessions has only one major paragraph in the Confession of 1967 (9.44) that addresses this issue that has haunted and troubled our church and nation.

In embracing the Confession of Belhar, by adding it to our Book of Confessions, we will be affirming the purpose and plan of God from before the foundation of the world. And that was "to unite" or "gather" up all things in Jesus Christ. (Ephesians 1). In the history of Israel and in the life, death and resurrection of Jesus Christ, God acted to make peace, to reconcile humanity to God's self and us to one another. This, God accomplished by breaking down dividing walls of hostility and reconciling "Jew and Gentile, slave and free, male and female, black and white, rich and poor". In the blood of Christ God made peace and incorporated us into a new humanity called to live as the Church of Jesus Christ, to the glory of God, for the healing of creation and history. (Ephesians 2–4)

This new humanity was called to become a spiritual temple in the Lord in which every disciple was to be included for the sake of participating in the church's mission of "doing justice, loving kindness, and of walking humbly with God." To the church in Corinth Paul wrote, "All this is from God, who reconciled us to himself through Christ, and has given us the ministry of reconciliation. So, we are ambassadors for Christ." 2 Corinthians 5:16–21

The central words of the Confession of Belhar, *"unity, reconciliation, and justice"* are at the heart of the Bible's Gospel. The PC (USA) needs to be claimed by these words and by the hope they promise. The Confession of Belhar speaks to us, convicts us, calls us, empowers us, reconciles us, unites us, and stirs new beginnings. The renewal of the church will depend on our being reformed anew by biblical truth and the Holy Spirit. We live in a time in which our church and nation are deeply divided into threatening camps. We are fragmented. The message of God's eternal plan to stoop to the poor, the lowly, the powerless, and the oppressed for the sake of healing human brokenness, of calling us together, and leading us to participate in God's work is good news indeed.

The *Accompanying Letter to the Confession of Belhar* says,

"We make this confession not as a contribution to a theological debate nor as a new summary of our beliefs, but as a cry from the heart, as something we are obliged to do for the sake of the gospel in view of the times in which we stand."

It is in this spirit that I want to add the cry of my heart. I grew up in northwest Texas in the last days of "separate but equal" law. During the first 20 years of my life blacks lived on the other side of town, had so called "separate but equal" schools, went to the back of the bus, were not allowed to sit at the soda fountain, had colored waiting rooms and drinking fountains and faced bleak economic futures. The African American family suffered the consequences. We were racists. I was a racist, even though rationally I knew better. The Civil Rights movement of the 1960's under the leadership of M.L. King, Jr. troubled and inspired me. His Letter from A Birmingham Jail convicted and melted my heart.

When I was in graduate school in California, after seminary, while working on a Ph.D. in Government, I came out of a seminar one evening with a fellow student who happened to be black. We were talking in the parking lot and became aware that we were about the same age. He grew up in a black farming community near my hometown. We might as well have been raised in separate countries. He shared with me that his dad had been a Southern Baptist black preacher. His father lived in a world in which he had no justice. He and his family were not considered equal to mine. He said that his dad preached against Jews almost every Sunday. The racism that his dad experienced he simply passed on to another racial group. As he told me the story he began to weep. I wanted to cry. We had been so near, yet so far from one another. The system that oppressed him was also oppressing me, wounding me, scarring my heart, and was, by in large, being neglected by the white established church. No, consciously or unconsciously, aided, and abetted!

For the most part I suspect that white Christian America has accepted a gospel with a hole in it. We have heard the good news and tended to opt for the salvation of our souls not realizing that the mission of God will not be complete before our souls and our societies are made right by God's grace. Between the "already and the not yet" of the New Creation I want our church to be a lighthouse of the gospel and to walk into the fullness of our confession that *"Jesus is LORD"*.

Let's listen to the Confession of Belhar, take it seriously, pray over it, teach, and preach it, and add it to our Book of Confessions. It's time to add our collective cry from the depths of the heart of our church!"

The core writing team for a new Accompanying Paper for Belhar met in Atlanta just as one of the winter vortex fronts came through Georgia. When I arrived at the Atlanta airport and stepped outside to catch the bus to my hotel, I felt frozen. I had multiple layers of clothing on under my sport coat and overcoat and I was still freezing. It was clear and the wind was blowing, and it was frigid. At the outdoor bus station people were waiting for buses wearing next to nothing. I felt sorry for them.

My paper was the basic text that needed to be perfected and edited. The result follows:

The Accompanying Letter to the Confession of Belhar
   from the 221st General Assembly of the Presbyterian Church (U.S.A.)

On the adoption of the Confession of Belhar.

The Presbyterian Church (U.S.A.) is again facing a critical time in its history. We are rent apart by division and schism, we have yet to directly confront and confess the racism that has been a significant force in our own history, and we have shown a failure of resolve to make courageous stands for justice. We believe that the Confession of Belhar, a profound statement on unity, reconciliation, and justice in the church, comes to us as a word from God for this time and place for the PC(USA).

We understand confession as both the church's response to human sin and as witness to our faith. Confession by the church is necessary because sin is present in social injustice and our conscious or unconscious participation in human suffering. Confession is not a way to cast aspersions or in any way denigrate, castigate, or delimit any person or group of persons. We the church are called to confess sin because the Word of God as revealed in and through the life of Jesus Christ and the Holy Scriptures calls us to bear witness to a just, loving, and compassionate Creator.

The Confession of Belhar calls us to renew our understanding and confessional affirmation of the "one triune God, Father, Son, and Holy Spirit." The confession centers us in the reality of the Holy God of creation, the covenant, and the prophets, who was incarnate in Jesus Christ. The Spirit fills all who have come to know God through the grace of our LORD Jesus Christ, the love of God the Father, and the communion of the Holy Spirit. As the Confession of Belhar affirms, the God whom we worship and serve has gathered us, protected us, and cared for us through the Word and Spirit. *"This, God has done since the beginning of the world and will do to the end."*[21]

The Confession of Belhar is particularly helpful to our common life as Presbyterians for two reasons. First, it comes to us in a time of Kairos in South Africa, when the church dared to speak with unusual clarity. It can help the PC(USA) speak and act with equal clarity. Second, it focuses the church's confession on its own life. It is far too easy for the church to look outside of its walls and find fault, all the while ignoring the sin in its own life. Belhar focuses the church's attention on the way its own life and witness has fallen short of the gospel.

Unity.

We believe that the gospel of God calls the entire universal church into the unity of the one triune God. At the heart of the Creator God revealed in Scripture is the invitation to enjoy the fellowship of the personal God who is one, yet three. The LORD whom we confess has a purpose and plan for the cosmos into which we have all been born by God's providence. We learn from Scripture of " . . . the mystery of [God's] will . . . set forth

---

21. *The Confession of Belhar*

in Christ, as a plan for the fullness of time, to gather up [unite] all things in him, things in heaven and things on earth" (Eph. 1:9–10).

To this end, Jesus, the incarnate Son of God, fully human and fully God, offered us new life when he gave his life for us through his incarnation, his crucifixion, and his resurrection. This new life broke down dividing walls of hostility within humanity, transforming hatred into love and making unity a mandate from God. Unity is God's will for humanity, beyond the differences of Jews and Gentiles, slave and free, male and female, educated and uneducated, rich, and poor, and beyond social categories of races. All who heard the good news and believed in God through Christ the Savior were incorporated into the new humanity. Through the abiding presence of the Holy Spirit, those who trusted in Jesus Christ became members of the household of God and experienced themselves as being built together spiritually into a dwelling place for God. This spiritual temple called "the church" was given a mission of proclaiming, living, making visible, and extending the good news of the New Creation in Christ (Eph. 2:11–22).

Presbyterians have confessed this gospel from the early years of our history in America. Yet we have had great difficulty of living into the gift of God's unity and mission revealed and made possible through the cross of Jesus Christ. Like our brothers and sisters in South Africa, we have been afflicted by the division of the church along racial, political, cultural, theological, and class divisions.

In South Africa the system of "apartheid," or separation of the races, divided both nation and church into separate spheres. The Reformed Churches of South Africa justified this division and developed theological rationales for this division so that blacks and whites were not allowed to come to the same Lord's Table. The white settlers who came from Europe to the tip of the African continent came with a vision of a Promised Land that required either the removal of the native Africans or the separation of the races for the sake of racial purity, spiritual well-being, and economic development. The spiritualized gospel adopted by the white church focused upon the saving of souls but had lost its prophetic word and mission for the healing of the divisions caused by human sinfulness.

Reformed/Presbyterian Christians who came to the New World of the North American continent carried with them a sense of their own election and privilege. They too came to a "Promised Land" of new beginnings, seeking freedom and opportunity for themselves. They brought with them an understanding of the gospel that was not whole, that did not understand the completed work of Jesus Christ upon the cross, and that called for the church to be visibly one. To complicate matters, to develop the New World's economic base, lands and workers were needed. Native Americans were removed from their lands and African slaves imported to be a source of cheap labor. Human persons were oppressed, defined as property, and denied basic human rights. The church embraced a spiritualized gospel that justified the enslavement of people forcefully and violently captured and held in dehumanizing slavery for the good of white masters and landowners. Every aspect of American culture became divided. Slaves were only counted as 3/5ths persons under the new Constitution of the United States. God's election, interpreted as social privilege, became a theological justification for chattel slavery and racial segregation.

Privileges based on race, wealth, gender, class, and power became institutionalized and legalized. As a result, we have witnessed to the eleven o'clock hour of Sunday morning as the most segregated hour of life in the United States of America. We Presbyterian Reformed churches found ourselves in betrayal of the gospel of Jesus Christ, in our own internal worship, fellowship, and witness. We continue to live under the specter of racism, classism, sexism, and division, which remain as enduring conflicts and challenges for both church and culture.

Beyond the issues of race and class, Presbyterians in the United States of America have, from the beginning, been troubled by differing theological world views and practices. We have been willing to divide repeatedly. Political ideologies, hermeneutical theories, racial prejudices, economic ideologies, and powerful personalities have driven wedges between believers, causing congregations to divide and to seek new affiliations of like-minded believers. *Old School/New School* believers separated and debated theology. Racial theologies divided the church and nation into north and south and led to the American Civil War. Brothers and sisters went to war reading the same Bible and praying to the same God with the confidence that God was on their sides. Fundamentalists and Modernists did battle over issues of biblical and scientific interpretations. The divisions over ordination of women remained present into the past century. For the last quarter of the 20th century, the Presbyterian church has argued and divided over human sexuality and how to read its Scriptures in these matters. Once again, the reality of diversity has threatened to divide us so that the visible unity of the church now hangs by a slender thread.

We believe that the PC(USA) needs to be called to the unity taught and proclaimed in the Confession of Belhar. Belhar's witness to the unity of God, the unity created by the good news of Jesus Christ and the power of the Holy Spirit, calls us to the hard work of spiritual transformation and surrender to the way of Jesus Christ who came to unite all believers in the visible communion of the body of Christ, the church.

Belhar asks us to look first at ourselves when faced with church division, rather than moving quickly to blaming those with whom we are separated. It is far too easy to look at the other and blame them for division. Belhar directs us to look at our own behavior that has led to disunity. What is the log in our own eye?

Reconciliation.

The Confession of Belhar reaffirms the vision of mission articulated in the Confession of 1967: that God in Christ has done what we could not do for ourselves. The Apostle Paul wrote to the Corinthian church, "All this is from God, who reconciled us to himself through Christ, and has given us the ministry of reconciliation; that is, in Christ God was reconciling the world to himself, not counting their trespasses against them, and entrusting the message of reconciliation to us. So, we are ambassadors for Christ, since God is making his appeal through us; we entreat you on behalf of Christ, be reconciled to God" (2 Cor. 5:18–20).

In the 1960s, the Presbyterian Church (U.S.A.) confessed its faith in the reconciling power of God in the context of a society being driven apart by racial divisions, issues of war and peace, poverty and abundance, and by anarchy in sexual relationships.

The Confession of Belhar reaffirms this witness, but more specifically calls the members of this church, the corporate structures of the church, and the deep divides that still haunt us all, to be claimed by the gospel of God, who alone can bring us together as one family of Christ.

We believe that all who have trusted in Jesus as Savior and Lord, been baptized into the fellowship of Christ's church, have been welcomed to the LORD'S Table. At the LORD'S Table, we receive by faith the presence of the resurrected LORD. His spiritual presence feeds us with bread and wine. At his Table we are reconciled to God, united as races, tribes of peoples speaking different languages, and representatives of many nations. We are Jew and Gentile, male and female, rich and poor, black and white and every color. We are blue and red, Democrat and Republican, Independent, Conservative and Progressive, Protestant and Catholic and Orthodox. We share in the LORD'S Table as a foretaste of the Reign of God.

In Christ, the hope of glory, we are members of the one family of God. We are brothers and sisters in Christ. And like all human families, we have our differences; we engage in conflicts. We often agree to disagree. We at times are arrogant; other times we are humble toward one another and serve one another. At each moment in time, we live by the forgiveness of sins. Over time we come to realize that our life together is only in and through the grace of our Lord Jesus Christ. This side of the perfection of the New Creation we will all remain sinners and in need of spiritual transformation.

Nevertheless, Christians are called to be seekers of justice, peacemakers, reconcilers, mediators, who extend hospitality and love toward those with whom we differ. Down deep we are longing to embrace our calling, "with all humility and gentleness, with patience, bearing with one another in love, making every effort to maintain the unity of the Spirit in the bond of peace. There is one body and one Spirit, just as you were called to the one hope of your calling, one LORD, one faith, one baptism, one God and Father of all, who is above all and through all and in all" (Eph. 4:2–6).

Therefore, as God's reconciled people we have promised not to break the covenant in which we are bound through the body and blood of our LORD Jesus Christ. At reunion we attempted to create the PC(USA) as a reunited church in the absence of confessing the sin that had created our original division. In the last several decades, we in the Presbyterian Church (U.S.A.) have become increasingly separated into different political, economic, and theological camps. More than ever, we need to be claimed by the gospel of God's reconciling love. This gospel allows believers to come together, knowing that we have more in common that unites us, than what divides us.

We American Presbyterians have not been able to fully confront our own past regarding race. The fact is that both streams of the PC(USA), southern and northern, used theology to justify permanent inequality in church and society. A theology that grew out of giving all glory to God became justification for divinely sanctioned inequality, particularly directed at African

Americans. To fully embody God's ministry of reconciliation, we Presbyterians must confess that we have used God against others in our own church and commit ourselves to new patterns of relationship.

Reconciliation implies repair of that which has been broken. Our verbal and written confessions, while important, are far less than adequate means of repairing the harms done, restoring the losses, and reconciling the relationships that have been historically distorted. Concrete steps are required to produce the healing that we so desperately want and need.

The Confession of Belhar calls us to renew the covenant, to embrace one another as members of one family of God. Jesus Christ calls us to a costly discipleship of dying to ourselves so that we might allow his light to shine through us as a witness into the darkness of our world.

Justice

Jesus began his public ministry in his hometown synagogue in Nazareth (Luke 4). He read from the Scripture of the day, Isaiah 61. "The Spirit of the LORD is upon me, because he has anointed me to bring good news to the poor. He has sent me to proclaim release to the captives and recovery of sight to the blind, to let the oppressed go free, to proclaim the year of the Lord's favor" (Lk. 4:18-19). Then he announced that in the reading of this Scripture, on that day, it had been fulfilled. He was God's Spirit anointed Messiah who had been sent to inaugurate the Year of Jubilee, the year in which wrongs would be righted, wounds be healed, sins forgiven, slaves set free, sight restored, lands returned to their rightful heirs. It was a day of new beginnings. The kingdom of God was at hand in the person and words of Jesus. With his coming in the power of the Holy Spirit, God's vision of justice and social righteousness were breaking into a troubled and unjust world.

Isaiah 61 was Jesus' mission statement, and it became the mission statement of the church, "to be repairers of the devastations of many generations." His mission was God's project of healing the cosmos, making right ancient wrongs, reversing the injustices of human society, of lifting the poor and humble and bringing down the high and mighty, ("to be repairers of the devastations of many generations"). His mission was not only to the lost sheep of the house of Israel, but also to believing Gentiles who would welcome his good news. Not all received Jesus, but to as many as turned around and believed, he gave the right to become the children of God (John 1).

As Jesus launched his mission, the poor, the sinners, the wounded, the oppressed, the blind, and the tax collectors gladly welcomed him. It was those whose privilege was threatened by transformation who rejected Jesus. They realized that he was turning the world upside down in a new day of justice and righteousness.

As the ambassadors of Christ's reconciling love, the apostles, the sent ones, often met resistance and persecution. Many gave their lives to advance the reign of God in their announcement of the good news of God's gracious presence and new life for those who repented and believed.

We are being called to launch this mission again in our place and time. While the Confession of Belhar arose from the struggle of South African Christians to give witness to the Gospel amidst the injustice of apartheid, we are also being called to give witness in the face of injustice here among us in the U.S.A. We see that injustice in the faces of thousands of First Nation peoples who still live in dire poverty on reservations; in young African American men who are incarcerated disproportionate to their percentage of the population; in the "legal limbo" status of immigrants, and in both native born Latinos who are subject to question in virtually every quarter of the nation; in public policies such as "stop and frisk" and "stand your ground" that put poor, black and brown young men at risk in the public square.

The Presbyterian Church (U.S.A.) confesses its commitment to God and to the biblical principles of unity, justice, and reconciliation because in times like these in which we live, we need to remind ourselves and others of our discipleship to Christ and follow God's mission in the world.

Some will no doubt say the Presbyterian Church (U.S.A.) already has confessions for the reasons identified herein and more. But we say that these are unique times in the United States of America. The winds of polarization blow strong and threaten the body politic as never before. There is a not-so-subtle dangerous intermingling of God and nation that makes discerning the difference between the two difficult. Historic Reformed theological values are under constant attack. The forces of evil tempt followers of Christ to walk in the spirit of disunity, conflict, and injustice. As we claim the church's earliest confession, *JESUS IS*

LORD, we put on notice, every principality and power, that the only Sovereign in heaven and earth is on the move.

We, therefore, close with the ringing affirmation found in the final words from the Confession of Belhar:

JESUS IS LORD.

To the one and only God, Father, Son and Holy Spirit, be the honor and the glory forever and ever.

When presented to the G.A. Committee, that committee refused to present our Accompanying Paper to the G.A. There was a strong feeling among some conservatives that Belhar was a trojan horse that would make its way into the Book of Confessions and provide theological support for gay and lesbian ordination and marriage on the grounds of civil rights and issues of justice/love. The truth was that human sexual issues regarding ordination and same gender marriage never came up in our committee. Nevertheless, once conservative advocacy groups injected this possibility into the public debate it was almost impossible to have a rational discussion about Belhar and racial justice.

One of the Ruling Elders of LPC was greatly offended that I had participated in the Belhar Task Force. He was convinced that this was a sign that I was joining the Progressive camp of the larger church. For me, Belhar was totally about racism, apartheid, justice, and reconciliation. The PCUSA has been infected at the grass roots by racial prejudice. One does not have to look far back in our American history to see the evidence of this in both south and north. We are still a segregated denomination. M.L. King Jr. was addressing pastors like me in his Birmingham Letter. In my own soul I feel the pain of racial attitudes that I do not understand and which I must confess and seek to heal.

The good news was that a two-thirds vote of the Presbyteries added the Confession of Belhar to the Constitution of the PCUSA. I spoke to the G.A. committee and listened carefully to the discussion and debate. It was disheartening to hear such spin on the Letter and the Confession. The debate was a prelude for the polarization of American political life of 2016 to the present. Since a black man and his family lived in the White House, deep fear, threat, anger, and irrational prejudices have built walls of hostility between the races.

I recommend Stephen Haynes book, *The Last Segregated Hour*, which traces the difficulties of integrating a Memphis, Tenn. Presbyterian College and the pressures brought upon the leadership of the college by members of the Second Presbyterian Church. While serving on the GANC, I came to know Melva Costen, one of the black Presbyterian saints of the south, a wise seminary professor and leader in the larger church. She was married to James Costen, an African American Presbyterian pastor and seminary president who was elected as Moderator of our denomination. The stories she told of their early years in ministry in a segregated south were informative and enraging. America needs to be awakened to our history and to our continued struggle to move toward the fulfillment of the values of our Declaration of Independence. Yet, Thomas Jefferson who wrote this treasured American document was a founding father and slave owner. He fathered children with one of his slave women to whom he was not married. The heritage of slavery, of the Civil War, of Reconstruction, of Jim Crow, of "separate but equal", of the Civil Rights struggles, needs to be understood and theologically interpreted as the consequences of human sin and social injustice. We have a long way to go, but I believe we have made slow progress. The Confession of Belhar will provide a foundation for study and spiritual growth on issues of Scripture and the mission of the church in a troubled world. I am thankful for what I learned from colleagues.

At the time of this writing, it is June 2020. America has experienced a series of deaths of young black men from gun violence and other tactics at the hands of the police. The world is in the midst of a pandemic caused by the coronavirus. Thousands of persons in the U.S.A. have died and many more thousands have been seriously ill in all States. The whole world has been impacted and under quarantine. There is no vaccine yet. The disease is a mystery, and the politicians blame others for their lack of response. Face masks have been required and have been politicized. The spread began in China and quickly moved to all parts of the globe. The economy has been adversely impacted and millions of people are out of work. Especially hard hit has been the African American community.

In the last ten days a black man from Minneapolis was arrested by four white policemen. In the process they took George Floyd down on the street and in front of cameras choked or squeezed the life out of him. His cry was that "I cannot breathe!" One of the officers pressed his knee into his throat for over 9 minutes. Even as George cried for his mother while dying, the white police officer showed no empathy. In front of the world, he murdered him. His fellow police officers watched and did not intervene on Floyd's behalf. All four have been fired from the police force and charged with murder. Protests and riots have broken out in cities around the world. The nation was already on edge because of police violence. The pressure has been building and has now exploded.

"BLACK LIVES MATTER" has been chanted by diverse crowds of white, black, and brown people. Some have used the protests as opportunities to loot, to steal, to burn, and to destroy property. The National Guard has been called into help control the crowds. The President of the U.S., Donald Trump, has failed to provide reconciling, healing leadership. He called the governors of States "weak" and said their job was to dominate and to control. He threatened to bring in Federal forces to protect the American people. He had the D.C. Federal forces clear the street in front of the White House and then marched to the front of St. John's Episcopal Church for a photo op holding a Bible. The nation exploded in protest. Southern Baptist evangelical preachers affirmed his bold stand with the Bible, but many other Christian leaders and politicians condemned his behavior.

Apparently, the President thinks he is the higher law and that he has the power to dominate and to control all who contest his interpretation of the U.S. Constitution. This is an election year and Democrats and Republicans do not know how the pandemic, the economic reversal, the police violence, and the national protests will play out. It is a dangerous crisis. The evangelical church has little to say because its leadership is highly supportive of Donald Trump. They see him as their hero of "law and order". They are the base of his following. They believe God is on their side and that their moral vision will prevail.

But his behavior and speech have brought protest and efforts to impeach him. Churches are divided and pastor's take sides at their own peril. Anger is running deep with each side puzzled at Christians in divided camps. These forces have closed businesses and churches. Many are saying that the nation and the church are at a turning point, that things will never be the same.

If only the Presbyterian G.A. had not only approved the Belhar Confession but had also embraced the Task Force Accompanying Letter, it may have helped the PCUSA find a way to address the undergirding American sin of "Racism". Our Letter opened a door for the truth to inform the American conscience and to empower the church to address its own involvement in maintaining the institutional racism it has aided and abetted by its denial and reinterpretation of Scripture and the Reformed tradition. Now, the Protestant evangelical and mainline denominations will need to face up to their own accountability for the deep roots of our social discontent. It will require us to repent of *"white supremacy and social privilege"*. American change is not waiting for us. People of many colors, races, languages, religions, and gender identities are becoming the majority of our demographics. If we do not wake up soon and fine the way to a new community characterized by love and justice, the nation could conceivably split even as in 1861. God forbid! But there will be no peace without justice!

Schism in the PCUSA

The internal conflicts of the PCUSA came to a head in the first decade of the 21st century. With the option of congregations and presbyteries deciding who they would ordain or marry, the polarization of the church into divided camps could no longer be resisted. Fundamental issues had come to the surface of our covenant community. What did we believe and think about Jesus Christ? What was the authority of the Bible and how was it to be interpreted around the great issues of money, sex, and power? What was the gospel? Was there enough unity within our diversity to bond us together in love and mission?

Within our Presbytery of Los Ranchos at least ten of our churches began to secretly plan their leaving together. The assumption was that together they could press the Presbytery to respond favorably, but alone the Presbytery might not allow them to separate. Several of our largest, wealthiest congregations were among the ten. As the result of lengthy discernments within the Presbytery and within their congregations, straw votes were taken favoring departure. LRP voted to allow a discernment for the churches that would choose to ask God's guidance. The Presbytery appointed members of the Presbytery to meet with the same numbers of members from local congregations and to do a serious, prayerful study of the issues and concerns for the sake of resolving the complaints. I was appointed to the discernment committee for St. Andrews Presbyterian Church in Newport Beach. Candie Blankman, John Griffin, and I worked with four members of St. Andrews. Rick Kannwischer, the St. Andrews pastor, also participated.

What we found was that the pastor, Rich Kannwischer, had conducted a series of Town Hall meetings for the purpose of making the case for departure. They were simply seeking for permission to leave the PCUSA by paying the smallest amount of money possible to the Presbytery. The fact was that Presbyterian polity dictated that local churches held their property in trust for the mission of the PCUSA. This was the wealthiest church in the Presbytery. They presented themselves as in great financial need. This put me in an awkward place. My best friend in the Presbytery is John Huffman, their retired pastor. While he had voiced great concerns about the theological drift of the denomination, especially regarding human sexual ethics, he had always been a devoted churchman who would not have led St. Andrews out of the PCUSA. I knew he was not an advocate of leaving the PCUSA. He had not pressured me to take a position on the cost of leaving. It would have been wise of me to not accept a position on this team given the compromising friendships and hopes that a separation would not occur. My co-dependency got the best of me.

Through our friendship of many years, John and I had grown to trust one another. We shared in depth on many subjects, one of which was the financial condition of our mutual churches. John had developed friendships with men who had deep financial resources and who promised to share with the church they had grown to love through John. There were two special families who loved John and what he represented in the Newport Beach community of faith. They had promised to give $12.5 million to the church as soon as the dismissal was complete so as to avoid additional fees to the Presbytery. I knew this and I assumed members of the St. Andrews discernment committee knew this also. Were they holding back in disclosing these promises that would soon bring blessing to the church? I thought they would honestly disclose the financial potential within the church.

As the larger discernment committee reviewed the reported financial position of the church reflected in the documents they presented, I was faced with an ethical dilemma. Should I reveal what I knew and confront the representatives from St. Andrews? I wanted to honor my relationship with John and not betray any confidences which he had entrusted to me. I was sure that Rich Kannwischer also understood the nature of these promises. Still, I sat upon what I believed to be true, and we reached an agreement with St. Andrews that was embarrassing for me and should have been for the St. Andrews team. Ultimately, I argued that the Presbytery ought to strike deals with the ten churches seeking dismissal that would promote their mission and build positive relationships for the future in case they might desire to reenter the friendly fellowship and mission of Los Ranchos Presbytery. We hoped they would as they would see we could be trusted to be a safe place for ministry.

Our Presbytery Executive had preached a sermon in the Presbytery in which he shared he hoped the secular media would report on how we loved each other as reflected in the Presbytery's gracious dismissals. I have since concluded that his sermon did not consider the hardnosed business approach of the sophisticated laypeople with whom we were dealing. I was naïve and could not see that the Presbytery was being rolled for the financial benefit of the congregation. This was simply a real estate deal in which the Presbytery lost out of a sincere desire to be the gracious larger body of Christ.

Whatever Rich Kannwisher's motives were, I believe that he was allowing a vocal minority of church members to lead him in the direction of schism, not schism on hostile terms, but with sweetness and light, to imagine a new future for St. Andrews with little care for the larger PCUSA. I had many friends at St. Andrews. I could not imagine St. Andrews departure. What was important to the St. Andrews folks was to be allowed to leave at the lowest cost! I wanted to please these people whom I loved and with whom Laguna had shared mission in Los Ranchos. When I read their church discernment papers, I was stunned.

Clearly, they were indicting the PCUSA and our Presbytery. They demonized the PCUSA and glorified ECO. They argued that the PCUSA had become apostate and was heretical. Rich was charming and clear in his presentations of why they needed to depart for the sake of their purity, theological integrity, and missional hope. They desired to be identified with "like-minded" Christians and churches for the sake of the truth of the gospel.

St. Andrews was the leading church in our Presbytery. John Huffman and I had paid our dues over many years as faithful presbyters and made strong evangelical, biblical, and Reformed commitments. We were two of the major leaders within the Presbytery. When it came time for me to speak to one of their Town Hall meetings and to make a case for staying in the PCUSA, Rich allowed me about seven minutes after their larger committee had made a twenty-minute case for why they were compelled to depart. The denomination was publicly indicted in the town hall. I was embarrassed. As best I could, I spoke my truth in love. I pleaded with them not to take this step. In the question-and-answer time Rich, perhaps not realizing it, mocked me with a comment about future weddings we might do together. At the one wedding we did together at LPC the groom was a baseball player and Rich jokingly tossed him a baseball in the middle of the service. As the host pastor, I was shocked. Many of my friends from St. Andrews were at the wedding. After the wedding some surrounded me in the transept of the church and tried to make a case for understanding why Rich, as a young pastor, could not spend the rest of his career in an apostate denomination. This was not a great after wedding conversation, but they were eager to make their point to me.

When we were finished with the Town Hall meeting of the discernment process, a man in the congregation told me that if all the pastors in the PCUSA were like John Huffman and I that they would not be wanting to leave, but as far as he was concerned, the majority of PCUSA pastors were not straightforward about the biblical message. Afterward, our Presbytery executive told me that he wished he had the courage to say what I did. St. Andrews requested dismissal from the PCUSA with its property. The Presbytery, after a long debate, released them for well below the appraised value of the property.

I was invited to speak at a Town Hall meeting of Trinity United Presbyterian Church of Santa Ana. Gary Watkins, pastor of Christ Church Huntington Beach, made the case for leaving and I made the case for staying. We had an excellent discussion, and I appreciated the opportunity to present a paper I had written and to engage in dialogue with questions from the floor. Later, I was invited to speak at a large Town Hall of the Irvine Presbyterian Church. I had chaired the Presbytery committee that organized the Irvine Church in the late 1970s.

San Clemente Presbyterian Church hosted a series of discussions about staying or not staying in the PCUSA. John Huffman and I spoke at one of them. At a larger gathering I was paired with Steve Marsh of Geneva Church, Laguna Hills, against Rich Kannwisher and Jackson Clelland of Mission Viejo. That evening the St. Andrews "White Paper", or case for leaving, had already been distributed and read by those desiring to withdraw from the PCUSA. It felt like a pep-rally for leaving. Rich spoke first telling the congregation about the apostasy of the PCUSA. He spoke with such charm and clarity that I was again angered and could barely speak. As far as I was concerned, he was not being straightforward about the reality of the PCUSA.

The case he made I could have made when I was taken under care of the Los Angeles Presbytery as a young student moving toward gospel ministry. Rich had been a lifetime Presbyterian. He revealed a sense of entitlement with a perspective of privilege. He had inherited this church. I had chosen this imperfect struggling Reformed body of believers. It was not my desire or inclination to betray my ordination vows of doing mission within and through this denomination. To me that was unspeakable, and it tore at my heart. I could not understand how Rich could be leading Saint Andrews out of the Presbytery and trying to do it in a way that would ultimately weaken, if not destroy, Los Ranchos. This was our leading congregation and their influence within the Presbytery pulled many members and congregations to seriously discern the possibility of schism. Of course, the argument was that the denomination had already left them. Out of conscience they could not remain in an apostate denomination.

Finally, a group of Los Ranchos leaders crafted a Letter to the Presbytery arguing that no more churches were to be released without paying the full value of their properties. This caused a stir, but saved the remaining churches hoping to leave on the second wave of departures. I had developed a conviction that it was time that some of us stood up for Los Ranchos and the PCUSA. I'll never forget the evening that Tom Erickson and I met with the Mission Viejo session to make a case for staying. The two main issues, although they had a litany of PCUSA sins, were divestment in corporations doing business with Israel, and gay ordination and same-gender marriage. Thankfully, after facing the fact that they could not afford to leave, they remained and made peace with the Presbytery. The Presbytery was grateful for this turn.

The truth was that all the churches could have remained and done ministry with the rest of us. They could have saved a lot of money. In the long run the Presbytery received around 10 or 11 million dollars from the departing churches. It was tragic, good news/bad news, and from my perspective, strong pastoral leadership could have calmed the storm. Many brothers and sisters, in my opinion, betrayed their ordination vows, but justified their actions.

After SAPC was released, they received the ten-million-dollar gift. They paid off their loan and paid around three million to the Presbytery for a campus that was probably worth thirty to fifty million, if not more. One of their arguments was that they had paid for their property and buildings and therefore, the Presbytery had little to say about it. The assumption was that LRP ought to quickly dismiss St. Andrews to ECO with whatever payment that would be acceptable to them and LRP. After dismissal, they launched another fund drive for updating their campus and, as I understand, received around twenty-two million in total. John Huffman was responsible for twelve and a half million of the twenty-two. I was told that Rich preached that he had raised all this money, but the truth was that John Huffman was the pastor whose pastoral care and preaching had made these promises possible.

The hardest thing to understand was not that Rich Kannwischer led them out into ECO. Rather, when the Peachtree Presbyterian Church in Atlanta called him to become their pastor, he accepted their call, and left St. Andrews, a congregation now filled with deep pain and lack of trust. He moved to Atlanta and back into the PCUSA. The congregation in Newport Beach was flabbergasted and wounded by his betrayal which he rationalized as God's call to him. The move meant that he returned to the PCUSA to pastor the largest church in the denomination.

Los Ranchos Presbytery has come out of this troubling time, and we are recovering from our brokenness and grief. It seemed to me that a great deal of all that we had worked to achieve on behalf of the mission of God went up in smoke. Presbytery meetings are much calmer now, but there is still a sense of loss in being separated from those who left us and whom we loved. No amount of money will ever make that right or ease the pain.

I print in this memoir a couple of the papers I wrote and delivered. They help flesh out some of my convictions and concerns. I humbly present them as examples of how a pastor moved through conflicted times and painful losses in a time of great and rapid change. These were not efforts to justify my feelings or to present myself as righteous in comparison to those who left. Basically, I wanted to inform the members of LPC and of Los Ranchos as to my convictions and concerns.

Report to Laguna Presbyterian Church on the PCUSA

Report on the PCUSA by Dr. Jerry Tankersley
  Pastor, Laguna Presbyterian Church
  Presbytery of Los Ranchos
  June 30, 2013

My Personal History in the PCUSA.

I was ordained as a pastor in the United Presbyterian Church in the USA in August of 1963. This August will mark the 50th anniversary of my ordination. Since I was a graduate of Fuller Theological Seminary, the Presbytery of Los Angeles required me and others to take an additional year in a Presbyterian Seminary to ensure that we understood Reformed theology and polity and would be faithful leaders and not promoters of schism. I did the extra year at Princeton Theological Seminary and earned a Th.M. in History of Doctrine.

Fuller Seminary was founded by some who came from fundamentalist, schismatic traditions that had troubled the denomination in the past. The policy of the Los Angeles Presbytery, along with many other presbyteries across the USA, reflected a lack of trust in the theological world view of any faculty or graduate of Fuller. What the Presbytery did not completely realize was that Fuller had become a seminary committed to the integrity of all faithful expressions of the Christian faith, and in particular the Presbyterian Church. At Fuller we were encouraged to enter the mainline denominations with the purpose of loving and serving them, even though they were not perfect. When I took my ordination vows, they were as important to me as my marriage vows. They were not to be easily broken. I knew that I was linking my life with a church that had been on a long journey with strengths and weaknesses that I would need to accept, celebrate, and in which to seek the spiritual transformation of my own life.

Presbyterians in American Culture

The Presbyterian Church had good reason to be concerned about leaders who might advocate for separatist movements. It had watched this process at work for two hundred fifty years. The history of the Presbyterian Church from the earliest part of the 1700's had been one of conflict, division, reconciliation, and reunion caused by differing views of Scripture, truth, essential tenets of the Reformed faith, and their application to the ever changing circumstances confronting the nation as it expanded into the frontier. Like the nation, the church struggled with issues of authority, race, war, poverty, wealth, violence, scientific discovery, property rights, justice, civil rights, and the allocation of power.

Presbyterians and Christians of all kinds immigrated to America to experience freedom of religion. The truth was that they all carried the infection of original sin. They were unable to escape mistrust of others and outright denial of the rights of other believing Americans. Before long Presbyterians were dividing and seeking to perfect the church.

Since the early 18th century Presbyterians were at the forefront of many of the social, political, economic, and cultural controversies that divided and united the citizens of the United States. King George of England called the American Revolution the Presbyterian rebellion. That was a fair judgment. The quest for autonomy, personal freedom, and space to build a new nation and church divided Americans into factions, parties, states, nations, religions, associations, fellowships, denominations, and congregations seeking the blessings of freedom and life together without fear of the other. That journey has continued to this day as we are seeing the search for freedom and unity lived out anew in our time.

Presbyterians and Challenging Changes

For the past 50 years the great social chasms that have opened in western culture have had to do with issues of post-World War II America. Our Confession of 1967 in the Book of Confessions (the First Part of our Church Constitution) named them as: racial discrimination, war and peace, wealth and poverty, and anarchy in sexual relationships. The Confession of 67 called the church to God's mission of reconciliation through the proclamation of the gospel of Jesus Christ in the pursuit of love, justice, and peace. We have sought to overcome what Richard Sterns of World Vision named *"the hole in our gospel"*.

During these years we have had a front row seat to several social upheavals and cultural changes in both church and society. The generations born after WWII have seen governments struggling to tell the truth about war. We have listened to nightly body counts from distant places and seen the faces and names of our fallen children posted on the nightly news. We have experienced the social unrest of the 60's and 70's with the loss of trust in political authority. Each decade seemed to have been branded by slogans that caricatured the decade: "I'm not a crook," "Greed will save America", "Turn on, Tune in, and Drop out", "the Me Generation", "The Culture of Narcissism", "The Age of Addiction", etc. Through the years we have felt betrayed by the spiritual and moral failure of authorities. Many believe that our institutions have been unable to cope due to human weakness. We long to realize a new utopia where all is made right only to be repeatedly disappointed by what and in whom we have trusted. Now in this new millennium Americans are divided into separate camps and civility has been lost.

For the past 35 years the emerging issue for the PCUSA has been the heated debate about human sexuality and behavior regarding our ordination standards and understanding of marriage and family. Within our parish we have seen families struggling to keep the doors of communication open. Our youth have come of age in a narcissistic culture committed to "drugs, sex, and rock and roll". We were one of the earliest cities in America that experienced the rise of sexually transmitted viruses that led to STD's and to the plague of AIDS. Whether we were comfortable with it or not many families within our city and church were pressed to deal with stresses that previous generations may not have faced. We soon realized that we were not alone and that churches and presbyteries across America and throughout the western world were facing the same issues we were confronting. Amazingly, we have come through these times and our youth have excelled with the strong support of parents who were committed to academic success and hard work.

With all these social and cultural changes our information technology has exploded. We live in the information age with the awareness that "big government" may be watching us. We have become anxious about privacy. Since 9/11 we live in the Age of Terrorism and wonder if we will ever again feel secure. How much military power will it take to secure us? How long and how wide will our border fences need to be to keep the aliens out? We long for the good ole days not knowing how to get back to foundational truths and communities, nor how exactly to move forward into a New Age of hope.

It was inevitable that gender identity and behavior become major issues for all Christian churches, Catholic, Protestant, and Orthodox. Indeed, these have become perplexing and dividing issues for the larger culture. Now these issues have come to the halls of the US Congress, to the White House, and to the US Supreme Court. They have also risen to the halls of Presbyterian General Assemblies, Presbyteries, and congregations. Research into the development of gender identity and behavior has continued. We have learned much. There is still much to learn. Biological life remains a mystery.

The Presbyterian Church has from its beginning valued education and has established colleges and seminaries committed to leading in the alleviation of ignorance and prejudice. We have built hospitals around the world and sent medical personnel along with educators and servants of all kinds for the work of God's kingdom. We have been passionate about training educated pastors and teachers. In the process, the two-thousand-year tradition of the Christian church has frequently been explored, questioned, and reformed by new discoveries and deeper insight into the Scriptures and into the benefits of modern science.

Since 1978, Presbyterian General Assemblies have been asked by interest groups within the church to affirm a growing societal consensus that Christian persons of different sexual orientations and behaviors ought to be allowed and welcomed into church membership with the same membership rights as other members, i.e., to be ordained as teaching and ruling elders, to baptize their children, and to be married. That is, if they possessed gifts and responsible behaviors consistent with biblical and confessional standards of morality. I could never have guessed that my ministry would be during decades of conflict, anger, and fear related to so many fears.

Two years ago, when a majority of presbyteries approved the principal of "local option standards" regarding ordination standards for congregations and presbyteries, I wrote a Pastoral Statement that was affirmed by my fellow staff pastors and a majority of our session. It stated what I think is the teaching of both Old and New Testaments and that is that human sexual relationships were intended by God to be celebrated and enjoyed within the covenant of marriage between one man and one woman. That also means that I support ordination to church office only for those who are able and willing to live according to the biblical standard of "fidelity and chastity" whether married or single. This applies to either heterosexual or homosexual Christians.

Most recently, our congregation was one of thirteen PCUSA congregations chosen to participate in the PCUSA's new Theology of Marriage curriculum pilot project. In seeking to moderate the discussion of twenty of our very bright, intelligent, and committed disciples, I found myself understanding how deep our differences run and how passionately we are committed to our convictions. I honor them all whether I agree with them or not.

As a pastor I am aware that many of our fellow citizens and church members have been caught up into the chaos of the larger culture's sexual anarchy. I am convinced that the church's mission is to extend compassion, understanding, forgiveness, and the hope of new beginnings in right relationship with God and others. In the early 1980's the gay mayor of our city appointed me to the city's first AIDS Education Task Force. I learned a lot. I became friends with many in the gay community. We worked together for the peace and well-being of our city. (Jeremiah 29:4–7) I provided pastoral care for many dying persons with a disease that no one understood and about which there was much fear. I read many books and listened to many lectures. I participated in some painful public confrontations between persons and groups who could not agree about either heterosexual or homosexual conduct.

I believe, as our church constitution affirms, in "freedom of conscience". There are faithful members of our congregation who do not agree with my interpretation of Scripture in the matter of sexual ethics. There are member families who have responsible gay or lesbian children, brothers, or sisters. I respect their sensitivities and convictions and seek to love all persons and families. All believers are my brothers and sisters in Christ. I want all people, whatever their life experience, to be welcome in our church. But such inclusivity within the church is a threat to some.

We may not be of one mind on all issues. I am sure that will not happen until Jesus returns to perfect the creation. Until then we are called to "clothe ourselves in love which binds everything together in perfect harmony." (Colossians 3:14) In between the first and second coming of Jesus we will need to speak the truth in love, to agree, to disagree, to argue, to debate, to dialogue, and to patiently wait until God's Word and Spirit brings about a resolution to heartfelt differences. No church can escape this challenge. Those who withdraw from the PCUSA seeking like-mindedness will inevitably confront their differences and be required to patiently forbear as they work together to build their fellowship. The truth is that all who transfer their churches into other Reformed denominations will also transfer their strengths and weaknesses, their gifts, and their sins. Until the New Creation of God's kingdom comes there will be no realized utopia on planet earth.

Theology of the Church

What this means to me is that I am committed to being at the table of fellowship within the PCUSA in dialogue with Scripture and our Book of Confessions until the Word of God, the Holy Spirit, and our Reformed tradition makes it clear that I should do otherwise.

I hold to a biblical and Reformed doctrine of the church that informs me that the church is made up of "saints and sinners" at the same time. The flesh and the Spirit are in conflict in every believer's heart and in the heart of the church. If we begin to focus upon one behavior, that we call sin, we will be in trouble. Indeed, we could choose from a long list of sins that we could easily see in others. It is much harder for us to see the beam that is in our own eyes. As baptized believers we have been forgiven and welcomed into a community within which we may grow in the grace and the knowledge of the Lord. In this fellowship the Word and the Spirit of God seeks to transform us and to impart to us each the mind of Christ.

I believe that Jesus was right when he warned his disciples about "weeding the field filled with wheat and weeds". (Matthew 13:24–30) Only the angels of God know how to do this, and they will do it at the end of time, but until then, if we try to remove from the church the weeds of sin, we will likely rip up a lot of good plants. This does not mean that I oppose church discipline. Indeed, John Knox, the Scottish Reformer, said that the three signs of the true church are that the "Word of God is preached, the Sacraments are administered, and discipline in the faith practiced." (*The Scots Confession, Book of Confessions,* 3.18).

The Movement Toward Dismissal from the PCUSA

I want you to know and most of you do, that there is a growing group of congregations within the PCUSA who have decided to seek dismissal from us. Since January there has been a process of discernment within Los Ranchos Presbytery about these matters. Not all churches have participated. The Presbytery has not required any church to engage in this process. At our session retreat in January, I told LPC session about this and asked them if they wanted to engage LPC in a process of discernment about our continuing relationship with the PCUSA. They were unanimous that we are a healthy congregation and that our calling is to invest our energies in God's mission through the PCUSA. I was thankful and proud of them.

I believe that changing the label of our denomination will not enhance our mission. It would likely introduce the toxin of division into our church family system and weaken us. You may not agree. And that is fine, but this is where I am, and I believe your elected session also. However, it is a session's responsibility to discern these matters in conversation with your pastors and the leadership of Los Ranchos Presbytery.

I have been told that at least ten of Los Ranchos' congregations will soon ask the Presbytery to enter a process of dismissal to some other Reformed body of like-minded believers. Pastors, groups of pastors and lay members have, it seems to me, put the PCUSA publicly on trial and have accused it of being "apostate, heretical, and corrupt". The issues that have been lifted are these:

"the authority and interpretation of Scripture",

"the nature of Jesus Christ as Son of God",

"whether or not Jesus Christ is the only Savior of the world",

"the refusal of the PCUSA to uphold its Constitution and to discipline those who violate its polity," and

" the teachings of the Scriptures and our Reformed Confessions on marriage, family, and sexual identity and behavior."

It is alleged that whatever the PCUSA says we believe we do not believe or practice. While we have an excellent *Book of Confessions* (now endorsed by ECO and the Fellowship of Presbyterians) and other documents approved by the denomination, (Hope in The Lord Jesus Christ), the church authorities are so diverse in their interpretations that little guidance can be given to address conflicts. Corporately, it is alleged, the PCUSA is filled with hypocrites who do not believe our ordination vows or Confessional truths. It is argued that we do not hold our heretics accountable, and we do not discipline those who violate their vows. These assertions are filled with partial truths, and they paint the whole church with a broad brush which I do not believe to be true. I know too many faithful Presbyterians of different political camps across the PCUSA who love God and seek to glorify God and who are deeply disturbed by these generalizations.

It is true that the PCUSA has been losing members consistently over the last 50 years. This growing loss of members in western mainline denominations is being attributed to a lack of theological integrity and committed discipleship. The facts are that the PCUSA since reunion in 1983 has dropped in membership from 4.3 million members to just over 1 million. Many explanations for this loss have been suggested. This loss of membership has been accompanied by an increasing mistrust and even hostility toward religion in the western world. Almost all Christian churches, including the Southern Baptists, are showing membership losses in the U.S. Amazingly, in the southern hemisphere of the earth, in the poorer parts of the world, Christianity is growing more rapidly than any other religion.

The Need for Biblical and Theological Renewal.

I share our critics concerns. Something is happening in western culture that is rapidly marginalizing the church. I suspect it can be attributed to many causes. Nevertheless, I strongly believe that the authority of God speaks through the Scriptures of Old and New Testaments. Every level of the church needs to surrender itself or place itself under the authority of the LORD who inspired the writers of the Bible and who still speaks through the written, spoken, and living Word.

The Scriptures witness to the God of Israel incarnate in Jesus Christ. They reveal that Jesus is the "way, the truth, and the life and that no one comes to the Father except through faith in him." (John 14:6) The witness of Scripture is that at the cross of Jesus, God made peace through the blood of Jesus, reconciled us to himself and us to each other. At the cross atonement for humanity's sin was made, dividing walls of hostility broken down, and Jews and Gentiles were incorporated into one new humanity, the Church of Jesus Christ, filled with the Spirit of Christ for sake of doing God's mission. (Ephesians 1 to 6)

The Scriptures reveal that in Jesus the Christ the heart of God's love was made known. On the Day of Pentecost, the love of God was poured into the church's heart and the believer's souls through the power of the Holy Spirit. This Word and Spirit mediate a new standing in grace to those who believe in Jesus. The believer is given the gift of the righteousness and holiness of Christ and then called to become who they are in Christ. (Romans, Galatians, Ephesians) But in this lifetime the process of sanctification is never complete. In good and bad days, we still live by grace, repent of our sins, and seek the mind and will of Christ. We do not know everything. We see dimly as in a mirror. Knowledge puffs up, but love builds up. (I Corinthians 8 and 13) The Scriptures promise that the LORD, who is the Spirit, will one day transform us and conform us to the image of Christ. (Romans 12:1-2; 2 Corinthians 3:18)

Those baptized into Christ have confessed that Jesus is LORD of body and soul. He owns us and is restoring us to the persons he intended us to be from the beginning. It is always progress and not perfection. The Living LORD is the head of the church.

Of course, this means that our bodies are temples of the Holy Spirit. The Spirit gives us new hearts. Jesus comes to live within us. Therefore, we do not want to do anything that will grieve the Holy Spirit. That means that how we express our sexuality, how we use power, how we spend our money, and how we use our time are stewardship responsibilities. In every dimension of our lives, we seek to please God and to live for the glory of God. Discerning God's will and doing it becomes the priority of our lives. As a Spirit filled people of God the mission of God shines forth into a spiritually darkened and lost world. We are sent forth to be God's kingdom people.

I pray that the church's identity and mission may be strengthened and empowered. Christians of all kinds need to wake up to what is happening for the sake of seeking spiritual renewal in a world not unlike the days of Noah. (Matthew 24:36–44) There are many places in our world where we can see the ruins of a culture that lost its reason for being and slowly was destroyed from within. Only God knows if this is western civilization's future. God will have his church, but will we be anything more than a historical footnote or a building ruin?

Los Ranchos Discernment

On Saturday, June 15, 2013, the Los Ranchos Presbytery approved its policy of discernment regarding a congregation's dismissal with church property. Some of you may not know that our Book of Order says that all properties of the local church are held in trust through the presbytery for the mission purposes of the PCUSA. Therefore, a presbytery cannot dismiss a congregation to another Reformed body without a careful consideration of the market value of the congregation's property. The presbytery has a fiduciary responsibility to the national church, the PCUSA, to guarantee that the mission purpose and programs of the larger church are fully protected from any congregation voting to withdraw from the denomination without making a good faith payment on the value of the property. *Book of Order G-4.02*

"The Trust Clause reflects our understanding of the church as a communion of saints across time, with responsibilities both to those who came before and those who will follow. When a congregation seeks to leave the PCUSA, it is breaking what is often a significant historic relationship; it is also departing from a fellowship in which its officers have participated, by whose polity they have pledged to be governed, and with which many members may feel bonds of affection." *Tom v San Francisco (Decision of the General Assembly of the PCUSA)*

For those congregations seeking dismissal from the PCUSA, our presbytery's property policy will now require that each congregation's session enter a time of discernment with a presbytery team to discern what is in the interest of congregation, presbytery, and the PCUSA. Financial considerations will need to be considered. There is no one formula as to how these negotiations will be considered. Once an agreement has been reached then it will be brought to the floor of the Presbytery for discussion, debate, amendment, and a final vote. As you may imagine, this is likely to be a painful process that if not handled wisely could lead to wounds in the family of faith for many years. May God have mercy upon us! Nothing arouses passions like money and property and its control. Please pray for our Presbytery.

Those who advocate schism accuse the western church of hypocrisy when it comes to truth and obedience to the essential tenets of the gospel of Christ. It is true that we live in a postmodern, post-Christian world that is highly suspicious of any ultimate truth. The larger culture celebrates "open-mindedness" and "tolerance" with the encouragement "to live and to let live". Our children are taught in the public education system in America that we live in a pluralistic, secular, deeply divided world, and that we could find ourselves continually at war if we seek to impose upon others our own subjective values and world views.

My Convictions About Schism

One of the books that shaped my theological reflection about the church was written by President Edward John Carnell, the President of Fuller Seminary and my Professor of Christian Ethics in the late 1950's. He made some very important points about the Classical View of the Reformed church. *The Case for Orthodox Theology*[22]

First: All other things being equal, a Christian should remain in the fellowship that gave him spiritual birth.

Both Jesus and Paul remained faithful to the Jewish Temple and to the Synagogue. Even though Jesus was rejected by a portion of his family, he never stopped loving and praying for the Israel of God and the Church. He prayed that his disciples would all be one even as he and the Father were one. (John 17). All people would know that they were his disciples if they had love for one another. (John 13:35). Jesus died for his church and for the world. The cross stands over us all. The Holy Spirit has

---

22. Carnell, *Case for Orthodox Theology*, 133–137.

inspired our confession of faith that Jesus Christ, through his life, death, and resurrection, is our Savior and LORD, the only way to the Father . The inspiration for spiritual formation has come to me through spiritual directors committed to the PCUSAs and our life together. This theology of the church is taught in our *Book of Confessions*.

Secondly, A Christian should judge the claims of a church by its official creed or confession, not by the lives of its members.

It is likely that there are teaching and ruling elders in the PCUSA who are not of one mind on the list of essential tenets of the Reformed faith. From the early 1700's we have argued about forcing all leaders of the church to subscribe to a list of essentials. We all believe that there are essentials, but we have learned that freedom of thought and interpretation of biblical texts are foundational. Any time we have sought to create a like-minded church, a perfect church, we have ended up with heresy trials that divided committed Christians.

Our confessions have rejected perfectionism and settled for progress in growing into the grace and truth of the revelation we have received in Jesus Christ, the living Word of God, to whom the Scriptures bear unique and authoritative witness. The authority of Scripture is the Holy Spirit, the Spirit of God, the Spirit of Christ, who inspired the writers of Old and New Testaments and who continues to speak the Word of God through the written Word and proclamation of the Word.

My hope for the church would be that we will keep our heads and our hearts in the Scriptures of Old and New Testaments as we are guided in their interpretations by the *Book of Confessions*. As long as the historical creeds and confessions guide, they lead us to the authority of the One Sovereign God, three persons, Father, Son, and Holy Spirit. They lead us to the fulfillment of the promises of God to Israel in the life, death, and resurrection of Jesus Christ. They inspire within us the confession of faith that Jesus is LORD. They call for the peace and unity of the church. The ordination vows for elders and deacons in the PCUSA commits us to these essentials of the Reformed faith.

The prophets of the Old Testament raged against Israel's unfaithfulness, but never once advocated that a righteous remnant separate from the larger elect people of God. The Apostle Paul addressed many issues of sin in the Corinthian church, but never advocated schism from the body of Christ. Just the opposite, he argued for the unity of the body of Christ, for the use of the gifts given by the Holy Spirit, and for the better way of love.

He had the humility to confess that all our knowledge is partial and that we see reality only dimly. Paul called the church to grow up into spiritual maturity, a maturity that could embrace, accept, forgive, and work for reconciliation. Yes, a maturity that could call the church to have the mind of the servant Christ and to love as we have been loved. Paul knew he had not yet arrived, but he was inspired by the Spirit to know the fullness of the grace and power of Christ's death and resurrection. (Philippians 2 and 3)

I believe that the Apostle would have written a firm word to many of us who have tried to fight and to win in the battles of church and culture. At the end of the day, we may discover that we have done more harm and left much more wreckage than we could have imagined. This is true for all sides in our conflicts. This includes progressives and conservatives. I need and we all need to repent of our willingness to discount our brothers and sisters and even to destroy the unity of the church for the sake of establishing our moral superiority and our political power.

Edward John Carnell ended his discussion of *Orthodoxy* by asking how we determine if a denomination may rightfully be called a church. He answered,

Is the gospel taught in the creed or confession?

He argued that if the system of doctrine taught in Romans and Galatians is reflected in its creeds and confessions the true church is to be found. If a denomination departs from this gospel, it forfeits its right to be called a church. Our *Book of Order* states the great Protestant watch words: *Christ alone, Grace alone, Faith alone, Scripture alone.* These great doctrines the PCUSA has enshrined in its Constitution, and we are called to live into the reality of justification by faith alone in the promises of God and sanctification in the Spirit of Christ.

Is the gospel free?

What he asked was whether the preachers and teachers of the church were free to proclaim the gospel. Our answer must be "Yes!" Martin Luther was not free to preach the gospel of Romans and Galatians in the Roman Catholic Church of the 16th century. He did it anyway and was excommunicated. He never intended to leave the church. Therefore, until I am commanded by the PCUSA not to preach the good news of God's grace, I will be a faithful member of this denomination.

Is the Christian free to protest abuses?

"He must speak against abuses with power and grace. And if his words fail to effect a change, he must patiently wait for a new opportunity to speak. He may not take the law into his own hands by provoking schism, for formal judgment belongs to God, not man."[23]

Our denomination is filled with good Protestants. We surely have the right to protest. The question is what we do while we wait for our protests to bear fruit. Maybe they never will, but surely, we must speak and live in such a way that our trust in God's faithfulness is manifest.

Thirdly, Separation from an existing denomination is justifiable on only two criteria.

Eviction.

In our own time, no one is being evicted from the PCUSA. We are free to preach and to live the gospel. We can protest.

Apostasy.

"If a denomination removes the gospel from its creed or confession, or if it leaves the gospel but removes the believer's right to preach it, the believer may justly conclude that the denomination is apostate. Before the believer takes a settled attitude one way or another, he must bring his convictions to the touchstone: he must seek the counsel of the brethren and the wisdom of classical theology. A spirit of divisiveness is not prompted by the Holy Spirit, for love is the law of life, and love remains unsatisfied until all who form the body of Christ are united in one sacred fellowship."[24]

I want you to know that I do not want my legacy to be of leading our congregation out of the PCUSA. For me that would violate all that has directed my ministry since my ordination. My family was evangelized by the Presbyterian Church in Amarillo, Texas. As a ten-year-old, I was baptized into this covenant family. During seminary days I suddenly awakened to the truth that the Presbyterian Church was my spiritual family. It has nurtured my spiritual life, imparted truth, and grace to me, and allowed me to serve Jesus in many ways and places. Never has the denomination told me I could not preach the Scriptures or proclaim the gospel of Christ. I have discovered that an evangelical leader in our denomination may stand for its highest offices. What seems important for all groups in the PCUSA is whether we are committed to the church and loyal to its theology and polity. Freedom of thought and openness to learn is valued. When the church no longer allows this freedom but seeks to enforce conformity to a position that is not advocated

---

23. Carnell, *Case for Orthodox*, 135.
24. Carnell, *Case for Orthodox*, 137.

in Scripture or our Confessions, then I will quietly withdraw from the PCUSA. But we are a long way from that.

I believe, have taught, and proclaimed the revealed truth of God. This truth is personal. It was manifest in the person of Jesus Christ. His life, death, and resurrection reveal God's rescue plan for humanity. Christian knowledge and truth have been revealed by the Word and Spirit of Christ. His light of truth illumines our way in the darkness. His truth points to the only way to a blessed or happy life. I make no apologies for defending and proclaiming the values and the spirituality of the kingdom of God. God's mission is being advanced in the world. Standing on tip toe in faith, hope, and love, we long to see the final and complete day when heaven and earth totally and perfectly overlap and interconnect in the fullness of the New Creation in eternal life.

Report by Dr. Jerry Tankersley

Pastor, Laguna Presbyterian Church, June 30, 2013

Paper for Trinity United Presbyterian Church.

Dear Trinity friends,

It was the summer of 1956 and I and two of my best friends decided to travel from our home in Amarillo, Texas, to Okla. City, Okla., to hear Billy Graham. In our first year of university, we had each come to a deeper faith in God. It was a thrilling time for me to have my two buddies with whom I had grown up from childhood to come to share my faith. They encouraged me and I encouraged them. It was a formative season. My parents had given to me a new Chevy and we were having the time of our lives.

That Saturday evening was youth night at the Graham Crusade. I still have that evening branded into my memory and heart. He preached on a text from Ezekiel 22:23-31. Ezekiel the prophet had been commissioned by the Lord to speak a word of prophetic truth to the nation of Israel. He spoke of the unfaithfulness of Israel. He called the people to a spiritual repentance that was both good news for the nation's soul, but also a call to social justice and righteousness on behalf of the kingdom of God.

The key verse that Billy preached on was verse 30,

"And I sought for anyone among them who would repair the wall and stand in the breach before me on behalf of the land, so that I would not destroy it; but I found no one." Ezekiel 22:30

Billy said that the Lord was still seeking for young men and women who would have the courage to publicly commit themselves to repair the broken walls of Jerusalem, who would stand in the breach before the Lord on behalf of the land. When Billy gave the invitation for us to come forward with the promise to stand in the middle of the brokenness of his people and to rebuild the life of the church and the nation, I heard the call. But if it had not been for my friend Mike nudging me in the side and saying to me, "Jerry, we have to go forward", I would not have gone. I had some reserve about embarrassing myself before others. It took the Lord poking me in the side to get me to promise my life to serve as a peacemaker at the center of the world's conflicts and to seek to heal the wounds and to rebuild the walls of the world and of the ruined life of humanity.

The three of us went forward. As I stood before the platform looking up at Billy, I began to see in tunnel vision. Suddenly, I knew I was in a watershed moment in which my life would change forever. I stood there crying my eyes out realizing what a dangerous calling I was receiving. For years I had been pressed by my parents to stand between them for the sake of mediating their marital disputes and wars. I had learned a lot about mediation and conflict resolution. I had become a raging co-dependent. I had succeeded, but now I think I realized that I had been providentially prepared for a call to a ministry of peacemaking, of standing in the breaches and during deep conflicts, anxiety and fear, for the sake of healing the human condition. That calling has put me in painful places of vulnerability. This evening I feel like I am standing in another breach hoping to repair the wall, to be an agent of God's reconciling love.

I am honored to share my convictions with you about staying in the PCUSA. Over the past 40 years you have been a valued colleague in ministry and in helping to develop the mission of the Presbytery of Los Ranchos. I have admired your leadership, your evangelical passion, and theological vision. I went to India and to Kenya with Dick Grace and with others of your congregation. Laguna Presbyterian Church is grateful to you for training and sharing with us leaders like Kathy Sizer and Linda White. When I heard that Trinity was one of the congregations seeking dismissal from LRP, I felt the loss and realized that our presbytery life and mission would never again be the same if you left. I am sure that the majority of your congregation has already decided its future course. My thoughts about staying in the PCUSA will likely have little impact upon those who are determined to leave, but since I was invited to do this, I will speak my heart and mind to you.

First, why stay in the PCUSA? Because there are important biblical and theological reasons to remain in this part of the Reformed body.

We affirm what the Biblical revelation has taught us and that is that God has a purpose and plan for our cosmos, for human history, and for his people. From the beginning of the human story we learn that the humans fell away from right relationship with God and with one another. They hid from the presence of God and were burdened with shame and guilt. The first couple was driven from the Garden of Eden to live East of Eden. They were cut off from the Tree of Life. The family was divided. They were separated, estranged, alienated from God and from one another. They lived under the bondage of sin and death. Soon Adam's family grew into a civilization and culture that was divided into hostile families, tribes, peoples, and nations. God's original intention of a peaceable kingdom had been transformed by unbelief, pride, disobedience, and rebellion, into a fallen world in which peace had been lost and violence characterized human existence. The tempter seemed to have won a great victory.

The good news was that the Creator God did not give up on all that he loved and created. The rescue was begun. The story of salvation took shape in the midst of human brokenness and sin. The Lord God called Abraham and Sarah to become the father and the mother of a multitude of nations and promised to bless them and to make them a blessing. From the beginning of God's initiative, it was God's grace that was at work in the midst of human sin. The Sovereign God was committed to fulfilling his covenant promises to reconcile the world to himself and the human family with itself.

Even in exile, God had not forsaken his people. He sent Nehemiah to rebuild the wall of Jerusalem during surrounding dangers and warnings. In anxiety and fear, the people under Ezra/Nehemiah rebuilt the destroyed Temple of God.

God's salvation story in the history of Israel came to fulfillment in the birth, life, death, and resurrection of Jesus Christ, the Son of God. In his perfect obedience he reversed Adam's disobedience. In his death upon the cross God made peace through the blood of Christ, the Second Adam, and bore the judgment our sins deserved. He broke down dividing walls of hostility and reconciled us to the Father. Jews and Gentiles, male and female, educated and uneducated, slave and free, rich and poor, were reconciled into one new believing humanity and baptized into the one family of Christ for the sake of being ambassadors for Christ in taking the message of healing to all the nations.

I believe that the Apostle Paul's Letter to the Ephesians clearly stated the purpose and plan of God at work in human history. Listen,

"With all wisdom and insight, he has made known to us the mystery of his will, according to his good pleasure that he set forth in Christ, as a plan for the fullness of time, to gather up, or unite, all things in him, things in heaven and things on earth." Ephesians 1:9–10

Therefore, the church was constituted as one body of Christ, filled with the Holy Spirit, called to become who God had created us to be from the beginning, a bright shining light of truth, justice, grace, holiness, and love. To fulfill God's mission the fellowship of the church would need to live into the unity of the Spirit in the bond of peace. The members of the church were to live with humility, gentleness, and with patience, bearing with one another in love.

"There is one body and one Spirit, just as you were called to the one hope of your calling, one Lord, one faith, one baptism, one God and Father of all, who is above all and through all and in all." Ephesians 4:1–6

Each member of this family was blessed with the mind of Christ, the new life of the rule of God, the reality of the indwelling Christ, who promised over time to conform us to his own image and to empower us to be the children of God living in peace, unity, and purity, in the holiness of God's gift of new life.

In the Gospel of John, chapter 17, we are allowed to listen in to the very heart of the Son of God as he prayed for those who were to be his disciples. His central concern was that we might be one, even as he and the father were one. They were one in fellowship, one in love, one in peace, one in mission. Yes, the unity within the very being of God was the fellowship of love into which all God's people were invited to enter. To do so was to abide in Christ and to manifest the fruits of the Spirit. We worship the Holy One of Israel, the one triune God, Father, Son, and Holy Spirit.

The reason that I recapitulate this biblical theology of the unity of God, the unity of the people of God, and the unity of

The Highways To Louisville And Beyond

the mission of God is that we may be reminded of what is at the very heart of the movement of the reign of God in human history. Paradise was lost, walls of the City of God breached, but God acted to restore paradise in and through the sacrifice of the Lamb of God, Jesus. He purchased us with his own blood. Now we belong to him and to his body. His passion and mission must become the passion and mission of God's people. God's promise is of a New Creation in which the original righteousness of the unity of all creation will be perfectly restored and all will be made right to the glory of God and the joy of heaven and earth in the New Jerusalem.

As we consider our staying a united people of God in the PCUSA, these great biblical themes ought to be first and foremost in our believing and doing the will of God. In fact, this Reformed tradition is confessed in our Book of Confessions, the first part of the Constitution of the PCUSA. Some say that there has been a theological drift in the PCUSA. Not so, if we seriously read the Confessions. Discerning the will of God must place God's purpose and plan for creation and history at the forefront. One of the essential tenets of the Reformed tradition is the unity of the one God and reflected in the unity of the people of God. To act to sever this unity within any fellowship will have profound implications for the congregation, presbytery, and surrounding community. The unity of the church is central to our witness to the gospel in a fragmented, chaotic, and lost world. The world will know we are Christians by the integrity of our love for one another.

Secondly, why stay in the PCUSA? Because we promised in our ordination vows to remain faithful to the covenant with God and our covenant as the people of God.

We live in a culture of promise breakers, not promise keepers. Somewhere deep in the recesses of our minds, we carry a vision of loving someone else if they are young enough, rich enough, smart enough, thin enough, well enough, and agreeable enough. When the other does not meet our needs, we decide we will trade the old model in and move upward to a new model that will love us as we need and who will fulfill our "wish dreams". Then we set about seeking to conform the other to our expectations. When that fails, we begin the process again. We divorce and seek a new relationship.

Kay and I just celebrated our 46th wedding anniversary. On our wedding day we made covenant promises to God and to one another that we would faithfully live together as husband and wife throughout our life journey. It is an amazing thing that a man and a woman can make such promises. This journey takes place one day at a time during happy and trying circumstances, as long as we both shall live. Those who have been married for a while know that relationships are not easy. In fact, none of us based on human will has the capacity to keep the promises we made. Why? We are sinners.

But the Christian covenant of marriage is a commitment and act of the will. "Husbands love your wives as Christ loved the church." Ephesians 5. What this means to me is that when two Christians make covenant promises we are trusting the power of God's Spirit of love to inform and to inspire our loving.

This will mean that over many years there will be both success and failure. What will matter is if we cast ourselves upon the mercy of God, accept one another in our differences, forgive one another in our failures, and patiently endure by God's grace the long journey? The Holy Spirit within the believer's heart empowers this fidelity. The miracle is that love heals, and joy restores. I remember hearing Tony Campolo speak to the National Presbyterian Pastor's Sabbath gathering. He shared the journey that he and his wife of many years had experienced. In particular, he said that she was strongly in favor of gay ordination and same gender marriage. He said he was on the opposite side. But he said, they had not divorced over this difference. Why? Because they loved one another and were not about to let this ruin their marriage, even though it was important to each of them.

Dietrich Bonhoeffer wrote the classic book on Christian community. It was entitled, *Life Together*. He celebrated the gift of Christian community. But he said all of us come into community with "wish dreams" of what we expect the community to be. We work hard to make our brothers and sisters conform to our "wish dreams". Finally, we discover it does not work. Our "wish dreams" are shattered and we are profoundly disappointed. I was stunned to read that Bonhoeffer said that the sooner our "wish dreams" are shattered the better. Why? Because then we begin to discover that we have life together only in and through the grace of our LORD Jesus Christ.[25]

I was ordained fifty years ago as a twenty-six-year-old assistant pastor at a church in Los Angeles. I was green, right out of

---

25. Bonhoeffer, *Life Together*, 18 to 39.

Fuller and Princeton Seminaries. I thought I had all the answers. One day my wife of five years told me she no longer loved me, and she disappeared. I was 26 and wanted nothing more than to make that marriage work. I thought my life and especially my ministry were over. I had failed. I knew all about the grace of God in my head, but I did not believe that the church was big enough and gracious enough to hold on to me, one of its wounded servants. What happened was life transforming. The Presbytery of Los Angeles that had ordained me a few months before investigated, counseled, prayed, and voted to affirm my continuing status as a pastor. In that act the church gave back to me my life and calling. I received grace, not cheap grace, but life transforming grace, the costly grace of God.

For over 40 years I have given thanks to God whose love would not let me go. It was the Presbyterian Church that mediated grace to me a sinner and picked me up with hope. God has been faithful to me and to the church. My heart is ever bonded with the PCUSA. It did not divorce me. I will not divorce it in its brokenness and painful diversity.

Thirdly, why stay in the PCUSA? Because the people of God, the church of Jesus Christ, have never been perfect.

Billy Graham was right when he said that if you are seeking to join the perfect Christian church, the moment you join it, it will be imperfect.

Check out the history of Israel in the Old Testament. The people were called to be the holy people of God, yet Israel's history is a history of both faithfulness and unfaithfulness. At times it seemed that there were none who were righteous. But along the way, there was a righteous remnant. The prophets called the whole nation back to God and covenant faithfulness, but not once did they ever call the remnant to separate from the larger covenant community. Through the prophet's words, the LORD held the nation accountable and in God's mighty acts in Israel's history the LORD disciplined his people. But there was never an exodus called for from the covenant family.

Likewise, Jesus did not separate from Israel. He worshiped in the Temple and synagogue. He interpreted the law of God. He proclaimed that the kingdom of God was at hand in the fulfillment of God's promises in his life. He called people to take up their cross and to surrender themselves to a disciplined life together and mission. In losing their lives they would find their lives. He allowed persons the freedom to choose if they would follow him. He called people to go and sin no more. To the very end he knew his disciples were debating among themselves which one of them was the greatest. He told them that Satan was sifting them, dividing them, under the rubric of religious leadership, veiling their sinful ambitions. He taught them that they were not to weed the garden of the kingdom of God. The wheat and the tares could only be separated by the angels of God on the last day. If his disciples tried to do the job, they would rip up the good and the bad plants. (Matthew 13:24-30)

At the end of his journey, it was the religious leadership of the people that he loved that demanded that Rome kill him. Better for one person to die for the nation than for the nation to be destroyed!

The Apostle Paul prayed for the unity of the church of Christ. In Corinth he faced a church that had almost every manifestation of sin within its fellowship. Nevertheless, Paul addressed them as saints. He confronted their sin and called them to repentance, to faithfulness and to transformation, but not once did he seek to divide that church. He knew the church was filled with forgiven sinners who still struggled with the weaknesses of their sinful hearts. Yet, they were one in Christ. Christ could not be divided. The Apostle applied the sharp - edged sword of the Word of God and the Holy Spirit. Paul's shattered "wish dreams" for the church never made him strike out in an anger that would have been more of his flesh than the Spirit of Christ. He suffered for and with the church. He was perplexed. He prayed for the church. He taught the church. He worked for the reconciliation and healing of the church. He never gave up. Why, because love never ends. (See John Calvin, Institutes of the Christian Religion, Book IV, chapter 1.7-29)

Paul understood what Bonhoeffer later taught that when we begin judging and accusing one another we end up accusing God who has given to us our brothers and sisters. The PCUSA is not a perfect church. We have major disagreements. We read the Bible through different eyes and grids. We have our heretics. We have our noted sinners on the left and the right. But we also have a multitude of faithful, forgiven, disciples who have worked for this church, prayed for this church, given to this church, since the beginning years of Presbyterian history. The great events of American history have divided us. The imperatives of unity have drawn us back together until the next crisis.

I have listened to former moderators of the GA loudly fighting in the halls of the GA. There have been times in which I have questioned how I could stay in covenant with this family. I wanted to separate, but the better angels of my nature have always whispered into my soul to be patient, to forbear, to forgive, to stay in fellowship, even when every human inclination has been to run. I am so glad that I chose to stay. I do not want my legacy as a pastor to be that of leading an exodus out of an imperfect church that will never arrive at perfection until the fullness of the New Creation. To leave would be to betray God's calling in my life.

In between the first and second coming of Jesus we will need to speak the truth in love, to agree, to disagree, to argue, to debate, to dialogue, and to patiently wait until God's Word and Spirit brings about a resolution to heartfelt differences. No church can escape this challenge. Those who withdraw from the PCUSA seeking like-mindedness will inevitably confront their differences and be required to patiently forbear as they work together to build their fellowship. The truth is that all who seek release of their churches into other Reformed denominations will also transfer their strengths and weaknesses, their gifts, and their sins. Until the New Creation of God's kingdom comes there will be no realized utopia on planet earth.

Fourthly, why stay in the PCUSA? We need to stay for the sake of God's mission in our broken and wounded world.

God needs a united witness and service, not just for those inside the church, but also for those who are waiting and watching from the outside of the church's life. In this regard, I find myself agreeing in several ways with Pope Francis of the RCC. He has confessed that his church has been preoccupied with issues of Christian morality, i.e., "abortion, homosexuality, same gender marriage, ordination standards". Sounds like the PCUSA. While we have struggled with our internal divisions and arguments, we have neglected to see that there is a wounded world lying beside the road and left for dead. The walls of the City of God have been breached. Is there anyone who is willing to stand in the breach for the sake of healing the church?

The Pope has argued in his recent interview in the Jesuit magazine, *America*, that the church needs to open its eyes and ears to the needs of our world for the mercy, compassion, and grace of God that are central to the gospel of Jesus Christ. It is not that morality is unimportant, but that moral passions can so capture our attention that we fail to see that our world is filled with sheep without shepherds. Pope Francis has asked the church to consider if anyone can fulfill the claims of Christian morality if they have not first been converted to Christ and begun to live their lives under the Lordship of Christ? Therefore, he has called the church to a new Christ-centeredness, to the good news of the gospel, to a servant mission of finding the lost and restoring them to wholeness in the fellowship of a people who live by God's amazing grace.

He said the church is a field hospital in the battlefield of this sin-sick world. The cries of the wounded are everywhere. People need the balm of Gilead that alone can heal the sin sick soul. Francis said of his church that we have gone about checking the cholesterol of the wounded when what was really needed was the immediate healing of wounds, the proclamation of Jesus Christ in whose touch sins are forgiven, bodies made whole, and hope restored.

Over the past 41 years in Laguna Beach as a pastor I have found my mind and heart stretched and transformed. I have come to a deeper appreciation for the work of pastoral ministry. I have placed myself under the authority of Jesus Christ as he is revealed through the Word of God. He is my Savior and my LORD. From the San Diego GA in 1978 I have been at the center of the human sexuality debate. I have not changed my mind about God's intentions in creation for the faithful union of one man and one woman in the covenant of marriage. Nor am I willing to change our ordination standards. The only difference now is that each presbytery and congregation will have to study, pray, and decide its convictions on this matter.

Some will disagree with my convictions. In fact, some of the most gifted and committed disciples of Christ at LPC disagree with my reading of the Bible. But I am not about to separate from them. I need them and they need me. I am not prepared to divide my beloved congregation over this. A sizable group of our families have gay or lesbian children. All our neighborhoods have same gender families. We know them. They are human and they have the same aspirations as others. How will we reach them if they perceive that up front they will be rejected in the name of God?

The larger church has never required me to do anything that violates my conscience as it is informed by the Word and the Spirit of God. I do not believe it ever will. The issues that trouble us will need to wait for resolution. In this moment we

ask for the fruits of the Spirit to grow in our lives so that we can be the faithful people of God.
    Rev. Dr. Jerry Tankersley

This entry was posted in Reflections on the PCUSA, Uncategorized. Bookmark the permalink.

CHAPTER 10

The Highways into the Storms

2016 to 2020

On January 21, 2016, my 102-year-old Mother died in a Lubbock, Texas, nursing home. Over the years in my travels from west to east I often visited Mom for 2 or 3 days at a time. Her last 10 years were difficult to watch as she aged and became totally dependent on twenty – four – hour care. My sister could not manage it. I could not. On one visit, at 5 a.m., she rolled out of her bed at her home. She was a tiny thing and I thought I would pick her up and place her back in bed. She was dead weight, and I could not get her off the floor. At 5 a.m. I had to call a man to come over and help me lift her body back into bed. I began to realize that being a caregiver was complicated. Thanks be to God for the nursing home in Lubbock that helped her, my sister, and I so much. Thanks be to God that there was a social welfare network that provided for her during those dark days and that we did not have to sell her house. We exhausted every financial resource she had and were at the mercy of the State of Texas. Finally, my sister was allowed to inherit the house. When she died, she passed it on to her son, Brad. I was happy that all of us together were able to help Mom to the end of her life.

When she passed, I went to Lubbock to conduct her memorial service at the cemetery chapel. I was not sure I could emotionally handle the service, but God gave to me the courage and the strength to honor her and to preach the gospel. Tears did not incapacitate me. I loved Mom. Her life was difficult, but also good. I had officiated at her marriage to

Bruce Kattman a number of years before at the Presbyterian Church near downtown Lubbock and not far from where I was born on Ave. M. She used to tell me that she could hear me preaching in Laguna Beach, even though she was in Lubbock, Texas. I know she was proud of me.

It was a windy West Texas day, clear, but cold. The chapel had a glass window that allowed me to look across the alcove at the mausoleum site where her coffin was to be placed next to Bruce's. The wind was swirling the leaves in circles next to the chapel window. I thought to myself that this was a parable for the winds of chaos and change that had blown through our family from time to time. I think about Mom often and I miss her, but I am glad her suffering is over and that she is with the LORD. She was never a church person, but she was a believer. In the fulness of time I hope that our family will be healed of its brokenness and that we will know the height, the depth, and the fulness of God's healing love. I am thankful that Mom and Dad brought me into the world and did their best to encourage my life journey. My desire is to now surrender the family to God, to trust in the Creator's goodness and promises, and to look forward to heavenly reunion.

Political Context of 2016 – 2020

For the past four years the life of the larger church and national culture have been shaped by the Presidency of Donald Trump. The Republican contest of 2016 was surprising in its lack of civility. Donald Trump destroyed all his Republican competition. He used angry language, personal put downs, factual lies, and bombast to eliminate the competition of candidates seeking to be decent in their speech. Clearly, he was courting the favor of an angry base who have felt left out of enjoying the benefits of the elite and smug left wing of the U.S.

Trump's character was revealed as lacking in moral standards. It was evident to me, if not to others, that he was an adulterer, a dishonest businessman, a narcissistic egomaniac, and a person willing to do and to say anything he wanted to win and to be great, on his own terms. His presidential behavior, from my perspective, has been an embarrassment to our nation. His nationalism has disrupted American leadership among the nations. His arrogant assertions and self-centered pride have lifted him up in word and deed to illustrate what the Bible calls sin. He captured the anger, the lack of trust, the envy, the racism, the ignorance, and the economic selfishness of his base who had been called "the deplorables" by Hilary Clinton. This was an unfortunate name to attach to Trump supporters. Moderate Republicans and Democrats doubted he could be elected. But he was elected in the electoral college but lost the plurality of votes in the nation. He claimed the national vote was rigged. He became President of the United States.

What has been remarkable, and perplexing, is that conservative Protestant Church members overwhelmingly voted for Donald Trump. Many progressive evangelicals saw through his rhetoric and chose to not vote for him or Clinton. I have great respect for those who took a deep breath and voted for Trump. I am grateful for the stance that *Christianity Today* took in response to Trump's character. Any democratic political order will only function properly if trust is shared broadly among fellow citizens. That trust must be modeled by the nation's leadership. For the sake of drawing out the goodness of American character it is necessary for the nation's leadership to model that goodness and to call it forth. Our better angels need encouragement to show up.

President Trump promised to pack the Supreme Court with conservative judges who would reverse *Roe v. Wade* and therefore eliminate the practice of abortion in all the States. At the General Assembly of the PCUSA in 1991 in Milwaukee, Wisconsin, I was a commissioner. At that gathering a new study and recommendation on Life and human birth was presented. The study was well done and if approved would have given support for the "pro-choice" position regarding a woman's right to choose. I voted against the paper with regret. Nevertheless, it was passed. I was in the minority as a supporter of the Pro-Life position. It was not that the G.A. was approving abortion. Rather, it was seeking to give guidance to a church community seeking to provide a graceful and compassionate understanding for the complex issues involved.

It seemed to me that the political parties were seeking to politicize the issue and to use it as a wedge to divide. Even though I was in the minority on that vote, I was not about to boycott or to leave the denomination. The interesting thing is that in all my years in ministry only one woman has come to me, her pastor, seeking ethical guidance on birth issues. It has never been a debated issue at LPC. My very conservative mother would never have taken a pro-life position, even though she had profound gratitude to God for the gift of her children.

Donald Trump embraced the Russian leader Putin and indicated that he did not believe the Russians interfered with the 2016 election, even though our nation's intelligence agencies insisted that they did. He proclaimed there was a "deep state" trying to remove him from office. He was determined to drain the swamp in Washington D.C. He became an advocate of conservative religion and invited ultra-conservative pastors to the White House promising to support their political agenda. He passed a tax bill through the Congress giving major tax breaks for the wealthy and the giant corporations. He promised to build a Wall on the southern border of the U.S. to stop the flow of illegal immigrants from Mexico and Central America. He promised that Mexico would pay for the wall. The reality is that American taxpayers are paying for his wall. He attacked people of color and called them degrading names. Indirectly, he supported White Supremacists and called them good people. In doing so he embraced the Klu Klux Klan's agenda. The NRA rejoiced in his support of the Second Amendment. His will to power and his willingness to lie caused the media to examine his statements in detail. His breaking of international ties with American allies began to destabilize the post-WWII arrangements that have by in large kept the peace.

Trump was impeached by the Democratic House of Representatives for his abuse of power but was acquitted by the Republican Senate. Having been acquitted he commenced to fire everyone he thought disloyal to him personally. At every point the Republican leadership has supported him and refused to hold him accountable to the Constitution and the law. The conservative church leadership of America has argued that they were not electing a pastor to be President. Trump has emerged as an example of a demagogue willing to use his power to destroy his enemies, anyone not approving his actions. Money, Sex, and Power have driven Trump's words and behaviors. Trump was seen as a John Wayne macho man whose rugged masculinity was exactly what was needed in order restore law and order and to place women under the authority of male leadership.[1]

The result is that America has become even more divided into Blue and Red States, conservative and progressive interest groups. Even our T.V. channels are seen as propaganda for the left or the right. CNN, MSNBC, and FOX have interpreted reality and been either pro or con Trump. Trump has accused the mainstream media of dispensing "Fake News". His has been a post-modern administration that has caused many

---

1. Du Mez, *Jesus and John Wayne*

to question if there is any objective truth to report. Depending on one's assumptions about reality, facts may be spun to justify one's ways.

Since the beginning of 2020 the world has been afflicted with the Covid-19 virus. China blames the American military for releasing the virus in China. The U.S. President blames the Chinese government for the virus. Thousands have died or suffered. The citizens of America have been asked to "Shelter in Place" for the sake of stopping the spread of this pandemic. By this date, one hundred thousand plus Americans have died and there will likely be many more. It has been estimated that by Easter 2020 that more than five hundred thousand Americans will have lost their lives to this virus. Many in Trump's political base have refused to wear masks to protect themselves and others from infection.

The Churches of America have closed and gone online. The economy has almost come to a complete shut down and millions of people are out of work. Trump, the pro-business President, has done everything he could do to reopen the economy for the sake of his re-election. Not only that, but he has had good reason to promote the opening of the economy. All our lives and the well-being of our institutions depend upon a healthy economy. But at times it has seemed the economy is seen as more important than the health of a frightened nation with a President that will not wear a face mask. He was tardy in responding to the crisis and even has been in denial of the warnings of the scientists. Representatives of his political base are carrying arms publicly to protest the threat of losing their perceived rights to bear arms, to assemble as they choose, and to refuse to wear masks.

Social media is filled with propaganda and prejudice promoting one side or another. The nation and the church are more divided than since the Civil War of the 19th century. Elections are won by narrow margins that may then be contested as rigged. Depending on the news channel one chooses, our worldviews are different and that makes it difficult for us to have calm conversations about the issues.

Therefore, pastors and church leaders are faced with caring for divided congregations of fearful people most of whom are blaming the other camp for the threat to American health and culture. It remains to be seen what the financial impact will be upon the nation's churches. No doubt, many will close, as will many small businesses. This is cause for concern and raises questions about the nation's values and spirituality. Our citizenship commitments will be tested. Our generosity of spirit will be called upon to respond. Anxiety and fear grow in the American heart.

People hoard toilet paper and food. It has been almost humorous watching market shopping carts filled to overflowing with toilet paper and food. When panic takes hold, anything may happen. This is the political, economic, and spiritual crisis that afflicts the western world and especially America in the year of 2020. Read Ron Sider's, *The Spiritual Danger of Donald Trump.*

"BLACK LIVES MATTER" has been chanted by diverse crowds of white, black, and brown people. Some have used the protests as opportunities to loot, to steal, to burn, and to destroy property. The National Guard has been called in to help control the crowds. The President of the U.S., Donald Trump, has failed to provide reconciling, healing leadership.

Apparently, the President thinks he is the higher law and that he has the power to dominate and to control all who contest his interpretation of the U.S. Constitution. This is an election year and Democrats and Republicans do not know how the pandemic, the economic reversal, the police violence, and the national protests will play out. It is a dangerous crisis for the nations, but also for our nation, and especially for mainline Christian denominations. The evangelical church has little to say because its leadership supports Donald Trump. They see him as their hero of "law and order". They are the base of his following. They believe God is on their side and that their moral vision will prevail.

His behavior and speech have brought protest and efforts to impeach him. Churches are divided and pastors take sides at their own peril. Anger is running deep with each side puzzled at Christians in divided camps. These forces have closed businesses and churches. Many are saying that the nation and the church are at a turning point, that things may never be the same.

I was asked to join the Board of Trustees of the New Theological Seminary of the West. Soon we are zooming to discuss the future of theological education. Enrollment in seminaries is down. Debts are large. There are few jobs in churches for seminary graduates. Church memberships are falling. This may become the winter of our discontent or a permanent new normal that will require major adjustments to how we do church and theological education. On July 8, 2020, I gave this devotional to the Board of the NTSW:

NTSW 070820 Devotions by Dr. Jerry Tankersley

Romans 8:18–27

I have been reading and reflecting upon N.T. Wright's new book entitled,

God and the Pandemic, A Christian Reflection on the Coronovirus and Its Aftermath.

All of us have been impacted by the suffering of the world. Wright invites our attention to Romans 8:18–27.

I have found myself lamenting about our world and its physical, political, economic, and spiritual condition.

The Apostle Paul suggests in Roman's 8 that this is the normal Christian experience. He argues that the whole creation, including ourselves as those in Christ, groan inwardly longing to see the fulness of the New Creation. In this present time, we are in labor pains. We are waiting and longing for the birth of the fulness of Life, the redemption of our bodies.

I find myself groaning.

I groan about the violence of the last century, the most violent century in human history with almost constant warfare. How many wars have we fought as the Great and Final Holy War? How many more wars will we need to experience before Isaiah's visions of peace is fulfilled?

I groan over the continuing racism that afflicts persons, cultures, and nations.

Do Black Lives Matter? We paint the slogan on our streets, but every young black person who walks through his or her neighborhood knows the pain of fear when stopped by a police officer. Just when we thought we had overcome racism the old white privilege and superiority strikes and there is injustice. I lament this!

I groan over the suffering humanity continues to experience due to natural evils: earthquakes, fires, floods, droughts, diseases, viruses, cancer, mental illnesses, poverty, hunger, starvation, homelessness, and on and on.

I groan the lack of political leadership to help us through. Character, Facts, Truth, Compassion, Wisdom, Vision, seemed to have died in the marketplace of spin, self-interest, arrogance, narcissism, and outright falsehoods. We are therefore frozen in place, unable to see, to feel, to respond, and to bring healing. We are powerless. I find myself groaning.

I groan for the church, the body of Christ, that continues to be deeply divided, polarized, compromised, powerless to speak a Word from God of healing and hope.

I groan for the vulnerabilities of our theological seminaries. Fewer students; overextended financially; searching for market share. Little prospect for a job once graduated.

The Highways Into The Storms

I groan for a denomination that had 4.3 million members in 1980 and now has around 1 million members. The general population has grown, but the church in the western world does not know how to love those on the outside into the family of faith.

I groan over the human refusal to accept responsibility for behaviors that are destructive of life. So many have refused to wear masks, to wash their hands, or to maintain social distancing for the sake of others and themselves.

I groan over this season of my life, with aging pains, with a spouse who is ill with Parkinson's, with a heightened awareness of my own mortality and of the loss of dear friends. I groan with anxiety and fear.

Tom Wright asserts that we need to listen to our groaning, to our labor pains. Why? Because the Spirit of Christ within us is also groaning, lamenting, and lifting the deep sighs of our hearts into the presence of the one triune God, Father, Son, and Holy Spirit. We ask, "where is God in the midst of all this groaning and longing for the fulness of life?" Christ is present praying with us and for us in the ambiguities and suffering of life. He is interceding for us. He has become one with us, sharing the fulness of our humanity without sin, but now seated at the right hand of God praying for us, assuring us, causing us to remember that the promises of God will come to fruition. Nothing can separate us from the love of God revealed in Jesus Christ.

Wright says that the mission of God through us is our listening, praying, and working in the power of the Holy Spirit on behalf of a groaning humanity. He closed his book with these words,

"Perhaps that is how we are bound to live: glimpsing what ought to be, then struggling with the way things are. However, the only way to live with that is to pray with that; to hold the vision and the reality side by side as we groan with the groaning of all creation, and as the Spirit groans within us so that the new creation may come to birth."

"We urgently need statesmanlike, wise leadership, with prayerful Christian leaders taking a place alongside others, to think with both vision and realism through the challenges that we shall face in the coming months." [2]

This is not the first challenge to American society, to business, to religion, to education, indeed, to the health of the nation. The 20th century

---

2. Wright, *God and the Pandemic*, 74–75.

was full of wars, economic depressions, prosperity, and pandemics. It appears the COVID 19 virus may threaten the whole world and make a major impact upon our earth's warming climate. It would be easy to argue that we are living in a fragile time with apocalyptic dangers. So, what do we do?

For over 50 years I have refused to endorse political candidates. At times the pressure within me and from beyond me have been great. I have assumed that neither of our major political parties held the keys to inaugurating the golden age of perfect peace and righteousness. I have believed that both parties have good people within them, as well as self-centered greedy ideologues. Both parties have used culture wars to gain votes. Economic ideologies have clashed. Polarization has increased. Civil discourse has become almost impossible without the other side taking offence and separating. Not only the nation is in danger of cultural and civic tearing, but also the church. Nevertheless, I have never used the church's pulpit to direct the voting choices of people who may know more than I know.

2020 presents a major challenge for the Christian Church. There are several important political/value issues that need to be studied, debated, and acted upon. The nation is in a time of crisis related to race. Regularly we see young black men killed by police officers with impunity and without compassion. Since the advent of the pandemic, racial prejudice toward Asians has grown and innocent Asians have been attacked on the streets of our cities. I believe that most police and firemen, servants of the State, are good, moral, and caring people. I believe we need law and order and that the police powers entrusted to the 50 States and the Federal Government are necessary for human political order and justice. We enjoy a revered Constitution and legal system.

The spirituality of America's original sin of slavery and racism are still powerful forces seeking to define political parties and economic policies. Conflicts and angry clashes are seen in our streets. Protests and riots rage from decade to decade when their driving passions find expression in abuses of power. Thus, "Black Lives Matter", "Enough is Enough". As a people we are called to support our values and methodologies of doing justice, walking with humility, and kindness for the sake of the greater good. Only now is the City of Tulsa, Oklahoma, awakening to what happened to its black citizens in 1921. We pray that unity, reconciliation, and justice may come from this awakening.

I have read, prayed, taught, and preached from the Bible for over 50 years. I know and believe the message of the book. I am still seeking to place myself under the authority of this written Word and historic witness to God's justice/love. I believe God spoke his Word to the world in these ancient writings and that we risk destroying ourselves, our human orders, and freedoms, by neglecting the way of God's wisdom that was incarnate in Jesus of Nazareth. The "principalities and powers" are fallen and need to be called to repentance and life. This is part of the mission of God through the church in all its rich manifestations.

I realize that I risk alienating many of my Republican and Democratic Presbyterian friends. I regret that. If I am wrong, I repent. It is not my intention to wound anyone whom I love and have served over many years. I am a patriotic citizen of the United States who pleads for the nation to live into its aspirations articulated in the Declaration of Independence. I love the Constitution. I have celebrated our nation's triumphs and wept over its failures.

Because I am first and foremost a citizen of the kingdom of God and pray for the fullness of God's kingdom to come on earth, I cry out to the President to read the Bible and to believe in the kingdom of God's peace, justice, and love. I invite him to understand that his ultra-conservative base may have a limited understanding of the truth of God's salvation. Perhaps, our nation may have a new birth of faith, freedom, hope, love, and justice out of this time of great mistrust and unrest. It is as President Lincoln said in his Second Inaugural speech, that, "we all read from the same Bible and pray to the same God". Now it is time for a new and deeper reconciliation to find expression in a new unity for the sake of lifting up all people as members of one new humanity reconciled at the cross of Jesus and filled with the Spirit of God's peace and truth.

I want to affirm that this is a time for us to be steadfast and immovable in the work of living faith, hope, and love. God is sovereign. The kingdom of God has already come, but not yet here, in its fullest sense. The fullness of New Creation will come in God's time. We are called to be faithful builders upon the foundation of Jesus Christ the Rock. (1 Corinthians 3; 15:58) Jesus is coming again! Our LORD, come!

We believe that God's judgments are upon this fallen world. But God loves this world and can bring its reconciliation and restoration to fullness of life. We do not know what that will mean or how long it will take, but in this resurrection hope we find courage to go forward. In this interim time of waiting, we exercise our stewardship responsibilities as we engage in spiritual warfare with all the armaments of which the Apostle Paul wrote in Ephesians 6.

We live in dangerous times. In November 2020 Joe Biden, the Democrat, was elected President of the United States. Donald Trump has refused to accept that he lost the election and has continued to contest the results. On January 6, 2021, Trump stirred up a mass D.C. rally to violently attack the nation's Capital to interfere with the Congress's ratification of the electoral college vote. People were killed. Many were injured. The Presidents provocative speech was denied, but for anyone watching and listening, it was clear that the President was largely responsible for the violent attack. With the pandemic raging and political climate more polarized, the well-being of the nation is threatened. This cultural and political divide has brought suffering into the life of the church. May God have mercy and may we find a way to reconciliation and peace!

CHAPTER 11

The Highways to the New Jerusalem

I TURNED 80 ON MAY 31, 2017. In early June, my wife Kay, hosted a surprise birthday party at church after our Sunday evening Chancel Choir concert. It was catered by La Serena and was a complete surprise for me. As Kay and our son, Jeff, spoke to the gathered people, my heart was warmed. On my 50th birthday, Kay had hosted a party for me, and my Laguna Beach friends, in our home's back yard. The pictures of those parties have functioned as reminders of my family's love for me. On September 9, 2017, Kay and I celebrated our 50th wedding anniversary. On September 17, 2017, the church gathered at the Hotel Laguna for a celebration dinner of the church's 100th anniversary. That evening we burned the church's mortgage papers and were debt free. We had raised nearly 15 million dollars for the project. It was a miracle through a devoted people and a faithful leadership through difficult times.

On October 14, 2017, Kay had a stroke that exacerbated her Parkinson's Disease. The stroke occurred while she was up at 4:30 a. m. I happened to get up and I found her seemingly asleep on our family room couch. This was nothing new; she had often awakened, moved about the house, and visited the refrigerator in the middle of the night. I tried to awaken her, but I could not stir her. I was half asleep and returned to bed. In a while I went back to her and noticed that the left side of her mouth was drooping. Stroke came to my mind, but my denial and sleepiness paralyzed me from calling 911. Finally, about 7 a.m. I called 911. The paramedics came and took her to Saddleback Hospital. Quickly, they diagnosed stroke before I arrived. Dr. Suzuki from UCI was on his way. They discovered a blockage in her right carotid artery. The doctor was able to remove the blood clot from her brain. On December 11, 2017, at

UCI Hospital, he installed a stent in the carotid. There was some small lasting damage, but the trauma caused her Parkinson's symptoms to progress. After the initial three days at Saddleback, she spent two weeks at the Mission Hospital Acute Rehabilitation Unit. That really helped, but for the past three years her recovery has been up and down from day to day. She has not lost hope, nor have I. Gradually, we have come to acceptance. No more denial of our mortality. The body wears out. She has lived longer than anyone in her family. I have longevity in my family, but who knows?

At the January 2018 Laguna Presbyterian Church Session retreat, I announced that I would be retiring. I had prayed that God might give me the courage to speak to this issue at the retreat. The door opened and I did it. It was one of the most difficult things I have ever done. I had invested 46 years into the life of this church and community. But I had experienced a growing sense that I had completed my work. By God's grace the church congregation had slowly grown in this island space of Laguna Beach. The people had come together; the buildings had been restored; LPC was debt free; we had demonstrated the love of God to the world; and I was turning 81 on May 31, 2018. Thankfully, with Kay's encouragement, we had lived conservatively, paid off our house, and accumulated some savings. Together with the Church Pension and Social Security, we trusted that we could retire.

I notified the congregation that I would retire on June 30, 2018. From January to June, I met with small groups of the church members to share my love for them and what I believed about the future. Together we had grown into one of the healthiest churches within the PCUSA. God had been faithful and honored our planning, praying, and hard work. In this pulpit I had learned to preach. The people had listened and responded. The church was ready to live into the challenges of its future. I asked them to honor my successor in the way they had honored and supported me. I knew they would. I would do the same. For years I had prayed for whoever the next pastor would be.

There were several newspaper articles written about me and my 46 - year ministry in Laguna Beach. A big celebration party was planned for early June. It was held at the Laguna Niguel, El Niguel Country Club. Over 300 people came. There was a great dinner and program. My 92-year-old mentor, Gary Demarest, spoke, together with John Huffman, Mike Regele, Virginia Grogan, Mary Canon, Craig Williams, Ed Sauls, Steve Donner; Steve Sweet, and Kathy Sizer. The choir sang. Beth Pinney and

Linda White led the music. Suzi Gordinier presented me with a painting of me preaching. I was grateful for her gift to me. Later, Daryle Lynn Cornelison painted me baptizing a baby as I had often done. I was moved with gratitude as Kay, and I were honored in every way. I was grateful that Kay was able to walk into the gathering with the help of her caregiver, Livier Corona. Our children, Jeff and Rachel, with our grandsons, Quinn Joseph and Luke Zane, were at table with us. Dr. Ron White came from Pasadena. Dick Grondhovd came from Central California. Larry Coulter was there from Texas. Dick Todd, Ken Kalina, and Dennis Tarr, members of my covenant group, were present. So many people I had loved and with whom I had shared joys and sorrows. It was a great evening.

I struggled with how I would end my preaching ministry in Laguna Beach. Years earlier the church had built an extension platform from the chancel into the nave of the sanctuary for the sake of my getting closer to the people in my preaching. That removable ramp became my preaching station where I learned to preach without notes and from the depths of my heart.

With the building rebuild the liturgical architect designed a curved extension of the chancel into the nave that brought me closer to the new curved pews. This was the place of experiencing the electricity of God's Word and Spirit over and over as I brought all my preparation and prayer to offer to the Lord and to his people. The chancel area was covered with Jerusalem marble. Into the marble was placed a design to mark my preaching spot. On that spot I was determined to stake my life for the truth of the gospel and the integrity of my life and ministry. To say goodbye to that sign of grace and truth was painful, but necessary. It had been my place of service, but in the deepest sense the design on the floor belonged to the LORD and to his people. My prayer was that the light of God's love would shine forth from this preaching station for the glory of God into God's continuing mission through whoever graced the spot. For the last eight years of my ministry, I walked from my chair to the center of the chancel to stand, to pray, and to proclaim God's Word. I am deeply grateful for this gift.

I was concerned about my biblical text selection for my final sermons. What would I say to this people I had loved and who had loved me? I chose several of the Apostle Paul's words from 2 Corinthians in which he laid out his heart and passion for the congregation that he had established and for which he had labored. He said to them some of what

I wanted to say to my beloved people in Laguna Beach. Paul's words are beautiful letters of love.

"For we are the aroma of Christ to God among those who are being saved. We are not peddlers of God's word like so many; but in Christ we speak as persons of sincerity, as persons sent from God standing in his presence" 2 Corinthians 2:14–17

I had become aware that many leaders in the larger culture and church had left behind aromas that were not pleasing. Across the years I had prayed that the aroma of Christ's truth, grace, peace, joy, and love would become associated with my years at the center and heart of our city. In one of my final sermons, I told my church family this concern of mine.

"Are we beginning to commend ourselves again? Surely, we do not need, as some do, letters of recommendation to you or from you, do we? You yourselves are our letter, written on our hearts, to be known and read by all; and you show that you are a letter of Christ, prepared by us, written not with ink but with the Spirit of the living God, not on tablets of stone but on tablets of human hearts." 2 Corinthians 3:1–6

We write letters not just with pen and ink or on our laptops. The Spirit writes through us. My writing of sermons and study papers were for the sake of building up the people of God. As I wrote on the hearts of my people, so the people wrote their truths and love into my soul. I am who I am today because of the letters that have been written into my life. Throughout eternity I will praise God for what has become embedded in my heart. The truth is that the Spirit of Christ has used the patience and affirmations of my people to touch me in the sacred places of my life experience.

"We have this treasure in clay jars, so that it may be made clear that this extraordinary power belongs to God and does not come from us." 2 Corinthians 4:7

How true this is. The preacher is but a broken clay jar. Yet, he or she is in the process of being mended by the gold of God's truth. The cracks in the jar have been made beautiful by the gold of God's graceful balm. Woe to the preacher and the congregation that have never seen and embraced this mystery of God's healing beauty. The Apostle Paul courageously shared with the churches he served the many weaknesses he had, the sufferings of his life, and the forgiveness he had received for being a blasphemer, a persecutor, and a man of violence. But God's grace had overflowed for him, and he had become a model for the mercies of God in the life of God's people. For this truth I am grateful. I have been able to open my heart about my own struggles and needs for grace. My people have repeatedly shared with me how much this has meant to them.

My teaching, preaching, and caring was the work of writing the Spirit's letter into the hearts and minds of my people. The position papers and letters I had written to the larger church concerning the great issues that were using us all were for the sake of my people, that they might know me and understand how great the love of God is for us. For years heaven and earth have overlapped and interconnected for me in their listening presence around the holy space built into the structure of our sanctuary.

"So, we are ambassadors for Christ, since God is making his appeal through us; we entreat you on behalf of Christ, be reconciled to God." 2 Corinthians 5:20

This was the theme verse of the 214th General Assembly for which I stood as a candidate for Moderator. This is the great truth of the church's identity and mission as together we represent the King. Our calling is to represent Jesus to the "principalities and powers" of the world. We have been given the King's message, "good news", for the sake of not only believing it, but also of living it. It has been such an honor to represent Jesus and LPC for 46 years. But I have not been alone. A great cloud of witnesses has surrounded me to support and to celebrate the mission. Through the multitude of witnesses with whom I have served the light has shined into the darkness.

My last Sunday to preach was June 24, 2018. Again, it was a moving time of celebration of our ministry together. The church was full at the two morning services. A representative of Orange County Supervisor Lisa Bartlett's office was with us to present me with a framed Proclamation from the Orange County Board of Supervisors. I think Lorna Cohen had written it from some material I gave her. It was called *"A Legacy of Divine Ministry"*. It articulated all that I had sought to be and to do over many years. The congregation had given a love offering and it was presented to us. Who could have thought that God would have called a boy from West Texas to a lifelong journey with Jesus who had set his face to go up to Jerusalem? The LORD was faithful to the calling even through years of hard work together with many others, who pulled for me, loved me, prayed for me, forgave me, and held up my arms as I faced threatening enemies, dark valleys, and foggy mountain passes of temptation, struggle, and accomplishment.

The Son has risen, and the light of God's kingdom has shined upon us. I will forever praise the LORD for saving me, rescuing me, welcoming me home, comforting me, disciplining me, teaching me, blessing me, transforming me, and sustaining me in faith, hope, and love. The Good Shepherd has named, called, and carried me. I trust that he will raise me on the final day of resurrection and that I will be with all the saints whom I have loved.

Life in Retirement

In January of 2018 my spiritual director, Wilkie Au, a former Jesuit priest and professor at Loyola Marymount, recommended that I prepare for retirement by working through the Ignatian Prayer exercises again. He shared that there was an interim director at the Center for Spiritual Development in Orange by the name of Father Patrick Howell. Pat, a Jesuit, had been centered in Seattle, Washington, and was recently retired from Seattle University. I arranged to meet with him weekly for six months and to do a shortened form of the Exercises.

Pat was a gift to me. He was a man of God who had suffered much over the years. He had written a book about his emotional breakdown and his hospitalization that was required. Through much hard spiritual and psychological work, he had recovered, and God had used his struggles to help many. Now in his mid-70's he was doing interim work. He had six months in Orange, and I was able to meet weekly with him and to talk through the Ignatian Prayer Exercises with him. I had previously prayed my way through them during extended periods of reflection and discernment and they had deepened my life with Christ.

I shared with Pat the changes coming in my life. I was retiring at age 81. My wife had been diagnosed with Parkinson's in 2012, and then she had a stroke in October 2017. Pat suggested that I was in a "perfect storm" and that it was good that I was reaching out for help. Together we reflected on various weekly scripture readings and shared our lives. He encouraged me to read Ronald Rolheiser's, *The Holy Longing, The Search for a Christian Spirituality*. I had already read parts of the book. Byron Beam had given me the book several years before. Especially, Father Pat encouraged me to read the chapter on the Paschal Mystery. Rolheiser wrote,

The Highways To The New Jerusalem

"Christian spirituality does not apologize for the fact that, within it, the most central of all mysteries is the paschal one, the mystery of suffering, death, and transformation. In Christian spirituality, Christ is central and central to Christ, is his death and rising to new life to send us a new Spirit. This is the central mystery within Christianity." [1] . . .

"The paschal mystery, as we shall see shortly, is a process of transformation within which we are given both new life and new spirit. It begins with suffering and death, moves on to the reception of new life, spends some time grieving the old and adjusting to the new, and finally, only after the old life has been truly let go of, is new spirit given for the life we are already living."[2]

"There are five clear, distinct moments within the paschal cycle; Good Friday, Easter Sunday, the forty days leading up to the Ascension, the Ascension, and Pentecost. Each of these is part of a single process, an organic one, and each needs to be understood in relation to the others to make sense of the paschal mystery. Each is part of one process of transformation of dying and letting go to receive new life and new spirit."

In caption, the paschal cycle might be diagrammed as follows: [NL 1–5]

1. Good Friday . . . " the loss of life---real death"
2. Easter Sunday . . . " the reception of new life"
3. The Forty Days . . . " a time for readjustment to the new and for grieving the old"
4. Ascension . . . " letting go of the old and letting it bless you, the refusal to cling"
5. Pentecost . . . " the reception of new spirit for the new life that one is already living"[3] [/NL 1–5]

Put into a more colloquial language and stated as a personal, paschal challenge for each of us, one might recast the diagram this way: [NL 1–5]

1. "Name your deaths"
2. "Claim your births"
3. "Grieve what you have lost and adjust to the new reality"
4. "Do not cling to the old, let it ascend and give you its blessing"

---

1. Rolheiser, *Holy Longing*, 142.
2. Rolheiser, *Holy Longing*, 147.
3. Rolheiser, *Holy Longing*, 147.

5. *"Accept the spirit of the life that you are in fact living"*

"This cycle is not something that we must undergo just once, at the moment of our deaths, when we lose our earthly lives as we know them. It is rather something we must undergo daily, in every aspect of our lives. Christ spoke of many deaths, of daily deaths, and of many rising and various pentecosts. The paschal mystery is the secret to life. Ultimately our happiness depends upon properly undergoing it." [4] . . .

1. *"The death of our Youth . . .*
2. *The death of our Wholeness . . .*
3. *The death of our Dreams . . .*
4. *The death of our Honeymoons . . .*
5. *The death of a Certain Idea of God and Church . . .* "[5]

"Knowledge alone cannot save us. When St. Augustine coined that phrase nearly seventeen hundred years ago, he meant it as a principle of truth, but he was also writing a commentary on his own life. Augustine, as we know, had two conversions, one in his head and the other in his heart. At age twenty-five, he converted to Christianity, intellectually. After years of experimenting with various pagan philosophies and ways of living, he was now convinced in his head that Christianity was correct. The rest of him, however, was not as willing a convert. For nine more years, until he was thirty-four years old, he was unable to bring his moral life into harmony with his intellectual faith. It was during these years that he not infrequently prayed his infamous prayer: 'Lord make me a good and chaste Christian, but not yet.'" [6]

The spiritual journey is not just a quick dash. It is a long marathon, and it requires that the runner have spiritual resources to sustain the long obedience in the same direction. This is the process of Transformation. Along the way I have learned that knowing the truth and having my intellect converted is not enough. I have needed to experience the presence and the power of the Holy Spirit. I have needed to have my heart converted so that I might radically trust the promises of God in ever deeper ways.

4. Rolheiser, *Holy Longing*, 148.
5. Rolheiser, *Holy Longing*, Selected titles, 148 – 162.
6. Rolheiser, *Holy Longing*, 213–214.

For some period, my spiritual director, Wilkie Au, encouraged me to read Peter Enns, *The Sin of Certainty, Why God Desires Our Trust More Than Our 'Correct' Beliefs*. This is a brilliant personal story of a man who knew the truth but required years of following Christ to trust the knowledge of God revealed in Scripture. This is the conversion of heart of which Augustine wrote. Knowledge has a way of puffing up. Only Love builds up. (1 Corinthians 8:1–3) Often to learn this mystery one's belief system must be tested. In such times one learns in both heart and mind that trust allows the journey to continue. I remember that Clarence Roddy, my professor of preaching at Fuller Seminary, would say, "I feel sorry for you men who have never had an experience that transcended your theology." I was only beginning to learn what he meant.

It has taken me the rest of my life to faithfully pray that the "highways to Zion" might be built into my heart. I am still learning to surrender to this way without having all the answers. It is liberating to become aware of the mystical presence and power of God available through letting go and letting God be LORD of my heart and mind. For so long I was satisfied with having the right answers in my head without struggling with the mixture of faith and doubt, success and failure, and many other paradoxes. I confess that pressing my knowledge into the mold of peaceful surrender of the heart has not been easy. But more than ever I am living this truth.

On the bookshelf of my office at home I keep the book written by Franciscan Richard Rohr, *The Wild Man's Journey, Reflections on Male Spirituality*. Inside the book I have kept the letter of instructions all the men received for a five – hour theological reflection and journaling time while alone. We were given these five messages to reflect and to write about:

Life Is Hard
You are Going to Die
You Are Not that Important
You Are Not in Control
Your Life Is Not About You.

For five hours I prayed and wrote my commentary about these five messages. I was alone in Box Canyon at Ghost Ranch, New Mexico. As we each finished the time alone, we were to go to the irrigation pond on the ranch and baptize ourselves into this reality. It meant submerging ourselves into the dark cold water in the name of the Father, the Son, and the Holy Spirit. This ritual was powerful in my powerlessness. But I have not exhausted its meaning. On a regular, almost daily basis I have lived with the truths of the 12 Steps of AA. Surrendering control of others and of my own life to God has brought repeated miracles of inner peace and well-being for all those afflicted by my need to control their lives.

Spiritual direction from two Jesuits has helped my troubled soul surrender to the mystery of life and death. The head is vital for guiding the heart, but the heart is the soil in which the fruit of the Spirit grows. Through the brokenness and cracks of our lives the light shines and illumines the darkness within. Jesus comes to our heads and our hearts to show the way of truth, love, freedom, and peace.

When I worked through the Ignatian exercises with Father Howell, I faced that my life had become a perfect storm. It was as if I had worked my hardest to accomplish my goals in a calling that allowed me to work until I was 81. I was on a fastmoving escalator that carried me to the exit on June 30, 2018, and then I landed in a new season of my life. What had died needed to be grieved. I have grieved yet always aware that my sense of loss continued and needed to be processed. In the words of John 21 someone had put a belt around my waist and taken me to a place I could not easily accept or enjoy. I had to leave my beloved parish after a 46-year pastorate of sheer joy and personal achievement. My wife, the source of much joy and wisdom was seriously ill and I did not know if I would lose her also. In January 2019 my younger sister died. I was unable to attend her funeral at the graveside in Texas. By phone we had spoken words of love for each other. She asked me about her destiny in heaven. Was it true that when she died that she would go to be with Jesus? I told her that this was my faith for myself as well as for her. In death we go to sleep in Jesus only to awaken in his arms.

My friend, Tom Boyd, from Amarillo, had suggested to me that I enroll at Westmont College. I did so, but from December 1957, I never saw Tom again. God had brought guidance to me through Tom. Within the last five years I received the Westmont College magazine and read that Tom had died. I went online in search for him. I discovered his obituary posted on a mortuary's website in Houston, Texas. I posted a tribute to him and my admiration for him. I was sorry that we had not connected for 50 plus years. To my amazement his wife emailed me and told me their story. When he had turned 70, they had a big party and had tried to find me but had failed. She wanted me to know how much Tom admired me. He had suffered from Parkinson's disease. His final words to her were his desire to go to sleep and to awaken in Jesus' arms. These were my words to my sister. I look forward to seeing my friend and my sister again in the New Creation as all of creation is held in Jesus' arms.

For me, the journey has continued into a new season. Was my life over? I had to face my own mortality and live into the angst of a season I had not experienced. Of course, there were times of suffering along the way when I was afraid my life was over before it had begun. There were the years of not knowing if our son would make it through his adolescent years. There were vocational challenges and disappointments. There was my bout with Prostate Cancer and the six-week period it took for me to regain my strength. There was the PCUSA schism that wounded me and caused me to rethink and to seek a glimpse of God in that separation. There were historical events that shattered my worldview and dreams. There was the truth that my youth had passed me by, that the years had become like passing months on my calendar. My future years were numbered and limited, and my mortality could not be avoided.

In June 2018 the Los Ranchos Presbytery required me to sign its Separation Policy statement that established a boundary line between me and Laguna Presbyterian Church. This happened at the end of worship in a congregational meeting. The Clerk of the Session brought the document to me, and I signed it in the pulpit before the congregation. It meant I could not be in worship or participate in any pastoral duties until a new pastor was called, established, and invited me to return to the fellowship of the Laguna Church. Our Presbytery requires all its retiring pastors to keep this promise of separation. I knew this and fully expected to keep the promise. Former pastors, because of their close pastoral relationships, may make it difficult for new pastors to be accepted and welcomed.

I understood that this would be necessary, but difficult. I did not appreciate how difficult it would be to separate myself from my beloved people, from the fellowship of my staff, and from the community that had sustained my life for many years. It has been like a death for me. It has meant letting go and letting God take care of the people who have been like members of my family. I have felt plunged into an experience of grief and spiritual, emotional pain.

We had decided to remain in our Laguna Beach home and to retire in this space we loved. It has been in the silence of my home office, surrounded by my books, and artifacts I have collected that Christ's presence and power have become more real. Many days have been spent in reading and writing this spiritual autobiography. God has given this season to me to reflect upon my journey and to seek to reframe it. I am grateful for this fruitful season in my life.

Before retirement I had bookshelves built into our garage. My books, collected over many years, are jammed into those shelves, and sit waiting for me to read them again. Alas, I do not have enough time to attend to these gifts to me and my discipleship over many years. But they are there. On top of the shelves sits the church bulletins and sermon notes from over 60 years of preaching. I could spend another 50 years revising and reflecting on my feeble words and wisdom insights for my people. I look at all of this with gratitude to God for what I have learned and even for all the theological and interpretive errors I have committed. Geoffrey Bromiley, my church history professor at Fuller Seminary, said on one occasion, "there has never been a perfect sermon preached." We are but imperfect, mortal persons, called into the service of the kingdom in hopes of the LORD completing in us what he began. What joy and meaning has come to my being from the hard work of seeking to rightly interpret the revelation of God's servants from across the years. The walls of my garage have heard many sermons over the past 46 years as I have sought on Saturday evenings to work the manuscript words into my memory for the sake of preaching them on the LORD'S Day.

Since Kay's stroke in 2017 the people had brought food to our home. The expressions of love had been wonderful, and we were thankful. On July 1, 2018, we asked the church members to no longer do this, as grateful as we were. We needed to make it on our own, but this was a major adjustment for us. I think they were ready to cease, as were we. Nevertheless, the journey of transition from pastor to friend was necessary. Gradually, I have learned to cook as well as to clean and to provide care for Kay. When we married, we promised to be there for each other as long as we both lived. There have been moments of intense joy and insight into life and death. There has been conflict, anger, love, tears, anxieties, and fears. At times, the loneliness of the transition has crept in upon me as well as her. She has continued to go to church, as she has been able, and has found friendship and joy in this continued relationship.

There have been many night times of helping her from bed to the bathroom. Watching her struggle has brought pain and longing for what had been. Often, I have seen the presence of Jesus in her body, and soul suffering, yes, the human condition glimpsed through the lens of God's compassion. My patience has been strained. Anger at the human condition has sometimes overwhelmed me and I have said things that have hurt her and me. I have asked for her forgiveness, and she has been gracious. I have needed compassion and acceptance for myself as well as for her. I have hoped that I would outlive her so that I could provide care, but that is the way of the cross for each of us. Our love for God and for each other has deepened as we have lived out our marriage vows.

I understood that this was a necessary transition for us to make. The worst loneliness happened when I attended other churches in the Presbytery. It was like recovering from a death. Many times, widows and widowers have shared with me that they could not return to worship alone, where they had shared meaningful times with their deceased spouses. So, it was for me. Kay was still alive, but I had to worship alone in another place. The churches were welcoming and encouraged me to become a part of their fellowships. It was strange to not be leading in worship. I loved each of the churches I attended, but I felt that I stuck out like a sore thumb as I was in worship alone and feeling grief. On Christmas Eve December 24, 2018, I went by myself to a nearby church. Previous Christmas Eves I had preached four times and returned home exhausted but thankful for the privilege of bearing witness to hundreds of attendees searching for the meaning of the season and for the love, peace, and joy promised in the birth of Jesus. Now I was alone, and the night was full of longing. I remembered a retired pastor telling me years ago that it was a lot more fun upfront than in the balcony. I was seated in the distant back pews seeking to hide from my own pain that first retired Christmas Eve.

LPC has not yet called a new pastor. Later this year I believe they will, and this will be good for them and for me. Gareth Icenogle has been the interim pastor. He has been very warm to me and me to him. I have not wanted to say or to do anything to interfere with this process for the church or for me. I have kept my promises as I said I would. Gareth has invited me back for special times, and I have returned with Kay, but it has been difficult for me and probably painful for some members of the church. So, we move on. Recently, I was delighted to learn that my associate pastor, Dr. Steve Sweet, was called to be the next pastor. He is a gifted pastor and interpreter of the Scriptures. For twenty – six years he blessed me, my family, and the church as our senior associate pastor. His many gifts will lead Laguna Presbyterian Church into its future. The work of the kingdom continues.

The church belongs to God. Jesus Christ is the one foundation. He is the head of the body, his church, and we pastors are but shepherds and stewards of his dearly beloved flock who are on their way to the New

Jerusalem doing the mission of God along the way. Yes, working to build the New Jerusalem into this beautiful and broken city. I believe there is a great cloud of witnesses who urge us on in faithfulness in good and bad times. One person plants the seed; another waters the seed; but it is God who gives the growth. (1 Corinthians 3)

A few months ago, I received the message that Father Patrick Howell, a few years younger than me, had returned to Seattle, and died not too long afterwards. During our six months of visits, we had often spoken of our mortality. I had read the book he wrote about his mental breakdown and his long journey toward recovery. His vulnerability had helped me deal with my own human fragility. Years before in praying the Psalms, I had come upon Psalm 90. The Psalmist prayed,

> "You turn us back to dust, and say, 'Turn back, you mortals.' For a thousand years in your sight are like yesterday when it is past, or like a watch in the night. You sweep them away; they are like a dream, like grass that is renewed in the morning; in the morning it flourishes and is renewed; in the evening it fades and withers.
>
> For all our days pass away under your wrath; our years come to an end like a sigh. The days of our life are seventy years, or perhaps eighty, if we are strong; even then their span is only toil and trouble; they are soon gone, and we fly away.
>
> So, teach us to count our days that we may gain a wise heart.
>
> Have compassion on your servants! Satisfy us in the morning with your steadfast love, so that we may rejoice and be glad all our days."

The psalmists prayed their death anxieties and fears. They spoke the truth that Jesus lived as he approached the cross and the end of his earthly life. He left his beloved disciples but promised to come to them in a new and powerful way. Nevertheless, he asked his heavenly Father to remove the cup of suffering from him. On Easter Sunday we celebrate that God raised him from the dead and that he has poured out his Spirit upon us to teach, to comfort, and to empower us. I cling to Frederick Buechner's words: "Death is not the end; the end is Life." He made this claim based on the promises of the gospel.

It is by the words of Christ and the apostles that we live. "In life and in death we belong to God." "Whether we live or whether we die, we are the LORD'S". "Nothing can separate us from the love of God." "To live is Christ and to die is gain." In high school I had a plaque on my bedroom wall. It read, "Only one life will soon be past; only what is done for Christ will last." Even then I must have been searching for comfort and courage to let go and to let God.

At Princeton in the summer of 1990, I read Frederick Buechner's powerful story in *The Sacred Journey*. He summarized his own spiritual journey. I have loved this:

> "For Adam and Eve, time started with their expulsion from the garden. For me, it started with the opening of a door. For all the sons and daughters of Eve, it starts at whatever moment it is in which the unthinking and timeless innocence of childhood ends, which may be either a dramatic moment, as it was for me (at ten years of age his father committed suicide), or a series of moments so subtle and undramatic that we scarcely recognize them. But one way or another the journey through time starts for us all, and for all of us, too, that journey is in at least one sense the same journey because what it is primarily, I think, is a journey in search. Each must say for himself what he searches for, and there will be as many answers as there are searchers, but perhaps there are certain general answers that will do for us all.
>
> We search for *a self to be*. We search *for other selves to love*. We search for *work to do*. And since even when to one degree or another we find these things, we find also that there is still something crucial missing which we have not found, *we search for that unfound thing to, even though we do not know its name or where it is to be found or even if it is to be found at all*. (I think he was speaking of God.)"
>
> "To journey for the sake of saving our own lives is little by little to cease to live in any sense that really matters, even to us, because it is only by journeying for the world's sake—even when the world bores and sickens and scares you half to death—that little by little we start to come alive. It was not a conclusion that I came to in time. It was a conclusion from beyond time that came to me. God knows I have never been any good at following the road it pointed me to, but at least, by grace, I glimpsed the road and saw that it is the only one worth traveling." [7]

C.S. Lewis ended his autobiography, *Surprised by Joy*, with these observations,

> "When we are lost in the woods the sight of a signpost is a great matter. He who first sees it cries, 'Look!' The whole party gathers

---

7. Buechner, *Sacred Journey*, 58, 108.

round and stares. But when we have found the road and are passing signposts every few miles, we shall not stop and stare. They will encourage us, and we shall be grateful to the authority that set them up. But we shall not stop and stare, or not much; not on this road, though their pillars are of silver and their lettering of gold. 'We would be at Jerusalem.'

Not, of course, that I don't often catch myself stopping to stare at roadside objects of even less importance."[8]

When Kay and I were younger, we hiked portions of the John Muir Trail in the High Sierras. Out in the wilderness with limited amounts of energy and food, with constant danger from exhaustion, bears and weather, we often had to make the choice of the trail that would take us to our planned destination. Frequently, we came to a place where two trails went in different directions. I remember the relief we felt when we discovered a sign pointing to our day's goal. We were always looking for the sign with "John Muir Trail" carved into it with the number of miles still to be walked until we could lay our heads down for a good night's rest. So, it is in the Christian's journey of life. Choosing the right highway and trusting the posted signs are important for the success of the journey.

Thankfully, we were accompanied by Dick and Carol Maxwell. He was a tall gentle guide and encourager. Carol was a joy and an inspiration. When in doubt, Dick would pull out his trail map and plot the way. At night around the fire, he would produce his flask of "Jack" and we would relax into a deep sleep and needed rest.

Kay has always teased me about our first trip to Europe where I was driving and trying to choose the right way. One night in Cologne, Germany, we checked into our hotel, and then drove to have dinner in a German speaking restaurant. I remember the waitress struggling to interpret the German menu. She was so patient with me, and we finally ordered successfully. On the way back to our hotel I got lost. We wandered seemingly in endless circles. I got angry and Kay said, "lost my salvation". How embarrassing. Somehow, after endless frustration we found our way. It was a lesson. Pay attention to your maps. Get them out on the hood of the car if necessary. It helps to have a co-pilot to guide and to inspire the Way. If not a husband or wife, then surely, the living LORD Jesus Christ, who by his Word and Spirit, has promised to journey with us into the fulness of Life with God and all the saints.

---

8. Lewis, *Surprised by Joy*, 238.

My spiritual director, Wilkie Au, shared with me this Prayer for Old Age that was prayed at a Jesuit gathering. I am deeply grateful for this prayer. LORD help me to live this prayer.

> Prayer for Aging
>
> All Gracious God, you have given me all I am and have, and now I give it back to you to stand under Your will alone. In a special way I give You these later years of my life.
>
> I am one of those called by You into old age, a call not given to all. not given to Jesus, not given to most in our world today. I humbly ask You, grace me deeply in each aspect of the struggle.

As my physical eyesight weakens,
may the eyes of my faith strengthen,
that I may see You and Your love in everything.
As my hearing fails, may the ears of my heart
be more attentive to the whisper of Your gentle voice,
As my legs weaken and walking becomes more difficult,
may I walk more truly in Your paths,
knowing all the while that I am held in the embrace of your love. As my mind becomes less alert and memory fades
may I remain peaceful in You,
aware that with You there is no need for thought or word.
You ask simply that I be there, with you.

> And should sickness overtake me, and I be confined in bed, may I know myself as one with Your Son as he offers his life for the salvation of the world.
>
> Finally, as my heart slows a little after the work of the years, may it expand in love for You and all people.
>
> May it rest secure and grateful in Your loving Heart until I am lost in You, completely and forever. Amen.

– Sr. Moya Hanlen

Bibliography

Au, Wilkie. *The Enduring Heart, Spirituality for the Long Haul*. New York: Paulist, 2000.
Au, Wilkie, and Noreen Cannon. *The Discerning Heart, Exploring the Christian Path*. New York: Paulist, 2006.
———. *Aging With Wisdom and Grace*. D'Arcy, New York: Paulist 2019.
Au, Wilkie. *Prayer for Aging*. Hanlen, Moya, Sister. Personal sharing from Wilkie Au.
Bosch, David. *Transforming Mission, Paradigm Shifts in Theology of Mission*. Maryknoll, New York: Orbis Books, 1996.
Bonhoeffer, Dietrich. *Life Together*. New York: Harper and Row, 1954.
Brecht, Arnold. *Political Theory, The Foundations of Twentieth-Century Political Thought*. Third Printing, Princeton: Princeton University Press, 1959.
Brownson, James V. *Bible, Gender Sexuality, Reframing the Church's Debate on Same-Sex Relationships*. Grand Rapids: Eerdmans, 2013.
Brunner, Frederick Dale. *Commentary of the Gospel of Matthew*. Grand Rapids: Eerdmans, 2007.
Brueggemann, Walter. *Praying the Psalms, Engaging Scripture and the Life of The Spirit*. Second Edition, Eugene: Cascade Books, a division of Wipf & Stock, 2007.
———. *Message of the Psalms, Augsburg Old Testament Studies, A Theological Commentary*. Minneapolis: Augsburg, 1984.
Buechner, Frederick. *Telling Secrets*. New York: Harper Collins, 1991.
———. *The Sacred Journey*. San Francisco: Harper and Row, 1982.
———. *The Magnificent Defeat*. San Francisco: Harper Collins, 1985.
Bunyan, John. *Pilgrims Progress in Today's English*. Retold by Thomas, James. Chicago: Moody, 1964.
Brooks, David. *The Second Mountain, The Quest for a Moral Life*. New York: Random House, 2019.
Carnell, Edward John. *The Case for Orthodox Theology*. Philadelphia: Westminster, 1959.
Carpenter, Humphrey. *The Inklings, C.S. Lewis, JRR Tolkien, Charles Williams, and their friends*. Boston: Houghton Mifflin, 1979.
Calvin, John. *Institutes of the Christian Religion, Book IV, chapter 1.7 to 29*. Philadelphia: Westminster, 1960.
Cowper, William, and Henderson, Gerald, S; Thomas. "His Way", *The Hymnal for Worship and Celebration*. Waco: Word Music (Word Inc.) 1986.
Enns, Peter. *The Sin of Certainty, Why God desires Our Trust More Than Our Correct Beliefs*. New York: Harper Collins, 2016.
Evans, Craig., and Sanders, James A., *Luke and Scripture: The Function of Sacred Tradition in Luke-Acts*. Minneapolis: Fortress, 1993.

Fitzgerald, Frances. *The Evangelicals, The Struggle to Shape America.* New York: Simon and Schuster, 2017.

Fleming, David L. S.J. *Draw Me into Your Friendship, The Spiritual Exercises, A Literal Translation and A Contemporary Reading.* Saint Louis: The Institute of Jesuit Sources, 1996.

Ford, Michael. *The Wounded Prophet.* First Edition, New York: Doubleday, Image Book, 2002.

Fosdick, Harry Emerson. *The Autobiography of Harry Emerson Fosdick, The Living of these Days.* First Edition, "The Fundamentalist Controversy," Chapter 7, "Ideals That Have Used Me." Chapter 10. New York: Harper and Brothers, 1956.

Frost, Robert. "The Road Not Taken." *The Norton Anthology of American Literature, Second Edition, Volume 2.* New York: WW Norton, 1985.

Gagnon, Robert A. *The Bible and Homosexual Practice: Texts and Hermeneutics.* Nashville: Abingdon, 2001.

Gerson, Michael. "Sermon on Second Corinthians 4:1 to 6." Washington National Cathedral, February 3, 2019.

Hays, Richard B. *The Moral Vision of the New Testament, A Contemporary Introduction to New Testament Ethics.* San Francisco: HarperCollins, 1996.

Haynes, Stephen. *The Last Segregated Hour: The Memphis Kneel-Ins and the Campaign for Southern Church Desegregation.* Oxford: Oxford University Press, October 2012.

———. "If You Board the Wrong Train, American Christians, Dietrich Bonhoeffer, and Donald Trump." Edited by Sider, Ron. *The Spiritual Danger of Donald Trump.* Chapter 13, Eugene: Cascade, 2020.

Hemmingway, Ernest. *The Complete Short Stories of Ernest Hemmingway.* The Finca Vigia Edition, New York: Scribner, Simon, and Shuster, 1987.

Howell, Patrick J., S.J. *Reducing the Storm to A Whisper, The Story of a Breakdown.* Canada: Pine Orchard Imprint, Ulyssean, 1985, 2000.

Huffman, Jr., John A. *A Most Amazing Call, One pastor's reflections on a ministry full of surprises.* 2011.

Jenkins, Jerry. La Hay, Tim. *Left Behind Series, Volume 1,* Carol Springs: Tyndale, 2020.

Jenkins, Philip. *The Great and Holy War, How World War 1 Became A Religious Crusade.* New York: Harper One, 2014.

Kierkegaard, Soren. *Fear and Trembling.* Translated with introduction by Alastair Hannay. London: Penguin Classics, 1985.

Lapierre, Dominique. *The City of Joy.* Translated from The French by Kathryn Spink, Garden City, New York: Doubleday, 1985.

Lewis, C.S. *Surprised by Joy, The Shape of My Early Life.* New York: A Harvest/HBJ Book, Harcourt Brace, and Jovanovich, 1955.

———. *The Chronicles of Narnia. The Magician's Nephew.* Book 1 or 6. New York: HarperCollins, 1955 and 1983 renewed.

———. *The Chronicles of Narnia.* Book 1 or 2, *The Lion, The Witch, and the Wardrobe.* New York: MacMillan, 1950.

———. *The Chronicles of Narnia.* Book 2 or 4, *Prince Caspian, The Return to Narnia.* New York: MacMillan, 1951.

———. *The Chronicles of Narnia.* Book 3, *The Horse and His Boy.* New York: HarperCollins, 1954.

———. *The Chronicles of Narnia.* Book 7, *The Last Battle.* New York: Macmillan, 1956.

———. *The Chronicles of Narnia. Book 4 or 5, The Voyage of the Dawn Treader.* New York: HarperCollins, 1952, Renewed 1980.
———. *The Chronicles of Narnia. The Silver Chair, Book 6.* New York: HarperCollins, 1953 and 1981.
———. *The Four Loves.* New York: Harcourt Brace Jovanovich, 1960.
———. *Mere Christianity.* San Francisco: 1952 and 1980, Harper, 2001.
———. *The Screwtape Letters.* New York: MacMillan, 1951.
———. *The Great Divorce.* London: HarperCollins, 1946.
———. *Selected Literary Essays.* Edited by Walter Hooper, "The Vision of John Bunyan," Cambridge: Cambridge University Press, 1969.
———. *An Experiment in Criticism.* Cambridge: Cambridge University Press, 1961.
———. *The Problem of Pain.* HarperCollins Edition, San Francisco: 1940, 1996, 2001.
———. *The Weight of Glory.* HarperCollins, San Francisco: 2001.
Lindsey, Hal. with C.C. Carlson. *Late Great Planet Earth.* Grand Rapids: Zondervan Academic, 1970.
Loconte, Joseph. *A Hobbit, A Wardrobe, and A Great War, How J.R.R. Tolkien and C.S. Lewis Rediscovered Faith, Friendship, & Heroism in the Cataclysm of 1914-18.* Nashville: Nelson, 2015.
Marsden, George M. *Religion and American Culture, A Brief History.* 3rd Edition, Grand Rapids: Eerdmans, 2018.
Martin, James, S.J. *Jesus, A Pilgrimage.* New York: HarperCollins, 2014.
Mays, James L. *Psalms. Interpretation Commentary, A Bible Commentary for Teaching and Preaching.* Louisville: John Knox, 1994.
McGarrahan, Eunice. *A Study of the Belhar Confession and Its Accompanying Letter.* Office of Theology and Worship, General Assembly Council, PC(USA), 21162 08 001.
Meacham, Jon. *American Gospel, God, The Founding Fathers, and the Making of a Nation.* New York: Random House Trade Paperback Edition, 2007.
Mendelsohn, Daniel. *An Odyssey, A Father, A Son, and an Epic.* New York: Alfred Knopf, Borzoi, 2017.
Marshall, I. Howard. *The Gospel of Luke, A Commentary on the Greek Text. (New International Greek Testament Commentary)* Grand Rapids: Eerdmans, 1978.
Muggeridge, Malcolm. *A Twentieth Century Testimony.* Nashville: Nelson, 1978.
Murphy, Nancey. *Beyond Liberalism and Fundamentalism, How Modern and Postmodern Philosophy Set the Theological Agenda. The Rockwell Lecture Series,* Rice University, Valley Forge: Trinity, 1996.
Newbigin, Lesslie. *The Gospel in a Pluralistic Society.* Grand Rapids: Wm. B. Eerdmans and World Council of Churches, 1989 and 1991.
Nicholi, Jr., Dr. Armond. *The Question of God; C.S. Lewis and Sigmund Freud Debate God, Love, Sex, and the Meaning of Life.* New York: Free, 2002.
Nouwen, Henri J.M. *The Wounded Healer.* New York: Doubleday Image, First Edition, 1972.
———. *The Inner Voice of Love, A Journey Through Anguish to Freedom.* First Edition, New York: Image, Doubleday, 1996.
———. *in the Name of Jesus, Reflections on Christian Leadership.* Chestnut Ridge: Crossroad, 1989.
O'Conner, Elizabeth. *Journey Inward, Journey Outward.* New York: HarperCollins, 1975.

Office of Theology and Worship, Hope in the Lord Jesus Christ. PCUSA.

———. *The Relationship Between Christians and Jews.* PCUSA.

Office of the General Assembly, Presbyterian Understanding and Use of Holy Scripture, Position Statement adopted by the 123rd General Assembly. (1983) of the PCUSA.

Office of Theology and Worship, PCUSA, "Between Millennia, What Presbyterians Believe About the Coming of Christ". Louisville: 2001.

Office of Theology and Worship, PCUSA, "Christians and Jews: People of God, A Theological Understanding of the Relationship Between Christians and Jews". Church Issues Series, No. 7, Louisville: 2002.

Peterson, Eugene. *The Jesus Way, a conversation on the ways that Jesus is the way.* Grand Rapids: Erdman, 2007.

———. *A Long Obedience in the Same Direction, Discipleship in an Instant Society.* InterVarsity, 2nd Edition, 20th anniversary ed. 2000.

———. *Answering Prayer, The Psalms as Tools for Prayer.* San Francisco: Harper & Row, 1989.

———. *The Message, John 1, The Bible in Contemporary Language.* Nave, Colorado Springs, Colorado, 2002.

Pitt-Watson, Ian. *Preaching: A Kind of Folly.* Louisville: Westminster John Knox, 1978.

The Constitution of the PCUSA, Part 1, The Book of Confessions.

The Book of Order, Part 11.

Regele, Michael. *Science, Scripture and Same-Sex Love.* Nashville: Abington, 2014.

Rogers, Jack. *Jesus, the Bible, and Homosexuality.* Louisville, KY: Westminster John Knox, 2009.

Rogers, Jack B. and McKim, Donald K., *The Authority and Interpretation of the Bible, An Historical Approach, First Edition.* San Francisco: Harper and Row, 1979.

Rohr, Richard., and Joseph Martos. *The Wild Man's Journey, Reflections on Male Spirituality, Revised Edition.* St. Anthony Messenger, Cincinnati, Ohio. 1996.

Rolheiser, Ronald. *The Holy Longing, The Search for a Christian Spirituality.* New York: Doubleday, a division of Random House, First Edition, 1999.

Sanders, James A., *God Has a Story Too, Sermons in Context.* Philadelphia: Fortress, 1979.

———. *Torah & Canon.* Philadelphia: Fortress, 1972.

———. "From Isaiah 61 to Luke 4." In *Christianity, Judaism, and Other Greco-Roman Cults, Studies for Morton Smith at Sixty.* Leiden: Brill, 1975, pp75 to 106.

———. "Hermeneutics." *Interpreter's Dictionary of the Bible.* Suppl. V. 402. Nashville: Abingdon, 1976.

———. *Luke- The Theological Historian.* Nashville: United Methodist Communication Board, 1981.

Shakespeare, Wm., Macbeth. *The Pelican Shakespeare.* Edited Alfred Harbage.

Shilts, Randy. *And the Band Played On, Politics, People, and the AIDS Epidemic.* New York: St. Martin's, 1987.

Sizer, Stephen. *Christian Zionism: Road map to Armageddon?* UK: IVP Academic, 2006.

Small, Joseph D., Rosenthal, Gilbert S. *Let Us Reason Together, Christians and Jews in Conversation.* Witherspoon: 2010.

Sider, Ronald. Ed. *The Spiritual Danger of Donald Trump, 30 Evangelical Christians on Justice, Truth, and Moral Integrity.* Eugene: Cascade 2020.

Snyder, Timothy. *Twenty Lessons from the Twentieth Century.* Tim Duggan Books, Penguin Random House. 2017.

Bibliography

Snyder, Alan, quoted C.S. Lewis. *The Trouble with X.* Ponderingprinciples.com. January 26, 2019.

Theological Task Force on Peace, Unity, and Purity of the Church, to the 217th General Assembly. 2006.

Tankersley, Arthur Jarrell. *Preaching the Christian Deuteronomy, Luke 9:51 to 18:14.* Professional Project submitted in partial fulfillment of the requirements for the degree of Doctor of Ministry, School of Theology at Claremont, May 1983.

———. Ecclesio Website. *"Why the Confession of Belhar?"*

———. *"A Metaethical Analysis of American Theories of Jurisprudence."* A Dissertation submitted to the Faculty of Claremont Graduate School in partial fulfillment of the requirements for the degree of Doctor of Philosophy in the Graduate Faculty of Government, Claremont, 1970.

———. Unpublished *Journal.* 2001, 9/11/01.

———. Presbyterian Outlook. *"PCUSA and Israel".* 2004.

———. *"Fostering Peace Through the Abrahamic Religions: The Promise and the Pitfalls."* Basel, Switzerland, 2010.

———. Report on the PCUSA. June 30, 2013, written for Laguna Presbyterian Church, included in manuscript.

———. *"Unpublished paper for Trinity United Presbyterian Church of Santa Ana."* California, September 29, 2013.

———. *"Task Force for the Confession of Belhar. The Accompanying Letter for 221st General Assembly of the PCUSA."* Edited by Task Force. Included in manuscript.

———. Unpublished sermon. *"Amos and Amaziah: Amos 7 and 8."*

———. Unpublished sermon. *Psalm 130.* July 8, 2006.

Tiede, David. *Prophecy and History in Luke-Acts.* Philadelphia: Fortress, 1980.

Tisby, Jemar. *The Color of Compromise, The Truth About the American Church's Complicity in Racism.* Grand Rapids: Zondervan, 2019.

Tolkien, JRR. *Lord of the Rings. The Fellowship of the Ring. The Two Towers. The Return of the King.* 50th anniversary. New York: HarperCollins, 2004.

Via, Dan O., and Gagnon, Robert A.J., *Homosexuality and the Bible, Two Views,* Minneapolis: Fortress, 2003.

Vines, Matthew. *God and The Gay Christian, The Biblical Case in Support of Same-Sex Relationships.* New York: Convergent. 2014.

Volf, Miroslav. *Free of Charge, Giving and Forgiving in a Culture Stripped of Grace.* Grand Rapids: Zondervan, 2005.

Westover, Tara. *Educated, A Memoir.* New York: Random House, 2018.

Wehner, Peter. *The Death of Politics, How to Heal Our Frayed Republic After Trump.* New York: Harper One, First Edition, 2019.

Weiser, Artur. *The Psalms, A Commentary, Old Testament Library.* Westminster, Philadelphia: Fourth Edition, 1962.

Willard, Dallas. *The Spirit of the Disciplines, Understanding How God Changes Lives.* Harper, San Francisco: 1991.

———. *The Divine Conspiracy, Rediscovering Our Hidden Life in God.* San Francisco: Harper, 1998.

Wink, Walter. *Naming the Powers: The Language of Power in the New Testament. Vol 1.* Philadelphia: Fortress, 1984.

———. *Unmasking the Powers, Vol. 2, The Invisible Forces That Determine Human Existence.* Philadelphia: Fortress, 1986.

———. *Engaging the Powers: Discernment and Resistance in a World of Domination.* Philadelphia: Augsburg Fortress, 1992.

Wright, N.T. *Surprised by Hope: Rethinking Heaven, the Resurrection, and the Mission of the Church.* New York: HarperCollins, 2008.

———. *How God Became King, The Forgotten Story of the Gospels.* San Francisco: Harper One, 2012.

———. *The Day the Revolution Began, Reconsidering the Meaning of Jesus' Crucifixion.* First Edition, San Francisco: Harper One, 2016.

———. *God and the Pandemic, A Christian Reflection on the Coronavirus and its Aftermath.* Grand Rapids: Zondervan Reflective, Reviewed by Arthur J. Tankersley for Board of Trustees of the New Theological Seminary of the West, July 8, 2020.

———. *Broken Signposts, How Christianity Makes Sense of the World.* New York: Harper One, 2020.

———. *Evil and the Justice of God.* Downers Grove: InterVarsity, 2006.

Yoder, John Howard. *The Politics of Jesus.* Grand Rapids: Eerdmans, 1972, 1994.

www.ingramcontent.com/pod-product-compliance
Lightning Source LLC
Chambersburg PA
CBHW070909100426
42814CB00003B/110